Politics of Cross-Cultural Reading

NEW COMPARATIVE CRITICISM

PETER LANG

Oxford · Bern · Berlin · Bruxelles · Frankfurt am Main · New York · Wien

Politics of Cross-Cultural Reading

Tagore, Ben Jelloun and Fo in English

MARION DALVAI

For Marzieh

Thanks for your friendship and your interest in my work

Marion Dalvai

PETER LANG
Oxford · Bern · Berlin · Bruxelles · Frankfurt am Main · New York · Wien

Bibliographic information published by Die Deutsche Nationalbibliothek.
Die Deutsche Nationalbibliothek lists this publication in the Deutsche Nationalbibliografie; detailed bibliographic data is available on the Internet at http://dnb.d-nb.de.

A catalogue record for this book is available from the British Library.

Library of Congress Cataloging-in-Publication Data

Dalvai, Marion, 1975-
Politics of cross-cultural reading : Tagore, Ben Jelloun and Fo in English / Marion Dalvai.
pages cm -- (New comparative criticism ; 3)
Includes bibliographical references and index.
ISBN 978-3-03-431881-5 (alk. paper)
1. Literature, Modern--20th century--History and criticism--Theory, etc. 2. Literature--Translations into English--History and criticism. 3. Literature and society. 4. Tagore, Rabindranath, 1861-1941--Translations into English--History and criticism. 5. Ben Jelloun, Tahar, 1944---Translations into English--History and criticism. 6. Fo, Dario--Translations into English--History and criticism. I. Title.
PN771.D35 2015
809'.04--dc23

2015011585

Cover image by Chiara Tomasi

ISSN 2235-1809 (print)
ISBN 978-3-0343-1881-5 (print)
ISBN 978-3-0353-0733-7 (eBook)

Hochfeldstrasse 32, CH-3012 Bern, Switzerland
info@peterlang.com, www.peterlang.com, www.peterlang.net

This publication has been peer reviewed.

Printed in Germany

Contents

Acknowledgements

This book started out as a doctoral project at Trinity College Dublin where I was the recipient of a Trinity Long Room Hub scholarship within the *Texts, Contexts, Cultures* programme. At the university of Dublin, I am most grateful to Peter Arnds, my supervisor, for helping me to develop my arguments, encouraging me to persist with them and accompanying the work through several drafts. Caitríona Leahy and Cormac Ó Cuilleanáin read and commented on an early draft of what has become the theoretical part of the book. Many thanks are due to my internal and external examiners, Moray McGowan (Dublin) and Susan Bassnett (Warwick) for a viva that turned into a wide-ranging and stimulating discussion of the field.

I thank Nivedita Sen (Delhi) and Sreejata Guha (Kolkata) for our conversation about translation theory and practice, and Hans Harder (Heidelberg) and Habib Zanzana (Scranton) for sharing their work on Tagore and Ben Jelloun. Sofia Jamaï (Casablanca) kindly tracked down and posted to me material from a Moroccan academic publisher.

Participants at the 'Comparative Literature/World Literature' conference at Simon Fraser University, Vancouver (March 2011), 'Voices in Translation' conference at the University of Copenhagen (November 2011) and the 'Tagore: The Global Impact of a Writer in the Community' conference at Edinburgh Napier University (May 2012) listened to what I had to say about Ben Jelloun, Fo and Tagore and helped clarify my work by their questions and comments. A portion of Chapter 5 appeared in *Authorial and Editorial Voices in Translation*, edited by Anna Wegener and Hanne Jansen. I would like to thank the editors for their permission to reprint it.

My talented friend Chiara Tomasi created the cover image. Grazie mille!

At Peter Lang, I would like to thank Hannah Godfrey, Alessandra Anzani and Jasmin Allousch.

Finally, endless thanks go to my partner, Andrew Cusack, who gave generously of his time to discuss and proofread my work. This book is also about the silenced voices beside the author that fundamentally shape the books we read. It would not be what it is today without Andrew's unwavering support, constant encouragement and active interest in my research over the past six years.

A Note on Language

Readers may notice a discrepancy in the spelling of the terms world literature and *Weltliteratur* in this book. I do not use capital letters to distinguish the paradigm and the teaching practice of world literature and opt for italics when using the German term. When quoting other scholars I reproduce their preferred way of spelling.

I transcribe Bengali words phonetically, using the most commonly accepted (usually Sanskritized) forms. Arabic words are also transcribed phonetically.

Unless otherwise indicated, all translations are mine.

INTRODUCTION

Reading World Literature in English

English is a global language, indispensable in commercial, academic and general life. Its preeminent position is nowhere more visible than on the international publishing market: between 1979 and 2004, the share of publications written in English rose from 40 to 60 per cent of the world literary fiction market.[1] However, only a small percentage of these English-language publications were translations. In 2010, Edith Grossman painted the following bleak picture:

> In the English-speaking world [...] major publishing houses are inexplicably resistant to any kind of translated material at all. The statistics are shocking in this age of so-called globalization: in the United States and Britain, only 2 to 3 percent of books published each year are translations, compared with almost 35 percent in Latin America and Western Europe.[2]

Data collected since 2008 by Three Percent, an online initiative based at the University of Rochester that aims to raise awareness of the low number of translations into English, confirm that in the United States translations make up around 3 per cent of all works published yearly, with fiction and poetry usually averaging around 0.7 per cent.[3] A recent report that collected data for three sample years (2000, 2005 and 2008) for the UK and Ireland

1 See Susan Pickford, 'The Booker Prize and the Prix Goncourt: A Case Study of Award-Winning Novels in Translation', *Book History*, 14/1 (2011), 221–40. Here 221.

2 Edith Grossman, 'A New Great Wall. Why the Crisis in Translation Matters', *Foreign Policy* (May/June 2010) <http://www.foreignpolicy.com/articles/2010/04/26/a_new_great_wall> accessed 5 October 2014.

3 See 'Three Percent: A Resource for International Literature at the University of Rochester <http://www.rochester.edu/College/translation/threepercent/index.php?s=database> accessed 8 October 2014.

found that translations of fiction, drama and poetry titles here proved to be 'a little higher than the often-cited 3% figure, and consistently greater than 4%.'[4] However, we cannot ignore that English functions as a source language for many other literary languages while relatively few works of fiction, drama and poetry written in other languages are translated into English. A 2010 overview of fourteen European languages and book markets found that two out of three translated books typically are from English originals.[5] Clearly, English is less permeable to translation than other major literary languages. Edith Grossman explains this by saying that the 'English-language market is the one most writers and their agents crave for their books'.[6] Writers and agents are not only attracted by the profits to be made on the English-language market; they perceive translation into English as a catalyst for translation into further languages. The power and attractiveness of English-language publishing and its relative impermeability to other languages entitles us to ask: what are we reading when we read literature in English translation promoted as 'foreign literature', 'international literature' or 'world literature' – literature understood as not 'one's own', either one's national literature or literature written in one's mother tongue? The asymmetry in favour of English described above makes the exchange with literature written in languages other than English rather unbalanced.

In the last twenty years, literary translation into English has grown an impressive 18 per cent, according to a forthcoming study commissioned by

4 Jasmine Donahaye, 'Three Percent? Publishing data and statistics on translated literature in the United Kingdom and Ireland' (2013) <http://www.lit-across-frontiers.org/wp-content/uploads/2013/03/Publishing-Data-and-Statistics-on-Translated-Literature-in-the-United-Kingdom-and-Ireland-A-LAF-research-report-March-2013-final.pdf> accessed 5 October 2014. Quote on page 4.

5 'As a rule of thumb, two out of three translated books are from English originals, with German and French well behind at 7 or 8 percent each, and all other languages falling far behind'. Miha Kovač, Rüdiger Wischenbart, et al., 'Diversity Report 2010: Literary Translation in Current European Book Markets. An Analysis of Authors, Languages, and Flows', 41. <http://wischenbart.com/page-30> accessed 5 October 2014.

6 Edith Grossman, *Why Translation Matters* (New Haven and London: Yale University Press, 2010), 14–15.

Literature Across Frontiers, a European Platform for Literary Exchange, Translation and Policy Debate founded in 2001 and based in Wales. While an increase in the number of works translated into English certainly looks like good news, the overall increase in the number of books published in English in the same period realistically means that the proportion of translated works has remained unchanged.[7]

The dominance of English on the publishing market is also reflected in the academic field. The majority of recent influential academic works that critically engage with the concept of world literature and teaching practices have either been written in English (*What is World Literature?* and *How to Read World Literature* by David Damrosch; John Pizer's *The Idea of World Literature: History and Pedagogical Practice*; *Debating World Literature*, edited by Christopher Prendergast; Mads Rosendahl Thomsen's *Mapping World Literature: International Canonization and Transnational Literatures* and Emily Apter's *Against World Literature*) or have been translated into English in order to ensure a wider impact (Pascale Casanova's *The World Republic of Letters* or Elke Sturm-Trigonakis's *Comparative Cultural Studies and the New* Weltliteratur). While most of these works deal with world literature as a field of study and teaching, my book has a different focus: it aims to show how that field of foreign/international/world literature is constructed by agents making decisions and by the rhetorical strategies used to justify and explain these decisions. In this book I use the term 'politics of world literature' to refer to the selecting and rhetorical work of agents as they shape the fields of publishing and academic discourse. My work complements the studies published to date: it analyses agents and factors involved in constituting the field of world literature in English translation and investigates the ambivalent position of English as a roadblock to

7 See Dalya Alberge, 'British Readers Lost in Translation as Foreign Literature Sales Boom', *The Guardian*, 24 August 2014. <http://www.theguardian.com/books/2014/aug/24/british-readers-translations-foreign-literature-sales-boom-stieg-larsson-jo-nesbo> accessed 21 January 2015. The report was not released in September 2014 as announced in the article but will be launched in 2015 instead. It will be interesting to see how the increase in translated titles is reflected in the overall percentage translated books occupy in the English-language book market.

international visibility and as a necessary intermediary vehicle for other literary languages. Put rather pointedly, the guiding question of this book might be formulated thus: how can one explain the increasing academic interest in world literature in the English-speaking world when *de facto* there is rather little world literature available in English translation?

While the rest of the study is concerned with the historical manifestations of specific reception processes, the first two chapters develop a multifaceted model of that international literary space containing the object widely known as world literature that takes into account the text's location in its producing culture and the agents' location in the receiving culture. My method combines *reception studies* (Wolfgang Iser, Hans Robert Jauss and Peter Rabinowitz) with *polysystem theory* (Itamar Even-Zohar) and *rhetorical hermeneutics* (Steven Mailloux). The study proceeds from the working assumption that meaning is not an exclusive property of the text (a material object) or of language (an abstract concept). Meaning is negotiated in a complex interpretive process that involves an act of *sense making* (understanding) as well as an act of *making-sense-to-others* (persuading). Like meaning, *authority* and *authenticity* do not reside at one site ('the original' or 'the author') but are distributed among various agents participating in the production and positioning of a literary text.

Chapter 1 briefly outlines the emergence and persistence of the term 'world literature'. I engage in more detail with the discursive politics underpinning several definitions of 'world literature' (Damrosch, Pizer, Casanova, Rosendahl Thomsen, Sturm-Trigonakis and Apter) before introducing the first two components of my model: polysystem theory and reception studies.

Chapter 2 introduces the third and final essential element to my model, rhetorical hermeneutics, and engages more deeply with the agents who shape texts in translation – publishers, translators, adaptors, editors, literary critics and academics – before moving on to a discussion of the importance of literary prizes for the contemporary international book market. As a final point, I briefly outline two central concepts that emerge in all discussions of translated texts: authorship and authenticity.

In Chapters 3 to 5, I apply the model developed in Chapters 1 and 2 to three works translated into English that are commonly described and promoted as 'world literature': *The Home and the World* by Rabindranath Tagore (1861–1941), *The Sand Child* by Tahar Ben Jelloun (born in 1944) and *Accidental Death of an Anarchist* by Dario Fo (born in 1926). Choosing which texts to use as case studies proved one of the more difficult decisions when planning this book. At first glance, there may not be any obvious links between the three case studies, and at times Tagore, Ben Jelloun and Fo may seem to sit slightly uneasily together, much like travellers in a railway carriage, thrown together by chance and studiously ignoring each other.[8] But in a sense the canon of world literature is rather like a railway carriage whose occupants are brought together by chance, travelling on different journeys but sharing the same vehicle. The railway metaphor points to another working assumption guiding this study: that inclusion in the canon of world literature is to a significant degree a matter of contingency. As I intend to show, this chanciness is a function of the situatedness of agents and their temporal agendas. In the case studies, I engage with the strategies and methods of decision-making and the discursive practices of several agents responsible for the way in which *The Home and the World*, *The Sand Child* and *Accidental Death of an Anarchist* are presented to the English-speaking readership. My focus varies in each case study in order to show the versatility of my model which can be applied either to give a bird's-eye view of the reception of a literary work over a relatively prolonged period of time (Tagore), or to 'zoom in' on one particularly insightful aspect of reception, such as the academic criticism on a specific work (Ben Jelloun) or a close reading of the paratextual and metatextual commentary provided by agents other than the author within the covers of a published text (Fo).

Chapter 3 reconstructs the complex reception history of Rabindranath Tagore's novel *The Home and the World* in the English-speaking West. The first Asian writer to receive the Nobel Prize for Literature in 1913, Tagore was reduced to a marginal figure in the English-speaking West by 1960. I present some reasons for the decline in Tagore's literary reputation and compare the reception of Tagore's work in the English-speaking West with

8 I would like to thank Moray McGowan for suggesting the metaphor of the railway carriage in conversation.

that in several European countries. Finally, I proceed to agents and factors responsible for the reintroduction of Tagore into the canon of world literature in its English implementation over the last thirty years. Tagore's fate is interesting because it shows that consecration, the process by which an author is admitted to a canon, is reversible.

Chapter 4 focuses on a single aspect of the reception of Tahar Ben Jelloun's 1985 novel *The Sand Child*: academic criticism written in English. The chapter concentrates on specific readings of Ben Jelloun's novel as well as on the cross-fertilization between individual critical readings and between critical discourses across cultures. Establishing which lines of argument are accepted as meaningful and which arguments put forward in French are acknowledged or adopted in English-language Ben Jelloun criticism allows one to discuss why claims of a professedly disinterested engagement with literature, on the one hand, and the location of academics within specific institutions and the wider academic field, on the other, are often at variance.

Chapter 5 concentrates on the paratextual and metatextual commentary provided by editors, translators and adaptors of English-language versions of Dario Fo's *Accidental Death of an Anarchist*. I reconstruct the specific translation and adaptation strategies, and link these to the wider politics at work in the transposition of theatre texts and theatrical traditions.

The conclusion argues that, when dealing with works of world literature in translation, we need to take into account a text's transnational trajectory and the changing positions of politico-cultural agents towards that particular text: in short, we need to acknowledge the *processual* nature of all cultural transfers in order to be able to do justice to both the *effect* and *affect* of literature in translation (the text's effect on the reader and the affective relationship of text and reader). I also engage with a matter that rather unexpectedly emerged in the course of writing this book: a preoccupation with authenticity and faithfulness shared by many agents who shape literary works in translation and argue for their value within their reading communities. Finally, the conclusion points out several ways in which scholars and general readers interested in world literature can be empowered to become agents for change themselves.

CHAPTER 1

'The Universal Possession of Mankind'? The Discursive Politics of World Literature

During the eighteenth century, literary magazines and collections published in cultural centres across Europe provided a growing reading public with more and more translations, not only of Greek and Latin classics but also from other – mainly, but not exclusively, European – languages. Over the decades, they contributed to the 'eventual development and confirmation of a corpus of classic fiction (presented in, for example, many nineteenth-century collected editions) that would include foreign works in translation'.[1] As Gillespie argues, this intensification of literary translation actually enabled the establishment of a separate English literary canon over and against the classics.[2] In other European countries the canon was expanding along similar lines, integrating translations of modern European works and non-European literature. In Germany, book production expanded by 50 per cent between 1750 and 1800 and steadily grew in the nineteenth century, more than tripling in the twenty-five years between 1820 and 1845 to over 14,000 titles per annum, thanks to Friedrich Koenig's high-speed press and the advent of the steam engine.[3] Many of these books were translations. It is no coincidence that Johann Wolfgang von Goethe proffered his widely

1 Stuart Gillespie, 'Translation and Canon-Formation', in Stuart Gillespie and David Hopkins, eds, *The Oxford History of Translation in English* (Oxford and New York: Oxford University Press, 2005), 7–20. Here 15.

2 Ibid., 7–8.

3 See Lynne Tatlock, 'Introduction: The Book Trade and the "Reading Nation" in the Long Nineteenth Century', in *Publishing Culture and The 'Reading Nation': German Book History in the Long Nineteenth Century* (Rochester, NY: Camden House, 2010), 1–21. Here 4–5. Germany produced more book titles per annum than any other nation worldwide in the nineteenth century.

quoted sentence about world literature after a long life of reading translations from dozens of languages and after a recent, intense engagement with translations from the Chinese: 'National literature is now a rather unmeaning term; the epoch of world literature is at hand, and everyone must strive to hasten its approach'.[4] There is more to Goethe's call for a new era in literature than a sudden realization that literature can be a window onto the world or, indeed, facile universalism. Goethe developed his idea of *Weltliteratur* in a speech written for a conference of scientists held in Berlin in 1828 (though the speech was not actually delivered):

> If we have ventured to proclaim a European, indeed universal Weltliteratur, then this does not simply mean that the different nations become acquainted with each other and their products, for it has already existed in this sense for a long time, is continuing and is more or less renewing itself. Rather, what is meant is that the living, striving men of letters get to know each other and feel spurred to act socially through inclination and a sense of a common public spirit.[5]

Here, Goethe argues for the creation of an ideal community that will further specific modes of literary circulation and cross-fertilization, thus shifting the focus towards the production and producers of literature. While Goethe argues for an ideal community of *litterateurs*, I am interested in the actual modes of cross-cultural circulation of literary texts as well as the politico-cultural role played by agents besides the author (translators, editors, publishers, reviewers, critics and academics) in these processes.

The term *politics*, Jacques Rancière points out, is often equated with the exercise of power. Yet, the simple existence of power structures or of regulatory laws is not enough for power to be exercised: 'What is needed is a configuration of a specific form of community. Politics is the construction

4 Johann Wolfgang Goethe, *Conversations with Eckermann (1823–32)*, transl. John Oxenford (New York: North Point Press, 1984), 133.

5 Johann Wolfgang von Goethe, *Sämtliche Werke. Briefe, Tagebücher und Gespräche* ['Frankfurter Ausgabe'], 40 volumes, ed. Friedmar Apel, Hendrik Birus et al. (Frankfurt/Main 1986–1999), 25: 79. Translation quoted from John Pizer, *The Idea of World Literature. History and Pedagogical Practice* (Baton Rouge: Louisiana State University Press, 2006), 60.

of a specific sphere of experience in which certain objects as posited as shared and certain subjects regarded as capable of designating these objects and of arguing about them'.[6] In the context of cross-cultural reading, therefore, politics refers to 1) the sphere of experience shared by readers in the receiving culture, 2) *strategies* and *methods* of decision-making processes within specific reading communities, as well as 3) the discursive practices that follow from these decisions. While politics shapes every single reading process, it becomes more visible in the reading of translations, as this type of reading has to negotiate various degrees of foreignness that in turn bring to the fore quite specific interpretive and discursive strategies.

Reception historians investigate a series of visible factors that shape the reception of literary works.[7] For first time publications, they may record the reasons why a work is selected for publication in the first place, how it is transformed (through various forms of rewriting, such as editing and adaptation), what impact the text has on the literary elite (literary critics, academics, journalists) and on the general reading public (numbers of copies sold and inclusion in book club discussions, for example). Literary texts might also enter cultural and social discourse on several levels: they

6 Jacques Rancière, *The Politics of Literature* (Cambridge and Malden, MA: Polity Press, 2011), 3. Similarly, Gayatri Chakravorty Spivak advocates that rather than attempting to depoliticize literary discourse (an impossible task), we should develop a raised awareness of the politicized character of any cultural discourse. Gayatri Chakravorty Spivak, *Death of a Discipline* (New York: Columbia University Press, 2003), 4. For a detailed analysis of ideology at work in the writings of Eagleton, Booth, Kristeva and others, see Gayatri Chakravorty Spivak, 'The Politics of Interpretations', in *In Other Worlds: Essays in Cultural Politics* (New York and London: Routledge, 2006), 161–83.

7 Reception processes 'become manifest in a wide variety of forms: in the selection and transformation of the works, the attention given to them by publishers, reviewers, essayists and academics, the reactions of the buying and reading public, their modes of entry into cultural discourse, their inclusion in literary histories and schoolbooks, their intertextual and intermedial transmission, and in their influence on poetics and even on social thought'. Els Andringa, "For God's and Virginia's Sake Why a Translation?" – Virginia Woolf's Transfer to the Low Countries', *Comparative Critical Studies*, 3/3 (2006), 201–26. Here 201.

become part of school and university curriculums and might be included in literary histories and anthologies. Works of literature sometimes have an intermedial effect (film adaptations, radio plays or even computer games) and they might be discussed in a variety of forums (newspapers, television shows or literature blogs). Finally, they influence other literary texts; and – if they are innovative rather than conservative – might also change poetic and aesthetic categories. All of these manifestations of reception are tangible and help the literary critic interested in reception history to gain a more complete overview of the impact that a literary work has not only on the literary field, but also on the cultural field in general at a given time in history. If there is an absence of these visible factors, if a text has no or little impact on the larger culture it is (being) embedded in, this might be an indication of a text not fitting the politico-cultural agenda of that particular time and place (especially if this text is 'redeemed' later on or in a different cultural system through translation). The reception history of translated works of literature consists of all the factors mentioned above with the addition of a further level of analysis, that of one or several translations of the literary text available in the receiving culture.[8]

At any given moment in time, there exist a variety of communities engaged with (world) literature, whether we conceive of them in very concrete terms – university literature classes, book clubs – or in a more abstract sense – the 'British' or 'Western' readership.[9] Reading communities

8 Translation is, in fact, a major form of rewriting a text. See André Lefevere, 'Why Waste Our Time on Rewrites? The Trouble with Interpretation and the Role of Rewriting in an Alternative Paradigm', in Theo Hermans, ed., *The Manipulation of Literature* (London and Sydney: Croom Helm, 1985), 215–43. Lefevere asserts that '[t]ranslation can no longer be analysed in isolation but it should be studied as part of a whole system of texts and the people who produce, support, propagate, oppose, censor them' (237).

9 These communities are not Stanley Fish's interpretive communities, however. Fish's 'affective stylistics' is based on the assumption that it is the reader that invests a text with all of its meaning. Each reader is part of an interpretive community and reads, or rather *writes* a text, according to established and well-accepted rules within this community. Fish defines *interpretive communities* as 'made up of those who share interpretive strategies not for reading (in the conventional sense) but for writing texts,

develop what Jonathan Culler calls specific kinds of *literary competence*: they 'internalize the "grammar" of literature which permits [them] to convert linguistic sequences into literary structures and meanings'.[10] Culler argues that we make sense of a literary work following an established set of rules of whose existence we are more or less aware, and he suggests that these rules are the result of a negotiation between past and present culture. The rules of interpretation do, of course, change from culture to culture and from one historical period to another; thus a text is never approached without specific preconceptions and assumptions.[11] The rules of interpretation described here form a habitus in the sense defined by Bourdieu: 'both a system of schemata of production of practices and a system of perception and appreciation of practices'.[12] However, Culler does not clearly address the issue of how readers internalize the 'grammar' of literary structures and meanings or how this literary grammar relates to other modes of being and understanding. We shall return to this issue in Chapter 2.[13]

Within such a community of readers, some agents will possess more discursive authority than others. Discursive authority is the ability to make other members in the shared sphere of experience conceive of a given object in one's preferred way. It also entails the ability to neutralize or render ineffective critics who question one's interpretation. All analysis of discursive

---

for constituting their properties and assigning their intentions. In other words, these strategies exist prior to the act of reading and therefore determine the shape of what is read rather than, as is usually assumed, the other way around'. Stanley Eugene Fish, 'Interpreting the *Variorum*', in David Finkelstein and Alistair McCleery, eds, *The Book History Reader* (London and New York: Routledge, 2006), 450–8. Here 451.

10 Jonathan Culler, *Structuralist Poetics: Structuralism, Linguistics and the Study of Literature* (London: Routledge Classics, 2002), 132.

11 Culler, 'Literary Competence', in Jane P. Tompkins, ed., *Reader Response Criticism. From Formalism to Post-Structuralism* (Baltimore and London: The Johns Hopkins University Press, 1992), 101–17. Here 116.

12 Pierre Bourdieu, *The Logic of Practice* (Cambridge: Polity, 1990), transl. Richard Nice, 131.

13 The influence of French Structuralism is apparent in Culler's choice of words. The concept of a *sign system* with a clear *grammar* that readers internalize is undoubtely indebted to thinkers such as Lévi-Strauss, Foucault, Todorov and Barthes.

practices must focus on the two dimensions of discursive authority: the discursive (what is said) and the performative (how it is said and in what setting).[14] 'Community' here is also a performative discourse in the sense described by Homi Bhabha: 'As a category, community enables a division between the private and the public, the civil and the familial; but as a performative discourse it enacts the impossibility of drawing an objective line between the two'.[15] In Chapters 3 to 5, I will analyse a sequence of rhetorical performances in which various agents invested with discursive authority produce and assign meaning and status to a particular work of literature and its author. But let us return to the discursive politics that surround the term 'world literature'.

The term that Goethe coined, *Weltliteratur*, was the expression of a developing cultural awareness in the nineteenth century that was also linked to budding modern forms of capitalism in the West. Yet, far from Imperialist projects of the kind that later comparatists such as Macaulay would advocate, Goethe's project situates itself in the idealist, humanist tradition.[16] Goethe believed that literature would in the future be the medium for an open discourse among nations (understood, in Herder's sense, as cultural and linguistic communities, each characterized by a specific *Volksgeist*). Understanding among cultures would increase, also thanks to more foreign literature being made available to readers in translation. Goethe saw 'Weltliteratur' as an opportunity for greater understanding rather than for the imposition of cultural hegemony. However, his endeavour does not

14 'Discursive authority' is a term often used when speaking about public policy. For one example of its use, see Maarten Hajer and David Laws, 'Policy in Practice', in Michael Moran, Martin Rein, and Robert E. Goodin, eds, *The Oxford Handbook of Public Policy* (Oxford: Oxford University Press, 2006), 409–25.

15 Homi K. Bhabha, *The Location of Culture* (London: Routledge, 1994), 235.

16 See Thomas Babington Macaulay, 'Minute on Indian Education (1835)', in Mia Carter and Barbara Harlow, eds, *Archives of Empire: From the East India Company to the Suez Canal* (Durham and New York: Duke University Press, 2003), 227–38. Macaulay states that all Indian students should be made to read English literature, claiming that the latter is of much higher quality than their national literature.

reduce the indeterminacy of the two words making up the term 'world literature'.[17]

The 'world' in 'world literature' can be understood in at least three ways: as a principle of universality underpinning all human endeavour; it might refer to a (perceived) linear tradition that has formed the Western mind and therefore consists of a relatively limited number of 'Great Books' or it might mean global or planetary in a more postcolonial fashion. Similarly, the term 'literature' is mostly understood in a strict Eurocentric manner, in one of two ways: literature as *belles lettres*, aesthetically formed writing which aims to cultivate taste and which, for a long time, relied on a high degree of emulation of the classics; or, with the advent of literary history,

17 I discuss several book-length studies of world literature later on in this chapter. The last decade has also seen several special journal issues on world literature, such as *New Literary History*, 39.3 (Summer 2008), edited by Ralph Cohen entitled *Literary History in the Global Age*. Four articles have 'world literature' in the title and several more engage with the concept even if they might use alternative terms, such as 'transcultural literary history' (Anders Pettersson). See also *Neohelicon*, 38.2 (December 2011), guest-edited by Ning Wang and entitled *Comparative Literature: Toward the (Re) construction of World Literature; Modern Language Quarterly: A Journal of Literary History*, 74.2 (2013), entitled *What counts as world literature?*, edited by Caroline Devine and B. Venkat Mani as well as a two issues of *CLCWeb: Comparative Literature and Culture*, 15.5 and 15.6 (both December 2013): the first edited by Marko Juvan entitled *World Literatures from the Nineteenth to the Twenty-First Century*, and the second edited by Graciela Boruszko and Steven Tötösy de Zepetnek entitled *New Work about World Literatures*. Also see collections of essays on world literature, such as *Debating World Literature*, edited by Christopher Prendergast; *The Routledge Companion to World Literature*, edited by Theo D'haen, David Damrosch and Djelal Kadir (Abingdon and New York: Routledge, 2011); *World Literature. A Reader*, edited by Theo D'haen, César Domínguez and Mads Rosendahl Thomsen (Abingdon and New York: Routledge, 2012); and *World Literature in Theory*, edited by David Damrosch (Oxford and Malden, MA: Wiley Blackwell, 2014). There are also several influential individual articles and book chapters such as Franco Moretti, 'Conjectures on World Literature', *New Left Review*, 1 (2000), 54–68; Pascale Casanova, 'Literature as a World', *New Left Review* 31(2005), 127–36 and Hendrik Birus, 'The Goethean Concept of World Literature and Comparative Literature', in Steven Tötösy de Zepetnek, ed., *Comparative Literature and Comparative Cultural Studies* (Lafayette: Purdue University Press, 2003), 11–22.

literature as 'condensed, and indeed exemplary, bodies of social and cultural documentation'.[18]

World literature: Aesthetically formed writing or an inventory of socio-cultural documents?

Pascale Casanova claims that the initial step towards the constitution of an international literary space came with the formation of the first European states in the sixteenth century. The intellectual struggle for the recognition of vernacular literature over and against Latin reached its first culmination in the French *Pléiade* and du Bellay's *La deffence et illustration de la langue françoyse* in 1549. The second step saw the (re)invention of self-consciously national languages in the late eighteenth and early nineteenth centuries, while the third and last stage was decolonization.[19] Casanova also provides a chronology of when various members joined the international literary space:

> Previously confined to regional areas that were sealed off from each other, literature now emerged as a common battleground. Renaissance Italy, fortified by its Latin heritage, was the first recognized literary power. Next came France, with the rise of the *Pléiade* in the mid-sixteenth century, which in challenging both the hegemony of Latin and the advance of Italian produced a first tentative sketch of transnational literary space. Then Spain and England, followed by the rest of the countries of Europe, gradually entered into competition on the strength of their own literary 'assets' and traditions. The nationalist movements that appeared in central Europe during the nineteenth century – a century that also saw the arrival of North America and Latin America on the international literary scene – generated new claims to

18 Stefan Hoesel-Uhlig, 'Changing Fields: The Directions of Goethe's Weltliteratur', in Christopher Prendergast, ed., *Debating World Literature* (London and New York: Verso, 2004), 47.

19 See Pascale Casanova, *The World Republic of Letters* (Cambridge, MA and London: Harvard University Press, 2004), 46–55.

> literary existence. Finally, with decolonization, countries in Africa, the Indian subcontinent, and Asia demanded access to literary legitimacy and existence as well.[20]

Not only is the chronology advocated here doubtful: where, for example, do we insert Indian and Chinese literature written before decolonization? Was there no exchange between cultures inside and outside Europe before the sixteenth century? What are the confines of Europe? And most importantly, are literary assets and traditions only ever assets of written language and traditions of aesthetically formed ways of writing? In Casanova's portrayal, literature is the perfect apolitical space in which literary genius and talent are automatically recognized, and the only currency is aesthetic value, a value narrowly defined by agents sitting in the centre of the literary world. There seems to be no need to distinguish 'literature' from 'world literature' in this universe, as truly important works will be recognized as such and will be automatically included in the canon, irrespective of their origins.

The second definition of literature as an archive or inventory of socio-cultural documents waiting to be studied is equally based on Western standards. The underlying suggestion is that cultural comparison through literature is in fact objective. Goethe claimed that 'poetry is the universal possession of mankind, revealing itself everywhere and at all times in hundreds and hundreds of men'.[21] 'Poetry', here, stands for language: similarly to Herder, Goethe believed that all human beings used language to express themselves. In what was perceived as a logical deduction from this claim, many thinkers argued that as poetry – and, by extension, literature – truly was the universal possession of mankind, it could be objectively compared, judged and valued. This claim to objectivity works on several levels: on an aesthetic level, Kant's postulate of pure and disinterested aesthetics functions as a guarantor of objective universality.[22] On an epistemological

20 Ibid., 11.

21 Goethe, *Conversations*, 133.

22 Immanuel Kant, *Critique of Judgment*, transl. Nicholas Walker (Oxford: Oxford University Press, 2007). Kant describes four key features of aesthetic judgments: they are *disinterested* (we take pleasure in an object because we judge it beautiful, rather than finding it beautiful because we see it as pleasurable); they are *universal*

level, the possibility of knowledge of other cultures, the ability to absorb their literature is never doubted: the appropriate application of methods of abstraction will result in the correct interpretation. The methods of hermeneutic interpretation adopted, however, are again Eurocentric in character: the books of the Great Tradition are established as models against which newcomers from other cultures have to measure up in terms of content, genre, style and literariness. Ultimately, the adoption of these literary standards influences one facet of what Thomas Richards has called the *imperial archive*, 'a fantasy of knowledge collected and united in the service of state and Empire'.[23]

While literature is increasingly understood as an archive, the aesthetic component that had shaped the previous understanding of literature as *belles lettres* continues to be present, if only in enfeebled form as genre poetics loses its binding quality. As a result, 'the [...] archival endorsement [of the term 'world literature'] invites an ever wider range of readings, while its weak aesthetic impulse suggests more selection'.[24] Two conflicting views of world literature emerge: world literature should include more – no less than the entire world! –; yet it should also only include 'good' literature or masterpieces, however one may define these. This insoluble tension is also visible in twentieth century discussions about canons of (world) literature.

On one hand, we have a school of thought that sees literature as a perfect ahistorical and apolitical space. Examples range from T. S. Eliot's definition of the 'classics' as an imagined, utopian corpus of great works that comes together thanks to an epistemological master pattern of excellence, to Harold Bloom who argues against the politicization of literature and presents a guide to the twenty-six essential writers of the ages that have

(we expect others to agree with our judgment); they are *necessary;* and *'purposive without purpose'* (beautiful objects affect us as though they had a specific purpose, although they do not).

23 Thomas Richards, *The Imperial Archive: Knowledge and the Fantasy of Empire* (London and New York, 1993), 6.

24 Hoesel-Uhlig, 32–3.

shaped the Western canon.[25] On the other hand, we have a variety of different voices (Feminist, New Historicist, Marxist and Postcolonial) arguing for the importance of analysing the position of literature and literary agents within specific power structures, thus shifting the focus from the text to the context of production and reception: for such critics, canons of (world) literature are always closely linked to specific power structures, and literary works do in fact represent the 'reality' that bore them.[26] Deconstruction stands somewhat aside from all other approaches to literature, in its scepticism about the coherence of meaning, authorial intention and the mimetic function of literary texts. A rapprochement among the different stances on the nature of literature is not in sight, even as the last twenty years have seen an increase in theoretical discussions regarding the nature and scope of world literature.

As will emerge most clearly in the case study of Tahar Ben Jelloun in Chapter 4, several literary critics who believe that literature has a mainly documentary function read literary texts as authentic representations of a given reality or culture. In this approach, literary texts are not perceived to be very different from historical, sociological and ethnographic documents: they allow us to gain a better understanding of a clearly defined 'other'. However, as Wolfgang Riedel points out, there is a danger in equating literary texts with the culture they are thought to represent, as this stance tends to neglect the aesthetic component of literature and therefore fails to acknowledge the distinction between literature and other discourses,

25 Thomas Stearns Eliot, 'Tradition and the Individual Talent', in Lawrence S. Rainey, ed., *Modernism: An Anthology* (Malden, MA and Oxford: Blackwell, 2005), 152–5. Harold Bloom, *The Western Canon: The Books and School of the Ages* (New York and London: Harcourt Brace, 1994).

26 For an overview of the canon formation dispute, see John Guillory, 'Canon', in Frank Lentricchia and Thomas McLaughlin, eds, *Critical Terms for Literary Study* (Chicago and London: The University of Chicago Press, 1995), 233–49. For a liberal viewpoint, see Barbara Herrnstein Smith, *Contingencies of Value: Alternative Perspectives for Critical Theory* (Cambridge, MA and London: Harvard University Press, 1988). See also David Damrosch, 'World Literature in a Postcanonical, Hypercanonical Age', in Haun Saussy, ed., *Comparative Literature in an Age of Globalization* (Baltimore: Johns Hopkins University Press, 2006), 43–53.

such as history, sociology or ethnography. Riedel argues that a literary text is not a document but rather a commentary on the culture and reality it stems from, written with the benefit of aesthetic and reflective distance.[27] The concept of commentary is a useful tool in world literature as it allows one to relativize the idea that the main value of literary texts in translation from different cultures is to provide privileged knowledge of those cultures.

Since the 1970s, more non-Western critical voices have participated in the constitution and interpretation of world literature; as a consequence, world literature syllabuses in colleges worldwide have changed considerably. This process of canon change stimulated by the participation of new critical voices can be seen as fulfilling Rosendahl Thomsen's postulate of literature as a 'system of communication':

> 'Canonization' is [...] not the use of power to determine curricula, or an idiosyncratic scholar's projection of his or her own preferences onto a general idea of what literary history should be. Canonization should instead be seen as the complex social mechanism where numerous agents – readers, critics, teachers, publishers, etc. – take part in a continuing conversation about what has value as literature. Some agents are more powerful than others, but one can look at literature as a vast system of communication about what interests people, and how we respond to texts by strangers and integrate new perspectives on the world. Canons are not static, but they do offer ample resistance to idiosyncratic statements such as 'Forget Shakespeare, focus on Jonson,' or 'No one should bother to read *Gilgamesh*.' As such, canonization can be an important starting point for exploring the structures of literary cultures and the cross-cultural influences.[28]

27 See Wolfgang Riedel, 'Literarische Anthropologie: Eine Unterscheidung', in Wolfgang Braungart, Klaus Ridder, and Friedmar Apel, eds, *Wahrnehmen und Handeln: Perspektiven einer Literaturanthropologie* (Bielefeld, Germany: Aisthesis, 2004), 337–66, esp. 350–2. In the German context, 'anthropology' is understood as a philosophical discourse (the theory of man) rather than the common English-language notion of 'ethnography'.

28 Mads Rosendahl Thomsen, 'World Famous, Locally: Insights From the Study of International Canonization', 6 March 2014, in *The 2014–2015 Report on the State of the Discipline of Comparative Literature*. <http://stateofthediscipline.acla.org/entry/world-famous-locally-insights-study-international-canonization#sthash.83d8lv6F.dpuf> accessed 1 February 2015.

While we are far from a balanced understanding of what world literature is or should be, the developments of the past few decades seem positive overall. The (sometimes heated) discussions about canonization and what constitutes 'classics' of literature, about the cultural politics at work in literary centres in the West and in the so-called periphery, and about the value of translation have shown that, while far from perfect, a critical engagement with the concept of world literature is still necessary and fruitful. As the next section clearly shows, one needs to account for both the idealizing aims of a project such as world literature and the politicized results of this project.

Perspectives on world literature: Damrosch, Casanova, Pizer, Rosendahl Thomsen, Sturm-Trikonatis and Apter

In English-language academia, the renewed interest in world literature started in the 1990s and has given rise to a large number of articles and books on the subject since the early 2000s. Interestingly, the 1995 Bernheimer report on the state of the discipline of comparative literature did not mention world literature as an important subfield. By 2006, the key term used in the title of the ACLA report had changed from 'multiculturalism' to 'globalization', and world literature loomed large as a category that could not be ignored in Saussy's report.[29] Surveying the profusion of recent publications on world literature would be a major task in its own right. In an effort to convey the range of influential views of world literature as concisely as possible, I have in this section opted for a synoptic overview of six book-length studies on world literature that have appeared since the start of the new millennium.

29 See Charles Bernheimer, ed., *Comparative Literature in the Age of Multiculturalism* (Baltimore: Johns Hopkins University Press, 1995) and Haun Saussy, ed., *Comparative Literature in an Age of Globalization* (Baltimore: Johns Hopkins University Press, 2006).

Damrosch (2003)

The introduction of David Damrosch's *What is World Literature?* focuses on several interlinked issues: the relationship between Goethe and Eckermann (the recorder of Goethe's famous assertion about world literature), the career of the term since Goethe's time, and ways in which to limit the scope of world literature. The rest of the book, divided into three parts – 'Circulation', 'Translation' and 'Production' – is a representative cross-section of Damrosch's understanding of world literature which is defined as possessing three distinct qualities: it is an elliptical refraction of national literatures; it is literature that gains in translation; it is a mode of reading, a form of 'detached engagement with worlds beyond our own place and time'.[30]

Not having access to the original language of a work of world literature is 'actually irrelevant to the [work's] existence abroad. *All* works cease to be the exclusive products of their original culture once they are translated; all become works that only "began" in their original language.'[31] An interesting case in point is Eckermann's own text. The initial reception of the *Conversations* in Germany was poor despite the fact that is was published by the renowned Brockhaus publisher. However, the book did well in it numerous translations, especially in English. Margaret Fuller published a first abridged translation in 1838. After a sequel was published in German in 1848, John Oxenford expanded Fuller's translation and integrated material from the sequel. This new translation was published in 1850. However, while the German original lists Eckermann as author and is entitled *Gespräche mit Goethe*, Oxenford changes the title to *Conversations with Eckermann* and makes Goethe the author. Oxenford also considerably reduces Eckermann's presence in the text, curtailing his autobiographical introduction and omitting large chunks of the text, especially when Eckermann seems to take the

30 David Damrosch, *What is World Literature?* (Princeton: Princeton University Press, 2003), 281.

31 Ibid., 22.

spotlight away from Goethe. After Oxenford it became standard practice for editors of the *Conversations* to rework those parts pertaining to Eckermann and to accord full respect only to the quotations from Goethe.

Damrosch's cross-section of world literature includes varied authors, texts and genres such as the *Epic of Gilgamesh*, Aztec poetry, Kafka, P. G. Wodehouse, Milorad Pavić's *The Dictionary of the Khazars*, Rigoberta Menchú's *testimonios* and Mechthild von Magdeburg's mystical writings.

Damrosch shows how the reception of a foreign text is often a struggle and can swing from one extreme to another: the initial efforts at understanding *Gilgamesh* displayed 'a high degree of assimilation toward the already known (most especially the Bible and its history)' while recent editors and translators 'have not always been very successful at understanding and conveying the epic's cultural difference'.[32] Similarly, until recently, post-Conquest Aztec literature that was collected and loosely translated by Spanish clerics tended to be read 'backward toward the pre-Conquest period [while] European elements in the sources were read forward as early stages in the region's march toward independence'.[33] Some of the Nahuatl poetry collected has survived only by pure chance; the surviving texts contradict the traditional view that native Mexican culture ended abruptly upon the arrival of the Spanish.

The case of a papyrus containing Egyptian love poems acquired by Chester Beatty in the late 1920s elucidates issues such as the relatively short lifespan of translations and the struggle between domestication in translation and a desire to keep culture-specific references. In the chapter on Kafka, Damrosch investigates a similar matter: how shifts in the interpretation of Kafka's texts in German and English have affected the recent translations of Kafka. Freudian and existentialist interpretations that accentuated the alienated individualist responding inwardly to modernity have been supplanted by historicist interpretations of Kafka as a representative of Prague Jewry and as a representative of a 'minor' literature in Deleuze and Guattari's sense.

32 Ibid., 40.

33 Ibid., 83.

Mechthild von Magdeburg translated a theological feeling into a passionate mysticism inspired by medieval love poetry. Her first two translators were clerics who translated her writings from Low German into Latin and into Middle High German. While doing so, they rearranged material by subject matter, tried to direct the reader's attention to particular passages and muted 'both eroticism and criticism of Church authorities'.[34] The Middle High German translation was only rediscovered in 1861, but would have to wait until the twentieth century to reach a broader reading public. Evelyn Underhill (whom we will meet again in Chapter 3) and Lucy Menzies introduced the German mystic to the English-speaking readership. Mechthild's use of erotic imagery has become more visible in contemporary translations but 'no translation has yet done justice to [her] many-sided work'.[35]

The case of Milorad Pavić's *The Dictionary of the Khazars* shows how some recent books have been produced *as* world literature, with an international audience in mind, while at the same time not being able to escape the pressures of local context. This is a metafictional work indebted to Borges, the *Arabian Nights* and Danilo Kiš. The text features completely different endings in different translations. Its political content, linked to Serbia, however, has largely been ignored or misread. Damrosch argues that while it is important to understand cultural subtexts 'a book of world literature has its fullest life, and its greatest power, when we can read it with a kind of *detached engagement*, informed but not confined by a knowledge of what the work would likely mean in its original time and place, even as we adapt it to our present context and purposes'.[36] Similarly, Rigoberta Menchú's *testimonios* have been mistaken for autobiographies in a Western sense and she has been accused of fabricating events. Added to the genre issues, Damrosch highlights the question of authorship: Menchú has distanced herself from Elizabeth Burgos, who still holds the author's rights for *I, Rigoberta*. For her second *testimonio*, Menchú enlisted the help of several

34 Ibid., 174.

35 Ibid., 184.

36 Ibid., 277. Emphasis in the original.

writers all of whom are mentioned in the original. In the English translation – which also rearranges chapters and cuts the text by 20 per cent – Menchú appears as sole author.

In the conclusion, Damrosch reiterates the importance and value of translation and his definition of world literature as a mode of reading: 'Traveling abroad [...] a text does indeed change, both in its frame of reference and usually in language as well. In an excellent translation, the result is not the loss of an unmediated original vision but instead a *heightening* of the naturally creative interaction of reader and text'.[37] The mode of reading advocated by Damrosch 'can be experienced *intensively* with a few works just as effectively as it can be explored *extensively* with a large number'.[38]

Casanova (2004)

Pascale Casanova's *La République mondiale des lettres* appeared in the French original in 1999; its English translation, *The World Republic of Letters*, appeared in 2004. Casanova's aim is to 'restore a point of view that has been obscured for the most part by the "nationalization" of literatures and literary histories, to rediscover a lost transnational dimension of literature that for two hundred years has been reduced to the political and linguistic boundaries of nations'.[39] Casanova consciously chooses the term 'world republic of letters' over 'world literature': this republic is 'a literary universe relatively independent of the everyday world and its political divisions, whose boundaries and operational laws are not reducible to those of ordinary political space'.[40] Casanova conceives of the literary universe in very similar terms to Braudel's 'economy-world' (*économie-monde*): a

37 Ibid., 292.
38 Ibid., 299.
39 Casanova, *World Republic*, xi.
40 Ibid., xii.

dimension whose temporality is distinct from that of the realm of politics, and governed by long-term cycles rather than short-term events. Spatially this universe is characterized by its literary capitals (most importantly Paris, but London and New York, too) and clearly divided into central and peripheral zones. This world has its own present, 'the literary Greenwich meridian'.[41]

Casanova also acknowledges her indebtedness to Bourdieu's sociology of literature and his notion of a 'field'. When it comes to success on the literary or cultural market, Bourdieu sees the literary and cultural fields as heteronomous (that is to say, interdependent with social, economic and political spheres of life). It is only where consecration (intended as the field-specific application of criteria of value) is concerned that the literary and cultural fields have gained a relatively high degree of independence from the social, economic or political domains. Contrary to Bourdieu who analyses well-defined literary and cultural fields firmly located in time and space, Casanova sees the whole transnational space of world literature as a single literary field – hierarchically structured, but a single field nonetheless – which functions according to well-established rules.

I have already mentioned Casanova's view on how the international literary space came into being above: literary authority and recognition depend on the formation and development of the first European states in the sixteenth century; Africa, Asia and the Indian subcontinent only join the international literary space with decolonization. There is a clear hierarchy between central and peripheral literary space, but this hierarchical structure is not linear or focused on a single dominant centre. Furthermore 'if literary space is relatively autonomous, it is also by the same token relatively dependent on political space'.[42]

According to Casanova's model, literary texts only have one way of entering the canon: consecration in one of the capitals of the literary universe.

> The consecration of a text is the almost magical metamorphosis of an ordinary material into 'gold', into absolute literary value. In this sense the sanctioning authorities

41 Ibid., 4.

42 Ibid., 115.

> of world literary space are the guardians, guarantors, and creators of value, which is nonetheless always changing, ceaselessly contested and debated, by virtue of the very fact of its connection with the literary present and modernity.[43]

All participants in the international literary space share a belief in the value of literary capital, of 'spiritual gold' and because of this shared belief it is 'possible to measure literary practices against a standard that is universally recognized as legitimate. Literary capital so surely exists, in its very immateriality, only because it has [...] objectively measurable effects that serve to perpetuate this belief'.[44]

Translation and criticism are both processes of establishing value, a particular type of consecration. The translation into a particularly dominant language (French for a very long time, and more recently English) is valued more than translation into other languages. In characterizing a writer's work, Casanova argues, one needs to pay heed to two aspects: the place the work occupies within its native literary space and the place occupied by the native literary space within world literary space.

The inhabitants of the literary centres are usually unaware of their role in producing a common standard for measuring literary time that unifies the literary space through competition. Casanova sees those literary fields located in the centre(s) as possessing greater autonomy than peripheral fields since they are the furthest removed from a political struggle through literature. This is why literary fields in the centre 'reduce foreign works of literature to their own categories of perception, which they mistake for universal norms, while neglecting all the elements of historical, cultural, political, and especially literary context that make it possible to properly and fully appreciate such works'.[45]

Casanova sees literary prizes as the lowest form of literary consecration, 'a sort of confirmation for the benefit of the general public'.[46] Casanova also argues that the Swedish Academy simply ratifies many judgements made in

43 Ibidem, 126–7.

44 Ibid., 17.

45 Ibid., 154.

46 Ibid., 147.

the longstanding literary capital, Paris: 'France remains the most regularly honored nation, with twelve prizes [...]) but also, and above all, the prizes awarded to Faulkner, Hemingway, Asturias, and García Márquez, all of whom were first discovered and celebrated in France'.[47]

Part II of Casanova's book consists of six chapters that investigate writers representing 'minor' literatures, writers who can be described as assimilated or rebelling against the literary capital, Irish writers, translated writers and 'the revolutionaries' (Dante, Joyce and Faulkner). Unlike Damrosch Casanova does not perform any close readings but makes rather sweeping statements regarding dozens of writers of international renown, from William Faulkner, W. B. Yeats and Franz Kafka to Ngũgĩ wa Thiong'o, Mário de Andrade and E. M. Cioran.

In the conclusion, Casanova argues again for the importance of making literature a temporal object: scholars should place literature in its historical time and then show how it managed to gradually tear itself away from the temporality of history towards a temporality of its own, an autonomy that allows literature to 'escape the ordinary laws of history'.[48] This newly created temporality has led to the creation of an autonomous literary space endowed with its own regulations. Paradoxically, time is both the sole source of literary value and the source of the inequality of the literary world. By drawing attention to the 'deprived and dominated writers on the periphery of the literary world', Casanova hopes to have created 'an instrument for struggling against the presumptions, the arrogance, and the fiats of critics in the center, who ignore the basic fact of the inequality of access to literary existence'.[49]

47 Ibid., 153. Since the publication of Casanova's book, another two French writers have been awarded the Nobel Prize: Jean Marie Gustave Le Clézio (2008) and Patrick Modiano (2014).

48 Ibid., 350.

49 Ibid., 355.

Pizer (2006)

Pizer's aim in *The Idea of World Literature: History and Pedagogical Practice* is twofold: to trace the history of the term *Weltliteratur* as a discursive concept in Germany and to discuss the practice of 'World Literature' as taught in the United States, with the ulterior motive to argue for the introduction of a metatheoretical approach in the teaching of world literature at US universities.[50] The twofold focus is necessary because

> as a distinct, coherent concept, Weltliteratur, despite its obviously cosmopolitan essence, was most fully and consistently articulated in Germany; it is, essentially, a German paradigm. But if Weltliteratur as a discursive paradigm is most closely and profitably associated with Germany, 'World Literature' *as a pedagogical practice* is almost exclusively to be found in the United States.[51]

Pizer provides his readers with a historical overview of the context that gave rise to Goethe's concept of *Weltliteratur* and describes its history in the German-speaking world. Pizer argues that one needs to understand Goethe's pronouncement about the imminence of a new epoch in literature as the result of a lifelong literary practice and against the specific backdrop of the politics in Europe in the first three decades of the nineneeth century, on one hand, and in opposition to Romantic perspectives on foreign languages, translation and universality/cosmopolitanism (viewed as markedly German attributes), on the other.

In the nineteenth century, Pizer sees Heinrich Heine as the '*only* mediator of Weltliteratur *as Goethe understood it* to have received international recognition.'[52] Karl Marx and Friedrich Engels's *Communist Manifesto* also advocated a new *Weltliteratur* observing that 'in the age of international interdependence, intellectual productions of individual nations are shared by all [and] national narrow-mindedness and one-sidedness

50 Pizer, 3.

51 Ibid., 85. Emphasis in the original.

52 Ibid., 13.

become impossible'.[53] However, the events of 1848 and the subsequent nationalist project in Germany meant that the project of national literature was prioritized over *Weltliteratur* and cosmopolitanism. The second half of the nineteenth century saw the publication of several anthologies of world literature in German that emerged out of a sense that Germany could be 'a great mediator among world cultures' but also out a sense of cultural superiority.[54]

In the early twentieth century, Goethe's *Weltliteratur* was eyed with suspicion and interpreted rather narrowly, either as an oldfashioned model that needed to yield a focus on the nation state (Friedrich Meinecke), an interest solely in the internationalization of the literary market (Ernst Elster), or derided as a leveling out of artistic talent and cultural specificity (Thomas Mann). With the rise of Nazism, however, Thomas Mann changed his view. In a 1932 article entitled 'Goethe as representative of the Bourgeois Age', Mann argued that his country stood in dire need of Goethean cosmopolitanism. 1946 saw the publication of Fritz Strich's influential *Goethe und die Weltliteratur* [Goethe and world literature] which reflects the global hopes of its time of a 'transnational aesthetic exchange on a universal scale', with an exchange among European literatures as the first stage and the integration of the rest of the world at some later stage.[55] Influential works on *Weltliteratur* in the 1950s fluctuate between Anni Carlsson's embrace of the concept as encompassing 'those works which transcend national, temporal, and linguistic borders and address a universal audience' and Erich Auerbach's fears that the allegedly homogenizing tendencies would flatten out cultural traditions.[56] Pizer goes on to discuss Hans-Georg Gadamer's and Hans Robert Jauss's influence in literary studies in Germany and their view of *Weltliteratur* in the 1970s before giving a brief overview of the revival of the term after the fall of the Berlin Wall.

53 Ibid., 65.
54 Ibid., 68.
55 Ibid., 72–3.
56 Ibid., 73.

In the section on the pedagogical practice of World Literature in the United States, Pizer writes a brief overview of the subject and its fortunes in US academia: it was first employed by scholars such as Richard G. Moulton and Philo M. Buck who were both comparatists but, following the Second World War, world literature courses where texts were taught in English translation rather than in the original languages (a practice reserved to comparative literature) expanded rapidly. This sudden rise in popularity was met with scepticism and contempt, as Calvin S. Brown's 1953 essay entitled 'Debased Standards in World-Literature Courses' and Lionel Trilling's 1958 'English and American Education' clearly show. World literature courses survived the so-called 'theory years' (mid-1960s to mid-1980s) and profited from the canon debate that started in the 1980s. Throughout its career world literature with its use of anthologized material competed with 'Great Books' courses with their pedagogical emphasis on the study of whole works. Pizer believes that 'whatever one's stance on these curricular approaches, world literature should become *disentangled* from [these debates]' because it cannot

> lead to a profound insight into Western *or* Eastern civilizations. While Great Books courses presuppose educational depth, World Literature must focus on breadth. [...] It can only provide a nodding, indeed superficial acquaintance with the world's divisive literatures, but it can lead to an appreciation for this diversity at a time when Americans might find such diversity virtually imperceptible. At the same time, it must familiarize students with the increasing global trend toward cultural transnationalism.[57]

Pizer believes that providing students with a metatheoretical approach will raise their awareness of 'how Goethe's Weltliteratur paradigm is grounded in the dialectical relationship between cultural unity and multiplicity, universality and particularity' and therefore enable them to read world literature as reflecting both dimensions.'[58]

Pizer then uses the critical lens of *Weltliteratur* as a paradigm to perform a critical reading of two novels by Rafik Schami, *Damascus Nights*

57 Ibid., 109.
58 Ibid., 114.

[Erzähler der Nacht] and *Der geheime Bericht über den Dichter Goethe* [The Secret Goethe File, not yet translated into English] before discussing the metatheoretical methodology he uses in his own teaching and the pedagogical significance of emphasizing the dialectical nature of Goethe's concept of *Weltliteratur*: only then will world literature transcend 'the vagueness and indefinition' that many associate with the concept and the practice at present and also bring about 'a positive interdisciplinarity among departments traditionally associated with one national tradition.'[59]

Rosendahl Thomsen (2008)

Mads Rosendahl Thomsen sees *Mapping World Literature. International Canonization and Transnational Literatures* as an intervention in the world literature debate that 'ask[s] questions about how world literature is structured and evolving in the Western world.'[60] He sees world literature as a double paradigm: the study of internationally canonized literature and the ambition to include all kinds of literature. World literature is a developing field, he argues, 'that takes seriously both cultural globalization and literature that can be characterized as transnational' but it may also be seen as a subfield of comparative literature and postcolonialism.[61] Rosendahl Thomsen argues against framing world literature within the latter two approaches. Comparative literature is an inadequate frame for the following reasons: it seems to have lost most of its interest in literatures of the world; it has been too encumbered by theory since the 1980s; at the same time it undertheorizes situations 'in which there is too much to read.' Moreover, comparative literature has not yet reflected on its own transition 'from

59 Ibid., 149.

60 Mads Rosendahl Thomsen, *Mapping World Literature. International Canonization and Transnational Literatures* (London and New York: Continuum, 2010), 2.

61 Ibid., 5.

being nation-bound, to de facto working with a comparison of texts that have become internationally canonized.'[62]

While postcolonialism emphasizes the complexity and hybridity of identity construction, Rosendahl Thomsen highlights some aspects that speak against an integration of world literature into postcolonial studies: postcolonial literary criticism is mostly interested in the young countries that were former colonies and in their nation-building processes, but has so far failed to integrate the literature of 'the traditional centres of literature, the old colonizers'. Also, within the field, scholars advocating hybridity and those advocating authenticity – understood as a 'cluster of specific events and habits attached to a people and a nation, and perhaps also a language, whose sum is more unique than hybrid' – do not see eye to eye.[63]

There is a risk of world literature becoming world literature in English, especially when anthologies are used to teach the subject. At the same time, 'the range of literatures also needs a common language in order to be truly diverse'. Rosendahl Thomsen sees world literature as 'always balancing between idealism and realism: the idealism of a world of unlimited cultural exchange and diversity with respect for differences, and the harsh realism of what is actually being translated, sold, read and taught around the world.'[64]

Rosendahl Thomsen then expands on the centre-periphery model that informs both Franco Moretti's and Pascale Casanova's work. We need to include temporary sub-centres in the geography of world literature, he argues, in order to give credit to phenomena such as the Scandinavian influence on European literature between 1880 and 1900 and 'el Boom' of South American literature in the 1960s and 1970s, both of which were important but could not sustain their position in the international literary system.

Many scholars nowadays look upon the idea of canons with suspicion because the selections reflect power relations. While this is certainly true, Rosendahl Thomsen reminds us that it is the combination of countless

62 Ibid., 22–3.

63 Ibid., 25.

64 Ibid., 10.

individual selections by critics, literary historians, writers, teachers and general readers that make works canonical over time.

International canons consist of several constellations of works 'that share properties of formal and thematic character, where canonized works can bring attention to less canonized, but affiliated, works, and draw them into the scene of world literature'. What is needed is 'critical thought based on the mapping of social selection combined with a textual approach that seeks constellations across time and space'.[65] Rosendahl Thomsen mentions three such constellations that are also inherently transnational: Holocaust writing, migrant writing and works by authors that get instantly translated and published simultaneously in several languages, before engaging in more detail with migrant writers and Holocaust writers.

Migrant writers stand out in world literature simply because they have managed to create a space of their own that is not tied to national literatures. They also have

> a different relation to languages and book markets than most other writers. That they also share a number of common interests cannot surprise, either, but what is interesting is how they have combined their basic themes, that, with formal solutions which give a particular voice to their material, make them interesting, regardless of whether one reads for the artistic, or the cultural or historic aspect of literature.[66]

The Holocaust is the first object of historical memory that is truly cosmopolitan and a concern to readers without any direct connection to the event. But it is not the universality of its theme that makes this literature an important constellation of world literature: the international canonization of this kind of literature depends on the ethical problem of combining history with aesthetics. Holocaust literature is, of course, about memory but it is also about defeating trauma, warning future generations and comprehending contemporary transgressions.

Seeking and finding constellations based on formal and thematic similarities is not just an experiment, Rosendahl Thomsen concludes, it also

65 Ibid., 3.

66 Ibid., 101.

presents facts about the complex selection of canons. This approach has four advantages: it is realistic, innovative, pluralistic and didactic. By taking an interest in the details of literary history and the workings of the international literary system, one is able to reveal the 'finer web of literature'.[67]

Sturm-Trigonakis (2013)

In 2013, Purdue University Press published Elke Sturm-Trigonakis's *Comparative Cultural Studies and the New* Weltliteratur, a revised translation of the author's 2007 *Global Playing in der Literatur: Ein Versuch über die Neue* Weltliteratur, written in German. The theoretical framework used here is comparative cultural studies as developed by Steven Tötösy de Zepetnek, with a clear emphasis on interdisciplinarity, contextual approach and evidence-based methodology.[68] Sturm-Trigonakis describes Goethe's concept of *Weltliteratur* before asking in what way his concept can be applied to specific contemporary hybrid texts that do not fit the rigid paradigms of national philologies, such as Turkish-German literature, Chicano/a literature, and Maghrebian authors writing in French.

Sturm-Trigonakis reminds the reader that Goethe only used the term *Weltliteratur* eighteen times in his writing. Of these eighteen, only five appeared in print during his lifetime:

> three appear[ed] in the journal edited by him, *Über Kunst und Alterthum in den Rhein-und Maingegenden* [On Art and Antiquity in the Rhine and Main Regions] (1816–1832), in the issues covering the years 1827 and 1828. The other two are found in an essay planned for an issue in 1830, the ideas of which have been mentioned in Goethe's introduction to Carlyle's biography by [sic] Schiller, as well as in an edition of the *Wanderjahre* [*Wilhelm Meister's Journeyman Years*] dated 1829. The

67 Ibid., 142.

68 See, for example, Steven Tötösy de Zepetnek, 'The New Humanities: The Intercultural, the Comparative, and the Interdisciplinary,' in *Global Society*, 1.2 (2007), 45–68.

> other entries, unpublished during Goethe's lifetime – thirteen in his work and two in Johann Peter Eckermann's conversations – are directly or indirectly connected with articles in the journal *Über Kunst und Alterthum*.[69]

While the journal's print run was relatively small, it found readers in Britain, France and Italy. Sturm-Trigonakis sees the journal as a means for Goethe to 'pass on the cosmopolitanism of the eighteenth century to the nineteenth, despite the growing nationally conscious attitude of European nations: his idea of Weltliteratur constituted work in progress.'[70] Goethe was interested in a process of cross-cultural exchange and reciprocal reception which, Sturm-Trigonakis argues, would be impossible without translation. Consequently, *Über Kunst und Alterthum* devoted much attention to translation and translation criticism. In valuing cultural exchange over a limited focus on national literature, Goethe clearly rejected the agenda of Romanticism.

Yet, Sturm-Trigonakis argues, there is more to the concept than a longing for Enlightenment cosmopolitanism. The final years of Goethe's life saw 'a general acceleration, a cancellation of spatial distances, and technological innovations of unknown dimensions accompanied by a globally expanding communication and trade network' not unlike our recent past and one needs to see the concept of *Weltliteratur* against that backdrop. It should therefore be thought of as an ongoing process of communication between different (national) literatures, linked to new technical and economic achievements of Goethe's age and including a utopian moment that Goethe saw 'in the near future'.[71]

At the same time, Sturm-Trigonakis is critical of what she calls the functionalization of Goethe's *Weltliteratur* by US scholars such as Damrosch and Pizer – either as theoretical or methodological model – and states that 'while in some instances the "new" notion of world literature as proposed by comparative literature scholars in the US may well be appropriate and

69 Elke Sturm-Trigonakis, *Comparative Cultural Studies and the New* Weltliteratur (West Lafayette, Indiana: Purdue University Press, 2013), 8–9.

70 Ibid., 9.

71 Ibid., 12.

useful[,] Goethe's notion ought to remain a matter of literary history'.[72] Rather, the concept requires to be redefined in the age of expanding globalization: 'Since new problems call for new methods, it is time to mark with the idea of a NWL [New World Literature] both the connection to Goethe and at the same time the distance from him by bringing into view a changed cognitive grid of previously neglected research objects and linking them to one another in a manner different than usual'.[73]

The neglected research objects are works of what is usually called 'minority literature' or 'migrant literature'. Sturm-Trigonakis redefines this literature as NWL, a subsystem of the 'literatures of the world' that displays a set of criteria, namely: 1) bilingualism and/or multilingualism with a specific shift in focus 'from the hitherto overstressed [...] question of the linguistic competence of the author to the performance of language(s) in the actual text;' 2) content and thematic nature, 'which refer to the phenomena of transnationalism typical of globalization;' and 3) the presence of 'poles provoked by globality and transnationality' that bypass the national and focus on the regional and/or the local.[74]

The category of NWL allows for the systemic organization of hybrid texts beyond the confines of national philologies which are uncomfortable with their characteristics anyway, Sturm-Trigonakis argues. NWL 'has to be thought of as of equal rank to "national literature", because it does not derive its evaluation criteria from national literary specifics, but from its constitution as a transnational, independent system'.[75]

Sturm-Trigonakis analyses dozens of texts that exhibit the three criteria summarized above, among which Monica Ali's *Brick Lane*, Gloria Anzaldúa's *Borderlands/La frontera*, Assia Djebar's *Les Nuits de Strasbourg* [Strasbourg Nights], Hanif Kureishi's *The Buddha of Suburbia*, Jusuf Naoum's *Die Kaffeehausgeschichten des Abu al Abed* [Abu al Abed's Coffee House Stories], Michael Ondaatje's *Anil's Ghost*, Emine Sevgi Özdamar's

72 Ibid., 20.

73 Ibid.

74 Ibid., 65–6.

75 Ibid., 160–1.

Mutterzunge [Mother Tongue] and Salman Rushdie's *East West*. Tahar Ben Jelloun's *The Sacred Night*, the sequel to his novel at the centre of Chapter 4 of this book, does not qualify as NWL in Sturm-Trigonakis's eyes because 'despite the presence of the Arabic use of metaphors in this French-language text [...] in the text itself the oscillation between the transnational and the local has not been registered for all the metamorphoses and the border-crossings of the protagonist'.[76]

In the globalized world we live in, Sturm-Trigonakis concludes, it is necessary to analyse 'diversity with tools of systemic and contextual frameworks whereby the heterogeneity and complexity of new relations are observable'. Comparative cultural studies constitutes such an inter-disciplinary methodology as it applies frameworks developed in other disciplines (sociology, linguistics, history and cultural anthropology) to literary studies.

Apter (2013)

Also in 2013, Emily Apter published *Against Literature. On the Politics of Untranslatability*. It recasts some of Apter's earlier work in terms of the philosophical concept of 'untranslatables'. The concept is taken from the *Vocabulaire européen des philosophies: Dictionnaire des intraduisibles*, edited by Barbara Cassin and first published in 2004. Together with Cassin, Jacques Lezra and Michael Wood, Apter edited the English translation that appeared in 2014 as *Dictionary of Untranslatables: A Philosophical Lexicon*. The aim of *Against World Literature* is clearly stated in the introduction:

> to activate untranslatability as a theoretical fulcrum of Comparative Literature with bearing on approaches to world literatures, literary world-systems and literary history, the politics of periodization, the translation of philosophy and theory, the relation between sovereign and linguistic borders at the checkpoint, the bounds

76 Ibid., 66.

> of non-secular proscription and cultural sanction, free versus privatized authorial property, the poetics of translational difference, as well as ethical, cosmological and theological dimensions of worldliness.[77]

While Apter approves of the expansion of the canon and the critical engagement with translation that has resulted from the renewed interest in world literature she also expresses serious reservations 'about tendencies in World Literature toward reflexive endorsement of cultural equivalence and substitutability, or toward the celebration of nationally and ethnically branded "differences" that have been niche-marketed as "identities"'.[78] To counter-act these tendencies, Apter focuses on a cluster of issues that in her view do not get enough attention in recent comparative literature and world literature studies: non-translation, mistranslation, incomparabilty and untranslatability. The untranslatable is not directly opposite to the always translatable but rather a 'linguistic form of creative failure with homeopathic use'.[79]

In her attempt to redefine the paradigm of world literature as a pluralistic construct anchored in philosopy and geopolitics, Apter does not perform close readings of literary texts but rather uses examples from a variety of discourses: philosophy, theology, critical theory, film, and installations.

Apter elucidates what she means by untranslatables in Part Two of her book where she discusses specific keywords that do not translate easily or only as a creative failure into other languages: Ephraim Chambers's neologism 'cyclopedia'; 'peace'; the Portuguese 'fado' and 'saudade'; 'sex' and 'gender' in the translations of French feminist texts such as Simone de Beauvoir's *Le deuxième sexe* [The Second Sex]; and 'monde' as in the 2007 manifesto that aimed to do away with the term 'Francophone literature' and supplant it with '*littérature-monde en français*' [world-literature in French].

Several chapters are dedicated to critics who, in Apter's view, anticipated some of the issues she draws attention to: Erich Auerbach was particularly attentive to 'the untranslability of cultural expression and to

77 Emily Apter, *Against World Literature: The Politics of Untranslatability* (London and New York: Verso Books, 2013), 3–4.

78 Ibid., 2.

79 Ibid., 20.

discrepant literary traditions' and 'actually downplayed the equivalencies and similitudes cherished by comparatists'.[80] Edward Said saw translation as a kind of 'territorial loss, be it [of] cultural or geographic property' and argued for the need of a 'terrestrial humanism that tracks the history of forced relocation, exile and occupation'.[81] Apter also traces the alterations in Jacques Derrida's thoughts on translation from 1979 to the mid-1980s: the discussion shifts from an emphasis on the 'duty to translate' and a 'theology of translation' to 'untranslatability' as something 'endemic to the university institution that causes us to renegotiate the boundaries between self and institution, life and death, language and world'.[82]

Apter presents the case of Eleanor Marx's translation of Gustave Flaubert's *Madame Bovary* as the 'tale of a world literature classic in translation into whose folds the personal histories of its translators are secretly embedded'.[83] A translation, Apter argues, is always a 'worked and working text. No longer viewed as stable object owned by a single author, it emerges as a site of translational or editorial labor'.[84] Chastized as a bad translation by Nabokov, Marx's text nevertheless served Paul de Man as the basis for his 1965 translation for Norton. The resulting 'Substantially New Translation Based on the Version by Eleanor Marx Aveling' was also reused in Margaret Cohen's 2004 Norton edition. Paul de Man's daughter recalls that her father lost his review copy and according to another source, it was de Man's wife Patricia who did most of the work. De Man argued in the preface that the revisions had been extensive but a close comparison of the translations reveals that de Man stays relatively close to Marx's text and that the 2004 edition is also clearly indebted to her work. In the 2004 text, Flaubert is mediated by Marx, two de Mans and Cohen – a mediation that the average reader does not necessarily think about.

This case study leads Apter to ask questions about authorial ownership, authorship and intellectual property and translation as a legal form of

80 Ibid., 195.

81 Ibid., 220.

82 See Apter, 243.

83 Ibid., 266.

84 Ibid., 292–3.

plagiarism. In the penultimate chapter of the book, Apter investigates issues of ownership when it comes to cultural heritage: who owns an antique or a literary classic? Who has the right to speak about it, touch it or teach it? Apter calls on Bruce Robbins's idea of a *dispossessive ethics of reading* that

> challenges the presumptive self-interest and self-having assumed to condition the reader's relation to cultural property. This dispossessive stance casts World Literature as an unownable estate, a literature over which no one exerts proprietary prerogative and which lends itself to a critical turn that puts the problem of property possession front and center.[85]

Apter summarizes her aim again in the final chapter: 'to wean World Literature from its comfort zone [...] by pressing on what a world is, philosophically, theologically and politically.'[86] Scholars interested in comparative and world literature should focus not only on the expansion of canons or translation technologies but also on the abstract and untranslatable 'thanotropic projections of how a planet dies'.[87]

Systematizing world literature

The six monographs summarized above are a representative cross-section of academic criticism on world literature produced in the West in the last fifteen years. Each book takes up a very specific stance in relation to the term world literature and a more general view as to how to define world literature: a mode of reading, a paradigm for teaching and research, an overarching term for hybrid literature that exhibits very specific, narrowly defined traits. While there are some convergences and some clearly contradicting views on the usefulness of the concept or paradigm in contemporary

85 Ibid., 329.

86 Ibid., 335.

87 Ibid., 342.

literary studies in the six monographs, two important concerns emerge that seem fundamental in any critical engagement with world literature: 1) a particular stance on translation and consecration; and 2) an attempt to systematize works of world literature or the entire literary universe.

While there are works of literature written in English that are also sometimes described as world literature such as Anglophone colonial and postcolonial literature, most world literature we read is by definition translated literature. Damrosch claims that world literature gains in translation; he is also quite sensitive to the impact that a translator's input can have on a text in several of his case studies. Casanova sees translation as a particular type of consecration whereby the translation into a particular language (French or English) confers value on a work – this view chimes with Edith Grossman's quoted in the introduction.

The use of translated material in anthology form is an accepted practice for Damrosch and Pizer while Rosendahl Thomsen and Sturm-Trigonakis are more aware of the risk of world literature becoming a discipline mainly taught and talked about in English. Rosendahl Thomsen, however, also believes that a common language in which to talk about world literature might actually be beneficial. Sturm-Trigonakis acknowledges that translation was a major concern for Goethe but then takes a more traditional comparative approach to her case studies: she only works with texts she can read in the original; therefore she does not express any value judgements on translated texts.

As we have seen, Apter's critical lens is a philosophical concept, that of 'untranslatables', which expresses not the impossibility of translation but the creative linguistic failures that result from translation. Apter welcomes the translational turn in comparative literature (to which she contributed with her previous monograph, *The Translation Zone*) and returns to translation – not necessarily understood as literary translation – again and again in the course of her book. While most world literature scholars agree on the importance of translation, very few actually integrate translation theory into their works as I will do in this study.

Let us now return to Casanova as she links translation to consecration, another central aspect of my approach. What gets translated into the foremost literary languages? Only that which is thought of as displaying a particular kind of literary quality. Casanova seems to advocate *innovation* and *modernity* as the all-important defining element of literariness. She also asserts that the relative age of a literary culture is the condition of being able to 'claim a literary existence that is fully recognized in the present'.[88] By linking the 'age' of a culture to that of the post-Napoleonic nation, Casanova ignores the existence of many *de facto* older civilizations that achieved literary modernity without the supporting framework of a nation state for much of their literary history. Bengal, for example, can look back onto a rich literary existence that stretches back to at least the ninth century CE and therefore clearly should qualify as 'old'. It also saw a literary revolution, the Bengal Renaissance (circa 1860 to 1940) characterized by innovation and modernization.[89]

One of the consecrated writers Casanova uses as examples is the Bengali author Rabindranath Tagore, who is also at the centre of Chapter 3. Tagore was fifty-one years old when he was introduced to the literary scene in London in 1912. The London literary elite was fascinated by this 'sage from the Orient', and, thanks to the endorsement of some of its leading members (Robert Bridges, Thomas Sturge Moore, Ezra Pound and William Butler Yeats), Tagore was the first Asian writer to be awarded the Nobel Prize for Literature in 1913. Casanova argues that Tagore needed consecration in the West in order to be included in the canon of world literature, glossing over the fact that Tagore was established as a literary luminary in Bengal before he was 'consecrated' in London. Granted, the initial success in London and the subsequent Nobel Prize did make Tagore a more *visible* figure on the Western literary scene for a while – yet world literary space, I contend,

88 Casanova, *World Republic*, 89–90.

89 The oldest manuscript of Charyapada, the first known Bengali written language, is a collection of poems written between the ninth and the eleventh century. The palm leaf manuscript consists of 47 verses, written by over twenty poets that describe 'agriculture and particularly the importance of family, marriage and local ways'. Amaresh Datta, *The Encyclopaedia of Indian Literature, Volume One: A to Devo* (New Delhi: Sahitya Akademi, 2006), 647. On the Bengal Renaissance, see Subrata Dasgupta, *The Bengal Renaissance: Identity and Creativity from Rammohun Roy to Rabindranath Tagore* (Delhi: Permanent Black, 2007).

cannot simply be reduced to visibility or marketability in the West. While Tagore's works were unavailable in the English-speaking West for several decades, during that time they remained visible in India, other European and Middle Eastern countries (all undoubtedly members of the international literary space). This brings us to the second concern shared by the six monographs surveyed above: the systematization of world literature and/or international literary space.

Scholars attempting to systematize world literature do so out of a desire to make it an operable paradigm for literary study and escape the imprecision that has shadowed the term in the past. These systematizing efforts work on one of two levels (or on both): there is an attempt to describe the international literary space using system theory; and there is a conscious systematization of texts understood as a grouping according to thematic and structural criteria.

Damrosch does not call what he does systematizing, but he does present us with a specific group of texts that he calls 'his world literature'. A 'mode of reading' is still an attempt at delimiting world literature; out of the six approaches to world literature, Damrosch's system (if we want to call it that) is the most dynamic and open to agency. Casanova's model is the most elaborate out of the six monographs under review here. It focuses on the entire literary universe and not so much on the grouping of texts (this grouping tends to happen automatically in Casanova's view). As we have already seen, there are shortcomings to this metropole/province system: it does not allow for several parallel canons or for consecration in, or exchange between, locations outside the literary metropoles. Mads Rosendahl Thomsen picks up on this inadequacy and suggests supplementing the centre/periphery model with so-called 'temporary centres' that explain the intermittent importance of particular authors and works. Rosendahl Thomsen also attempts to systematize world literature texts grouping them into coherent 'constellations' for reading, teaching, and analysis. Sturm-Trigonakis also systematizes hybrid texts according to strict thematic and linguistic aspects with the aim to render NWL texts equals of traditionally defined 'national literature'. Diversity is best analysed with systemic and contextual tools, Sturm-Trigonakis argues, and while I intend to use such tools in the following case studies these are not necessarily the tools used by Sturm-Trigonakis.

Starting from the observation that the six case studies cited above share a concern with systematizing world literature and the international literary space it belongs to I have opted for a systemic approach that has been developed with a particular focus on literature. This approach is Itamar Even-Zohar's polysystem theory, an explanatory model for cultural phenomena widely used in translation studies, though not much employed by comparatists. In comparative literature Bourdieu's theory of the literary field and Luhmann's system's theory have attracted more followers.[90] In the following section, I explain Even-Zohar's model and illustrate its usefulness for this study as well as for other projects interested in reception processes.

Polysystem theory

Starting from the assumption that human society is always stratified, Even-Zohar sets out to elaborate a theory that would account not only for what we usually call 'reality', but also for different expressions of human thought: history, philosophy, sociology and literature. Any semiotic polysystem, be it history, language or literature, is a part of a larger polysystem, that of 'culture' and thus closely related to the whole and to the other components of this larger polysystem. 'Conceiving of literature as a separate semi-independent socio-cultural institution is therefore tenable only if the literary polysystem, like any other socio-cultural system, is conceived of as simultaneously autonomous and heteronomous with all other co-systems'.[91]

90 '[T]o some extent, this is due to the misconception that the more recent forms of system theory have superseded their polysystemic predecessor'. Philippe Codde, 'Polysystem Theory Revisited: A New Comparative Introduction', *Poetics Today*, 24/1 (2003), 91–126. Here 91.

91 Itamar Even-Zohar, 'Polysystem Theory', *Poetics Today* 11, no. 1 (1990), 9–26. Here 23.

The idea that polysystems possess some autonomy but are still related to a larger ensemble allows us to treat literature in its entire complexity and to address the paradoxical situation of its constantly shifting boundaries. Even-Zohar's approach is pragmatic and functional: it is based on the analysis of relations within and between different semiotic systems. Polysystem theory also provides a less simplistic and reductive approach to two questions: why do readers read the way they do? How is it possible to reach some degree of consensus in interpretation? Equally importantly, it provides a workable model for literature's interrelations with other discourses, as we shall see throughout this book.[92]

Rather than rejecting structuralist approaches to culture and society as static and synchronic, Even-Zohar argues that aspects of Russian Formalism and Czech Structuralism are characterized by a *dynamic* approach to structures. If one wants to describe how a system functions both in principle and in time, one soon realizes that 'a system consists of both synchrony and diachrony' and that it is by definition *heterogeneous* and *open*, and that its elements are *interdependent*.[93] In polysystem theory, heterogeneity is reconcilable with functionality because, rather than correlating them individually, Even-Zohar conceives of individual items or functions as constitutive of 'partly alternative systems of concurrent options'.[94] These systems are structured, they are indeed *hierarchies*, and there is a permanent struggle between the various strata, a constant change between centrifugal and centripetal motions. In a literary polysystem, the centre could be equated with dominant literary models or, indeed, an established canon

92 See Gerald Ernest Paul Gillespie, *By Way of Comparison: Reflections on the Theory and Practice of Comparative Literature* (Paris: Champion, 2004), 228: 'The advantage of general systems thinking is that it does not first require that a particular literature or set of literatures serve the individual scholar as the exclusive source of standards on which to base his or her conclusions or to perceive others' truth-claims. Rather, it allows the researcher to situate literary works in relation to the significant movements of elements in the repertory of any literature, including phenomena that exhibit intersystemic interferences, such as translation'.

93 Even-Zohar, 'Polysystem Theory', 11.

94 Ibid., 13.

of 'great books'. The movement towards and away from the centre explains why at a specific time in history a particular literary genre or author gains importance, thus moving towards the centre, or why they are slipping into oblivion, moving away from the centre.[95]

Each polysystem, however, does not only have one centre (standard language, canonized literature) and one periphery (dialects or non-canonical literature) but many parallel centres and peripheries. Also, elements might move not only within a polysystem (from one stratum to another) but also from one system into an adjacent system. Thus, an influential philosophical text will have an impact on the writing of literature and history, and developments in literature might influence other discourses. This holds true for the relationship between fiction and extra-literary reality, as well. Polysystem theory also offers a viable model for cross-cultural discourse in the way it describes the transfers within a system but especially between systems. I will repeatedly come back to the question as to why cross-cultural transfers take place in the first place and how these transfers are performed and actualized.

Ultimately, Even-Zohar suggests, all polysystems are conceived of as components of a 'mega-polysystem', one that organizes and controls several polysystems. However, polysystems are not clear-cut or forever bound to one specific form. Because of this, 'the very notions of "within" and "between" cannot be taken either statically or for granted'.[96] One of the prerequisites for any socio-cultural system to operate is heterogeneity. In polysystem theory, the law of proliferation not only seems to be *universally valid* but *necessary*: 'In order to fulfil its needs, a system actually strives to avail itself of a growing inventory of alternative options'.[97] In most literary polysystems there is a conscious lookout for new talent, new voices, new forms of literature, either from within or from other polysystems. Ultimately, the adoption of polysystem theory provides us with a tool to

95 Clearly, this centre is not a geographically definable centre, such as Paris or London in Casanova's *The World Republic of Letters*.

96 Even-Zohar, 'Polysystem Theory', 24.

97 Ibid., 26.

explain changing interpretations of literature as well as literature's relations to other discourses and cultures (polysystems in their own right) as well as its relations to 'reality' (the 'mega-polysystem').

One of the central notions in polysystem theory is that of the *repertoire*, 'the aggregate of rules and materials which govern both the *making* and *handling*, or production and consumption of any given product'.[98] The two levels described here (individual objects or elements and the rules or models they either reflect or labour against) always are at work in the transfer of literary texts from one cultural polysystem to another. Most importantly, however, the term *repertoire* has connotations of a certain freedom of choice. Thus, the interpretive options available to members of reading communities will inevitably be culturally determined, but members can actively choose from a variety of options available to them. The concept of repertoire allows for different coexisting viewpoints of literature: readers may opt to view literature as authentic documents that one can use as a socio-anthropological representation of a given culture or period in history, or rather see these as commentary (in Riedel's sense) or, at the other end of the spectrum, as self-sufficient aesthetic artefacts without a mimetic function.

Over the years, Even-Zohar has amended and expanded his model several times, also adapting Jakobson's Communication Scheme to deal with socio-semiotic polysystems in general and literary polysystems in particular. Even-Zohar explains the adapted scheme as follows:

> A CONSUMER may 'consume' a PRODUCT produced by a PRODUCER, but in order for the 'product' to be generated, then properly consumed, a common REPERTOIRE must exist, whose usability is constrained, determined, or controlled by some INSTITUTION on the one hand, and a MARKET where such a good can be transmitted, on the other.[99]

98 Itamar Even-Zohar, 'Factors and Dependencies in Culture: A Revised Outline for Polysystem Culture Research', *Canadian Review of Comparative Literature*, 24 (1997), 15–34. Here 20.

99 Ibid.

The scheme is easily applied to any act of reading literature: a reader (consumer) sitting somewhere in Britain picks up a book by, let us say, Charles Dickens (producer). In order for a 'successful' reading to happen, the reader must share a certain repertoire (common language, specific ideas about what a novel is or how characters are/should be described) with the author. Dickens' œuvre, however, is determined, constrained or controlled by, for example, a long tradition of Dickens scholarship and editing (part of Even-Zohar's *institution*, 'the aggregate of factors involved with the control of culture') of which the reader might or might not be aware. The reader is also influenced by his or her own schooling (another element of institution) and can only access reading material that is available on the market (which, quite like the institution, is defined as an intermediary force 'between social forces and culture repertoires').[100] The usefulness of this scheme for revealing points of friction in the reading of translations is apparent: what happens when we place other producers next to the author (editor, translator, adaptor)? What if the repertoire available to the reader does not necessarily correspond to the repertoire of the author? How will the co-producers of the translated text make sure that the text fits into what they perceive to be the repertoire of the receiving culture?

As far as my own research is concerned, thinking of works of world literature in translation as objects positioned within a flexible, multi-layered polysystem allows me to investigate different aspects: the struggle between high and low culture, the tension between centre and periphery, as well as claims of equivalence between original and translated texts. While Even-Zohar is mainly interested in literary models, my focus is different: as pointed out above, I concentrate on agents besides the author who shape the production and reception of translated works of world literature in specific receiving cultures. In the following section, I provide an overview of reception studies, the second of the three theories which, alongside Even-Zohar's polysystem theory and Steven Mailloux's rhetorical hermeneutics (to be described in Chapter 2), form the foundation of my method.

100 Ibid.

Reception studies

> *It is the joint effort of author and reader which brings upon the scene that concrete and imaginary object which is the work of the mind. There is no art except for and by others.*[101]

The study of reception has been one of the dominant modes of literary criticism since the 1970s. Starting out in the Constance School with Wolfgang Iser and Hans Robert Jauss, reception theories have been gaining importance globally since the 1980s. Reception studies departs from the view prevalent in Romanticism of the author as literary genius and of the text as an integral work of art containing all the information for its decoding. Unlike text-centred criticism, reception studies focuses on the act of reading (*aesthetics of reception*) and on the historical reception of literary texts (*reception history*).[102] By focusing on the contextualization of both the production and the reception of literature, as well as on the *performative* character of the reading process, reception theories provide literary studies with the conceptual and methodological tools to address issues such as plurality and cross-cultural discourse. Significantly, reception theory is an operational model that also functions as a theory of the literary text. I agree with Jonathan Culler's argument that

> to stress literature's dependence on particular modes of reading is a firmer and more honest starting point than is customary in criticism. One need not struggle [...] to find some objective property of language, which distinguishes the literary from the non-literary, but may simply start from the fact that we can read texts as literature and then inquire what operations that involves.[103]

101 Jean-Paul Sartre, *Jean-Paul Sartre: Basic Writings*, ed. Stephen Priest (London: Routledge, 2001), 264.

102 See Wolfgang Iser, *How to Do Theory* (Oxford: Blackwell Publishing, 2006), viii: 'Reception Theory focuses primarily on two points of intersection: the interface between text and context, and that between text and reader'.

103 Culler, 'Literary Competence', 116.

Reception theory is a pragmatic and functional approach that not only acknowledges the fact that all our efforts to interpret literature are intrinsically linked to the situatedness of the interpreter/reader; it is based on that very observation. In its pragmatism and functionality, it is quite easily integrated with polysystem theory. Reception theory also provides us with a viable definition of the literary work that focuses on not only one or two of the three elements of literary communication (author – text – reader), but on all of them. The literary work is not just a vehicle that communicates an author's meaning or a self-referential and self-contained unit of meaning; it becomes, in Sartre's words, the product of the 'joint effort between author and reader'. It is exactly this joint effort that allows reception history to mediate former and current understandings of a literary text. Reception theory revalues the historicity of the literary work, a quality that text-centred literary criticism largely ignores. Only by emphasizing the performative character of the reading process can we account for both the historical context of the creation of the text (which includes the author's biography) and the reader's own being in time. Only by considering both will we be able to achieve what Jauss calls the 'coherence of literature as an event'.[104]

As James Machor points out, the practice of reception studies moves 'beyond theoretical critique and acknowledges, explains and justifies the very different interests, contexts and interpretive communities that compose our pluralistic society'.[105] The study of literature as a social polysystem of (inter)actions raises questions about what happens to literature and the manner in which it is written, published, distributed, read and judged.

104 Hans Robert Jauss, *Toward an Aesthetic of Reception* (Minneapolis: University of Minnesota Press, 1994), 22.

105 James L. Machor, 'Introduction' in James L. Machor and Philip Goldstein, eds, *Reception Study: From Literary Theory to Cultural Studies* (New York: Routledge, 2001), ix–xviii. Here xiii.

Reception aesthetics

While most of my research is concerned with reception history, an overview of the key concepts of reception aesthetics, the actual steps performed by individual readers, is necessary at this point as it provides a larger critical context into which to integrate our findings. Reception theorists such as Wolfgang Iser, Hans Robert Jauss and Peter Rabinowitz approach different facets of the reading process.

The activity of reading is more challenging than both author- and text-centred approaches to literature imply. Reading is challenging in as much as it does not mean applying the right rules in order to get the right meaning out of a text originally developed by a single author. Reading does not mean *close reading* in the tradition of New Criticism, either. Reading is complicated because it means having a starting point; it implies many abilities, such as being able to paraphrase and making sense of the words, sentences, paragraphs and pages in front of us. Reading means raising expectations that are either fulfilled or denied. Reading means looking for coherence, by focusing on certain elements and ignoring others. There is no one-way traffic in reading; there is an interaction between text and reader, a virtual dialogue. Readers are not passive recipients who reproduce an already established meaning; they actively participate in the making of meaning.[106]

Until the advent of reader response criticism, one of the most neglected facts in literary history was that 'readers need to stand somewhere before they pick up a book and the nature of that "somewhere" [...] significantly influences the ways in which they interpret (and consequently evaluate) texts'.[107] Every reader has a *horizon of expectations* that will be either fulfilled

106 'One should conceive of meaning as something that happens, for only then can one become aware of those factors that precondition the composition of the meaning'. Wolfgang Iser, *The Act of Reading: A Theory of Aesthetic Response* (Baltimore: Johns Hopkins University Press, 1980), 22.

107 Peter J. Rabinowitz, *Before Reading: Narrative Conventions and the Politics of Interpretation* (Columbus, Oh.: Ohio State University Press, 1997), 2.

or denied. Hans Robert Jauss introduced the term as one of the major devices by which to integrate history and aesthetics of reception. By horizon of expectation, Jauss means 'an intersubjective system or structure of expectations, a "system of references" or a mind-set that a hypothetical individual brings to a given text. All works are read against some horizon of expectation'.[108] The horizon of expectation in Jauss's theory is an adaptation of the concept of *horizon* in the phenomenology and hermeneutics of Edmund Husserl and Martin Heidegger but mostly of Gadamer's concept of *horizon* as our limited perspective on reality.[109] Yet, a *horizon* is not a closed standpoint, it actually is something into which we move and which moves with us.[110] Jauss adopts Gadamer's view of *understanding* as a process of fusing the present horizon with a past horizon (*Horizontverschmelzung*). This procedure of projecting one horizon onto another, be it a past horizon or a culturally different one, is a basic presupposition for any act of interpretation. Because Jauss conceives of the reading process as the opposite of an arbitrary series of purely subjective impressions, our present reading and interpretation of a determined text is part of an evolution, is inserted in a bigger system of reference. Jauss's theory concentrates on devices in the literary text that trigger signals and memories and bring the reader 'to a specific emotional attitude'. Thus, '[a] literary work, even when it appears to be new, does not present itself as something absolutely new in an informational vacuum, but predisposes its audience to a very specific kind of

108 Robert C. Holub, 'Reception Theory: The School of Constance', in Raman Selden, ed., *The Cambridge History of Literary Criticism. Volume 8: From Formalism to Post-Structuralism* (1995), 319–46. Here 323.

109 '"to have a horizon" means not being limited to what is nearby but being able to see beyond it. A person who has an horizon knows the relative significance of everything within this horizon, whether it is near or far, great or small. Similarly, working out the hermeneutical situation means acquiring the right horizon of inquiry'. Hans-Georg Gadamer, *Truth and Method*, trans. rev. by Joel Weinsheimer and Donald Marshall (New York: Crossroad, 1989), 302.

110 'Der Horizont ist vielmehr etwas, in das wir hineinwandern und das mit uns mitwandert'. Gadamer, *Wahrheit und Methode. Grundzüge einer philosophischen Hermeneutik.* (Tübingen: Mohr, 1965), 288.

reception'.[111] Our initial horizon of expectations is constantly varied, corrected and altered during every interaction with the text and thus becomes a *syntagmatic horizon of expectations*.

Our assumptions about a literary genre and our knowledge of other works by a specific author create in us a certain expectation of what we are probably going to find in the text. As Rabinowitz points out, genre designation is extremely important and not an act that happens towards the end or after the reading process: 'some preliminary generic judgment is always required even before we begin the process of reading. We can never interpret entirely outside generic structures: "reading" – even the reading of a first paragraph – is always "reading as"'.[112] We always read a text as a novel, a poem or a journal. This activity of *reading as* is obviously related to our being a member of a specific reading community and our knowledge about authors, genres and literary style will undoubtedly vary, depending on our literary competence.

Once the reading process starts, most readers become more aware of the existence of assumptions and expectations, especially when they have to mediate between their initial assumptions and information provided by the text that might radically diverge from what they expected. Readers also use the information they get during the actual reading process to predict what could come next. Wolfgang Iser describes two essential factors in the interaction between text and reader: *gaps* and *negations*. Gaps are blanks left in the text for the reader to fill in:

> The blank [...] designates a vacancy in the overall system of the text, the filling of which brings about an interaction of textual patterns. [...] It is only when the schemata of the text are related one to another that the imaginary object can begin to be formed, and it is the blanks that get this connecting operation under way. They indicate that the different segments of the text are to be connected, even though the text itself does not say so.[113]

111 Jauss, *Aesthetic of Reception*, 23.

112 Rabinowitz, *Before Reading*, 176.

113 Iser, *Act of Reading*, 182–3.

Texts, therefore, are as much about what they communicate explicitly as they are about what they convey implicitly. Filling in gaps is a reading technique that all readers handle to a certain extent. What they fill the gaps with will largely depend on their literary competence and their skills, but in order to be able to proceed in the reading process, textual patterns *must* be connected. The text does not have to explicitly tell the reader to fill in the gaps because one of the major efforts readers make during the act of reading is to achieve coherence; therefore they automatically try to fill in the gaps they perceive in the text.

Without the reader bridging the gaps, there is no communication. The gaps are central axes for the text-reader relationship. Iser calls the other instance in the textual system where text and reader converge *negation*.

> Blanks and negations both control the process of communication in their own different ways: The blanks leave open the connection between textual perspectives and [...] patterns – in other words, they induce the reader to perform basic operations *within* the text. The various types of negation invoke familiar and determinate elements of knowledge only to cancel them out. What is cancelled, however, remains in view, and thus brings about modifications in the reader's attitude toward what is familiar or determinate – that is, he is guided to adopt a position *in relation* to the text.[114]

In Iser's description of the act of reading, the operational character of reception theory becomes apparent. Readers perform basic operations within a text (by filling in the gaps) and they have to adopt a position in relation to the text (by dealing with negations of their expectations). In this formulation of the reading process, elaborated in the 1970s, one can already see the germ of what Iser later calls *transactional loops*: 'what is mutually transposed is never fully in view but masked by symbols [...]. [I]nterpretation, owing to the trial-and-error pattern that structures transactional looping, becomes self-correcting'.[115]

114 Wolfgang Iser, *Prospecting: From Reader Response to Literary Anthropology* (Baltimore: Johns Hopkins University Press, 1989), 34.

115 Wolfgang Iser, *The Range of Interpretation* (New York andChichester: Columbia University Press, 2000), xi.

Readers with different starting points due to different historical and cultural backgrounds will perceive different sections of a text as gaps or interpret these gaps differently; what is perceived as negation also depends on the initial assumptions brought to the text. Thus, gaps and negations function as the latent or potential meanings in a given, overdetermined text. There are as many sections in a text that can be perceived as gaps or negations as there are potential meanings in a text. Whether they are perceived as such depends on the historical and cultural background of the readers.

While reading and after having read a text, readers perform a combination of three activities: *naming*, *bundling* and *thematizing*. Readers automatically tend to name what they have read (readers can name feelings described in a piece of writing, such as 'love', long before it is spelled out in the text); they bundle information which is dispersed in the text itself (they find analogies and parallels in both form and content), they thematize what they have read (they distinguish 'good' and 'evil' characters and those which are difficult to characterize, for example).[116] All of these activities are carried out in the name of *configuration* and *coherence*.

According to traditional criticism, it is the text that is either coherent or not: coherence is based almost entirely on textual, thus objective, factors. What reception theorists argue is that readers *want* texts to be coherent. Readers assume that texts are coherent, even if this coherence is not always given at the first approach to the text. In order to achieve a sense of coherence, during the act of reading readers fill in gaps, tame the surplus of information and bundle disparate sections of the text. Then, after having read a paragraph, a chapter, but especially after having finished the text, they give the totality a new, complete sense. This does not mean, however, that a text's coherence wholly depends on individual readers, either. Rabinowitz argues that

116 I am borrowing the terms *naming*, *bundling* and *thematizing* from Rabinowitz. See Peter J. Rabinowitz, 'Reading Beginnings and Endings', in Brian Richardson, ed., *Narrative Dynamics. Essays on Time, Plot, Closure, and Frames* (Columbus: Ohio State University Press, 2002), 300–13.

> coherence is more usefully discussed as an activity by readers rather than a property of texts[.] I am not arguing that the coherence that results is unintended by the author. The gaps found in the texts, in other words, are not necessarily either errors or even ambiguities – they may well be intended as opportunities to us to apply rules of coherence in some guided fashion. In fact [...] this is often one of the strongest ways an author can express his or her meaning.[117]

The striking claim here is that gaps are one of the most powerful ways in which authors can express themselves. That is not to say, however, that all of these gaps are perceived as such by every single reading community. Only an ideal reader would be able to see them for what they are and fill them in according to the author's wishes. However, thus conceived of, gaps are a powerful *locus* for the encounter and exchange between authorial intent and the reader's assumptions.

Although readers always read from a vantage point, they can change their assumptions while reading because their literary competence includes this feature as well. Because the literary text is not only a commentary on biographical, social or political concerns (a product of a specific historical period) but the *locus* of social formation as well, *Horizontverschmelzung* is a model for understanding the past while contemporaneously forming and being formed by the past.

The first generation of reader-oriented criticism is not necessarily interested in actual readers (as in empirical, flesh and bone readers living in time and space) but in two other types of readers. Essentially, reader-oriented theory distinguishes three different types of reader: the *actual reader* who reads in time and as part of a specific interpretive community (or several interpretive communities); the *textual reader* (Prince's *narratee*, for example), and a sort of *ideal* reader who 'would have to have an identical code to that of the author'.[118] The ideal reader is able to carry out an ideal reading of the text, by approaching the text with the right assumptions, by applying the right reading strategies and by arriving at the right conclusions. This extremely sensitive and erudite reader has been given many names:

117 Rabinowitz, *Before Reading*, 147.

118 Iser, *Act of Reading*, 28–9.

model reader (Eco), *superreader* (Riffaterre) *informed reader* (Fish), *implied reader* (Iser).[119] I find Peter Rabinowitz's distinction between *actual reader* and *authorial reader* more persuasive than the terms cited above.

> [Authorial reading] recognizes that distorting presuppositions lie at the heart of the reading process. To read as authorial audience is to read in an impersonal way, but only in a special and limited sense. The authorial audience has knowledge and beliefs that might well be extrapersonal – that is, not shared by the actual individual reader. [...] The authorial audience's knowledge and beliefs may even be extracommunal – that is, not shared by any community (and we all belong to several) of which the actual reader is a member at the historical moment of reading.[120]

Trying to understand something (more or less) remote, geographically and/or temporally, entails bearing a certain tension, as Gerald Bruns describes:

> What tradition preserves or rather entails is not a deposit of familiar meanings but something strange and refractory to interpretation, resistant to the present, uncontainable in the given world in which we find ourselves at home [...]. In a critical theory of tradition, tradition is not the persistence of the same [...]. The encounter with tradition, to borrow Gadamer's language, is always subversive of totalization or containment. For Gadamer, this means the openness of tradition to the future, its irreducibility to the library or the museum or to institutions of interpretation, in its refusal of closure or of finite constructions.[121]

In his description of the encounter with tradition, Bruns only refers to the fusion of horizons between past and present; but I believe that his

119 See Gerald Prince, 'Introduction to the Study of the Narratee', in Jane P. Tompkins, ed., *Reader-Response Criticism. From Formalism to Poststructuralism* (1980), 7–25; Prince 'Narratology and Narratological Analysis', *Journal of Narrative and Life History* 7 (1997): 39–44; Umberto Eco, *The Role of the Reader: Explorations in the Semiotics of Texts* (Bloomington: Indiana University Press, 1984); Michael Riffaterre, *La production du texte* (Paris: Seuil, 1979). Also see Fish, *Is There a Text in this Class?* and Iser, *The Act of Reading*.

120 Rabinowitz, *Before Reading*, 26.

121 Gerald L. Bruns, *Hermeneutics Ancient and Modern* (New Haven, CT: Yale University Press, 1992), 201–2.

argument holds true for cross-cultural reading, as well. There is always an element of *conflict* in engaging with the 'foreign' (however defined) because it entails experiences of negation of our assumptions and expectations. By interacting with other horizons and with other polysystems we realize that our consciousness is conditioned by habit. Still, we are able to interact with the translated texts and learn from the experience. Bruns describes the encounter with tradition as 'never an assimilation of what appears to be alien, but always a critical appropriation of otherness'.[122] This concept is similar to Iser's *impact* between cultures.[123] Reading literature is a very effective way of interacting with the past and other cultures – and it is an extremely challenging and dynamic experience.

Iser sees communication in literature as a 'process set in motion and regulated not by a given code but by a mutually restrictive and magnifying interaction between the explicit and the implicit, between revelation and concealment'.[124] The way Iser frames this interactive concept of communication in literature reminds one of his description of the process of cross-cultural exchange, formulated about ten years later, to which I will return in Chapter 2.

The interactive nature of the reading process constitutes a challenge.

> Faced with a text, the reader can transform the words into a message that deciphers for him or her a question historically unrelated to the text itself or to its author. This transmigration of meaning can enlarge or impoverish the text itself: invariably it imbues the text with the circumstances of the reader. Through ignorance, through faith, through intelligence, through trickery and cunning, through illumination, the reader rewrites the text with the same words of the original but under another heading, re-creating it, as it were, in the very act of bringing it into being.[125]

122 Ibid., 237.

123 See, for example, Iser, *Range of Interpretation*, 179: 'Converting the black box between cultures into a dynamism, exposing each one to its otherness, the mastery of which results in change'.

124 Iser, *Act of Reading*, 169.

125 Alberto Manguel, *A History of Reading* (New York: Viking, 1996), 211.

How specific texts are 'imbued with the circumstances of the reader' and how this can cause a 'transmigration of meaning' is not the concern of reception aesthetics with its interest in the *operations* in the interaction between text and reader. The second strand of reception theory, *reception history*, however, aims to analyse how the transmission of meaning changes over time and is thus more empirical in character.

Reception history

If aesthetics of reception is interested in the abstract idea of the reader and provides an explanation for the reading process *per se*, reception history is interested in real (flesh and blood) readers and their interpretations. Obviously, a certain type of reception history – or a new approach to literary history – is contained to some degree in Jauss's aesthetics of reception: the horizon of expectations in which the text was first published is different both from our own and all the other horizons of the readers between then and now. The text is an unstable mediator between horizons, interpretation becomes possible by the fusion of horizons and thus is a function of history. In this newly defined literary history, the reader has become, in Jauss's words, the arbiter [*Instanz*] of a new history of literature.[126] However, reception history is not exclusively literary history. It is, as I will show, an approach that focuses on how power structures in the politico-cultural field take shape and shift over time. Several disciplines in the humanities make use of forms of reception history: *inter alia*, book history, cultural studies, film studies, Bible studies and comparative literature.

Defined as 'the "missing link" of book history' and, I contend, of cultural studies at large, the actual reader has been grossly neglected until the last decade of the twentieth century, with the honourable exceptions of

126 See Hans Robert Jauss, 'Der Leser als "Instanz" einer neuen Geschichte der Literatur', *Poetica*, 7/3–4 (1975), 325–44.

Q. D. Leavis's *Fiction and the Reading Public* (1932), Richard Altick's *The English Common Reader* (1957) and Carlo Ginzburg's *The Cheese and the Worms: The Cosmos of a Sixteenth Century Miller* (1976).[127] What emerges from these works is that reading is both a *social* and an *individual* phenomenon. While the description of the act of reading, especially in Iser's work, theorizes the different steps necessary for an individual reader to make sense of a text, reading considered from the point of view of the history of reception is a social, communal act. Although they are made up of real, empirical acts, reception processes are difficult to investigate in their totality. The sources for this work are plentiful, yet their use is also problematic. Empirical evidence for reception processes is not easy to come by and very labour-intensive to evaluate. Also, the findings will always be fragmentary as they rely mainly on written sources that have been preserved and therefore do not provide us with the 'complete picture' (this, however, is a problem common to all historiography). Should this keep us from approaching reception history at all?

There are two tendencies amongst book historians when it comes to answering this question. There are scholars who agree with Robert Darnton who in 1990 claimed that 'the experience of the great mass of readers lies beyond the range of historical research' and then there are other scholars who have tried to prove Darnton wrong.[128] Some of these adopt a strictly empirical approach: Jonathan Rose, for example, moves the focus of inquiry away from the individual reader to the 'audience' in order to analyse how texts affect the intellectual lives of 'common' readers.[129] Similarly, Janice

127 David Finkelstein and Alistair McCleery, *An Introduction to Book History* (London and New York: Routledge, 2005), 100. Q. D. Leavis, *Fiction and the Reading Public* (London: Pimlico, 2000); Richard D. Altick, *The English Common Reader: A Social History of the Mass Reading Public, 1800–1900* (Columbus, OH: Ohio State University Press, 1998); Carlo Ginzburg, *The Cheese and the Worms: The Cosmos of a Sixteenth-Century Miller* (Baltimore: Johns Hopkins University Press, 1992).

128 Robert Darnton, *The Kiss of Lamourette: Reflections in Cultural History* (New York: Norton, 1990), 177.

129 See Jonathan Rose, 'Rereading the English Common Reader: A Preface to a History of Audiences', *Journal of the History of Ideas*, 53/1 (1992), 47–70.

Radway has conducted research with readers of romance novels or members of book clubs in an attempt to show the empirical impact of reading on the life of real people.[130] What some of these book history approaches lack or do not always state explicitly is a focus on those members of the reading communities invested with discursive, rhetorical power who play a part in deciding what is available to what readership at a determined moment in history.

In comparative literature, too, there has been a recent shift of attention towards reception studies. The second issue of *Comparative Critical Studies* in 2006 was entirely dedicated to this approach. In her introduction to the volume, Elinor Shaffer reviews the ongoing research project on the reception of British and Irish authors in Europe (which by now has published around two dozen books on the reception history of important English language writers on the European continent).[131] The breadth of this project underlines the importance that reception studies in general and reception history in particular have finally gained in the area as a means of analysing cross-cultural discourse. What has become clear over the last few decades is that the study of reception must include a study of translations and editions of the text, modes of circulation, bookseller's lists, as well as individual reactions (whether from literary critics or from general readers) but that it will also profit 'from scrutiny of its placement or operation within the polysystem of a particular culture'.[132]

Traditionally, the view has prevailed that literary works could only lose in translation. For as long as translators were regarded as the producers of

130 See Janice A. Radway, *A Feeling for Books: The Book-of-the-Month Club, Literary Taste, and Middle-Class Desire* (Chapel Hill, NC and London: University of North Carolina Press, 1997).

131 See 'The Reception of British and Irish Authors in Europe' <http://www.bloomsbury.com/uk/series/the-reception-of-british-and-irish-authors-in-europe/?pagesize=25> accessed 17 February 2015.

132 Elinor Shaffer, 'Introduction', *Comparative Critical Studies*, 3/3 (2006), 191–8. Here 191.

necessarily inferior copies (a view that still obtains) they were invariably relegated a position well below that of the authors in the hierarchy of literary value.

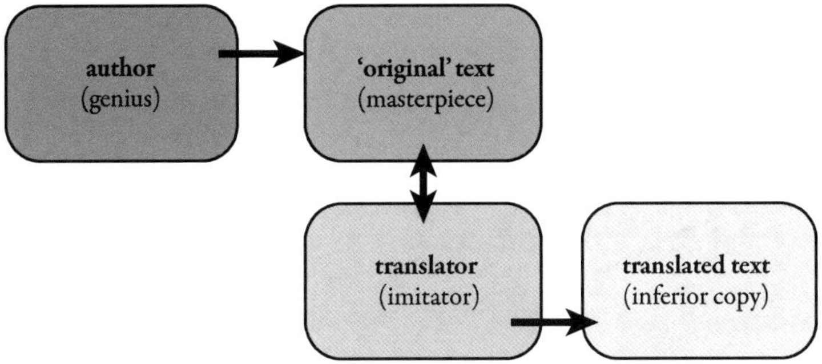

Figure 1: Traditional view of literary texts in translation.

As an alternative, I would like to offer a diagram that helps to visualize the agents and factors that shape cross-cultural reading. I need to acknowledge my debt to Robert Darnton's model of the communication circuit, one of the foundational models of Book History.[133] Darnton concentrates on several more agents than I do (printers, binders, suppliers, shippers and booksellers) but in the course of Chapter 2 it will become apparent why I have decided to focus on those agents whose functions are mainly defined by reading rather than taking into account the entire circuit.

133 The diagram has been reproduced in a variety of books. See, for example, Robert Darnton, 'What is the History of Books?' in Finkelstein and McCleery, eds, *The Book History Reader*, 9–26. The diagram is to be found on page 12.

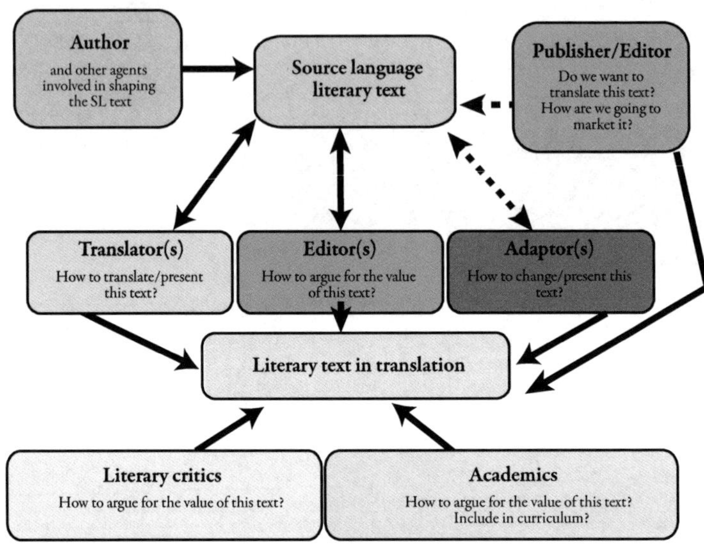

Figure 2: Agents involved in the shaping of literary texts in translation.

Each of the agents is constrained by several factors of milieu (summarized by Darnton under three headings: political concerns, intellectual influences, and economic and social conjuncture). All agents are, of course, first and foremost, *readers* of literature situated in a particular receiving culture and members of one or several reading communities, defined by a specific reading habitus. In a second step, some of these agents – authors, translators, and adaptors – produce literary texts. Some agents – translators, editors, literary critics, and academics – also produce texts about literary texts: translators' notes, introductions, afterwords, reviews and items of academic criticism such as articles in peer-reviewed journals, book chapters and monographs. The dotted arrows in the diagram stand for the possibility that publishers, editors and adaptors might not be able to read the original text but nonetheless need to make decisions regarding the shape of the translated/adapted text. As members invested with discursive power by their respective reading communities, all these agents actively shape the presentation and representation of translated works of literature in their receiving culture.

CHAPTER 2

Rhetorical Power and Symbolic Capital: The Middle Zone of Literary Space

Book history, Leah Price writes, 'is centrally about ourselves. It asks how past readers have made meaning (and therefore, by extension, how others have read differently from us); but it also asks where the conditions of possibility for our own reading came from'.[1] In Chapter 1, I have defined the international literary arena as a heteronomous polysystem. Within this polysystem, a focus on works of literature in translation allows one to illustrate some of the reading strategies deployed by specific readers invested with discursive authority as representative of how particular reading communities at a given time in history engage with the 'foreignness' of a text. Reception studies is a broad field, interested in many issues central to other fields of investigation in literary criticism and cultural studies: authorship and authenticity, publishing (including translation, editing and modes of circulation), writing as performance, reading as (inter)action, and the question of the specificity of literary discourse. In its pragmatic orientation, reception studies focuses on the self-cultivating subject (who, against all odds, should ideally strive to become a cosmopolitan, generous reader at relative ease in the realm of cross-cultural reading) and his/her position within a larger community. In this chapter, I link reception history to politico-cultural agency and explain in more detail what I mean by cross-cultural discourse and rhetorical power. I also focus on each of the

1 Leah Price, 'Reading: The State of the Discipline', *Book History*, 7 (2004), 303–20. Here 317.

agents involved in the production of a literary text in translation in more detail, pointing out the factors to consider when attempting to draw a map of influences that takes into consideration both rhetorical strategies and symbolic capital. Finally, I engage with two fundamental concepts that trouble agents working with literature in translation: the issues of *authority* and *authenticity*.

One of the interrogations at the heart of my study regards the degree to which agents who shape cross-cultural discourse are able to broaden their perspective when dealing with works of literature coming from a culture that is different from their own. Comparative literature as a practice stems from the belief in the possibility of successful acts of cross-cultural communication. However, there seems to be an inherent contradiction between the distinctness of cultures and cultural practices, on the one hand, and their comparability, on the other. If cultures are radically different, how can we engage with these differences without comparing texts in the sense of setting them up one against the other, thus falling into the trap of establishing arbitrary hierarchies? Should we not reject the notion of comparison altogether?

When one looks more closely at the criticism and rejection of comparative modes of investigation, much of the criticism is based on a definition of comparison in terms of *assimilation*, *equivalence* and *correspondence*: *setting one against another*. When comparison stands for the search for equivalence, the questions asked are: is it possible to translate one culture into another? If so, how best to translate a term, concept or philosophical tenet that one finds in the 'foreign' text into a corresponding term, concept or philosophical tenet in one's own culture? The use of the superlative here indicates that in traditional comparisons, one inevitably establishes hierarchies. If one cannot find a correspondence between two texts, then this is because one text is superior to the other. Instead of employing the notions of *translatability of cultures* and *correspondence* in my argumentation I use Wolfgang Iser's concept of *cross-cultural discourse* to avoid falling into the 'correspondence trap'.

Cross-cultural discourse

Wolfgang Iser draws a distinction between the concepts of *translating cultures* and *cross-cultural discourse*.[2] When talking about translating cultures, one assumes that it is possible to establish transcendental relationships between different cultures and that there is an overarching third dimension (an objective *tertium comparationis*) under which this translation is possible: a universal realm of meaning outside and independent of language.[3] Cross-cultural discourse, however, establishes itself as an interlinking network that does not base itself on correspondence and thus does not translate, transpose or assimilate one culture into another.[4] Still, it results in a gradual *impact* of and between cultural discourses.

> A discourse of this kind is not to be mistaken for a translation, as translatability is to be conceived of as a set of conditions that are able to bring about a mutual mirroring of cultures. It is therefore a pertinent feature of such a discourse that it establishes a network of interpenetrating relationships. These, in turn, allow for a mutual impacting of cultures upon one another, and simultaneously channel the impact. [...] The network itself is a web of mobile structures, functioning as an interface between different cultures.[5]

2 Wolfgang Iser, 'The Emergence of a Cross-Cultural Discourse: Thomas Carlyle's Sartor Resartus', in Sanford Budick and Wolfgang Iser, eds, *The Translatability of Cultures: Figurations of the Space Between* (Palo Alto: Stanford University Press, 1996), 245–64.

3 Traditionally, intercultural translation has always been linked to a more or less utopian vision of universalism and has defined languages (and subsequently, cultures) as elements of a shattered unity with the hope that this unity might be achieved (perhaps by finding the right vocabulary). Aleida Assman calls this ideal the 'regulative idea of the One' and rightly points out that until very recently, it has been the necessary framework for intercultural translation. For the impact of the story of Babel and the term Oneness (*Ekhad*) on the universalization of Western discourse throughout the ages see Assman, 'The Curse and Blessing of Babel; or, Looking Back on Universalisms' in Budick and Iser, eds, *Translatability of Cultures*, 85–104.

4 See Iser, 'The Emergence of a Cross-Cultural Discourse', 244.

5 Ibid., 248.

A mutual mirroring of cultures implies a binarism, a dialectic (the Self and the Other, the West and the rest of the world) in which one always has to choose a side. A network, on the other hand, allows us to consider multiple possibilities or variations – a repertoire, in Even-Zohar's sense. There is movement between the structures, a constantly shifting and changing discourse that is defined by a very specific patterning and repatterning of concepts. This practice works as follows: the receiving culture judges the foreign culture/text according to its own standards, thus trying to assimilate it. However, something in the foreign culture/text resists complete assimilation and readers in the receiving culture have to reshape their assumptions before making a renewed effort at understanding the foreign object. Iser calls this back and forth movement 'transactional loops':

> In such a back-and-forth movement, the hermeneutic circle operates in transactional loops, due to the fact that what is mutually transposed is never fully in view but masked by symbols. As there is no external reference for such a procedure, the looping can only be fine-tuned by continually scrutinizing what the transactional loops render tangible. Thus interpretation, owing to the trial-and-error pattern that structures transactional looping, becomes self-correcting.[6]

Rather than conceiving of the relationship between two cultural products issued from different backgrounds in a binary manner made possible by an overarching third dimension (*universality*), the method advocated here acknowledges a different kind of triangular nature in acts of cross-cultural reading: the source text, the translated text and the unstable, shifting meaning assigned to the translated text by means of transactional loops. In a never-ending chain of transactional loops, the reading becomes more varied and, ideally, more complete. Cross-cultural readings and cross-cultural conversations about literature undoubtedly are modulated and even distorted by uneven power relations that are usually also reflected in the rhetorical strategies deployed by the agents involved. My close engagement with the reception history of works by Tagore, Ben Jelloun and Fo in Chapters 3

6 Wolfgang Iser, *The Range of Interpretation* (New York and Chichester: Columbia University Press, 2000), xi.

to 5 sheds light on the workings of these transactional loops by comparing the reception of works of literature at different points in time and space, taking into consideration the situatedness of all agents involved.

Admittedly, handling an open, constantly changing system such as cross-cultural discourse is difficult and does not offer the prospect of exhaustive analysis. However, because all of our interpretations are embedded not only in a specific point in time and space but also linked to predominant modes of reading within specific reading communities, the idea and ideal of exhaustive analysis is necessarily utopian in character. Unlike most postmodernist stances, Iser's *cross-cultural discourse* acknowledges plurality to be one of the key factors while still allowing for the communication between different cultural systems to succeed. What impact does an acceptance of plurality in these terms have on the interpretive process?

In postmodernity, Aleida Assmann claimed in 1996, the focus on plurality and hybridity has had a considerable side effect: 'Concepts like communication and consensus have become unpopular. Bridges are no longer welcome because they hide abysses and rifts. The acknowledgement of alterity, the acceptance of difference, has become the foremost ethical claim'.[7] In 2006, Amanda Anderson argues along similar lines that 'identity', 'hybridity' and 'performativity' are subjective terms prevalent in literary and cultural studies used to 'imagine various ways in which one might enact, own, or modify one's reaction to the impersonal determinants of individual identity', determinants she describes as 'forms of self-understanding that revolve around sociological, ascribed understandings of group identity: gender, race, class, nationality, sexuality'.[8] Anderson points out that this approach neglects two elements which she considers important: characterological concepts and rhetoric. Anderson uses characterology not in the sense of 'general observations about epistemic practices that appear in psychological analyses' but rather in a pragmatist way: 'such an exercise [should] include a recognition of the historical conditions out

7 Assmann, 'Curse and Blessing of Babel', 99.

8 Amanda Anderson, *The Way We Argue Now: A Study in the Cultures of Theory* (Princeton, N. J. and Woodstock: Princeton University Press, 2006), 135.

of which beliefs and values emerge, as well as the possibility of the ongoing recognition of the many forces (psychological, social, and political) that can thwart, undermine, or delay the achievement of such virtues and goods'.[9] Anderson's characterology resembles Bourdieu's habitus in its focus on the variety of forces that impact the manner in which readers approach literary texts.

Reception history accords special status to the historical conditions that shape the production and reception of literary texts and also leaves room for a thick description of the habitus of individual agents and larger reading communities. Consensus building is very much dependent on the habitus of specific reading groups, and while all the categories pointed to by Anderson above (gender, race, class, nationality, sexuality) shape us as readers, we are also free to choose a particular reading community that interprets texts and literary currents in a way that we find either comforting and congenial to our own interpretive strategies, or, alternatively, stimulating and challenging to our interpretive strategies. In this model of intellectual engagement and consensus building, rhetorical elements play a considerable role. Before we move on to a description of rhetorical hermeneutics, let me briefly mention that in recent social theory and cultural philosophy, there has also been a gradual shift of focus away from diversity and heterogeneity towards similarity and homogeneity:

> The goal is to establish lines of solidarity across cultures opening them up to visions of new possibilities of transformation rather than freezing them into systems of bounded recognition. The dichotomizing hermeneutics of difference is replaced in such situations by an attitude of praxis, which does not remain at the level of only trying to understand each other but tries to move on to ways of arriving at sets of communicative practices in order to find a more acceptable common solution to our societal problems.[10]

9 Ibid., 118–22.

10 Anil Bhatti, 'Culture, Diversity and Similarity: A Reflection on Heterogeneity and Homogeneity', *Social Scientist*, 37/7–8 (2009), 33–49. For an approach in comparative literature that emphasizes the similarities rather than the differences between the Eastern and Western cultural and literary traditions, see Zhang Longxi, *Unexpected Affinities. Reading Across Cultures* (Toronto: University of Toronto Press, 2007). Like

In this approach, the focus is on praxis rather than on abstract theories of difference, and on communicative practices that labour towards establishing consensus on ways of interaction rather than a discourse of incommunicability across linguistic and cultural borders. Looking for similarity, clearly, is not the same as looking for equivalence: leaving aside abstract ponderings of cultural essentialism and unbridgeable differences which have made up much of the discourse about the 'Other', there is a conscious decision in this approach to focus on the practical tools of cross-cultural discourse.

Rhetorical hermeneutics

Reception theory is intrinsically historicized and socialized: the mediating process between a text and the reader depends on a whole set of time- and space-specific elements that come to the fore in actual reading processes. But how can one link this pragmatic experience with aesthetics? While it is true that reception theory develops from a functional method, it is nonetheless a theory that has been developed in aesthetic terms as well. Reception theory rejects most of the critical vocabulary of author- and text-centred criticism but in turn creates its own vocabulary. However, this apparent contradiction is easily solved if one adopts Richard Rorty's idea of vocabularies as *tools* to accomplish rhetorical purposes instead of the more traditional view that in hermeneutics one aims to find the ultimate vocabulary able to express truth and beauty beyond all others.[11] The results of rhetorical

---

Bhatti, Longxi advocates a practical rather than an abstract approach: 'The viability of East-West cross-cultural understanding must be shown rather than said, shown through concrete examples or citations, supported by textual evidence, rather than simply asserted in the abstract' (6).

11 Our vocabularies, Rorty suggests, 'have no more of a representational relation to an intrinsic nature of things than does the anteater's snout or the bowerbird's skill at weaving'. Richard Rorty, *Truth and Progress* (Cambridge: Cambridge University Press, 1998), 48.

hermeneutics should not be seen as possessing ontological significance, providing insight into the nature of human existence. Rather, the significance that results from using the tools of rhetorical hermeneutics is ontic, that is to say relating to the real and the factual.

Traditionally, the hermeneutic situation is conceived of as follows: The universe of linguistic possibilities creates the need for understanding or interpretation. Hermeneutic interpretation produces meaning and creates comprehension of the world.[12] In the realm of literature, there are at least three mutually exclusive ways of achieving this comprehension: by focusing on the text (formalist reading), by discovering the author's meaning (intentionalist reading) or by describing the ideal reader's experience (reception aesthetics in the narrow sense). The traditional approach to achieving 'correct' readings, therefore, assumes that 'an accurate theoretical description of the interpretive process will give us binding prescriptions for our critical practices, prescriptions that can ensure (or at least promote) correct readings'.[13] In any such a constellation, inevitably, 'the threatened "loss" of meaningfulness in cross-cultural interpretation [...] becomes a hermeneutic project for the restoration of cultural "essence" or authenticity'.[14]

The issue of latent meaning in any hermeneutical situation cannot be solved if not for the presence of another element, a rhetorical element, and an element of *persuasion*. Kenneth Burke claims: 'Wherever there is persuasion, there is rhetoric. And, wherever there is "meaning", there is "persuasion"'.[15] Being part of a reading community entails sharing a similar literary competence, as we have seen in Chapter 1. The ability to convince others of the validity of one's explanations and interpretations is part of this literary competence, as is the ability to judge whether somebody else's explanations are acceptable or not. The foundations of meaning are not

12 See, for instance, James Jasinski, *Sourcebook on Rhetoric: Key Concepts in Contemporary Rhetorical Studies* (Thousand Oaks and London: Sage Publications, 2001), 290.

13 Steven Mailloux, *Rhetorical Power* (Ithaca and London: Cornell University Press, 1989), 10.

14 Homi K. Bhabha, *The Location of Culture* (London: Routledge, 1994), 126.

15 Kenneth Burke, *A Rhetoric of Motives* (Berkeley and London: University of California Press, 1969), 172.

exclusively to be found in the text (as a material object) or in language (as a system of symbols) but they are *negotiated* in a complicated interpretive process that involves both an act of *sense making* (understanding) as well as an act of *making-sense-to-others* (persuading). Understanding a concept, a text for oneself and explaining what one has understood to others are intertwined in Steven Mailloux's *rhetorical hermeneutics*, 'a form of cultural rhetoric studies that takes as its topic specific historical acts of interpretation within their cultural contexts'.[16] Shared interpretive strategies in reading communities, therefore, must be seen as

> historical sets of topics, arguments, tropes, ideologies, and so forth which determine how texts are established as meaningful through rhetorical exchanges. In this view, communities of interpreters neither discover nor create meaningful texts. Such communities are actually synonymous with the conditions in which acts of persuasion about texts take place'.[17]

In my view, Mailloux's approach lends itself as an operational hermeneutic model because it shifts attention towards the historical struggle to determine the meanings of specific texts. As I will show in more detail in the following chapters, a focus on those agents in the literary polysystem who possess rhetorical power and are thus able to persuade others in their reading community of the validity of their claims, and on the changes in historical circumstances and potency of certain rhetorical arguments allows us to cover both individual and collective practices of understanding while avoiding unanswerable questions about the absolute literary value of a given text.

Rhetorical hermeneutics results from an intersection between rhetorical pragmatism and the study of cultural rhetoric. In Mailloux's model, culture is defined as the network of rhetorical practices that are extensions and manipulations of other practices (social, political, and economic), thus mirroring Even-Zohar's polysystem theory.[18] More importantly, though,

16 Steven Mailloux, 'Interpretation and Rhetorical Hermeneutics', in James L. Machor and Philip Goldstein, eds, *Reception Study: From Literary Theory to Cultural Studies* (New York: Routledge, 2001), 39–60. Here 47.

17 Ibid., 15.

18 Mailloux's theory also echoes Foucault's theory of discourses as bodies of knowledge.

in rhetorical hermeneutics argumentation is redefined as a *means* to a rhetorical end, not an end in itself. By allowing the rhetorical or persuasive element into the hermeneutic circle, differences in interpretation do not have to be explained in terms of wrong and right any longer. If rhetoric and hermeneutics are to be kept separate, then we must ask questions such as: where did past readers and scholars go wrong in their interpretation? How can we get it right? In rhetorical hermeneutics, the questions shift away from issues of value and judgement towards the functionality and modality of interpretation. How did readers and scholars of the past agree on the meaning of this text? What has changed that makes our interpretation different from theirs?

The argument for rhetorical hermeneutics seems to me even more convincing in a world in which different, very often contradictory, currents in literary theory have shown both the variety and the changing validity of interpretation. How are we to explain these changing interpretive practices if not by focusing on the different rhetorical and hermeneutical practices acceptable in different polysystems? An interpretation at a determined point in history and within a certain reading community has to be persuasive in that specific context. It will not and cannot be eternally valid, but it will always have to be persuasive in its own time and place. Although the vocabularies, as well as the literary competence of reading communities and whole polysystems will constantly and unstoppably change, human beings will still *want* and *have to* make sense of what surrounds them, for themselves and for others.

The pragmatism of rhetorical hermeneutics integrates well with the functionality of reception theory. By shifting the attention away from the search for the ultimate meaning or the best hermeneutic vocabulary towards the process of making sense and the rhetorical/persuasive element in interpretation, it provides us with an explanation for the ephemerality of interpretive acts while preserving the possibility of interpretation *per se* as well as the prospect of relating to the interpretive acts of others: even though we reach different conclusions in our reading, we still employ similar strategies. This kind of hermeneutics is pragmatic and functional as well as rhetorical, enabling us to share our viewpoints with the members of our reading community.

While my descriptive und pluralist method cannot offer a universally valid model for the processes that create literary reputation and literary obscurity, it focuses on certain agents and operations in the literary universe that critics can observe and compare. As a hermeneutic model, it is very explicit about the historical and rhetorical specificity of all acts of interpretation, including their own situatedness in time and space. I agree with Mailloux that 'rhetorical politics is inseparable from hermeneutics, and by necessary extension from ethics, epistemology, and aesthetics as well.'[19] Shifting the focus towards the rhetorical strategies that influence every single interpretation, however, does not diminish the real impact that particular interpretations might have:

> Taking a position, making an interpretation, cannot be avoided. Moreover, such historical contingency does not disable interpretive argument, because it is truly the only ground it can have. We are always arguing at particular moments in specific places to certain audiences. Our beliefs and commitments are no less real because they are historical, and the same holds for our interpretations.[20]

In the following section, I engage with an apparent paradox: although there are several agents who actively shape a text and influence the text's standing in a specific literary polysystem and although these agents are endowed with varying degrees of symbolic capital, they are very often also 'invisible' to the general reader.[21]

19 Mailloux, *Rhetorical Power*, 168.

20 Ibid., 181.

21 I use 'symbolic capital' in Bourdieu's sense. Symbolic capital is bound to individuals or institutions that hold positions of a certain prestige and are recognized as legitimate consecrating authorities within a given culture at a given time. See Pierre Bourdieu, *Outline of a Theory of Practice* (Cambridge: Cambridge University Press, 1977), 183. See also Pierre Bourdieu, *Distinction: A Social Critique of the Judgement of Taste*, trans. Richard Nice (London: Routledge, 1984).

Politico-cultural agents: 'Invisible hands' at work

The premise for any study of the manifestations of literary reception is the belief in the authority exercised by agents invested with rhetorical power in a specific culture at any given time. *Agent* is, of course, a sociological concept, designating 'an entity endowed with agency, which is the ability to exert power in an intentional way'.[22] In the case of literary production, it is not only the author who is able to exert power in an intentional way, but other agents' rhetorical power and symbolic capital are also important factors to consider. Far from being Casanova's autonomous literary authorities, the agents who shape the literary field are embedded in and bound by societal, economic and political elements in their lives. By virtue of their positions at university, in cultural institutions, in publishing houses and, in some cases, because of their ties to government, members of this intellectual elite influence what books are made readily available on the market. All agents are individuals who can 'simultaneously [be] the product of a given culture and the artisans of cultural change'.[23] In some extreme cases, an elite reading community invested with enough power at a given time in a given culture can also make or break the reputation of writers and thinkers, as we shall see in the case of William Faulkner further on in this chapter. However, by claiming that agents are steeped in a particular tradition at a particular time in history is not to ascribe all of their actions to those coordinates only. As Homi Bhabha points out, 'agency requires grounding, but it does not require a totalization of those grounds. It requires movement and manœuvre, but it does not require a temporality of continuity or accumulation; it requires direction and contingent closure but no teleology and holism'.[24]

22 Hélène Buzelin, 'Agents of Translation', in Yves Gambier and van Doorslaer, eds, *Handbook of Translation Studies* (Amsterdam and Philadelphia: John Benjamins Publishing Company, 2011), 6–12. Here 6.

23 Patrick Chabal and Jean Pascal Daloz, *Culture Troubles: Politics and the Interpretation of Meaning* (London: C. Hurst and Co., 2006), 69.

24 Bhabha, 185.

The illusion of a single-authored book soon fades as one reads the acknowledgements of any book, whether translated or not. (This is, of course, also the case with this book.) But how many readers bother to read the acknowledgements or, if they do, pause to reflect on the discrepancy between the one name on the cover and the number of people mentioned (and the number of people not mentioned) who have influenced the shape and the 'distinctive voice' of the book? Most general readers will still assume that when they read Salman Rushdie in the original English it is mainly the author's voice they are engaging with. Nearly as many readers, however, would still assume that very same thing when they read Salman Rushdie in French. The second (clearly marked) voice of the translator is blanked out; so are many other voices despite signs of the presence of other agents. Depending on the publishing strategies adopted, the translator will be named, quite prominently in some cases, less prominently in others. Depending on the perceived remoteness of a text (both historically and geographically), publishers may decide that explanatory introductions and notes are necessary. A novel by Cecelia Ahern or a sequel to *Bridget Jones's Diary*, for example, will not necessitate much critical apparatus. A student edition of Shakespeare's *Macbeth* will provide plenty of information to the reader, who then has the choice whether to delve into the information provided before or after reading the main text, or whether to ignore the critical apparatus altogether.

There are several 'invisible hands' besides the author who shape a text in translation.[25] Somebody needs to propose a book for translation based on the belief that it will sell and/or have a considerable impact on the target culture. Then somebody needs to look for a qualified translator. The translator translates the book into the target language, negotiating not only linguistic but cultural differences, as well. Somebody at the publishing house

25 The term 'invisible hand' was coined by Adam Smith as a metaphor to describe a concealed mechanism in which self-interested acts have unintended benign consequences, giving rise to spontaneous forms of social order. For a detailed discussion of the evolution of the term in Smith's writings and its use in later political theory, see Craig Smith, *Adam Smith's Political Philosophy: The Invisible Hand and Spontaneous Order* (London: Taylor and Francis, 2006).

needs to sanction this translation and decide whether the text can stand on its own or whether it needs a critical apparatus (which can take a variety of forms: preface, introduction, footnotes, postscript). Somebody must decide what sort of format or series the translated book should be published in and how to advertise it: 'classic of world literature', 'the French bestseller', 'from the winner of the Prix Goncourt'. In the twenty-first century, one could easily write off these labels as marketing strategies, and some of them are; yet it is also true that these labels are not just given by publishers interested in monetary profit but other agents whose symbolic capital depends upon the symbolic capital of the writers and books with whom they associate themselves. Also, decisions must be taken about established masterpieces and new writings from different cultures: which of these shall make it into the catalogue of a publishing house? In the case of a 'classic', is a new translation needed or advisable or will an older one do?

The agents in the field of world literature in translation, therefore, are responsible for one or more of the following activities: selection, translation, presentation, commentary and criticism. This is not the place for an extensive description of the publishing world in the twenty-first century or, indeed, the substantial changes that have occurred in the last decades in that world.[26] The roles described in the following sections are very broad sketches of the responsibilities and activities of the agents involved that will be complemented with more empirical detail in the case studies in Chapters 3 to 5. Another matter to consider is that although the positions of these agents will vary slightly from one polysystem to another there is enough common ground, I think, to work these functions into my model. In Italy, for example, publishing houses do not usually employ in-house readers; editors or freelance readers are expected to fulfil that role. In Germany,

26 For a recent comprehensive study of the fundamental changes in the publishing industry in the United Kingdom and the United States, see John B. Thompson, *Merchants of Culture: The Publishing Business in the Twenty-First Century* (Cambridge and Malden, MA: Polity, 2010).

the role of the reader is clearly distinguished from the role of the editor and for a very long time, the larger publishing houses employed in-house readers, although this is also changing.[27]

In his influential essay on book history, Darnton wrote: 'books belong to circuits of communication that operate in consistent patterns, however complex they may be. By unearthing those circuits, historians can show that books do not merely recount history; they make it'.[28] In the circuit of communications discussed in this study, I am particularly interested in those agents that occupy what – in a slight modification of James F. English's term *middle zone of cultural space* – I call the *middle zone of literary space*: agents involved in the publishing chain who shape the book prior to its publication (publishers, translators, editors and professional readers) and agents involved in positioning the published book within the literary field in the receiving culture once it has been published (literary critics and academics).[29]

27 The first 'Lektoren' appeared in German publishing houses of the 1790s. It was not until 1900, though, that the roles became institutionalized. Nowadays, the reader is becoming more of a product manager who needs to argue for the value of a literary product in economic as well as in aesthetic terms. Also, there is a trend in German publishing to work with freelance readers rather than employing them fulltime. See Ute Schneider, *Der unsichtbare Zweite: Die Berufsgeschichte des Lektors im literarischen Verlag* (Göttingen: Wallstein Verlag, 2005). For a general overview of the German literary marketplace, see Steffen Richter, *Der Literaturbetrieb. Eine Einführung. Texte – Märkte – Medien* (Darmstadt: Wissenschaftliche Buchgesellschaft, 2011).

28 Robert Darnton, 'What Is the History of Books?', *Daedalus*, 111/3 (1982), 65–83. Here 81.

29 James F. English, *The Economy of Prestige: Prizes, Awards, and the Circulation of Cultural Value* (Cambridge, MA: Harvard University Press, 2005), 12.

Publishers

The field of publishing is not uniform and publishing chains are not rigid. Even within a single cultural polysystem, the role of a publisher working at an internationally renowned corporation will differ from that of publishers at independent, smaller imprints who very often also work as editors.

The portrayal of publishers as mainly interested in profit and not necessarily in literary quality is virulent, especially in these last decades – ever since multinationals came to rule the English-language book market. However, as David Finkelstein points out, it is from the 1500s onwards that 'printers saw that money could be made from printed plays branded with named and known authors. Their authentication of "authoritative texts" could then be used to enhance their market value'.[30] I shall return to the issue of authentic and authenticated texts further on in this chapter, but would like to focus on the key functions of the publisher here.

John B. Thompson argues that publishers nowadays fulfil six key functions: 1) content acquisition and list-building; 2) financial investment and risk-taking; 3) content development; 4) quality control; 5) management and coordination; and 6) sales and marketing.[31] Other agents in the field, such as authors trying to get published or editors trying to push a particular book, often portray publishers in a negative light (as gatekeepers or filters who are unwilling to take too many risks). However, publishers do not only act as gatekeepers but in many cases play an active role in shaping individual works, on the one hand, and distinct literature lists, on the other. For the third and fourth functions, content development and quality control, publishers usually rely on the expertise of the editors, readers and copy-editors working for them. Ultimately, however, they have the final say if there happen to be contradictory opinions about a specific book. For

30 David Finkelstein, 'History of the Book, Authorship, Book Design, and Publishing', in Charles Bazerman, ed., *Handbook of Research on Writing. History, Society, School, Individual, Text* (New York and Abingdon: Taylor and Francis, 2008), 65–80. Here 71.

31 See Thompson, *Merchants of Culture*, 19.

management and coordination publishers usually rely on in-house production managers, controllers and copyright specialists. Sales and marketing are quite distinct activities but they are both

> concerned not simply to bring a product to the marketplace and let retailers and consumers know that it is available; they seek, more fundamentally, to *build a market* for the books. To publish in the sense of making a book *available to the public* is easy – and never easier than it is today, when texts posted online could be said to be 'published' in some sense. But to publish in the sense of making the book *known to the public*, visible to them and attracting a sufficient quantum of their attention to encourage them to buy the book and perhaps even to read it, is extremely difficult – and never more difficult than it is today. [...] Good publishers – as one former publisher aptly put it – are market-makers in a world where it is attention, not content, that is scarce.[32]

My three case studies, *The Home and the World*, *The Sand Child* and *Accidental Death of an Anarchist*, are all so-called backlist titles and longsellers: they are kept in stock and sold in relatively small numbers over years and decades, often in the same edition. Their market is limited in comparison to international bestsellers; the general reader's attention will go to the new publications stored in big baskets at a retail chain or a huge bookstore, often also part of a 'three for two' deal or heavily discounted. One may find each of the three books in specific sections of the bookstore, for example, 'Penguin Classics' for Tagore, 'Francophone Literature' or 'World Literature' for Ben Jelloun and 'Drama' or 'World Drama' for Fo. Sales of such titles might see a slight increase when an author receives an international prize or when an anniversary comes up. When Fo won the Nobel Prize in 1997 the Methuen Drama two-volume edition entitled *Dario Fo: Plays* was promptly reissued. *Accidental Death of an Anarchist* has been reissued several times in the last three decades in different translations that coincided with important new productions of the play. Each of these productions increased the visibility and marketability of both the play and the playwright. Ben Jelloun won the IMPAC Prize in 2004 for *This Blinding Absence of Light*. Readers drawn to this novel by the publicity

32 Ibid., 21.

that the IMPAC prize received also went back to his earlier novels, amongst which *The Sand Child.* While recent novels by Ben Jelloun are published in English translation by Penguin, *The Sand Child* and its sequel *The Sacred Night* were published by Harcourt Jovanovich Brace, and when the then independent publisher was taken over by General Cinema Corporation in 1991, the two novels were taken up by the Johns Hopkins University Press. As Ben Jelloun became more known internationally, the smaller publisher could no longer afford to participate in the bidding for the translation rights. However, the visibility of the Penguin translations has undoubtedly had a positive effect on the sales of the translations published by Johns Hopkins. While smaller publishers can scarcely retain authors whose novels become bestsellers, the fact that they first translated an author or a book will result in an increase in their symbolic capital.

In the case of Rabindranath Tagore, publishers exploited the sesquincentenary in 2011 to create a temporary surge in sales. In 2012, Tagore enthusiasts celebrated 100 years since the publication of the English translation of *Gitanjali,* a collection of religious poems that was the sensation on the London literary scene in 1912. This anniversary was accompanied by a timely new translation of the poems by William Radice. The year 2013 saw more celebrations due to the centenary of the awarding of the Nobel Prize and this occasion was also used to enhance the visibility of Tagore's books and boost sales.

In cases such as these, then, publishers will be persuaded to commission a new translation or a new edition when they believe that this will result in an increased – if only temporary – visibility of the product and that a new version of the text will result in higher sales volumes.

Translators, adaptors and editors as rewriters

André Lefevere defines as *rewriting* all those activities that influence the reception and canonization of works of literature: translation, anthologization, historiography, criticism and editing. I engage with literary critics and academics separately in the next section of this chapter but agree with Lefevere that all of these activities do in fact constitute different degrees of rewriting and appropriation; and that 'the men and women who do not write literature, but rewrite it [...] are, at present, responsible for the general reception and survival of works of literature among non-professional readers [...] to at least the same, if not a greater extent than the writers themselves'.[33] If a work of literature in translation is deemed to be opposed to the dominant poetics and ideology, the rewriters will either withhold the work until the circumstances have changed or rewrite these works until they are 'deemed acceptable to the poetics and the ideology of a certain time and place'.[34] Lefevere's view chimes with Lawrence Venuti's claim that translations for the middlebrow fiction market tend towards domestication: 'Since fluency leads to translations that are eminently readable and therefore consumable on the book market, it assists in their commodification'.[35] Very often translations are read as if they had originated in the receiving culture: they do not strike the reader as 'foreign'. In choosing my three case studies, I have consciously picked books that strike readers as markedly foreign. In these cases, most readers are aware if only peripherally that what they are reading is a translation and therefore there was at least one more agent involved in the creation of the text in front of them.

There seem to me two main, opposing types of reader response to literature in translation and, consequently, to translators: the translated status of a work is either ignored or decried. Most readers prefer to ignore the translated status of a text. The translator is invisible to such readers.[36] Alternatively, readers who emphasize the translated status of works of

33 André Lefevere, *Translation, Rewriting, and the Manipulation of Literary Fame* (London: Routledge, 1992), 1.

34 Ibid., 14.

35 Lawrence Venuti, 'Introduction', in *Rethinking Translation: Discourse, Subjectivity, Ideology* (London: Taylor and Francis, 1992), 1–8. Here 5.

36 The discipline of Translation Studies has repeatedly drawn attention to these two reactions to translations amongst the reading public. See, for example, Lawrence Venuti, *The Translator's Invisibility: A History of Translation* (London and New York: Routledge, 1995).

literature very often do so to point out what is wrong with the translation. Unfortunately, among this group, we find academics and literary critics with direct access to the original language who compare the source text and target text in terms of equivalence und inevitably end up establishing arbitrary hierarchies, mostly in favour of the source text. The translator very often is either ignored or held responsible for what is perceived to be a faulty translation or a misappropriation of the 'original' text. In the case studies on Tagore, Ben Jelloun and Fo we will see several examples of either strategy. Very often, rather than quoting from the published translation, academics will offer their own translations of extracts useful to their argument, further undermining the status of the published translation as a text that can stand on its own.

There is no consensus on what exactly constitutes an adaptation. In general usage, adaptations are very often understood as involving a switch from one medium to another (novel to film, cartoon to video game, novel to play). However, in the theatre, adaptations are versions of a translated play, often penned by a famous playwright who creates a culture-specific version that is related to but not strictly based – in a philological sense – on the original play. Here, the medium is still the same (drama) but because of its relative remoteness from the original, the text would not pass – or is consciously not marketed – as a translation. Considered as agents, adaptors generally seem to be accorded more freedom than translators, although they, too, cannot escape comparison of their work to the original. While translators must be effectively bilingual, adaptors can be monolingual. Some adaptation scholars deplore that the status of adaptors is lower than that of translators (their work is not a 'genuine' translation).[37] However, when the adaptor is a literary celebrity (Seamus Heaney or Jean Cocteau, for example, both of whom wrote adaptations of *Antigone*; or a famous poet translating Dante), the opposite might happen: the adaptation may

37 On different definitions of adaptation and the uneasy relationship between translation studies and adaptation studies at present, see Laurence Raw, 'Introduction', in *Translation, Adaptation and Transformation* (London and New York: Continuum, 2012), 1–20.

be viewed as a version that while retaining the essential character of the original is in some sense more fitted to the context of its reception. In such cases, the adaptor is perceived to be an expert in that type of literature and therefore expected to do a better job than somebody who is 'just' a translator. As a consequence, these celebrity adaptors are often much more visible to general readers than 'simple' translators. Celebrity charisma plays a significant part in legitimizing the translation in the eyes of general readers.

Editors become more visible for general readers when we are dealing with texts that are canonical in the sense that they are part of high school and university curriculums, as is the case with Tagore, Ben Jelloun and Fo. Certain books are edited by a prominent academic or specialist in the field. Dario Fo's *Accidental Death of an Anarchist* is published in the Methuen Drama series, edited by the late Stuart Hood, an academic and translator specialized in German and Italian literature. Series editors tend to pursue a specific strategy, both in the selection and presentation of texts in that particular series. While the kind of editing that positions a work within a series seems to be perfectly acceptable, editors who rewrite large sections of a work of literature are seen as transgressing unwritten rules.

Yet editorial interventions that substantially alter the shape of a book from its first to subsequent editions were accepted or at least tolerated even by illustrious authors in the nineteenth century. In one notorious case of rewriting, Jacob Burckhardt authorized an editor, Ludwig Geiger, to make substantial changes to successive editions of his *Civilization of the Renaissance in Italy*, first published in 1860. Geiger's interventions transformed Burckhardt's originally lithe essay [*Versuch*] into a weighty handbook that surveyed the state of contemporary Renaissance scholarship in a welter of excursuses and footnotes. It was only in 1922, following Geiger's death, that the *Civilization of the Renaissance in Italy* could be restored to the textual form of the first edition.[38]

In order to create a text that will fit the expectations of its intended readership in the receiving culture, translators, adaptors and editors play a

38 See Werner Kaegi, *Jacob Burckhardt: Eine Biographie*, 7 vols (Basel: Schwabe, 1947–82), III: 750–56.

substantial role that needs to be acknowledged. All kinds of rewriters (translators, editors, copyeditors, publishers) intervene in a literary text before it reaches the literary public and yet the resulting book is still vaunted as the product of a single person, a single voice, often a 'literary genius' rather than as the result of a collaboration, a very specific relationship between the named writer and his or her rewriters.

> Publishing industry etiquette and authors' sensibilities dictate that the details of this relationship should remain a private affair, particularly the degree of intervention, collaboration or re-writing that might occur. Indeed, various familial guardians and copyright holders, and the publishing industry's own publicity people, continually seek to contribute to maintaining this secrecy. Yet, every so often, anecdotes surface that raise questions about what a novel is and what an author might be – in a quite different way to the death of the author, and rise of the reader, announced by Roland Barthes.[39]

Before moving on to the agents who influence the literary standing of a book and its author after publication, let me give an example of editorial intervention that stirred up a controversy fifteen years ago, a controversy that was only recently revived.

'Bad' editing? Raymond Carver and Gordon Lish

A prominent example from contemporary literature of an uneasy engagement with textual interventions from agents other than the author is the case of Raymond Carver, recently reignited because of unabridged editions of his works being published in 2009. D. T. Max first described the problems with Carver's edited texts in the *New York Times Magazine* on 9 August 1998.

39 Keith Negus and Michael Pickering, 'Creativity and Cultural Production', *International Journal of Cultural Policy*, 6/2 (2000), 259–82. Here 275.

While Max was working on Raymond Carver's manuscripts in the Lilly Library at Indiana University for an article on the tenth anniversary of the author's death, looking at the manuscripts of stories such as *Fat* and *Tell The Women We're Going* he found pages full of editorial marks: 'strikeouts, additions and marginal comments in Lish's sprawling handwriting'.[40] Gordon Lish, Carver's first editor, played a significant part in the author's breakthrough. What Max came across in the manuscripts startled him:

> In the case of Carver's 1981 collection *What We Talk About When We Talk About Love*, Lish cut about half the original words and rewrote ten out of thirteen endings. 'Carol, story ends here', he would note for the benefit of his typist. In *Mr. Coffee and Mr. Fixit*, for example, Lish cut seventy percent of the original words.[41]

Carver had been particularly praised for his dry, concise writing style in his first collection of short stories. What emerges from Max's findings, however, is that that dry and concise style is due to Lish's interventions and not a characteristic of Carver's style. Who, then, is responsible for the success of the short stories – the author or the editor? Lish had repeatedly claimed that he was responsible for the final form (and the success) of many of Carver's short stories, but he had always been dismissed. Lish's claims were seen as acts of revenge after Carver changed editor and Lish lost his job after having championed several unsuccessful writers.

As he changed editor, naturally, Carver's style changed, too, but the difference between these two 'periods' in Carver's writing were explained in terms of biography. The Carver of the first short stories had known a hard life and his stories reflected his despair and sorrows. But then he became successful, met his second wife, and learned that life could be beautiful. Thus, his writing changed too. Apparently, 'most critics seemed satisfied by this literal-minded explanation: happy writers write happy stories'.[42]

40 D. T. Max, 'The Carver Chronicles', *The New York Times Magazine*, 9 August 1998, 34.
41 Ibid., 37.
42 Ibid., 36.

However, as emerges from some of Carver's letters to Lish, the author always felt uneasy about the situation: 'Please help me with this book as a good editor, the best [...] not as my ghost', he wrote in 1982.[43] Finally, he decided to change editor. Lish, then, asked his friends for help. Don DeLillo's answer is worth reporting in full.

> I appreciate, and am in sympathy with, everything you say in your letter. But the fact is: there is no exposing Carver. [...] Even if people knew from Carver himself, that you are largely responsible for his best work, they would immediately forget it. It is too much to absorb. Too complicated. Makes reading the guy's work an ambiguous thing at best. People wouldn't think less of Carver for having had to lean so heavily on an editor; they'd resent Lish for complicating the reading of the stories.[44]

DeLillo puts his finger on the problem: the centrality of the idea of *authenticity* in Western literary culture, an idea that has become linked to the concept of authorship, which I will discuss later. Carver's case is by no means an isolated one in Western literary history. The most famous example undoubtedly is Ezra Pound's revision of T. S. Eliot's *The Waste Land*. Eliot's reputation, however, was unblemished even after the publication of the manuscript in 1968 made clear how heavy Pound's touch had been. Thomas Wolfe's fame, on the other hand, has faded considerably after it was discovered how heavily his editor had curtailed his immensely long novels before publishing them.[45]

Carver had already included the long versions of some stories, such as 'A Small, Good Thing', in his later collection, *Cathedral*. Carver's second wife, the poet Tess Gallagher, for years campaigned for the publication of the original version of *What We Talk About When We Talk About Love*.

43 Quoted from Max, 'Carver Chronicles', 40.

44 Quoted from Max, 'Carver Chronicles', 40.

45 For a more detailed discussion of Wolfe's edited manuscripts see David Herbert Donald, 'Afterword: The Posthumous Novels of Thomas Wolfe' in *Look Homeward: A Life of Thomas Wolfe* (Cambridge, MA and London: Harvard University Press, 2002), 464–85. For an example of an unabridged version, see Thomas Wolfe, *The Good Child's River*, ed. Suzanne Stutman (Chapel Hill and London: The University of North Carolina Press, 1994).

When the original version was finally published in 2009 it was twice as long as the 1981 version. The extra text spells out much of what had puzzled and engaged readers of the 1981 text. The publication of *Beginners* sparked considerable interest in the literary sections of major English-language newspapers and it will certainly stimulate scholarly comparisons between the two versions of the text and a more general debate on the forces that shape literary texts.[46] While Carver's case certainly is extreme, perhaps it is time to acknowledge that literary texts are not exclusively, but very often, the result of a collaboration.

About his intervention in Eliot's *The Waste Land*, Pound once said: 'It's immensely important that great poems be written, but it makes not a jot of difference who writes them'.[47] However, publishing houses, editors and authors usually agree to keep the degree of intervention and collaboration secret because they are aware that 'the social character of this type of production has had consequences not only for the working lives of authors, but also for the judgment about the creativity of individual authors'.[48] The uneasiness in the Western readership mainly arises from the Post-Romantic perception of the figure of the author. Carol Polgrove, who worked on Carver's manuscript, points out that the modern reader generally exalts 'the individual writer as the romantic figure who brings

46 Tim Groenland describes how puzzling this case is for most readers: '*Beginners* fascinates because it poses a series of unanswerable questions, and cannot be read without consideration of these questions. How does literature, and indeed all art, come into being? Who owns the work? Who owns the legacy? What happens to work once it enters the public domain? The fact is, it is impossible at this remove to tell what Carver ultimately wanted, and this conflict of intentions seems emblematic of his ambivalent relationship to his own work'. Tim Groenland, 'My Words, Your Words', *Dublin Review of Books* 19 (2011). <http://www.drb.ie/essays/my-words-your-words> accessed 22 February 2015.

47 Tellingly, Carver quotes Pound's dictum in an interview. See Marshall Bruce Gentry, and William L. Stull, ed., *Conversations with Raymond Carver* (Jackson: University Press of Mississippi, 1990), 23.

48 Keith Negus and Michael Pickering, *Creativity, Communication and Cultural Value* (Thousand Oaks, London and New Delhi: Sage Publishers Ltd, 2004), 79.

out these things from the depths of his soul'.[49] The Romantic idea of the author is closely linked of the idea of genius; therefore, a text is seen as the product of geniality and not as the product of hard labour, or, even worse in the eyes of some, as the fruit of a collaboration. Ultimately, the text is seen as the author's *property* and any interference with it strikes readers as a transgression of the author's creation. I engage in more detail with issues of authority and authenticity later on in this chapter, and again in the case studies. Let us now turn our attention to those agents who influence the fortunes of writers once a work of literature is published.

Literary critics and academics

Rhetorical power is probably most visible in the intellectual circles of academia. Academic readers are drawn to certain theoreticians, say Michel Foucault, Julia Kristeva, Jacques Lacan or Giorgio Agamben, not just because of the content of their theories but also because of the rhetorical power that these theoreticians exercise. If scholars align themselves with critical approaches such as sociology, feminism, psychoanalysis or biopolitics it is because they are attracted not only by *what* is said but also by *how* it is said. All thinkers need to convince their readers that theirs is a better way of reading books, culture or the world at large than someone else's past or present reading:

> The rhetorical project for an emerging critical perspective necessarily involves a threefold strategy: providing persuasive, detailed interpretations of valued literary texts; presenting a strong case for the theoretical assumptions underlying the interpretive methods; and displaying a tight fit between the critical theory and the interpretive procedure.[50]

49 Quoted in Max, 'Carver Chronicles', 56.
50 Mailloux, *Rhetorical Power*, 33.

I have subsumed the two roles of literary critic and academic under one heading although they traditionally write for different readerships: literary critics direct their writings mainly at consumers while academics write for cultural producers. Traditionally, literary criticism in reviews was a viable career in its own right and there were people who would work nearly exclusively as critics without also pursuing an academic career. This is changing and most critics now are also academics and/or writers. This has resulted in a tighter network in which fewer books get reviewed. Reviews of new books in the reviewers' language are much more common than reviews of translations. The exceptions to this rule are retranslations of works by well-known authors.

Academics and literary critics shape the literary marketplace in a variety of ways: very often, a publisher will approach an academic to enquire about new titles in a language they are specialized in that are worthy of translation. Some academics also work as translators. However, it is by opting to teach specific books on their courses that academics ensure that there is a constant demand for those books kept on backlist and therefore ensure that certain titles do not go out of print so easily. The advent of print on demand from digital storage has made it easier for publishers to maintain substantial backlists. Still, as Lefevere put it, 'the classics taught will be the classics that remain in print, and therefore the classics that remain in print will be the classics known to the majority of people exposed to education in most contemporary societies'.[51] According to Lefevere, most high-brow literature in the English-speaking West is 'kept alive – somewhat artificially – by means of reading lists designed for institutions of (higher) education, which, in turn, guarantee a substantial turnover for the paperback lists of institutions publishing books'.[52]

As privileged consumers, both in terms of easier access to those publishers or subsections which specialize in 'high-brow' books, and in terms of their expertise in specific writers, cultures and periods, academics can considerably influence the reception of a foreign author. For example, it

51 Lefevere, *Translation, Rewriting*, 20.

52 Ibid., 21.

is largely due to the efforts of William Radice, a scholar now retired from the School of Oriental and African Studies in London, that Rabindranath Tagore is being better understood and valued in the English-speaking West. A poet himself, Radice has retranslated a substantial amount of Tagore's poetry (his latest success is a retranslation of the 1912 *Gitanjali* collection) as well as a considerable number of his short stories. Radice has also written extensively about Tagore and Bengali culture, thus providing Western readers with no direct knowledge of Bengali with access to this cultural sphere.

Besides their written engagement with literary texts (translations, paratexts, epitexts), academics fulfil another extremely important role: they perform and perpetuate certain ways of reading in their classrooms and fundamentally shape the way in which reading communities who invest them with discursive authority approach literary texts. One of Stanley Fish's teaching experiments illustrates the importance of this function.

Fish recounts the following anecdote: In 1971, he taught two different classes in the same classroom on the same morning: one in stylistics that investigated the relationship between linguistic and literary practice; the second one on English religious poetry of the seventeenth century. As part of an assignment for the first class, Fish had written the names of five linguists on the blackboard in the following manner:

Jacobs-Rosenbaum
Levin
Thorne
Hayes
Ohman (?)

Fish was not sure about the spelling of the last name which accounts for the presence of the question mark. When his second class arrived into the classroom, Fish had drawn a frame around these names and added 'p. 43'. He then asked his students to interpret this list of names as a mystic religious poem. The poem was immediately defined as a hieroglyph (in the shape of either a cross or an altar), Jacobs was linked to Jacob's ladder which symbolizes the Christian ascent to heaven. The ladder had, in this case, been replaced by a rose tree (Rosenbaum). The students then linked the rose tree to the Virgin Mary ('the rose without thorns'). Following these leads,

> the poem appeared to the students to be operating in the familiar manner of an iconographic riddle. It at once posed the question, 'How is it that a man can climb to heaven by means of a rose tree?' and directed the reader to the inevitable answer: by the fruit of that tree, the fruit of Mary's womb, Jesus. Once this interpretation was established it received support from [...] the word 'thorne', which could only be an allusion to the crown of thorns, a symbol of the trial suffered by Jesus and of the price he paid to save us all.[53]

The students further thought that 'Levin' was a double reference, to the tribe of Levi and to unleavened bread. 'Ohman' was read in three ways: either as 'omen' (the whole poem is about prophecy), 'Oh Man' (intersecting man's story with the divine plan) or simply 'Amen'. The question mark following the last name was explained thus: three names out of the six were Jewish, two recognizably Christian, and the ambiguity of the last name (underlined by the presence of the question mark) pointed towards the tension between the old dispensation (the law of sin) and the new dispensation (the law of love).

Because his students provided him with a coherent interpretation, Fish argues that as long as we believe we have a certain kind of text in front of us, we can interpret that text as such and will always be able to achieve a coherent interpretation. As I have pointed out in Chapter 1, we always read a text *as* a particular type of text – a novel, a poem, a play. Literary genres have certain – usually well identifiable – characteristics that help us to establish what kind of text it is and to therefore measure the text at hand against a repertoire of other texts we have already read. What makes Fish's experiment relevant here is that it shows how a reading community works: first, the members of a reading community work towards establishing an interpretation that will meet the consensus of other members of that particular group by using specific rhetorical strategies that they have

53 Stanley Eugene Fish, 'How to Recognize a Poem When You See One', in *Is There a Text in This Class?* (Cambridge, MA and London: Harvard University Press, 1998), 322–37. Here 324.

come to agree on over time; second, they instinctively trust Stanley Fish as the member with the highest degree of rhetorical power and therefore take his assignment at face value. Was Fish not in fact manipulating his students and therefore abusing the authority they had bestowed upon him? The unease one feels at the manipulation in this particular case points towards a larger issue.

We, as general readers, seem to expect rewriters *not* to abuse the trust that we, who do not have either the linguistic competence to read a translated work in the original or the in-depth knowledge to position a work in a larger context, have bestowed upon them. We expect translators, editors and publishers to respect and reproduce as closely as possible the 'essence' of a text, not to manipulate the text, not to 'falsify' or 'distort' the original meaning. We also expect academics and literary critics to provide us with tools that, again, will help us in our understanding, a 'better' understanding, of that text. The danger of such expectations is that we risk essentializing the original meaning of a text. Richard Rorty warns us that as readers we should 'assume that the works of anybody whose mind was complex enough to make his or her books worth reading will not have an "essence", that those books will admit of a fruitful diversity of interpretations, that the quest for "an authentic reading" is pointless'.[54] Paradoxically, most individual readers and most reading communities strive for exactly that 'authentic' reading experience, which perhaps explains why we have been so successful at blocking out the voices of the agents beside the author who also, and fundamentally, shape a literary text. We should, therefore, systematically think of world literature in translation as a 'cultural category produced through institutions and processes'.[55]

Before moving on to a discussion of literary prizes as institutions of literary consecration and their impact on the wider literary field, let me

54 Richard Rorty, 'Taking Philosophy Seriously', in Sean Burke, ed., *Authorship. From Plato to the Postmodern* (Edinburgh: Edinburgh University Press, 1995), 292–9. Here 299.

55 English, 311.

briefly mention where and how readers can engage with rewriters who are so influential in shaping the texts they read.

Agents made visible: Paratextual voices

Gérard Genette points out that literary works consist of a text, 'a more or less lengthy sequence of verbal utterances more or less containing meaning', which, however, very rarely appears on its own,

> without the reinforcement or accompaniment of a certain number of productions, themselves verbal or not, like an author's name, a title, a preface, illustrations. [...] The paratext of the work [...], always bearer of an authorial commentary either more or less legitimated by the author, constitutes, between the text and what lies outside it, a zone not just of transition, but of *transaction*; the privileged site of a pragmatics and of a strategy, of an action on the public in the service, well or badly understood and accomplished, of a better reception of the text and a more pertinent reading – more pertinent, naturally, in the eyes of the author and his allies.[56]

As a site of *transaction* and of *strategic pragmatics* shaped by various agents the paratext [para-, Greek for 'next to' and 'beyond'] varies from book to book. No book is completely devoid of paratext; but books vary greatly in the amount of paratext that they carry. In prefaces, introductions, translators' notes, publishers' notes, afterwords and footnotes, agents involved in the shaping of the text often engage with the historical context of the production of the text as well as with authorial intention in an attempt to further the understanding and appreciation of the literary text in question.[57]

56 Gérard Genette, 'Introduction to the Paratext', *New Literary History*, 22/2 (1991), 261–72. Here 261–2. For Genette's detailed engagement with paratexts, see *Paratexts: Thresholds of Interpretation* (Cambridge: Cambridge University Press, 1997).

57 According to Genette, paratext is 'always the conveyor of a commentary that is authorial or more or less legitimated by the author' (Genette, 'Introduction', 262). In literary studies, however, *paratext* has come to describe everything that accompanies

Depending on the intended readership of a given text, the quantity and diversity of paratext and the register of these paratextual contributions vary considerably, as we shall see in the case studies further on.[58]

Paratexts are either located in the same text (peritext) or at a distance from the text (epitext): the epitext is 'any paratextual element not materially appended to the text within the same volume but circulating as it were, freely, in a virtually limitless physical and social space'.[59] Analysing the verbal and visual material presented in the paratext is 'increasingly becoming integrated into empirical research on translated texts' as it allows researchers to 'focus on elements that bridge translated texts with their readers and therefore shape their reception in a major way'.[60] Chapters 3 and 5 will provide a substantial discussion of the paratextual apparatus of *The Home and the World* and *Accidental Death of an Anarchist*. In all three case studies, I will examine private and public epitexts such as interviews, letters, biographies, criticism and press coverage.

Having focused thus far on the different roles that the rewriting agents fulfil and where their activity is the most visible, I now briefly point towards an important factor that has shaped the middle zone of literary space in the last century: the advent of literary prizes.

---

and shapes the reception of a given text, whether it has been explicitly or implicitly legitimated by the author or not.

58 Urpo Kovala distinguishes four types of paratext: 'modest' paratext (basic information), commercial paratext (which advertises other books), informative paratext (which describes and contextualizes the work) and illustrative paratext (visual elements). See Urpo Kovala, 'Translations, Paratextual Mediation, and Ideological Closure', *Target*, 8/1 (1996), 119–47.

59 Genette, 'Introduction', 344.

60 Sehnaz Tahir Gürçaglar, 'Paratexts', in Gambier and Van Doorslaer, eds, *Handbook of Translation Studies*, 113–16. Here 113.

The symbolic capital of literary prizes

Over the past century, several literary prizes have become institutions of quite some importance. Starting with the Nobel Prize for Literature, the Prix Goncourt and Prix Fémina in France and the Pulitzer Prize in the United States in the early twentieth century, more literary prizes emerged (and some disappeared) all through that century, culminating in the richest literary prize to date, the IMPAC Dublin Literary Award, established in 1996.[61] Any literary prize is an institution, and 'institutionally, the prize functions as a claim to authority and an assertion of that authority – the authority, at bottom, to produce cultural value'.[62] This institutional aspect, however, is only one out of three fundamental functions of literary prizes. They also fulfil social functions – as a structural device in a competitive struggle for artistic recognition – and ideological functions – probing the notion of art as a domain separate from and perhaps superior to other domains of human life.

As I have already mentioned several times, Tagore was the first non-European writer to be awarded the Nobel Prize for Literature in 1913. Dario Fo received the Nobel Prize in 1997. Tahar Ben Jelloun is the recipient of the Prix Goncourt (1987) and several other French and international literary prizes, including the 2004 IMPAC Prize. I will return to the circumstances in which prizes were awarded to these authors and to the resonance of those awards in each case in Chapters 3 to 5. Here, I would like to briefly point out several interesting issues of a more general nature.

Since the inception of the Nobel Prize, it seems that the international literary market cannot do without awards.[63] In 1903, the Prix Goncourt was

61 The IMPAC Dublin Literary Award started as a joint venture between the IMPAC company and Dublin City Council. The prize still carries IMPAC in its name although the company no longer sponsors it.

62 English, 51.

63 The Nobel Prize is quite unique in its territorial reach and the wealth of the prize money. English calculated that the 1901 prize money corresponds to 750,000 dollars in 2005. Ibid., 54.

awarded for the first time and within months, the Prix Fémina was established as a counterpart to the all-male Académie Goncourt. Membership to the Académie Goncourt was 'reserved for "professional men of letters", thereby institutionalizing peer judgment as the key criterion in constructing literary respectability'.[64] By contrast, the Booker Prize, established in 1969, 'was to be judged by an annually selected panel, traditionally including a "man on the street". [...] This difference in jury makeup symbolically sites the power to award prestige not in a jury of peers but in the hands of the public'.[65] The situation has recently changed in France, after various scandals which revealed that up until the early 1980s 85 per cent of the jury members either worked for or were published by one of the three leading French publishing houses (Gallimard, Seuil and Grasset) and that more than half of the winners since 1969 were also published by one of these three publishers. The Prix Goncourt has now moved towards the UK and US model: as of 2008, the jury members are no longer allowed to be employees of a publishing firm.[66]

All literary prizes participate in what English calls an 'economy of prestige (the economy of symbolic cultural production)'.[67] This economy of prestige is characterized by a fundamental ambivalence: it is driven by aesthetic concerns (assessing the literary value of a given work) but inevitably causes reactions in other areas of the literary arena.

> The fundamental ambivalence here – whereby artists are at once *consecrated*, elevated to almost godlike status ('consecrations' being Bourdieu's favored term for cultural honors and awards), and *desecrated*, brought rudely down to earth by entanglement in a system of hard-nosed financial calculation, national or municipal self-promotion, and partisan, often petty politics – persists in cultural prizes to this day.[68]

64 Susan Pickford, 'The Booker Prize and the Prix Goncourt: A Case Study of Award-Winning Novels in Translation', *Book History*, 14/1 (2011), 221–40. Here 227.

65 Ibid., 228.

66 See Pickford, 'Booker and Goncourt', 232–3.

67 English, 75.

68 Ibid., 31.

Horace Engdahl, a former secretary of the Swedish Academy, stresses that the Nobel Prize is 'an award for individual achievements and is not given to writers as representatives of nations or languages nor of any social, ethnic or gender group. There is nothing in [Alfred Nobel's] will about striving for a "just" distribution of the prize, whatever that could be'.[69] However, as the reactions to the awarding of the Nobel Prize to, for example, Dario Fo (1997), Gao Xingjian (2000) and Orhan Pamuk (2006) have shown, the choices made by the Swedish Academy are often heavily criticized.[70] As we shall see in more detail in Chapter 5, many intellectuals in Italy did not consider Fo, an advocate of popular theatre, worthy of receiving a literature prize; instead, lists of more deserving candidates were compiled. The Chinese government hastened to state that the exiled author Xingjian was not a 'genuine' Chinese writer and congratulated France on having added one more writer to its long list of laureates. Similarly, voices from Turkey accused the Swedish Academy of awarding the prize to somebody who exoticizes Turkey to please his Western audience rather than recognizing 'true' Turkish literature. These reactions show yet another shade of a constant preoccupation that emerges from a thorough study of the reception of works of literature, a preoccupation with issues such as *genuineness* and *authenticity* which, in turn, are inherently linked to issues of *authorship* and *authority*.

69 Horace Engdahl, 'A Nobel Sensibility', *World Policy Journal*, 27/3 (2010), 41–5. Here 42.

70 Criticism regularly also comes from the academic quarter. However, the opposition to individual prizewinners or literary prizes in general is not doing the popularity of the awards any harm: 'Modern cultural prizes cannot fulfil their social functions unless authoritative people – people whose cultural authority is secured in part through these very prizes – are thundering against them. The vast literature of mockery and derision with respect to prizes must [...] be seen as an integral part of the prize frenzy itself, and not as in any way advancing an extrinsic critique' (English, 25).

Authorship and authenticity in Western thought

While a substantial part of literary and cultural criticism in the last two decades has argued for an inclusion of social and historical elements in literary and cultural discourse and the number of critics who perceive the text as an autonomous entity is decreasing, there is still a tendency to see the text as the author's property and not as the product of an interaction that involves several inputs from different sources (author, editor and/or translator and reader). Bourdieu has called this tendency an 'ideology of charisma', obscuring the view of agents in the field of cultural production.

> The 'charismatic' ideology which is the ultimate basis of belief in the value of a work of art [...] is undoubtedly the main obstacle to a rigorous science of the production of the value of cultural goods. It is this ideology which directs attention to the apparent producer, the painter, writer or composer, in short, the 'author', suppressing the question of what authorizes the author, what creates the authority with which authors authorize.[71]

There exists a particular strand in critical literary theory which sees literature as the expression of a writer's personality.[72] This approach claims a direct relation between a writer's mind and the work of art. A correlation between the two is present in classical rhetoric and poetics, as well as in seventeenth and eighteenth century criticism. However, with the advent of Romanticism, this approach to literature superseded others.

> Certain of these [Romantic] critics even went to distinguish between the personal attributes which an author projects directly into his work and those which he disguises and distorts in order to hide certain facts from his readers, or from himself.

71 Pierre Bourdieu, *The Field of Cultural Production: Essays on Art and Literature*, transl. Claude DuVerlie et al. (Cambridge: Polity, 1993), 76.

72 M. H. Abrams distinguishes three main orientations of critical theories: *mimetic* (which sees literature as imitation), *pragmatic* (literature has a purpose and is oriented towards the audience) and *expressive* (literature as the expression of the writer's personality). M. H. Abrams, *The Mirror and the Lamp: Romantic Theory and the Critical Tradition* (Oxford and New York: Oxford University Press, 1971).

> As a result we find the division of a work of literature into a surface reference to characters, things, and events, and a more important covert symbolism, which is expressive of elements in the nature of his author. Furnished with the proper key, the romantic extremist was confident he could decipher the hieroglyph, penetrate to the reality behind the appearance, and so come to know an author more intimately than his own friends and family; more intimately, even, than the author, lacking this key, could possibly have known himself.[73]

Even today, many Western readers seem heirs of Romanticism in this respect. The idea that a text reveals the essence of its author has become fundamental in the understanding of literature for most general readers. Some insist on this idea more than others. Elliot Engel, for example, calls himself a 'proud member of the school of biographical literary criticism', having always been truant from 'the Freudian, Marxist, deconstructionist, poststructuralist and other literary schools that seem to concentrate on illuminating the supposed genius of the critic while all too often ignoring and distorting the real genius of the famous writer'.[74] Clearly, Engel relates the term *author* to the romantic archetype of the untutored genius. Writing may be an art requiring genius, but it is also, perhaps primarily, a craft that can be trained, at least to a certain degree. At least that is what is assumed by the trainers of translators and the convenors of creative writing courses. A cursory overview of the changing definitions of the term *author* over time reveals that the idea of a literary work as the untouchable property of a single person is quite a recent development.

> In common usage, the term 'author' applies to a wide range of activities. It can refer to someone who starts up a game, or invents a machine, or asserts political freedom, or thinks up a formula, or writes a book. Depending on the activity and the application, the term can connote initiative, autonomy, inventiveness, creativity, or originality.[75]

73 Ibid., 228–9.

74 Elliot Engel, *How Oscar Became Wilde and Other Literary Lives You Never Learned About in School* (London: Robson Books Limited, 2005), xii.

75 Donald E. Pease, 'Author', in Frank Lentricchia and Thomas McLaughlin, eds, *Critical Terms for Literary Study* (New York: Octagon Books, 1995), 105–17. Here 105.

From Antiquity through the Middle Ages texts were customarily reproduced anonymously, without the least knowledge about their authors. There were exceptions, such as Homer and Virgil (the so-called *auctores*). Texts were reproduced and diffused because of their content, because of the effect they could have on the audience. Medieval censorship curtailed and manipulated the works of many philosophers of Antiquity in order to make them correspond to Christian ideology. Although it is true that from the very start, the idea of authorship has been related to the individual 'subject', we cannot disregard the fact that the common notion of 'individuality' in Western thought is linked to the Enlightenment and Romanticism.

Starting with print, one had to know the author's name of a piece of writing for simple legal reasons. But the naming of the individual responsible for a text is by no means comparable to the later emphatic link between individuality and originality. This becomes clear when we look at the etymology of the medieval term *auctor* on which the term *author* is based. According to Sean Burke, the Latin *auctor* derives from four terms, three of which do not imply any sense of textual mastery.

1. *agere* (to act or perform): this sense is close to the Medieval or Barthesian understanding of the author as acting through a text which in some way precedes its performance.
2. *augere* (to grow): for all its organistic resonances, it does not suggest that the text originates with its author but rather that it is preconstituted.
3. *auieo* (to tie): this term is derived from poetic lexicon and refers to the connective tissue (metre, feet) by which poets structure their verses. In many respects, this definition is similar to the Structuralist notion of *bricolage*, with authors seen as assemblers of codes.
4. *autentim* (from the Greek, 'authority'): this term is suggestive of authorship as hegemonic (*auctoritas* received from God and the Scriptural Canon).[76]

76 See Burke, *Authorship: From Plato to Postmodern. A Reader*, xviii.

Therefore, an author is a writer who does one or all of the following things: he performs the act of writing, bringing something into being, causing it to grow. Poets tie together their verses with feet and metres. An author's achievements command respect, but they do so for a variety of reasons. Respect may be due because God is speaking through the author or, as the Romantic revolution had it, because of the individual creativity and originality of the literary genius.[77] Similarly, rewriters perform the act of writing, bring something into being, in short: they also author and authorize texts. Yet, traditionally, their achievements only command grudging or partial respect.

Michel Foucault points out that '[t]he coming into being of the notion of "author" constitutes the privileged moment of *individualization* in the history of ideas'.[78] The peak of this development is the Romantic conviction that poetry is the creative expression of the individual. William Wordsworth wrote: 'Poetry is the spontaneous overflow of powerful feelings: it takes its origin from emotion recollected in tranquillity'.[79] The immediate act of composition for the Romantic poet *par excellence* has to be spontaneous and is therefore associated with sincerity and genuineness. The fundamental idea behind this concept is that one cannot lie to oneself on this first level of consciousness. Only on a second level does reflection set in and do the selective powers of memory operate. The author, for the Romantics, is an inventive, creative genius who creates an original, pristine, genuine and authentic work, both in form and content. Tampering with the authentic work of a genius automatically and inevitably reduces the work's value.

Authenticity is a concept that goes hand in hand with *authority* and *authorship*. The Greek *authentikos* translates as original, genuine or

77 On earlier theories of authorship, see A. J. Minnis, *Medieval Theory of Authorship: Scholastic Literary Attitudes in the Later Middle Ages* (Philadelphia: University of Pennsylvania Press, 2010).

78 Michel Foucault, 'What is an Author?' in Josué V. Harari, ed., *Textual Strategies: Perspectives in Post-Structuralist Criticism* (Ithaca: Cornell University Press, 1979), 141–60. Here 141.

79 Quoted from Stephen Charles Gill, *The Cambridge Companion to Wordsworth* (Cambridge and New York: Cambridge University Press, 2003), 109.

principal. It derives from the term *authentes* which is a composite of *autos* (self) and *hentes* (doer or being) and translates as 'one acting on one's own authority'. The Greek term already contains the germ of that individual and individualistic aspect of authorship that shapes the Romantic definition of an author. An authentic, original article is superior to any copy. In the domain of literary translation, consequently, any source text is automatically perceived to be superior to its translation. Also, a translator is not expected to act on his or her own authority, as it is the original that is authoritative in this case. In 1759, Edward Young expressed his discontent with the Neo-Classical emphasis on imitation and, in a prefiguration of Romantic ideas, argued that 'an imitator is a transplanter of laurels, which sometimes die on removal, always languish in a foreign soil'.[80] A genuine article is not corrupted from the original and is true to the intentions of the original (the implication being that truthfulness and sincerity reside exclusively in the originals). It is a widespread practice to set the organic quality of the original against the artifice of a translation.

From the Romantic focus on the writer's individuality there is a further development in the direction of Formalism. This step might not be evident at first, but actually the Romantic idea that a piece of writing contains an author's inner self is a prerequisite for the Formalist assumption of the autonomy of the text. If one can read an author's soul in a text, then all the necessary information has to be *within* the text itself. Out of this the notion of the text as a self-sufficient entity is easily developed and justified. The notions of authorship and of the text as stable entity are thus closely linked to one another, as Philip Cohen points out: 'The authorial orientation and the stable, closed text are less absolutes than the results of print technology, *laissez-faire* economics, and the Romantic/Modernist myth of the autonomous, creative artist'.[81] Michel Foucault has convincingly

80 Edward Young, 'From "Conjectures on Original Composition"' in Burke, ed., *Authorship. From Plato to the Postmodern. A Reader*, 37–42. Here 37.

81 Philip Cohen, 'Textual Instability, Literary Studies, and Recent Developments in Textual Scholarship', in *Texts and Textuality: Textual Instability, Theory, and Interpretation* (New York and London: Garland, 1997), xi–xxxiv. Here xv. Michel Foucault voices the same concern; the Formalist usage of the notion of writing 'runs

argued that modern literary criticism still relies on what he calls the author function (a specific classificatory function within narrative discourse) and that this author function is still defined by four criteria established by Jerome, the translator of the Bible. The author is used as 1) a 'constant level of value'; 2) a 'field of conceptual or theoretical coherence'; 3) a 'stylistic unity'; and 4) a 'historical figure at the crossroads of a certain number of events'.[82] There still is a strong resistance among general readers to integrate into this model or function other historical figures at the crossroads of a specific event, other agents who also assign value and coherence, and who contribute to the stylistic unity of a literary text in translation.

Authorship is, first and foremost, a matter of fixing a text. Finkelstein argues that the reproducibility of print results in the fixing of texts in a given form.

> This 'fixing' of print would become a key factor in establishing authority and trust in the figures (authors) who produced these works. It would create a new profession (authorship), bring forth an entire industry dedicated to promoting such a profession, and place the printed word at the centre of social communication.[83]

Assigning authorship to a single individual was a necessity: whoever signed a book was held responsible for its content; in the context of censorship and the proscription of books this was (and still is) no trivial matter. The authority derived from authorship has positive effects (from remuneration to social status) and negative effects (from recriminations to death threats, as in the case of Salman Rushdie and, more recently, Kamel Daoud). We need to be able to attribute a work to somebody (or several, but not too many individuals) whom we can hold legally and morally responsible. Yet, anyone who has ever published a piece of work, whether of creative or academic writing, knows that writing is a far more collaborative practice than is usually admitted or than is usually apparent from the acknowledgements. It is not merely a question

---

the risk of maintaining the author's privileges under the protection of writing's *a priori* status: it keeps alive, in the grey light of neutralization, the interplay of those representations that formed a particular image of the author' (Foucault, 145).

82 Foucault, 151.

83 Finkelstein, 'History of the Book', 77.

of attributability of a distinct voice, but rather of how much intervention by agents other than the author we as readers are prepared to accept. If there are too many agents involved in the creation of a text, which one of these agents is responsible for making the text 'unique' and 'authentic'? I should argue that some of the notorious uneasiness about translations stems exactly from an obsession with the uniqueness and authenticity of literary works.

The *author* and the *text* are often seen as an absolute authority, a *locus* of authenticity. Instead, I suggest that one should see the *author* and the *text* as demand-driven functions that are foregrounded so that we, as readers, do not have to remind ourselves of the complex processes that shape the books that we read. Instead of a simple, one way communication we have a complex process that involves a variety of crafters, politico-cultural agents with specific rhetorical power: translators, publishers, editors, reviewers, critics and academics. They all shape texts before they reach the reading public and have the power to include or exclude works from cultural discourse once they are published. I use the term 'crafter' because each of the agents involved in shaping the final product, a book of world literature in translation, is an adept of a specific tradition and each is endowed with a varying degree of authority by virtue of their socialization and training within a particular craft tradition whether it be that of literary scholarship, publishing or literary authorship.

The final section of this chapter shows how keeping in view the factors that I have outlined above (rhetorical strategies of particular agents and their preoccupation with authenticity) helps us to understand how the literary reputation of a now well-known figure of world literature, William Faulkner, was created.

Inventing an arch-American writer: The case of Faulkner

In the late 1980s, Lawrence H. Schwartz undertook an inquiry into the literary reputation and revival of one of the 'great' American authors of the twentieth century, William Faulkner. In Chapter 3 I develop a study along similar lines into the fate of Tagore in the English-speaking world. While Casanova argues that 'the road to worldwide recognition for William Faulkner [...] went through Paris' and while it is true that Faulkner was recognized earlier in France than in his own country, the issue of consecration is more complicated than Casanova admits.[84] This excursus on Faulkner will not only show agents and factors that Casanova's metropolitan and hegemonic model does not reveal but it will also introduce reception history, an approach to literature that is more process- and agent-oriented.

In *Creating Faulkner's Reputation. The Politics of Modern Literary Criticism*, Schwartz tries to explain the following conundrum: how could Faulkner, whose works, aside from *Sanctuary*, were all out of print in the United States at the beginning of the 1940s and who had been defined as a difficult-to-read, nihilistic writer, be hailed as a distinctly American moralist voice that expressed a new, post-war aesthetic hardly ten years later?[85] The central premise of Schwartz's study is similar to the thesis that underlies my work: 'The process of literary tastemaking can be isolated and identified, and [...] literary fame and reputation can be studied in the same way as any other historical phenomenon'.[86] Only if we acknowledge that literary fame and reputation are not exclusively based on a writer's talent or on a work's content and aesthetic qualities, but that they depend very much upon the favourable judgment of the agents involved in shaping the literary market, can we understand how such a sudden reversal of fortunes is possible.

Schwartz argues that shifts on four distinct levels are responsible for the making of Faulkner's literary reputation in post-war America: a shift in

84 Pascale Casanova, *The World Republic of Letters* (Cambridge, MA and London: Harvard University Press, 2004), 130.

85 O. B. Emerson conducts a similar inquiry but his focus is at once wider and narrower. While he includes literary criticism about all of Faulkner's writing from 1924 to 1954, he strictly focuses on literary reviews and articles thus ignoring other politico-cultural factors that are included in Schwartz's study. See O. B. Emerson, *Faulkner's Early Literary Reputation in America* (Ann Arbor, MI: UMI Research Press, 1984).

86 Lawrence H. Schwartz, *Creating Faulkner's Reputation: The Politics of Modern Literary Criticism* (Knoxville: The University of Tennessee Press, 1988), 3.

critical reception, commercial innovations, changes in the political agenda and the development of a new literary aesthetic.

First, there was a critical reassessment of Faulkner's work, led by critics such as Malcolm Cowley and Austin Warren. In the journals *Hudson Review*, the *Partisan Review* and the *Kenyon Review* as well as in the introductions to the republished volumes of Faulkner's novels, these critics propagated a different image of Faulkner from 1946 onwards, arguing that Faulkner had been misunderstood up to that moment and that he had simply been 'ahead of his time'. Thus, Faulkner became 'universalized as an emblem of the freedom of the individual under capitalism, as a chronicler of the plight of man in the modern world'.[87]

Second, changes in the publishing industry created a mass market for some of Faulkner's books, especially the ones considered more 'popular' (those containing plenty of sex and violence). On a pragmatic level, the economic success of these novels allowed Faulkner to concentrate on his other writing; this indirectly contributed to his international standing. More importantly, however, Schwartz sees Faulkner's revival as part of a bigger political project that involved the publishing industry. There was a conscious effort on the part of the USIA (United States Information Agency) to make American books more widely available, both in English and in translation. Spruille Braden, the assistant secretary of state, declared in 1946 that 'increased foreign circulation of American literature is essential to the success of American foreign policy, for it will do much to make the U.S. better understood abroad'.[88] Peter Jennison, another participant in the USIA programme, argued that books were not only industrial commodities but also 'unique conveyors in permanent form of a nation's thought, expression, achievements, and aspirations. And as such, they serve national policy as instruments of persuasion in the ideological context of the mid-twentieth century'.[89] This idea of the persuasive value of works of literature

87 Ibid., 4.

88 *Publishers Weekly*, Jan. 26, 1946, 603–4. Quoted from Schwartz, *Creating Faulkner's Reputation*, 51.

89 Chandler B. Grannis, *What Happens in Book Publishing* (New York and London: Columbia University Press, 1967), 280–1. Quoted from Schwartz, 51.

is, of course, linked to the persuasive power of the intellectual elite that is intent on convincing the wider reading public of the literary value of a given work and of the central importance of a given author. Against the backdrop of this political programme, Faulkner's revival cannot be explained away, as it were, in terms of strictly textual elements (plot and aesthetic aspects), or talent. Faulkner became a success after the Second World War not entirely on his aesthetic merits but also because his persona and his writing fit the wider politico-cultural agenda: as the symbol of Americanness, of anti-Communism and of traditional values.

Schwartz devotes the most substantial part of his study to the third aspect: the shifts in the cultural paradigm that accompanied the start of the Cold War. Schwartz convincingly argues that the American/capitalist intelligentsia had to rebut the claim that Communism, by promoting socially conscious literature linked to naturalism and realism, was working in the name of 'cultural democracy'. The Americans, therefore, had no choice but to insist on 'an elitist aesthetic – an aesthetic that claimed important literature was remote, complex, iconoclastic, and inaccessible, and required interpretation'.[90] Several major forces were responsible for this shift in the post-war American cultural paradigm and three were particularly influential in terms of Faulkner's revival: the New Critics, the New York intellectuals and the Rockefeller Foundation which 'came together in the 1940s to set a cultural agenda, and they used and promoted Faulkner for their own ends'.[91] It is because Faulkner was felt to be compatible with the cultural, aesthetic and intellectual needs of conservative liberalism in post-war America that his fiction was integrated into the new cultural paradigm. Looking for an alternative to the pessimistic disposition and the politico-ideological inclinations of French literary critics, such as Sartre and Malraux, Faulkner's defence of humanity, as expressed in his Nobel acceptance speech in 1949, perfectly fitted the new cultural paradigm being shaped in the US:

90 Schwartz, 5.
91 Ibid.

> I believe that man will not merely endure: he will prevail. He is immortal not because he alone among creatures has an inexhaustible voice but because he has a soul, a spirit capable of compassion and sacrifice and endurance. The poet's, the writer's duty is to write about these things. It is his privilege to help man endure by lifting his heart, by reminding him of the courage and honour and hope and pride and compassion and pity and sacrifice which have been the glory of his past. The poet's voice need not merely be the record of man, it can be one of the props, the pillars to help him endure and prevail.[92]

By pointing out the agents and factors that made Faulkner's reputation in the post-war United States, Schwartz's intention is not to belittle the literary value, however understood by critics, of Faulkner's writing. The specific type of reception history emerging from his study is not primarily concerned with the message or aesthetic qualities of a given text but with the interpretation of a given work or author at a particular time in history. Similarly, my aim in the three next chapters is not to diminish the literary achievements of Tagore, Ben Jelloun and Fo, but rather to shine a critical light on the intricate network of agents and factors that have shaped the reception of their works in English translation. There can scarsely be a more compelling example than the rise and fall of the 'first global superstar or celebrity in literature', Rabindranath Tagore.[93]

92 William Faulkner, *Essays, Speeches and Public Letters* ed. James B. Meriwether (New York: Random House, 1965), 120.

93 Amit Chaudhuri, 'Introduction', in *The Picador Book of Modern Indian Literature* (London: Picador, 2001), xvii–xxxiv. Here xviii.

CHAPTER 3

At Home in World Literature? Rabindranath Tagore's *The Home and the World*

Celebrated as a literary sensation as soon as he appeared on London's cultural scene in 1912, the then fifty-one year old Rabindranath Tagore (1861–1941) published a collection of poems, *Gitanjali* [Song Offerings], to which W. B. Yeats provided an effusive introduction.[1] The poems were widely praised by thinkers and writers with very different intellectual stances: Robert Bridges, Thomas Sturge Moore, Ezra Pound and Evelyn Underhill. Sturge Moore recommended Tagore for the Nobel Prize and in 1913, Tagore became the first Asian writer to receive the prize. The following years saw a rapid output of English translations of Tagore's work, among them that of the novel *Ghare Baire* (1916), translated as *The Home and the World* and published by Macmillan in 1919. In the West, there were no further editions of the English translation until 1985 when Penguin UK decided to publish the novel again. This edition was so successful that it was reissued in 1990; and in 2005 *The Home and the World* was published in a new edition.

Despite the fact that Tagore scholars have long deplored deficiencies in the translation and other editing choices, Penguin UK opted not to commission a new translation for one very specific reason: although Surendranath Tagore, Rabindranath's nephew, is named as the translator, in a letter to Macmillan the author stated that he was involved in the translation himself. Tagore's professed involvement was reason enough for the editors at Penguin UK to decide against a new translation. In the preface,

1 The name Tagore derives from the Bengali honorific 'thakur' meaning 'holy Lord'. While Tagore is universally known by this name outside India, he is referred to as Rabindranath in Bengal.

William Radice argues that the author's possible participation 'gives the translation an enhanced authenticity'.[2] In 2005, however, the same year Penguin UK republished the 1919 translation, Penguin India published a new translation of the novel by Sreejata Guha, called *Home and the World*. And the previous year, 2004, saw the publication of yet another translation, by Nivedita Sen, for Srishti Publishers. So why this sudden surge in Tagore translations into English in India? It is not merely a question of what Meenakshi Mukherjee deplores as 'a virtual scramble among English publishers in India to cash in on the brand name Tagore', as we shall see.[3]

After his meeting with Tagore in 1912, Yeats told Pound that the Bengali author was someone 'greater than any of us [i.e. Western writers]'[4] and in his introduction to *Gitanjali* he prophesied an extraordinary future for Tagore and his work. Yeats and Pound were convinced of Tagore's genius when they first met him; and in 1931 Albert Einstein called the Indian writer a 'Seer'. However, hardly thirty years later, in 1959, Edward C. Dimock was forced to admit: 'While Tagore lives today in Bengal as he did fifty years ago [...] for most non-Indians, he is no longer living. He is an isolated figure. For us, he is not part of a living tradition'.[5] In 1966, Nabaneeta Sen expressed regret about the fact that in the English-speaking West Tagore was no longer positioned among

2 William Radice, 'Preface', in Rabindranath Tagore, *The Home and the World*, transl. Surendranath Tagore (London: Penguin, 2005), viii.

3 Meenakshi Mukherjee, 'Tagore in the New Millennium', *The Hindu*, Sunday, 6 June 2004. <http://www.hindu.com/lr/2004/06/06/stories/2004060600160300.htm> accessed 22 February 2015. Mukherjee's article discusses the fact that three English translations of Tagore's novel *Chokher Bali* had been commissioned and published within several months from each other: one by Penguin, one by Srishti and one by Rupa and Co. Mukherjee clearly states that there was no need for what she defines a 'sudden and excessive interest' in that particular novel and attributes the appearance of the three translations to the extra-literary domain: English publishers in India wanting to cash in on the name Tagore.

4 Ezra Pound, 'Rabindranath Tagore', *Fortnightly Review*, 1 March 1913, 571–9. Here 573.

5 Edward C. Dimock Jr, 'Rabindranath Tagore: The Greatest of the Bauls of Bengal', *The Journal of Asian Studies*, 19/1 (1959), 33–51. Here 34.

the more important literary figures; and by the late 1980s, Mary Lago was forced to admit that 'in the West [...], Tagore is known to relatively few, and not all of those comprehend his immense significance as both a literary and a political figure'.[6]

In this chapter, I pursue five interconnected questions: 1) What factors were at play in the English-speaking Western world to reduce Tagore to a marginal figure in literature by 1960? 2) What has changed in the last three decades to allow the slow but steady reintroduction of Tagore into the English-language canon of world literature? 3) How does the reception of Tagore's works in the English-speaking West differ from that in European countries such as Germany, Italy, Spain, Portugal, Hungary and the territory of former Yugoslavia? 4) What institutions and individuals have visibly contributed to Tagore's reintroduction into the canon of world literature in translation? 5) How can one explain the different strategies adopted in the translation of *The Home and the World*, which, incidentally, has variously been condemned as 'a petit bourgeois yarn of the shoddiest kind' and lauded as '[Tagore's] finest single novel, [...] something like a Bengali version of Turgenev's *Fathers and Sons*' as well as 'the best picture of Bengal's time of political awakening'?[7]

Five years before his momentous voyage to London, the Indian National Council of Education in Calcutta invited Tagore to deliver a talk on comparative literature. Tagore instead decided to speak about *Visva Sahitya*. It is noteworthy that *sahitya* does not primarily refer to the written or published word as the term 'literature' does in Western

6 Nabaneeta Sen, 'The "Foreign Reincarnation" Of Rabindranath Tagore', *The Journal of Asian Studies* (1966), 275–86. Here 275. Mary M. Lago, 'Restoring Rabindranath Tagore', in Mary M. Lago and Ronald Warwick, eds, *Rabindranath Tagore: Perspectives in Time* (Basingstoke: Macmillan, 1989), 4–25. Here 5.

7 Gyorgy Lukács, 'Tagore's Ghandi Novel', in *Reviews and Articles from 'Die rote Fahne'* (London: Merlin Press, 1983), 9–11. Here 9. Seamus Perry, 'Rabindranath Tagore Revived', *The Times Literary Supplement*, 16 September 2011 <http://www.the-tls.co.uk/tls/public/article776938.ece> accessed 19 February 2015. Edward Thompson Jr, *Rabindranath Tagore – Poet and Dramatist* (Delhi: Oxford University Press, 1991), 246.

languages but rather means 'togetherness' and 'harmonious coexistence'.[8] Similarly, *visva* translates as 'all-encompassing', 'the whole world' and even 'the entire universe'. Tagore also used this term to name the university he founded at Santiniketan in 1921, Visva-Bharati (one possible translation is 'all-encompassing love of knowledge'). Although the term *Visva Sahitya* is conventionally translated as 'world literature' it clearly has an ampler sense, one acknowledged by Spivak in an exchange at the ACLA conference 2011, where a questioner appeared to suggest that *sahitya* be translated as 'self-realization'.[9]

One must not view literature as belonging to a particular time and space, Tagore argues, because

> we have to regard literature as a temple being built by the master mason, universal man; writers from various countries and periods are working under him as labourers. None of us has the *plan* of the entire building; but the defective parts are dismantled again and again, and every worker has to conform to that invisible plan by *exercising* his natural talent and blending his composition with the total design.[10]

Tagore sees world literature as an organic world, not an artifice, that surrounds the material world, the whole of humanity. It is not simply an accumulation of individual or national literatures, either: one should recognize 'a totality in each particular author's work, and [...] in this totality [...] perceive the interrelations among all human efforts at expression'.[11]

Tagore seems to have been the first person to propose world literature as a paradigm in literary studies in India and his ideas have fundamentally

8 See Bhavya Tiwari, 'Rabindranath Tagore's Comparative World Literature' in Theo D'haen, David Damrosch and Djelal Kadir, eds, *The Routledge Companion to World Literature* (Abingdon and New York: Routledge, 2011), 41–8.

9 Gayatri Chakravorty Spivak and David Damrosch, 'Comparative Literature/World Literature: A Discussion,' in David Damrosch, ed., *World Literature in Theory* (Malden, MA and Oxford: Wiley Blackwell, 2014), 363–88. Here 385.

10 Rabindranath Tagore, 'World Literature (1907)', in David Damrosch, ed., *World Literature in Theory* (Malden, MA and Oxford: Wiley Blackwell, 2014), 47–57. Here 55.

11 Ibid., 57.

shaped the discipline of comparative literature as it is practiced even today.[12] Well before his works became world literature via translation into Western and Indian languages, therefore, Tagore was interested in the concept. The aspirations to universal education and understanding through the medium of letters visible in the 1907 talk would grow into a major concern for the writer in the following decades. But let us return to *The Home and the World*.

As I have mentioned above, the novel was published in book form by Macmillan in 1919. English-language readers would have to wait for over sixty-five years, until 1985, for the novel to be published again; this time by Penguin, with an introduction by Anita Desai. We still find Desai's introduction in the latest UK edition (2005) along with a new preface by William Radice, additional notes, a chronology and a list of further reading. Significantly, in 1985, *The Home and the World* was considered a Penguin Twentieth Century Classic. Since 2005 the novel has been elevated to the status of a Penguin Classic, pure and simple. A classic, a great work of (world) literature is usually understood to be a timeless work, a mainstay of several societies and generations, one that in theory is continuously available, and not out of print for sixty years. While Tagore's writing has never been out of print in the original Bengali and, for example, in Arabic translation, for decades most readers in the English-speaking West did not have access to his works.

Tagore's writing initially underwent consecration – Casanova's *littérisation* – in one of the most important literary capitals, London, and Tagore won the Nobel Prize, which, according to Casanova, is the 'virtually unchallenged arbiter of literary excellence'.[13] In Casanova's model, once established as an important writer in a literary capital, Tagore should have attained literary immortality, entering the undying company of Nobel laureates. That a writer should fall out of this pantheon and into decades of oblivion is not

12 On the repercussions of Tagore's concept on the development of comparative literature in India, see Tiwari.

13 Pascale Casanova, *The World Republic of Letters* (Cambridge, MA and London: Harvard University Press, 2004), 147.

a development envisaged by Casanova. On closer examination it appears that Tagore was only forgotten in *parts* of the literary universe, for very specific reasons that are not exclusively linked to the world of literature; and he continued to be celebrated in other parts, as I will show. Here the concept of polysystem reveals its usefulness in the description of literary success and obscurity because it allows one to show how adjacent polysystems impinge upon the polysystem of literature.

As with Faulkner, there were a variety of factors that contributed to Tagore's 'disappearance' from the universe of world literature in English. At least five aspects were of utmost importance. First, one notices a shift in the critical reception of Tagore's work: initial enthusiasm quickly turned into harsh criticism for very specific reasons which I will briefly outline below. Second, Tagore and his publishers made particular commercial decisions in terms of what kind of books to translate and publish. Third, the political tensions between India and Great Britain played a considerable role, not only during Tagore's lifetime but also following Indian Independence. Fourth, Tagore's focus on universalism and world peace no longer fitted the political agenda in the West. Fifth, the development of a new literary aesthetic in Europe pushed Tagore's contributions to world literature translated into English out of focus.[14]

While he had been to England twice before, Tagore was fifty-one years old when he was officially introduced to the West as a writer and public figure by his friend, the painter William Rothenstein. That same year, Tagore published *Gitanjali* in English and 'on the strength principally of this volume' was awarded the Nobel Prize the following year.[15] This may strike us as strange but it only reflects the instructions given by Alfred Nobel in his will. He had explicitly specified that the Nobel Prize for Literature should be awarded not for a whole corpus of works but for an outstanding work published the previous year. Nobel's testament lists five criteria: the

14 Lago points towards some of these factors: 'Western preconceptions and misconceptions, facile romanticising, the intractable British-Indian conflict, and great changes in literary taste all contributed to Tagore's "falling out of grace" in the English-speaking world', (Lago, 'Restoring Tagore', 5).

15 See Lago, 'Restoring Tagore', 1.

prize shall go: 1) to those who shall have conferred the greatest benefit on mankind 2) during the preceding year; 3) no consideration shall be given to nationality; 4) the person who shall have produced in the field of literature the most outstanding work 5) in an ideal direction. In the opinion of the Swedish Academy, Tagore fulfilled these criteria in full measure.[16]

Both Sturge Moore and W. B. Yeats proofread and corrected the translation of *Gitanjali* from Bengali; Tagore asked Rothenstein to thank Yeats for helping his poems 'in their perilous adventure of a foreign reincarnation'.[17] Even a cursory comparison between the Bengali *Gitanjali* and the English *Gitanjali* reveals several noteworthy differences: there are 157 poems in the Bengali collection while there are only 103 in English. The poems in Bengali are in rhymed verse but are rendered as fluid prose in English. Furthermore, Tagore paraphrases freely, drops and adapts lines and merges several poems into one. One of the reasons why Tagore decided to rewrite his poems in English was that the translations of forty poems from *Gitanjali* done by Roby Dutta in 1909 did not please him: Tagore believed that rendering them in prose would be better, and he did so during his sea voyage to England.[18]

Tagore expressed some unease about verse translations also in other contexts. While translating a selection of the medieval poet Kabir's verse from Hindi into Bengali, Tagore wrote in a letter to Kshiti Mohan Sen, another translator of Kabir: 'I do not want to go beyond the original text to the smallest extent, even if, as a result, the spirit of the original is not fully explicated. That spirit may remain hidden a little – explaining too much may be limiting on that spirit – poetry and theoretical explication are different things altogether'. Sabyasachi Bhattacharya sees this as Tagore's manifesto for poetry translation and discourages the reader from looking for 'qualities of a creative piece of writing (or didactic explication)' in Tagore's

16 See Sture Allén and Kjell Espmark, *The Nobel Prize in Literature. An Introduction* (Stockholm: Swedish Academy, 2001), 7.

17 William Rothenstein, *Since Fifty: Men and Memories, 1922–1938* (London: Macmillan, 1940), 11.

18 See Tiwari, 46.

translations of Kabir.[19] However, when it comes to the translation of his poetry and prose works into English, Tagore does not always stick closely to the original. The reasons for this will become clearer as we progress.

Before we turn to *The Home and the World* and its reception in Europe, a look at the novel's reception in Bengal when it was first published is necessary. The novel was received with some harsh initial criticism both in Europe and Bengal, but for very different reasons.

A short-lived scandal: Initial reception in Bengal

Ghare Baire has three first-person narrators: Bimala, Nikhilesh and Sandip. Bimala marries Nikhilesh, a Bengali *zamindar*, who has just returned to India after his studies in England.[20] He feels strongly that his wife should come out of *purdah*, the private sphere reserved to women.[21] When Bimala

19 See Sabyasachi Bhattacharya, 'Introduction', in Rabindranath Tagore, *One Hundred Poems of Kabir* (Orient Blackswan, 2004), 1–29. Here 17. On the differences between the original Bengali poems and their English and German translations, see Hans Harder, 'Rabindranath Tagore, Übersetzen und (Miss-)Verstehen zwischen den Kulturen', *Translation as Cultural Praxis. Yearbook 2007 of the Goethe Society of India* (2007), 74–91.

20 Zamindar: 'In India, a holder or occupier (dār) of land (zamīn). The root words are Persian, and the resulting name was widely used wherever Persian influence was spread by the Mughals or other Indian Muslim dynasties. The meanings attached to it were various. In Bengal the word denoted a hereditary tax collector who could retain 10 percent of the revenue he collected. In the late 18th century the British government made these zamindars landowners, thus creating a landed aristocracy in Bengal and Bihar that lasted until Indian independence (1947)'. <http://www.britannica.com/EBchecked/topic/655661/zamindar> accessed 19 February 2015.

21 'The literal meaning of purdah is a curtain, but the term is used to designate the practice of secluding women from contact with men outside of the immediate family. This may be accomplished through virtual imprisonment in separate quarters in the home, veiling in public, and the provision of segregated public facilities. Seclusion has been practiced in many cultures, generally by elite groups; the practice is most

reluctantly steps out of her home into the world, she falls in love with Nikhilesh's friend, Sandip, the local leader of the *Swadeshi* movement.[22] Sandip is a passionate and active man, and thus the opposite of the peace-loving and somewhat passive Nikhil. Nikhil soon realizes that his wife has feelings for Sandip but, true to his principles, decides not to intervene. Bimala is left to choose between the two men alone. When she finally decides in her husband's favour, he has been fatally injured during the ongoing clashes.

Ghare Baire was published in serialized form in the journal *Sabuj Patra* [Green Leaves] between 1915 and 1916. At first, it caused a huge scandal amongst literary critics and the general readership in Bengal.[23] The novel was attacked on grounds of immorality, lack of loyalty towards the nationalist movement and even blasphemy. Many reviews and articles of the time were very harsh and Tagore felt compelled to react in writing twice.[24] Most Bengalis of the time found the novel debauched, and attacked it because of the triangular love it depicts. However, triangular love had been a common *topos* of Bengali literature since Bankimchandra Chattopadhyay

widespread today among the Muslim populations of the Middle East, North Africa, and Asia, and certain Brahmin castes in India'. Elizabeth H. White, 'Purdah', *Frontiers: A Journal of Women Studies*, 2/1 (1977), 31–42. Here 31.

22 In response to the partition of Bengal in 1905, Indian nationalists organized a boycott of goods produced abroad. Protesters burned foreign-made cloth and vowed to use only domestic (*swadeshi*) cloth and locally manufactured goods instead. This movement stimulated both Indian industry and nationalist protest. For a detailed account of the Swadeshi movement, see chapter 7 'The Nationalist Uprise' in S. N. Sen, *History of Freedom Movement in India (1857–1947)* (New Delhi: New Age International, 2003), esp. 92–107. The groundbreaking monograph on the movement remains Sumit Sarkar, *The Swadeshi Movement in Bengal, 1903–1908* (New Delhi: People's Publishing House, 1973).

23 For a more detailed account of reactions to the novel in Bengal between 1915 and 1994, see Jayanti Chattopadhyay, 'Ghare Baire and Its Readings', in Pradip Kumar Datta, ed., *Rabindranath Tagore's the Home and the World. A Critical Companion* (London: Anthem Press, 2005), 187–204.

24 Chattopadhyay, '*Ghare Baire* and Its Readings', 187.

(1838–1894).[25] Besides historical romances, Chattopadhyay 'also wrote domestic romances, which often featured triangular love plots that critically, with multiple perspectives, explored man-woman relations'.[26] In *Ghare Baire*, Tagore uses the same format as Chattopadhyay, but his novel has more psychological depth and integrates political and social issues as well. The authorial voice is completely absent; there is no mediation between the different voices in the novel. Two interlinking elements seem to have scandalized the contemporary readers in Bengal most: Bimala's voice is the most distinct one in the novel and this inevitably led to the discussion of a woman's place in society. Is Bimala the description of an authentic – let alone ideal – Hindu woman? In the minds of many contemporary readers her challenge to traditional rules governing a woman's place is society was unacceptable. In an article entitled 'The Object and Subject of a Story', written to counteract the violent attacks on the book, Tagore points out that 'Shakespeare has created many heroines, but nobody bothers to find out how far they represent the ideal English woman. Even the Christian clergy would not bother to grade them according to their Christian behaviour'.

However, it was not only the Indian reading public that speculated about Bimala's role as a representative of Indian women. In a review of *The Home and the World* in *The Church Times* (1 August 1919), we read the following: 'The central figure is Bimala; she may stand as typical of her native land, half emancipated from the bondage of ancestral traditions, easily infatuated by ideas, liable to be swept off her feet by blind enthusiasm for Swadeshi, a passionate, unstable and pathetic figure'.[27]

25 I use the Bengali spelling, *Chattopadhyay* (after Datta and other Bengali critics) although the surname is often spelled like the anglicized pronunciation, *Chatterjee*.

26 Pradip Kumar Datta, 'Introduction', in *The Home and the World. A Critical Companion*, 1–27. Here 9.

27 Quoted in Mohit K. Ray, 'Tagore on *Ghare Baire*: Aesthetics in Command', in Rama Kundu, ed., *The Home and the World. Critical Perspectives* (Delhi: Asia Book Club, 2001), 91–104. Here 97. 'The Mind of India. The Home and the World. By Rabindranath Tagore', *The Church Times*, 1 August 1919. Reprinted in Kalyan Kundu, Sakti Bhattacharya, and Kalyan Sircar, *Imagining Tagore: Rabindranath and the British Press, 1912–1941* (Kolkata: Shishu Sahitya Samsad, 2000), 320.

Furthermore, Tagore was accused of undermining Bengali nationalism because critics identified the character Nikhilesh with the author himself: Nikhilesh's criticism of the *Swadeshi* movement was seen as a direct reflection of Tagore's rejection of the nationalist movement. Finally, when Sandip makes a derogatory remark about the Hindu goddess Sita, Tagore is accused of irreverence. Tagore's answer to these accusations is that a work of literature must be seen as a work of art and not as a manual of moral instruction: 'The story of *Ghare Baire* reflects some aspects of modern sensibility of a writer of our modern age. But the reflection is a matter of art; it is not a part of the writer's intention to impart any education – good or bad'.[28] This was a revolutionary thought in Bengal where most people 'still favoured the nineteenth-century dictum that the novel was not only a personal communication from the author to the reader, but also a vehicle for delivering a moral message'.[29] This ideal notion was voiced by Jotindra Mohan Sinha (1868–1937) in an article written in 1920, in which he adopts Tolstoy's moral definition of a novel: 'A work of art that united every one with the author and with one another would be perfect art'.[30] Sinha also attacks what he calls the 'sick sentimentalism expressed by the three characters' who 'seem to be vomiting out their inner most thoughts, making the whole atmosphere heavy, filthy and full of foul smell'.[31]

However, the general outrage with *Ghare Baire* was not to last. In the late 1920s and early 1930s, younger Bengali authors started the Kallolian movement, named after the modernist magazine *Kallol* [Rippling Waves]. They wanted to challenge Tagore's authority but felt deep reverence for him at the same time. Bhabani Bhattacharya's 1927 article 'Rabindranath in Fiction' exemplifies the ambivalence of the modernists towards Tagore.

28 Quoted in Ray, 'Tagore on *Ghare Baire*', 93.

29 Chattopadhyay, '*Ghare Baire* and Its Readings', 193.

30 Chattopadhyay quotes Sinha who, in turn, quotes Tolstoy as follows: 'A work of art that united everyman with another and with one another would be perfect art'. Not only should the first 'another' read as 'the author', but Chattopadhyay seems to be (mis)quoting Militsa Greene's introduction to Tolstoy's *What is Art?* See Leo Tolstoy, *What Is Art?* (Letchworth: Bradda Books Ltd., 1963), xxiii.

31 Quoted in Chattopadhyay, '*Ghare Baire* and Its Readings', 196.

While rating *Ghare Baire* as one of the best novels not only in Bengal but in world literature Bhattacharya finds the characters 'full of Puritanism'. This view of Bimala differs completely from the one expressed by many critics only twelve years previously. Far from seeing her as unchaste and debauched, he describes her as a normal woman who, 'in spite of herself, is passionately attracted towards a man other than her husband'.[32]

In Bengal, in a sudden reversal of fortunes that is clearly linked to a politico-cultural shift initiated by a younger generation of writers, 'within one and a half decades of its publication the critical opinion on *Ghare Baire* had travelled from one end of the pole to the other'.[33] From this point onwards, the novel entered the canon of national literature in India. Critics and readers still struggled with the complexities of the novel, but the novel was no longer seen as immoral or irreverent.

Translation and editing choices

Ghare Baire was translated into English by Surendranath Tagore, Rabindranath's nephew, and was first published serially as *The Home and Outside* in the *Modern Review* in 1918 and then in book form in 1919. Although Surendranath is named as the translator, Rabindranath himself was involved in the translation – but to what extent is not clear. In a letter to Macmillan (5 November 1918), Tagore writes: 'A large part of it I have done myself and it has been carefully revised'.[34]

It is important to note how certain ideas about the structure and register of literature in the English-speaking West affected Surendranath and Rabindranath Tagore's editing choices. As far as structure is concerned, the English novel is divided into twelve chapters, unlike the Bengali text

32 Quoted in Chattopadhyay, '*Ghare Baire* and Its Readings', 198.

33 Chattopadhyay, '*Ghare Baire* and Its Readings', 199.

34 Quoted in Radice, 'Preface', viii.

which simply consists of twenty-three 'stories': ten narrated by Bimala, eight by Nikhilesh and five by Sandip. However, what is called a 'story' in English is not a story but 'atmakatha' in the original, which we might term an exhalation of spirit. Therefore, the division into chapters in the English version is 'planned according to the new developments in the plot' introduced in the English version.[35] As a result, the English novel seems more plot-oriented than the Bengali original which is usually described as a character-centred novel of ideas.

The editorial hand – whether Rabindranath's or Surendranath's – does not stop at a rearrangement of the narrative according to Western standards of plot orientation. It also censors parts of the original text. Certain sections of the Bengali text have not been translated into English, sentences and paragraphs that Tagore feared might upset the English readership of the time. In one scene, Sandip brags about how an Anglo-Indian girl was completely enthralled with him and in another scene, he claims that 'the shock of fear increases desire in women'.[36] Either Rabindranath or Surendranath decided to cut both of these sentences. Similarly, whenever a sentence could be read as overtly anti-British, the translator adds textual material to bring the discourse back into the personal realm of Bimala's relationship to the two men. In both the original and the translation, Sandip claims that he will worship Kali by setting Bimala on the goddess's altar of Destruction. However, in the English version, he adds: 'The way to retreat is absolutely closed for both of us. We shall despoil each other: get to hate each other: but never more be free'.[37] Here the excision may have been motivated by the fear of upsetting the English readers who might have read 'the altar of Destruction' as an incitement to overtly anti-British behaviour.

35 Tapobrata Ghosh, 'The Form of *The Home and the World*', in Datta, *The Home and the World. Critical Companion*, 68–81. Here 71.

36 See Ghosh, 'The Form of *The Home and the World*', 73.

37 Tagore, *The Home and the World* [Penguin UK], 84. For other examples, see Nivedita Sen's 'Translator's Note' in Rabindranath Tagore, *The Home and the World. Ghare Baire*, trans. Nivedita Sen (New Delhi: Srishti Publishers and Distributors, 2004), 312–16.

Finally, and most importantly, there is a significant difference in register. The Bengali language has two registers: the formal language called *sadhubhasha* that relies heavily on Sanskrit and the more colloquial *chalitbhasha*. Before *Ghare Baire*, Tagore had used *chalitbhasha* only in his diaries and personal letters, as well as in one epistolary short story, *Streer Patra* [The Wife's Letter]. *Ghare Baire* is the first novel to be written in the more colloquial form of Bengali – a significant step as 'its forms are used to explore [...] the making of the self'.[38] The impact of this innovation on the readership and the critics must have been immense and is perhaps comparable to Dante Alighieri choosing to write the *Commedia* in Tuscan dialect rather than in Latin. *Ghare Baire* is the first Bengali psychological novel with its own particular language, making a categoric break with established rules governing the use of the formal and informal registers of Bengali. The register in the English translation, on the other hand, is far from colloquial and innovative. It is difficult to determine what in the translation is Rabindranath's and what can be attributed to Surendranath but one thing is clear: the register and style are rather Victorian and far from revolutionary. The English translation must have read as quite old-fashioned in 1918 and 1919, at a time when parts of Joyce's *Ulysses* were already being serialized in England and America, showing to what revolutionary use the English language could be put.[39]

Is the difference between the language of the original and the translation due to the more 'floral' character of Bengali and the fact that Surendranath (or Rabindranath) did not possess enough linguistic competence to realize how old-fashioned their English sounded? This, at least, was the argument of many literary critics when confronted with the poor

38 Datta, 'Introduction', 8.

39 While *Ulysses* was not published in book form in the United States until 1933, some parts were serialized in the *Little Review* in New York from March 1918 until the autumn of 1920. In 1920, the last instalments of *Cyclops*, the whole *Nausicaa* and the first instalments of *Oxen and the Sun* were published. The Society for the Suppression of Vice lodged a complaint against the *Little Review* in October 1920. For more details see 'Appendix B', in James Joyce, *Ulysses*, ed. Jeri Johnson (Oxford: Oxford University Press, 1993), 740–5.

reception of the novel in the West. Thompson for example thought that these poor English translations were misrepresenting Tagore's work and affecting his reputation. In a letter to Tagore dated 17 November 1920, Thompson writes:

> As I have told you before, you – with great assistance from yr. publishers – have been yr. own worst enemy. [...] You have lost far more of yr. own force than you need have done. Then, had you trusted the West more, had you given a selection of yr. most imaginative stuff, you wd. have been rewarded.[40]

In his correspondence with Western friends and acquaintances, Tagore himself stresses the fact that he is not a native speaker of English.[41] In response to Thompson, Tagore writes in two separate letters: 'You are right in your diagnosis. I [have] become acutely conscious of cracks and gaps in my translations and try to cover them up with some pretty designs that may give them an appearance of wholeness' (20 September 1921). And: 'In my translations I timidly avoid all difficulties, which has the effect of making them smooth and thin. I know I am misrepresenting myself as a poet to the western readers' (5 August 1921).[42] It is perhaps ironic that such confessions of limited competence in English were expressed in such fluent letters.

The criticism expressed by Thompson seems to ring true for Tagore. It appears that the choice of register and other decisions may have been influenced by a very distinct idea about standards in the English novel. We can only speculate about the reasons that led Rabindranath and Surendranath to modify the English text in the way they did; they were evidently aware of certain expectations in the English readership that differ from those of

40 Uma Das Gupta, ed., *A Difficult Friendship. Letters of Edward Thompson and Rabindranath Tagore 1913–1940* (New Delhi: Oxford University Press, 2003), 126.

41 See, for example, his letter to W. B. Yeats of the 26 January 1913 in which he claims to be 'absolutely ignorant of the proprieties of your language'. Krishna Dutta and Andrew Robinson, eds, *Selected Letters of Rabindranath Tagore* (Cambridge and New York: Cambridge University Press, 1997), 165.

42 Letters reprinted in Das Gupta, *A Difficult Friendship*, 128–9.

Bengali readers.[43] While Tagore's command of the English language was remarkable, both his self-translations and the translations that initially were partly done by his followers at Santiniketan and Tagore-philes in Europe are not thought to compare to later translations of his works done more carefully, more slowly and according to a different philosophy of translation. However, blaming the two Tagores and their faulty translation for the decline in Tagore's literary reputation is too simple an explanation for the muted reception of *The Home and the World*.

A look at Tagore's works first published in English against his overall literary output is illuminating as it explains how the image of the 'sage from the East' could so easily develop: in all, Tagore published 251 books in Bengali, of which 139 were prose works including 67 collections of essays. Only 15 per cent of these essay collections deal with religious themes. Tagore's image as a spiritual leader might incline us to expect rather more of his output to be on religious matters than the 15 per cent of his essays that can be so classified. Between 1912 and 1966, 57 books by Tagore were translated into English, 37 of which in prose. Half of the prose books are 'books of essays'. Besides one book on Ghandi, all the others mainly or in large parts deal with religion or East-West questions.[44] One need not wonder, then, that for over fifty years, Tagore's image in the West was that of the 'wise man from the Orient'. As Edward Said points out, in its Orientalist

43 Harish Trivedi comments on the issue: 'The trouble with Tagore's own translations, as with those done by his Santiniketan associates under his own close supervision and revision, is that they diminish and emasculate the variety and vitality which constitute his unequalled greatness in Bengali. Tagore systematically left out much that was local, specific and original in his work for fear that it would prove unfamiliar and 'difficult' to an English reader'. Harish Trivedi, 'Introduction', in Edward Thompson Jr, *Rabindranath Tagore – Poet and Dramatist* (Delhi: Oxford University Press, 1991), 1–39. Here 11. Tagore himself provides a reason for this regular omitting of textual material: 'I find that English readers have very little patience for scenes and sentiments which are foreign to them; they feel a sort of grievance for what they do not understand – and they care not to understand whatever is different from their familiar world'. Tagore to William Pearson, the translator of the novel *Gora*. Dutta and Robinson, *Selected Letters of Rabindranath Tagore*, 310.

44 Sen, 'Foreign Reincarnation', 284–5.

attitude the West constructs an Orient from an external viewpoint to serve its own interests – this is where problems arise. Tagore's aphorisms and *Gitanjali* fit the image of wise man. Other – more political – writings, such as *Gora* or *The Home and the World*, do not fit that image.

Admittedly, Tagore helped shape this image or, at least, did not protest against this reductive image of the Sage. When Harald Hjärne, Chairman of the Nobel Committee of the Swedish Academy held the inauguration speech in 1913, he defined Tagore as 'a bearer of good tidings from that treasure house of the East whose existence had long been conjectured', blessed with 'the gift of prophecy' who places before the Westerner the culture that in 'the vast, peaceful, and enshrining forests of India attains its perfection, a culture that seeks primarily the quiet peace of the soul in ever-increasing harmony with the life of nature herself. It is a poetical, not a historical, picture that Tagore here reveals to us to confirm his promise that a peace awaits us, too'.[45] With Tagore's name clearly associated with mysticism and Oriental philosophy, the small percentage of his translated works that did not deal with these topics sank into oblivion. Between Tagore's death in 1941 and 1980, in the English-speaking West, his name was not associated with novels, theatre or short stories – aspects of his work for which he is celebrated in India.

A fragmented picture: Translations and publications in English

William Radice is one of the best-known contemporary translators of Tagore's poetry and short stories into English, despite his initial dislike of Tagore in English translation.

45 'The Nobel Prize in 1913. Rabindranath Tagore. Award Ceremony Speech' <http://www.nobelprize.org/nobel_prizes/literature/laureates/1913/press.html> accessed 17 February 2015.

> I did not, as some people have assumed, learn Bengali in order to translate Tagore, indeed I was so put off by his English works [...] that it would be truer to say that I started to learn Bengali *despite* Tagore. When inevitably as part of the postgraduate Diploma course I did at SOAS from 1972 to 1974, I read some poems and stories by Tagore in the original, the realisation dawned that he was a truly great writer, and I longed then to do greater justice to the variety and quality of the Bengali texts than he had been able to do himself.[46]

Radice reiterates, here and elsewhere, that the faulty translations of Tagore's work definitely played a role in hastening the writer's decline into literary obscurity in the English-speaking West. However, without considering the historical context in which these translations were written, it is easy to write Tagore off as untranslatable or, worse, as a bad writer. Mary M. Lago was the first Western Tagore scholar to point out that between 1913 and 1925, the period in which the initially passionate love affair of the English-speaking West with the Bengali writer gradually calmed down, there were several literal and literary breakdowns:

> literal because author, translators and editors were so often out of touch with one another at crucial stages of the work; literary because, although for more than a century Bengal had been the seat of British rule in India, there was a dearth of persons able to make a genuinely literary approach to modern Bengali literature.[47]

Not only were there hardly any qualified translators who could have given much needed advice and could compare the translations to the original, Tagore himself left the bulk of the translations, revisions and proofreading in the hands of a 'changing roster of persons in India and the West'.[48]

46 William Radice, 'Tagore the World Over: English as the Vehicle' (2006). <http://www.williamradice.com/Recent%20Events/Tagore_the_world_over.htm> accessed 11 September 2012. No pagination. When quoting from the article, I indicate the paragraphs instead of page numbers.

47 Mary M. Lago, 'Tagore in Translation: A Case Study in Literary Exchange', *Books Abroad* 46/3 (1972), 416–21. Here 416–17.

48 Lago, 'Tagore in Translation', 418. Between 1900 and 1930, there seemed to be an increased interest in Hindi, Urdu and Sanskrit amongst students of Indian languages but hardly any interest in Bengali. See ibid., 417.

Besides Tagore's own translations, at least fifteen people tried their hand at translating Tagore's works into English during his lifetime. The 1916 collection of short stories *Hungry Stones and Other Stories* provides the perhaps most impressive example of this practice. Besides Tagore himself, it names the following translators: Pannala Basu, Prabhat Kumar Mukherji, Sister Nivedita, E. J. Thompson and C. F. Andrews.[49] No wonder Tagore felt uncomfortable about the varying quality of his works in English translation. In a letter to Macmillan (13 January 1915), he writes: 'I am sending you some more of my stories done by various hands. They are of unequal merit and do not satisfy me. I shall depend upon you for their selection, also for corrections'.[50]

With several people working on the text, it was difficult to tell, even for Tagore, what had been his doing and what had been somebody else's. Considering Yeats' remark about the confusion about which corrections to one of Tagore's poems were his and which ones were Sturge Moore's, one can easily imagine a situation arising in Santiniketan where Rabindranath translated parts of and revised Surendranath's translation of *The Home and the World*.[51] Lago asks: 'Of all the translators and retranslators who worked on his poems, including, and perhaps especially, Tagore himself, who could unerringly draw the line between his own and others' contributions?'[52] As I have already indicated in my discussion of authorship and authenticity in Chapter 2, the unease expressed by Lago and others suggests that readers in most reading communities *want* and expect to be able to unerringly draw lines between the different agents involved in the creation of a translated

49 Charles Freer Andrews (1871–1940) was an Anglican priest who met Tagore at Rothenstein's house in 1912. He renounced his priesthood and joined an ashram at Santiniketan in 1914. He acted as Tagore's representative to Macmillan and also also became good friends with Mahatma Ghandi whom he accompanied to the 1931 Second Round Table conference in London.

50 See 'Appendix 3: Tagore's Writings Published from Britain between 1912 and 1941', in Kundu et al., *Imagining Tagore: Rabindranath and the British Press (1912–1941)*, 628–29. Dasgupta, *A Difficult Friendship*, 19.

51 See Lago, 'Tagore in Translation', 418.

52 On Yeats and Moore correcting Tagore's poems, see Lago, 'Tagore in Translation', 418.

work; or they would rather not admit that it is actually impossible to draw those lines.

While Tagore had accepted and appreciated the help that he got from Yeats and others when he first entered the literary world of the West, this relationship with his Western 'helpers' soon deteriorated for a number of reasons. It is certainly true that Tagore 'courted the friendship and engagement of elite intellectuals with whom he might develop and share ideas and common experiences, and who might further his project of East-West cultural and intellectual dialogue' but he was not willing to simply bow to every suggestion thrown his way.[53] In the second decade of the twentieth century, none of Tagore's advisers in Europe spoke Bengali, but there were many who thought they had a better understanding of what Tagore wanted to express and they sometimes tried (and succeeded) in pushing Tagore to change certain words and phrases. As early as 1913, Tagore seemed weary of this practice. In a letter to Thompson following a discussion regarding emendations suggested by Thompson to some of Tagore's translations, Rabindranath wrote:

> The pleasure I have of polishing [the poems'] English version is of different nature [from] that of an author revising his works for publication. Every line of these should be as closely my own as possible though I must labour under the disadvantage of not being born to your language. In such a case I have to be guided by my instinct, allowing it to work almost unconsciously without being hindered by more than casual suggestions from outside.[54]

Tagore's initial stance towards the English translations of his work seems to alternate between admitting that his linguistic skills might not be up to the task and that he appreciates help, on the one hand, and the frustration that none of his advisers have direct access to the Bengali original, on the other hand: 'When the meaning and music of [the] original haunts you it is difficult for you to know how much has been realized', he writes in a

53 Michael Collins, 'Rabindranath Tagore and the Politics of Friendship', *South Asia: Journal of South Asian Studies*, 35/1 (2012), 118–42. Here 119.

54 Dutta and Robinson, *Selected Letters*, 132.

letter to Ezra Pound in February 1913.[55] Tagore's ambivalent feelings about translation become evident in such exchanges. Just weeks before writing to Pound, Tagore feels obliged to apologize to Yeats for some corrections 'made at the instance of Mr. Andrews in *Gitanjali* when it was too late to submit them to [Yeats]' and expresses his hope that Yeats will revise the proofs of the second edition of the collections of poems in order to 'make all the restorations [he] think[s] necessary'.[56] What emerges from Tagore's correspondence quite clearly is that several of his advisers were pursuing their own agendas, as Lago points out:

> [I]t is highly unlikely that free verse translations by a Bengali lyric poet could negotiate with perfect ease their passage through the hands of Yeats the Celtic revivalist, Pound the iconoclast, Sturge Moore the neo-Hellenist, Evelyn Underhill the religious mystic and Robert Bridges the austere classicist who rejected free verse and all its ways.[57]

This is certainly also true of his prose translated into English: there is a significant difference in register and style between, for example, *The Home and the World* and *Gora*, translated in 1922 by William Pearson.

Tagore was also aggrieved by cynical comments about his having received the Nobel Prize simply because of Yeats's rewriting of most of the poems in *Gitanjali* and upset by Bridges's request to make 'verbal alterations' in these poems before including them in the anthology, *The Spirit of Man*.[58] Tagore's initial refusal to have a single word changed and his frustration with the suggestions coming from very different angles about how and what he should translate – in terms of poetry and other writings – have been explained by some critics as the offended sulking of a slightly arrogant man. Tagore's temper may have played a role but when one reads

55 Ibid., 106.

56 Ibid., 105.

57 Lago, 'Tagore in Translation', 417. Evelyn Underhill's most famous work *Mysticism. A Study of the Nature and Development of Man's Spiritual Consciousness* (1911) was the standard work on religious and spiritual practice until 1946, when Aldous Huxley's *A Perennial Philosophy* was published. Underhill helped Tagore with the English translations for *Songs of Kabir*, published in 1915.

58 See Lago 1972, 418.

his correspondence, a far more nuanced picture emerges. Less than eighteen months after the announcement of the Nobel Prize and less than three years after his sensational appearance on the English literary scene Tagore writes to William Rothenstein (letter dated 4 April 1915):

> Since I have got my fame as an English writer I feel extreme reluctance in accepting alterations in my English poems by any of your writers. I must not give men any reasonable ground for accusing me – which they do – of reaping advantage [from] other men's genius and skill. There are people who suspect that I owe in a large measure to Andrews' help for my literary success, which is so false I can afford to laugh at it. But it is different about Yeats. I think Yeats was sparing in his suggestions – moreover, I was with him during the revisions. But one is apt to delude himself, and it is very easy for me to gradually forget the share Yeats had in making my things passable. [...] If it be true that Yeats's touches have made it possible for *Gitanjali* to occupy the place it does then that must be confessed. At least by my subsequent unadulterated writing my true level should be found out and the faintest speck of lie should be wiped out from the fame that I enjoy now. It does not matter what people think of me but it does matter all the world to me to be true to myself. This is the reason why I cannot accept any help from Bridges excepting where the grammar is wrong and wrong words have been used. [...] PS: [...] In fact I am not so much anxious about mutilations as about added beauties which I cannot claim as mine.[59]

While Tagore initially did not object to his texts being worked on by several people, the canard about the Nobel Prize going to him mainly because of Yeats's input drove home in no uncertain terms that asking for too much help as a writer and poet was frowned upon in the West.[60] Instead, what was expected was an *original genius* of the Romantic kind. Indeed, Tagore was aware of the Western doubt regarding the authenticity of a text that was not the work of a sole person; and his gradual exclusion of London-based collaborators from the translation of his work into English should be seen in this light.

59 Dutta and Robinson, *Selected Letters*, 162.

60 See Lago, 'Tagore in Translation', 418: 'Valentine Chirol, in India in 1913 with a Royal Commission, was reported to have said in a mischievous speech to an assembly of Bengali Muslims that Tagore had won the Prize only because Yeats rewrote the poems. Tagore never forgot this canard'.

By 1921, Tagore was quite disillusioned with the difficulties involved in his self-translations and their reception. In a letter to Thompson in 1921, he wrote: 'I know I am misrepresenting myself as a poet to the western readers. But when I began this career of falsifying my own coins I did it in play. Now I am becoming frightened of its enormity and I am willing to make a confession of my misdeeds and withdraw into my original vocation as a mere Bengali poet'.[61]

Also, Tagore's relationship with Macmillan was becoming more and more strained and would basically come to a halt by 1925. The person in charge of proofreading and approving of the translations of Tagore's work was Charles Whibley (1859–1930), a journalist, critic and reader for the publishing house. He had no knowledge of Bengali but expressed doubts about the rapidity with which the translations reached him and the poor quality of most of them.[62] At the same time, because he did not read Bengali himself, Whibley did not feel in a position to help Tagore; and the translations were published with his and Macmillan's blessing.

Overall then, there were a variety of factors that contributed to the editing and translating choices not only of *The Home and the World*, but of all works by Tagore translated into English. Trying to adapt texts with a foreign audience in mind means labouring under certain assumptions of what will be acceptable to the target audience. Not knowing to whom to turn for qualified help played a role, as well as did assumptions about authorship and authenticity in the West. Tagore was aware of the expectations

61 Dutta and Robinson, *Selected Letters*, 254. On Tagore's exchange of letters with a variety of prominent members of the Western elite and the resulting misunderstandings, see Michael Collins, *Empire, Nationalism and the Postcolonial World: Rabindranath Tagore's Writings on History, Politics and Society*, Edinburgh South Asian Studies Series (London: Routledge, 2011). Collins also provides an insight into the difficulties of cross-cultural understanding in 'Rabindranath Tagore and the Politics of Friendship'.

62 In a letter to Macmillan, Whibley writes: 'I confess that there seems a danger of Tagore's spoiling his market by overproduction [...] What becomes of the legend of the exclusive and secluded poet?' Quoted in Mary M. Lago, *'India's Prisoner': A Biography of Edward John Thompson, 1886–1946* (Columbia: University of Missouri Press, 2001), 112.

that the European readership – both the intellectual elite and the general readers – had of an author. He was torn between wanting to fulfil these expectations and needing help with the translations and editing process. With hindsight, both Tagore and his publishers made doubtful choices. However, as stressed above, their choices are not enough to explain why the first Asian Nobel Prize winner sank into oblivion in the English-speaking West.

By the time Tagore decided to publish *Ghare Baire* in English, he was not only disillusioned with comments and suggestions coming from people who claimed to have his best interests at heart but were actually following their personal agendas. He was also involved in the establishment of Visva-Bharati, the university at Santiniketan, and worried about the political unrest in Bengal. 1919 is not only the year the book was published in English but also the year Tagore repudiated his knighthood after the Jallianwalla Bagh Massacre.[63] His decision to have a novel translated may have been prompted by frustrations when it came to verse translation and by the wish to show Western readers another side to the mystic poet and the public speaker focusing on spirituality and universalism.

63 The massacre is more widely known as Amritsar Massacre. On the massacre, see Stanley A. Wolpert, *A New History of India* (New York and Oxford: Oxford University Press, 2009), 751–2. On 30 May 1919, Tagore wrote the following letter to the Viceroy. The letter appeared in *The Statesman* on 3 June 1919: 'Your Excellency, The enormity of the measures taken by the Government in the Punjab for quelling some local disturbances has, with a rude shock, revealed to our minds the helplessness of our position as British subjects in India. The disproportionate severity of the punishments inflicted upon the unfortunate people and the methods of carrying them out, we are convinced, are without parallel in the history of civilized governments, barring some conspicuous exceptions, recent and remote'. For the full letter, see *The English Writings of Rabindranath Tagore*, ed. Sisir Kumar Das (New Delhi: Sahitya Akademi, 1996), 751–2.

Shifts in critical perception

The reception of *The Home and the World* needs to be put in context and contrasted with the initial reception of Tagore's *Gitanjali* in 1913. As Radice points out, the moment of Tagore's introduction to the West was characterized by a feeling of restlessness and disorientation, a feeling that worked in Tagore's favour:

> With the huge success of *Gitanjali*, it became apparent that many readers in Britain were tired of the cynicism of Oscar Wilde, embarrassed by the imperialism of Kipling, baffled by the experiments of early modernism: they wanted a different sort of writer, and judging by the response of the Nobel Prize Committee and the explosion in sales of secondary translations of *Gitanjali* across the world, it seems that many readers in other countries, in the frightening and disillusioning context of the First World War and its aftermath, wanted a new, sincere, beautiful, spiritual sort of writer too.[64]

Because spirituality was the first and foremost quality that readers in the West recognized in Tagore, that is what they were looking for in his other writings, as well. Tagore did contribute to the initial image of his poetry being universal and spiritual: in an effort to make his poetry more accessible, he discarded much of the local and political. The historical moment was favourable to that particular kind of reception. The influential members of the intellectual elite responsible for Tagore's initial consecration in London all were attracted to Tagore for very specific reasons; whether they saw parallels between Bengal and Ireland (Yeats), looked for inspiration in Eastern

64 Radice, 'Tagore the World Over', para. 7. In an article written in 1918, Professor C. H. Hereford explains Tagore's initial reception in similar terms: 'The literary and intellectual atmosphere here, in and after 1900, was stirred by a variety of influences which made for the welcome of one who brought the promise of a spiritual renaissance and conveyed it in an elusively delicate English style. [...] Reaction from the robust directness of realism had given a vogue to suggestion, reticence, and symbol. On the ethical side, the cult of Tolstoy and of St. Francis subtly prepared for and coloured the reception of the Indian poet'. C. H. Hereford, 'Rabindranath Tagore and His Work', *The Manchester Guardian*, 28 March 1918. Reprinted in Kundu et al., *Imagining Tagore: Rabindranath and the British Press, 1912–1941*, 308.

mysticism (Underhill) or were interested in exchanges about prosody and other poetic devices (Moore and Pound). Convinced of Tagore's greatness (although they arrived at that judgment via different routes) 'it was their reading of the Bengali poet and his culture that set the tone on the chorus of Western adulation of Tagore'.[65] However, it soon became clear that the image of Tagore as serene and spiritual Oriental did not correspond to the historical, 'real' Tagore: a man in his fifties whose literary career had already spanned more than thirty years and who also had quite distinct political ideas, expressed forcibly in the English press after the Jallianwalla Bagh massacre. Ezra Pound's reaction to Tagore singing *Sonar bangla* [Golden Bengal] provides a glance into why the political background to the plot of *The Home and the World* did not seem very credible to most Anglo-American readers.

> Pound almost understood it as a highly emotional patriotic rallying song: 'It is "minor" and subjective. Yet it has all the properties of action'. But he fell in with the political assumption that an Asian country cannot (or should not) possess a concept of nationhood: 'Sonar bangla', he wrote, 'must be the Bengalis "Marseillaise", if an oriental nation can be said to have an equivalent to such an anthem'.[66]

The Home and the World was received with mixed feelings in the Anglo-American intellectual elite of the time. Yeats had cautious praise for the novel and Tagore's autobiography but was disappointed in what he felt were poor translations of Tagore's poems.[67] By 1935, his initial enthusiasm for Tagore had vanished completely:

> Damn Tagore! We got out three good books, Sturge Moore and I, and then, because he thought it more important to know English than to be a great poet, he brought out sentimental rubbish and wrecked his reputation. Tagore does not know English,

65 Ana Jelnikar, 'W. B. Yeats's (Mis)Reading of Tagore: Interpreting an Alien Culture', *University of Toronto Quarterly*, 77/4 (2008), 1005–25. Here 1006. This is a lucid account of the manner in which specific politico-historical forces at work between 1912 and 1935 encroached on the relationship between Tagore and Yeats.

66 Lago, *'India's Prisoner'*, 88–9.

67 See Harold M. Hurwitz, 'Yeats and Tagore', *Comparative Literature*, 16/1 (1964), 55–64. Here 62.

> no Indian knows English. Nobody can write with music and style in a language not learned in childhood and ever since the language of his thought.[68]

Besides Edward Thompson, Evelyn Underhill, some of her fellow mystics and a few members of the *India Society*, nobody who had been very vocal about Tagore's genius and talent paid the literary output of the Bengali writer much heed after 1920. The language of the translations was awkwardly Victorian, the topics often lacked mysticism and otherworldliness, and the reviews were cruel.

E. M. Forster is very harsh in his judgment of *The Home and the World.* Although he finds the theme 'beautiful', he also states: 'Throughout the book one is puzzled by bad tastes that verge upon bad taste'. He calls Bimala's and Sandip's mutual attraction a 'simple boarding-house flirtation', completely ignoring that what might appear an innocuous flirt in England was thought to be outrageous in India, as the first reactions in Bengal clearly show. Most of all, Forster deplores the language, which he refers to as 'Babu sentences'.[69] Forster is quick in blaming the translation for his dislike of the novel: 'Was there some rococo charm that vanished in translation, or is it an experiment that has not quite come off?'[70] Forster concludes that this must be a failed experiment. Reception theory elucidates what happens in cases such as this: 'There are two ways of rethinking your reading experiences when a text fails to respond to the strategies with which it is approached: you can keep the text and change the strategy, or you can keep the strategy and toss out the text on the assumption that it is thin or incoherent'.[71] Forster did the latter: he rejected the text as did many readers in the Anglo-American world. Because they had a very narrow image

68 Allan Wade, ed. *The Letters of W. B. Yeats* (London: Rupert Hart-Davis, 1954), 834–5.

69 A derivation of *bapu* (father), the term *babu* is used in India to express respect towards men However, Forster is here referring to the then current deprecating usage of the word amongst British citizens to describe Indian clerks who wrote and spoke a distinctly 'Indian' English.

70 E. M. Forster, *Abinger Harvest* (Harmondsworth: Penguin, 1983), 365–7.

71 Peter J. Rabinowitz, *Before Reading: Narrative Conventions and the Politics of Interpretation* (Columbus, OH: Ohio University Press, 1997), 211.

of Tagore, it was difficult to classify *The Home and the World* alongside his more 'spiritual' and 'universal' writing.

In 1996, Andrew Robinson and Krishna Dutta published a biography entitled *Rabindranath Tagore: The Myriad-Minded Man*, trying to shine light onto aspects of Tagore's life not known in the West.[72] A truly myriad-minded man, Tagore wrote poetry, novels, plays and essays; he composed music and was a painter. He is credited with introducing the genre of the short story to Bengal and with shaping a new, modern literary language.[73] On a socio-political level, Tagore advocated education and rural development. However, the West was not interested in the polymath Tagore, but only in the 'wise man from the Orient'. To many, the Bengali writer was the personification of Eastern philosophy and mysticism – hardly more than

72 Krishna Dutta and Andrew Robinson, *Rabindranath Tagore: The Myriad-Minded Man* (London: Tauris Parke Paperbacks, 2nd ed., 2009). The standard Tagore biography until then had been Krishna Kripalani, *Rabindranath Tagore: A Biography* (Kolkata: Visva-Bharati, 1980. First edition 1962). Both of these biographies have been accused of being biased: 'Kripalani's biography [...] is one of the most flawed biographies of Tagore in circulation, stressing Tagore's alleged, though unsubstantiated, western leanings in a wholly unwarranted and unqualified way'. Michael Collins, 'Rabindranath Tagore and Nationalism: An Interpretation', *Heidelberg Papers in South Asian and Comparative Politics* Working Paper No. 42 (2008), 1–37. Here 32n164. Ketaki Kushari Dyson is critical of the Dutta/Robinson biography: 'Dutta and Robinson had a splendid opportunity to project an accurate and comprehensive picture of Tagore to English-reading audiences, but they did not make real use of that opportunity, and ironically, their book encouraged some of those very misconceptions about Tagore, and undervaluations of his achievements'. Ketaki Kushari Dyson, 'Rumbling Empires and Men Speaking to Storms'. <http://www.parabaas.com/rabindranath/articles/brKetaki_Collins.html> accessed 19 February 2015. For another, more concise and more recent biography of Tagore, see Uma Das Gupta, *Rabindranath Tagore: A Biography* (New Delhi: Oxford University Press, 2004).

73 While it is by now a commonplace that it was Rabindranath who introduced the short story into the Bengali canon, Susan Stanford Friedman points out that his sister Swarnakumari Devi 'published her volume of short stories before Tagore wrote any'. Susan Stanford Friedman, 'Towards a Transnational Turn in Narrative Theory: Literary Narratives, Traveling Tropes, and the Case of Virginia Woolf and the Tagores', *Narrative*, 19/1 (2011), 1–32. Here 13.

that. As Radice writes, '[i]n Tagore's lifetime, quite a lot can be attributed to his extraordinary aura and charisma. When people met him, they felt – as with Mahatma Gandhi – that they were in the presence of someone of immense inner balance and self-control'.[74] When Tagore's world travels ceased so too did the highly publicized meetings with political leaders and cultural luminaries which contributed at least as much as the published works to sustaining Tagore's charisma in the West.

Changes in literary aesthetics

Substantial changes in literary taste are another influential reason why Tagore nearly became a non-entity in the West. When Tagore first came to London, the circles he frequented projected a certain image of him that would not outlive the initial hype. Through the *India Society*, founded in London in 1910, Tagore became friends with Yeats but also with Evelyn Underhill, an exponent of British mysticism. Tagore's most fervent admirer and sponsor in Germany was Count Hermann Keyserling who had founded the *Schule der Weisheit* [School of Wisdom] in Darmstadt, a forum for intercultural exchange and a prominent institution in Weimar Germany. A great deal of the excitement about Tagore revolved around his person and *persona*, created in his lectures on universalism and world peace. There was also an interest in the spiritual poetry including *Gitanjali*, some plays and in the essays based on Tagore's lecture tours. Those writings that did not fit the spiritual and inspirational category attracted only marginal interest.

74 William Radice, 'Sum Ergo Cogito: Tagore as a Thinker and Tagore as a Poet, and the Relationship between the Two', *Asian and African Studies*, 14/1 (2010), 17–36. Here 21.

As Lago points out, literary tastes were already changing by 1925, the year Macmillan stopped publishing new works by Tagore:

> The bittersweet pastorals of the Georgian poets were replaced by a poetry of the here and now. […] Fictional sprawl was more and more frowned upon. Theatergoers demanded plays with contemporary interest. Now Tagore's delicate allegorical verse plays, his poems still in the *Gitanjali* vein, his fiction in which the Babu English seemed barely forced under by an editorial hand, struck many readers as dated and unfocused.[75]

Soon after Tagore's death, the remaining few faithful friends in the West passed away, as well: Underhill in 1941, Thompson and Keyserling in 1946. What was left were truncated translations and nobody capable of or interested in retranslating what seemed outdated and irrelevant to Western concerns in the aftermath of the Second World War. In the following decades, New Criticism would further move away from all Tagore was thought to represent, emphasizing the close reading of texts and raising the text above generalizing discussion and speculation about either authorial intention or social context. Someone like Tagore, who in Britain and in the United States was known mainly for the persona of 'the wise man from the East', did not excite much interest between 1930 and 1980. Most of his works sank into oblivion.

Was this true of other European countries, as well? With one exception, all initial translations into European languages base themselves on the English translation: for much of the twentieth century there were apparently no Europeans fluent enough in Bengali to attempt a translation from the original language. How did these agents involved in introducing Tagore into their culture present the text twice removed from the original and the writer himself?

75 Lago, 'Tagore in Translation', 421.

Translating the 'English' Tagore into other European languages and cultures

The majority of first translations of the works by Tagore into other European languages relied on the English text rather than the Bengali original. The latest French edition of *The Home and the World*, dating from 2002, for example, is a reprint of the 1921 French translation of the 1919 English translation.[76] The same is true for the German editions of *Das Heim und die Welt*, originally published by the Kurt Wolff Verlag in Munich (1920). The first translation by Helene Meyer-Franck was used for several later editions (second edition in 1961, third edition in 1978 and fourth edition in 1984, all published by the *Volk und Welt Verlag* [People and World Publishers] in East Berlin). The use of a translation based on the 1919 English text did not, however, impair the reception of Tagore in other countries.

> [M]aybe instinctively and unconsciously [Tagore] hit on a style that would enable his reputation to spread rapidly not only in the English-speaking world but elsewhere, because the style *was very easy to translate into other languages*. Universal in his imaginative reach, strongly impelled to speak for and to all humankind and not just to his fellow Bengalis, Tagore found in his English translation style a perfect vehicle for worldwide transmission. In recent years I have looked at translations of *Gitanjali* and other English books by Tagore in many languages: German, French, Spanish, Italian, Dutch, Swedish. They are all very faithful to the original, which in every case was the English version, *not* the original Bengali. This was true even of translations into Hindi, Tamil and other Indian languages with the honourable exception of Gujarati; where translators had eagerly started to translate Tagore directly from Bengali before he won the Nobel Prize.[77]

76 Rabindranath Tagore, *La maison et le monde*, trans. F. Roger-Cornaz (Paris: Petite Bibliothèque Payot, 2002). Roger-Cornaz (1883–1970) famously also translated *Lady Chatterley's Lover* into French.

77 Radice, 'Tagore the World Over', para. 8.

Before we deal with the specific reception of *The Home and the World*, I would like to give an example of a highly effective translation twice removed from the original.

Tagore in Spanish

In 'The Invention of an Andalusian Tagore' Howard Young explores the reasons for 'Tagore's fortunes in the Spanish-speaking world [which] defy simple summarization'.[78] This has to do with Spanish Orientalism, very much *en vogue* at the time, but more importantly it has to do with the fact that Juan Ramón Jiménez and his wife Zenobia decided to translate Tagore into Spanish.[79] In Young's opinion, Tagore may have found one of his most sympathetic translators in Jiménez. Nonetheless, Young quickly adds that the Spanish translations 'unwittingly helped contribute to the process of distorting Tagore, begun by the Bengali poet himself in his autotranslations'.[80] However, these 'distortions' did not harm Tagore's reception and fortune in Spain. Jiménez did not translate *The Home and the World* (which remained untranslated until the 1970s) but twenty-two other Tagore titles, among them *Gitanjali*, between 1913 and 1922. Some of these collections were revised in the 1930s.[81] All translations bore Zenobia's name (or, rather,

78 Howard Young, 'The Invention of an Andalusian Tagore', *Comparative Literature*, 47/1 (1995), 42–52. Also see Graciela P. Nemes, 'Of Tagore and Jiménez', *Books Abroad*, 35/4 (1961), 319–23.

79 Because Spain experienced direct Muslim influence for over 800 years, Mahmoud Manzalaoui insists on the differences between Franco-English and Spanish Orientalism. In Spanish Orientalism, 'the study of the East is precisely not a study of the Other, but a recovery of part of the Self'. Mahmoud Manzalaoui, 'Orientalism. Book Review', *Modern Language Review*, 75/4 (1980), 838–9. Here 838.

80 Young, 'Invention', 42.

81 See R. Johnson, 'Juan Ramón Jiménez, Rabindranath Tagore, and "La Poesia Desnuda"', *The Modern Language Review*, 60/4 (1965), 534–46. Here 540.

her initials), and as of 1918, they all sported a frontispiece that read: 'Unico traductor autorizado por Rabindranath Tagore para publicar sus obras en español' [Only translator authorized by Rabindranath Tagore to publish his works in Spanish].[82] Again, we catch a glimpse of the preoccupation with authority and authenticity in light of a multiplication of voices in translation. Jiménez's translations might have been 'distortions' but 'for decades, the Jiménez version of Tagore was Tagore for the vast Spanish-speaking world, functioning as the original, even though the original in this case was an English rewrite of Bengali'.[83] When Tagore rewrote his Bengali poems in English, he opted for prose rather than verse and simplified the ornate language of the original. Jiménez did not actually read English himself and thus had no direct access to the poems. His wife did, and so she would 'prepare a straightforward Spanish version that rigidly followed Tagore's word order and format' in English.[84] Then Jiménez would make this literal translation into a poem to his liking. This process:

> changes from interlingual, or translation proper, to intralingual, a rewording or working with signs in the same language. By paying particular attention to the rhythmic possibilities of Spanish prosody and exercising his own choices in diction, based on the conventions of European symbolism and on the writings of the Spanish Romantic poet Becquer, Juan Ramón [Jiménez] turned out the published version.[85]

From a traditional Western point of view that values authenticity of texts and considers them to be the property of a single author, this practice of translation seems disreputable. Whether one agrees with this practice or not, the outcome was indeed very successful. Jiménez's translations were so effective at meeting the aesthetic expectations of readers that Tagore remained an important author in Spain, and all other Spanish-speaking regions, especially South America, regularly published all through the

82 Quoted in Howard Young, 'In Loving Translation: Zenobia and Juan Ramón', *Revista Hispanica Moderna*, 49/2 (1996), 486–93. Here 489.

83 Young, 'Invention', 45.

84 Ibid., 46.

85 Ibid.

twentieth century, at a time when he was as good as forgotten in the English-speaking countries in the West.

The success of Tagore's poetry in the Spanish-speaking world completely overshadows the novels, which did not attract very many followers. *The Home and the World*, for example, went untranslated until the 1970s. While the novel was out of print for several years (the last imprint dated back to 1994), an independent Spanish publisher from Barcelona launched a new edition of the novel in early 2014.[86]

Tagore in Portuguese

The case of the Portuguese translation of *The Home and the World* is different from other European languages as even the first translation was made directly from Bengali. It also shows yet again how the efforts of a single individual can decisively influence the reception of a literary work.

A Casa e o Mundo was translated by the Goan writer Telo de Mascarenhas (1899–1979) and published in 1941 by the Lisbon publishing house *Editorial Inquérito*. It would see four editions in fourteen years. De Mascarenhas had founded the *Centro Nacionalista Hindu* in Lisbon in 1926 and saw the translations of modern Indian literature as acts of passive resistance towards the Portuguese colonial power and as a way to create a cultural pan-Lusitanian identity separate from the Portuguese Empire. In 1928 de Mascarenhas wrote an article on Tagore's views of nationalism in which he stressed the importance of *Ghare Baire* as a discussion of patriotism and nationalism rather than as the depiction of an unhappy love triangle.

The translation strategies are noteworthy: in a similar move to the English translation, the Portuguese translation [Portuguese Renaissance]

86 See 'La casa y el mundo' <http://www.plataformaeditorial.com/ficha/269/1/3725/la-casa-y-el-mundo.html> accessed 26 January 2015.

is also divided into chapters (albeit thirteen rather than the twelve in Surendranath's translation) and de Mascarenhas also decided not to translate certain parts of the text.[87]

Overall, the Portuguese reception of Tagore inserts itself within the efforts of a literary elite that believed in the necessity of active intervention in political life. These efforts first resulted in the formation of *Renascença Portuguesa* [Portuguese Renaissance], a literary association established in Oporto in 1910, and the *Grupo da Biblioteca* [The Library Group], which existed from 1919 to 1927. Political involvement was also important to the intellectuals contributing to the critical review *Seara Nova* [New Cornfield], founded by Jaime Cortesão, Raul Proença, Aquilino Ribeiro and Câmara Reys and published twice monthly from 15 October, 1921. Despite censorship, shortage of money and frequent arguments among the contributors, the review survived for decades and can count many Portuguese writers amongst its contributors, notably José Saramago and Luiz Francisco Rebello.[88] Sovon Sanyal argues that these Portuguese intellectuals were 'attracted by Tagore's universalism and search for unity of mankind in the midst of the all round spread of fascist doctrines in Europe. [...] Transcending all narrow racial, religious and national boundaries, Tagore emerged for them as a true internationalist'.[89] In a politico-cultural environment favourable to the message of Tagore's political novels, *The Home and the World* remained more visible to Portuguese readers over the decades than it was in the English-speaking West.

87 See Sovon Sanyal, 'A Casa e O Mundo: Telo De Mascarenhas's Translation of *Ghare Baire*', *Parabaas* Special Rabindranath Tagore Section (May 2012). <http://www.parabaas.com/rabindranath/articles/pSovon3.html> accessed 25 January 2015.

88 For an overview of the first forty years of Seara Nova and its impact on Portuguese society, see Gerald M. Moser, 'The Campaign of Seara Nova and Its Impact on Portuguese Literature, 1921–61', *Luso-Brazilian Review*, 2/1 (1965), 15–42.

89 Sanyal, para. 8.

Tagore in German

In Germany, *The Home and the World* became one of Tagore's best-known books. The German translation of *The Home and the World* by Helene Meyer-Franck for the publisher Kurt Wolff in 1920 is called *Das Heim und die Welt*. In June of that year thousands flocked to the grounds of the palace of the Grand Duke of Hesse in Darmstadt, the site of Keyserling's *Schule der Weisheit*, to hear Tagore speak. By 1920, Wolff had become a fervent promoter of Tagore, even though he was not immediately impressed by his literary genius according to an anecdote concerning the German publication of *Gitanjali*. This anecdote is worth telling as it shows the power struggle between different agents in the literary polysystem.

Willy Haas recounts that only one reader report was positive about Tagore's poems and that, as a consequence, Wolff had decided not to publish the collection. He had already asked for the manuscript to be sent back when he heard that Tagore had been awarded the Nobel Prize. To everyone's great relief, the manuscript had not left the local post office yet and the publication of the bestseller brought in a considerable profit.[90] In his recent publications on Tagore's impact on Germany, Martin Kämpchen has gathered the recollections of other people involved in the Wolff publishing house at the time which contradict Haas's version. In several letters as well as in an essay written for a radio programme in 1962, Kurt Wolff states that he had accepted Tagore's book shortly before the news of the Nobel Prize reached him. Kurt Pinthus, a reader at the publishing house, as well as another employee, Arthur Seiffhart, both recall events in a similar

90 Willy Haas, 'Lesehilfen für notorisch faule Leser', *Die Welt*, 27 December 1971. Quoted in Martin Kämpchen, *Rabindranath Tagore und Deutschland* (Marbach am Neckar: Deutsche Schillergesellschaft, 2011), 17–18. For an English-language account of Wolff's and other versions of the Gitanjali affair, see Martin Kämpchen, *Rabindranath Tagore in Germany: Four Responses to a Cultural Icon* (New Delhi: Indian Institute of Advanced Study, 1999), 66–74. Also see Harder, 'Übersetzen und (Miss-)Verstehen' and Radice, 'Tagore the World Over', both of whom reproduce Haas's anecdote without questioning its truthfulness.

fashion to Wolff. Kämpchen also found evidence that Haas may actually have joined the publisher only in the spring of 1914 which would mean that he could not have been present to witness events surrounding the acceptance or rejection of the manuscript in the first place.[91] But let us return to the German translation of *The Home and the World*.

Das Heim und die Welt clearly states that it is the 'einzig autorisierte deutsche Ausgabe. Nach der von Rabindranath Tagore selbst veranstalteten englischen Ausgabe ins Deutsche übertragen' [The only authorized German edition. Translated from the English version of the novel prepared by Rabindranath Tagore himself].[92] Not only do we notice the preoccupation with the author's authorization but the English version also only names Surendranath Tagore as the translator. Why would the German translator and/or the publisher decide to mislead their readers into believing that Tagore had single-handedly prepared the English translation? They must have felt that the German readership would worry about the authenticity of a translation twice removed from the original – which is why they stressed that theirs was the only *authorized* translation. Moreover, if readers believed that Tagore had himself authored the English version of *The Home and the World*, then that text had the status of an original and therefore a German translation, once removed from the original, would be perceived as more faithful, more valuable and thus more authentic than a translation twice removed from the original.

One of the earlier critics of the novel writing in German was Gyorgy Lukács. In the early 1920s, Lukács expresses a similar view to Forster's in his review of the German translation of *The Home and the World*, entitled 'Tagore's Ghandi Novel'.[93] Lukács claims that 'Tagore's enormous popularity among Germany's intellectual "elite" is one of the cultural scandals occurring with ever greater intensity again and again'. The novel is described as

91 See Kämpchen, 'Tagore und Deutschland', 14–18.

92 Rabindranath Tagore, *Das Heim und die Welt*, trans. Helene Meyer-Franck (Munich: Wolff, 1920), unpaginated page.

93 For a more detailed analysis of Lukács's criticism of Tagore, see Kalyan Kumar Chatterjee, '*The Home and the World.* Tagore's Ghandi Novel', in Kundu, *The Home and the World: Critical Perspectives*, 109–17.

'a petit bourgeois yarn of the shoddiest kind' and Tagore himself as 'a wholly insignificant figure [...] whose creative powers do not even stretch to a decent pamphlet. He lacks the imagination even to calumniate convincingly and effectively'.[94] One of the most influential Marxist literary critics at that time, Lukács approaches the text with a whole set of assumptions and expectations: he reads the novel looking for a clearly expressed political statement and thus finds nothing worthy in it, completely ignoring its psychological aspects and its genre (novel of ideas). When it comes to European writers, Lukács will occasionally admit that art does not always have to be political (as he does when talking about Dostoyevsky and Strindberg) but when confronted with *The Home and the World*, he expects Tagore to make a stronger political statement. As the novel does not correspond to his expectations, he opts to discard it instead of changing his interpretive strategy.

Meyer-Franck's translation of *Das Heim und die Welt* saw four editions between 1920 and 1984 – the last three in East Germany. The *Volk und Welt* publishing house was founded in 1947 and was the second most important publishing house in the GDR. Its initial aim was to publish Soviet literature in translation as well as anti-Fascist German literature. In the 1950s, the focus shifted to international writers. Over the decades, *Volk und Welt* included publications by forty Nobel Prize winners; Rabindranath Tagore was one of them. Tagore's name was proposed for inclusion in the publisher's catalogue on the strength of his work's status as the literature of the oppressed minority and of Tagore's anti-imperialist credentials.[95] However, the decision whether to publish the novel did not ultimately lie with the publisher. Other members of the cultural elite in the GDR were not quite sure about Tagore. *Das Heim*

94 Lukács, 'Tagore's Ghandi Novel', 9–11.

95 'Volk und Welt propagierte seit seiner Gründung den "anti-imperialistischen Kampf", mit "progressiver internationaler Literatur" und stellte sich auf die Seite der unterdrückten Minderheiten'. [Since its inception, *Volk und Welt* propagated the 'anti-Imperialist struggle' by means of 'progressive international literature' and took the side of oppressed minorities.] Siegfried Lokatis, 'Nimm den Elefanten – Konturen einer Verlagsgeschichte', in Simone Barck and Siegfried Lokatis, eds, *Fenster zur Welt: Eine Geschichte des DDR-Verlages Volk und Welt* (Berlin: Christoph Links Verlag, 2003), 15–30. Here 26.

und die Welt had to get the official approval by one of the 'Hauptgutachter' [monitors in chief] in the ministry of culture, Paul Friedländer, who was in charge of manuscripts considered potentially compatible with official socialism in the GDR. Friedländer was famous for a high rate of rejection, and he managed to block the publication of *Das Heim und die Welt* for three years.[96] Although the novel saw four editions and was widely read, some members of the intellectual elite were not convinced that its political content was concordant with the cultural policy of GDR and Soviet literature. Only one year after the publication of Meyer-Franck's translation, the Hyperion publishing house in in Freiburg, West Germany, published a new translation (from the English) by Emil and Helene Engelhardt.[97]

Between 1914 and 1925, Kurt Wolff's publishing house put on the market twenty-four editions of Tagore's work, including an eight-volume *Collected Works* in 1921. The last translation to appear in the publishing house was *Gora* in 1925.[98] Several works by Tagore were published on a fairly regular basis in the Federal Republic of Germany from 1925 until 1980:

96 'Paul Friedländer ('Der Autor kann vom Leser nicht verlangen, ihm in seine Gedankenwirrnis zu folgen…') entschied Monat für Monat über das Schicksal von 14 Manuskripten. […] Friedländers Stellungnahmen waren selten länger als drei Seiten, aber seine Abschußquote konnte sich sehen lassen. Er sorgte zum Beispiel dafür, daß 'Das Heim und die Welt' des Nobelpreisträgers Rabindranath Tagore 1961 mit dreijähriger Verspätung erschien'. [Month after month, Paul Friedländer ('The author cannot request the reader to follow the train of his confused thoughts…') decided the fate of fourteen manuscripts. […] Friedländer's reports were rarely longer than three pages, but his rejection rate was impressive. It was his doing, for example, that *Das Heim und die Welt* by Nobel laureate Rabindranath Tagore appeared in 1961, after a three-year delay.] Siegfried Lokatis, 'Ein literarisches Quartett – Vier Hauptgutachter der Zensurbehörde', in Barck and Lokatis, *Fenster zur Welt*, 333–8. Here 333.

97 As far as I am aware, this translation has not been reissued since. As well as translating several of Tagore's works from English into German, Emil Engelhardt had already published a biography of Tagore forty years earlier, in 1921, entitled *Rabindranath Tagore als Mensch, Dichter und Denker* [Rabindranath Tagore. Man, Poet and Thinker].

98 See Martin Kämpchen, 'Rabindranath Tagores Rezeption in Deutschland, Österreich und der Schweiz', in Gabriele Fois-Kaschel, ed., *Rabindranath Tagore. Ein anderer Blick auf die Moderne – Un autre regard sur la modernité* (Tübingen: Narr Francke Attempto, 2013), 17–37. Here 21.

aphorisms, some poems and short stories. Indologists working in West and East Germany – at, for example, the South Asia Institute at the University of Heidelberg, the South Asia Institute at the Humboldt University in Berlin or the South Asia Seminar at the Institute of Oriental Studies at the Martin-Luther University at Halle-Wittenberg – reminded and continue to remind the German public of the importance of Tagore. Again, a few prominent agents stand out in the struggle to maintain a certain level of visibility for Tagore's work, individuals who managed to interest the larger public in the Bengali writer. Martin Kämpchen is one of the most prominent figures both in terms of translation and Tagore criticism.[99] In East Germany, Gisela Leiste also translated directly from Bengali. Leiste published a translation of *Gora* in 2004, but *The Home and the World* is currently out of print in Germany – while it seems to be more *en vogue* in the English-speaking West.

Tagore in Hungarian, Slovenian and Croatian

Imre Bangha argues that 'Tagore's popularity in [East Central Europe] came in three waves between which there were periods of amnesia'.[100] The first wave started with the awarding of the Nobel Prize. What is worth

99 Besides the titles mentioned above, Kämpchen has also published *Rabindranath Tagore and Germany: A Documentation* (Kolkata: Goethe-Institut, 1991) and a short biography in German entitled *Rabindranath Tagore* (Hamburg: Rowohlt, 1992). For a concise summary of his findings, see 'Rabindranath Tagore and Germany: An Overview' in Sanjukta Dasgupta and Chinmoy Guha, eds, *Tagore. At Home in the World* (New Delhi, Thousand Oaks, CA and London: SAGE, 2013), 15–24.

100 Imre Bangha, 'From 82-Year-Old Musicologist to Anti-Imperialist Hero: Metamorphoses of the Hungarian Tagore in East Central Europe', *Asian and African Studies*, 14/1 (2010): 57–70. Here 58. Bangha refers to several studies on the reception of Tagore in Russia, Bulgaria and Romania which seem to confirm that, there too, the interest in Tagore manifested itself in three waves. In a revised chapter on the topic, Bangha urges Tagore scholars to move beyond the national framework when

mentioning in this regard is the reaction in the Balkan regions that formerly belonged to the Austrian-Hungarian Empire. As Ana Jelnikar shows, the initial response was 'largely dominated by extra-literary factors rather than any authentic appreciation of the writer's sensibility'.[101] There was a relief amongst the Slovene intelligentsia that the Nobel did not go to Peter Rosegger, 'whose name [...] was associated less with literary credentials than with an aggressive Germanization policy pursued against Slovenes in Southern Carinthia and Southern Styria'.[102] As a counter-example to the narrow-minded nationalist Rosegger, Tagore was praised for his universalism and spirituality.

The second wave lasted from the end of the First World War until the late 1920s, peaking in Tagore's visits to the region in 1926. The third wave came with the rediscovery of Tagore in 1955 and his celebration as 'an anti-imperialist hero in the communist bloc'.[103] This latter wave of popularity was in tune with the cultural politics of communist countries, whether in COMECON states like the GDR and Hungary or in the non-aligned Yugoslavia.[104] *The Home and the World* was anonymously translated from English into Croatian in 1922 and published serially, before Miroslav Golik retranslated the novel in 1944.[105] There are several recent Croatian translations of Tagore's poetry and short stories by Clara Gönc Moačanin, not directly from the Bengali but based on Radice's retranslations into English.

---

it comes to the reception of Tagore, especially in East Central Europe as such an approach will highlight the 'similarities and dissimilarities of Rabindranath's reception in these geographically small but culturally very rich countries'. Imre Bangha, 'Tagore's Reception and His Translations in Hungary', in Sanjukta Dasgupta and Chinmoy Guha, *Tagore. At Home in the World*, 25–37.

101 Ana Jelnikar, 'Sreçko Kosovel and Rabindranath Tagore: Points of Departure and Identification', *Asian and African Studies*, 14/1 (2010), 79–95. Here 83.

102 Jelnikar, 'Kosolev and Tagore', 83–4.

103 Bangha, 'From 82-Year-Old', 58.

104 For an analysis of the reception of Tagore in Croatia, see Klara Gönc Moačanin, 'Reception of Tagore's Work in Croatia', *Asian and African Studies*, 14/1 (2010), 71–8.

105 Ibid., 73.

On one side of the Iron Curtain, Tagore was described as a 'fierce enemy of petrified traditions and of fascism' and a 'friend of the Soviet Union, and a vociferous critic of British imperial oppression': in short, an anti-capitalist, anti-imperialist writer.[106] *The Home and the World* seemed to fit the political agenda and was therefore made widely available at a time when it was out of print in the English-speaking West.

As emerges from this brief overview, a combination of factors and agents kept Tagore more visible in several European countries than in the English-speaking West. Let us now return to *The Home and the World* in English translation.

Arguing for a specific translation: Paratextual engagement with authenticity

As I have mentioned at the beginning of this chapter, *The Home and the World* is currently available in its first 1919 translation as well as in two new translations. In this section, I concentrate on the paratextual apparatus in the three English translations available to date: Surendranath's translation (1919, 1985, 2005); Nivedita Sen's translation for Srishti (2004) and Sreejata Guha's for Penguin India (2005). In this particular analysis, I am interested in the different agents whose voices we can hear in the paratext and in their hermeneutical and rhetorical skills: how do they make sense of literature (their interpretation of the text) and how do they make sense to others (how do they persuade the readers of the value and validity of the translation in question)?

As pointed out above, Penguin UK opted not to commission a new translation for one very specific reason: Tagore's possible involvement in the translation. Let me quote from William Radice's preface:

106 Jozsef Blaskovics and Dusan Zbavitel, *Baren Basu: Zsoldosok* (Pozsony: Magyar Kiado, 1953). Translation quoted from Bangha, 65.

> In a letter to Macmillan of 5 November 1918, he wrote: 'My nephew Surendranath has translated the latest novel of mine which I think you will find fully acceptable. A large part of it I have done myself and it has been carefully revised'. This gives the translation an enhanced authenticity, as Tagore was by no means so attentive to Macmillan's editions of his other novels and collections of short stories.[107]

If Rabindranath's involvement makes the translation more authentic, do we actually need a new translation? Not according to the paratextual commentary provided by Radice in the Penguin UK edition:

> In recent years, critics with access to both languages have become more respectful of Surendranath's achievement, more aware of what a challenge the Bengali text presents to any translator, more willing to read his English not as 'dated' but as representative of its provenance and period. [...] It is a highly sophisticated piece of work, deserving respect, not patronage.[108]

And Anita Desai has the following to say in her introduction:

> Doubtless a more modern and colloquial translation could be made to suit the altered tastes of the times, but the truth is that Bengali is a highly rhetorical language. Bengalis are given to impassioned and extravagant speech as they are to radical politics, and Tagore wrote political essays from which he took whole sentences to place in the mouth of the central character, Nikhil. Clearly, it was to him a natural, not a contrived or literary, language. It belonged to its period, the Victorian. It was of a piece with such architecture as the Victoria Terminus in Bombay, and with the dark, looming furniture, fussy costumes and domestic trappings of that age, and must be seen in this context.[109]

The implication is that if one retranslates the text, it will be taken out of that Victorian context and this would result in the text losing authenticity. William Radice also claims that 'the translation itself has classic status and is unlikely to be wholly supplanted by a new translation'. What the 1919 translation should be used for, then, is 'closer comparison of the two

107 Radice, 'Preface', viii.

108 Ibid., xiii–ix.

109 Anita Desai, 'Introduction', in Tagore, *The Home and The World* (London: Penguin UK, 2005, xxi–xxviii). Here xxvi.

texts than has been attempted even by Bengali specialists in English'.[110] Surendranath's translation, Radice argues, is so complex that there is enough scope for research as it is. This is a view that Radice takes when it comes to all of the first translations of Tagore's work. He urges us to 'see [the initial translations done and supervised by Tagore] as part of his total œuvre, and a very important and lasting part because unlike translations by others – which can date and be replaced – Tagore's translations are *his own words*, and as such are as durable and authentic as his writings in Bengali'.[111] So how do we read these first, faulty translations? Radice suggests we do so

> sympathetically, not with constant reference to the original (a pointless exercise) but as self-standing literary creations in their own right. Critics such as Sukanta Chaudhuri or Sisir Kumar Das (editor of the Sahitya Akademi's English writings of Tagore) prefer not to see his translations as translations at all. Instead, they see him as a 'bilingual writer', whose 'translations' can be read as a sort of commentary on his Bengali works.[112]

Notwithstanding these arguments in favour of Tagore's autotranslations, there seems to be an overall trend to retranslate Tagore, a trend that is being led by Indian translators. This is also true for *The Home and the World*. In 2005, the year Penguin UK published the first translation complete with paratextual commentary arguing for the validity of this particular text, Penguin India published a new translation of the novel by Sreejata Guha, with an introduction and notes by Swagato Ganguly. And the previous year, 2004, saw the publication of Nivedita Sen's translation for Srishti Publishers.[113]

The retranslation of works by Tagore in India has been prompted by the decision of several Indian universities in the late 1990s to start teaching a range of literary texts by Indian writers in English translation. The

110 Radice, 'Preface', xiii.

111 Radice, 'Tagore the World Over', para. 9.

112 Ibid., para. 10.

113 Both the Srishti and the Penguin India covers feature stills from Satyajit Ray's 1984 film adaptation of the novel. The latest Penguin UK edition shows a woman's hands decorated with henna.

1919 translation of *The Home and the World* was one of the texts on the syllabus; three collections of critical essays in English on Tagore's novel have appeared since 2001.[114] While the essay collections refer to the prescribed 1919 translation on the syllabus by now several Indian universities use one of the two new translations of Tagore's novel.[115] If in Indian academia and in the Indian publishing industry there had persisted a similar deferential attitude towards the *author as possible translator* as emerges in the choices of William Radice and Penguin UK, we would not have these two new translations.

What arguments are presented to the reader in the paratextual apparatus of the 2004 and 2005 translations? Quite predictably, neither the Penguin nor the Srishti text mention Rabindranath's professed involvement in the 1919 translation. The blame is laid on Surendranath, the named translator, for what is considered an incomplete, defective translation. In her 'Translator's Note', Nivedita Sen states that she 'found Surendranath Tagore's translation inadequate not only because it leaves out some of the virtually untranslatable poetic prose; it also does away with important textual matter'. However, she also admits: 'Although it is easy enough to dismiss Surendranath Tagore's translation as archaic or incomplete, it is not as easy to render the entire original text in a reader-friendly idiom'.[116] Here, the translator is in good company: as I have pointed out above, many Tagore scholars have deplored the differences in register, content and structure between the Bengali and English versions of Tagore's work. In the second quote, we also have got an echo of what both Radice and

114 These are: Pradip Kumar Datta, ed., *Rabindranath Tagore's* The Home and the World. *A Critical Companion*; Rama Kundu, ed., *Rabindranath Tagore's* The Home and the World: *Critical Perspectives*; Saswati Sengupta, Shampa Roy, and Sharmila Purkayastha, eds, *Towards Freedom. Critical Essays on Rabindranath Tagore's* Ghare Baire/The Home and the World (Hyderabad: Orient Longman, 2007).

115 For example, the Department of History at the University of Delhi has prescribed Sen's translation for an MA course on Modern Indian History. Veer Narmad South Gujarat University has prescribed Guha's translation for a section of their MA programme in English.

116 Sen, 'Translator's Note', 312.

Desai say about the difficulties of translation from Bengali, and of translating Tagore in particular.

Similarly, the 'Publisher's Note' in the Penguin translation informs us that, in the 1919 translation

> Surendranath Tagore chose to leave out chunks of the poetic prose that *Ghare Baire* is embellished with, as well as some of the poetry written in the form of Vaishnava Padavali [hymns to Vishnu, M. D.], perhaps deeming these untranslatable. His translation also left out textual matter that is important to understanding the nuances of the characters, and collapsed Nikhilesh's two sisters-in-law into one. This new translation provides an English version of the full text of Rabindranath Tagore's *Ghare Baire*, and attempts to replicate the language of the original, with all its complexities, as closely as possible.[117]

The distinct rhetorical strategies at work are clearly visible: no mention of the author's professed involvement in the textual interventions that make the 1919 translation what it is and an avowal that the translation on hand is more faithful to the original in a philological sense, a more genuine article than Surendranath's efforts. Interestingly, all agents involved, whether sitting in India or in Europe, play one and the same trump card. That trump card is called *authenticity*. In all three translations an argument is made for that particular text possessing authenticity, or even enhanced authenticity. But which translation is more authentic: Surendranath Tagore's because of the author's professed involvement, or Sen's and/or Guha's translations which claim to stick more closely to the Bengali original? Is authenticity

117 'Publisher's Note', Rabindranath Tagore, *Home and the World*, trans. Sreejata Guha (New Delhi: Penguin India, 2005), unpaginated page. Vaishnava is a form of devotion to Vishnu, a supreme deity who can also take the human form of Krishna, that peaked in the sixteenth century. At the centre of the surge of Krishna devotion was the Brahman Chaitanya (1486–1533). Devotion is shown in songs, *kirtan*, which can be roughly distinguished into four groups: *samkirtan* (group singing), *nam-kirtan* (names of God), *padavali kirtan* (lyrical hymns) and *lila-kirtan* (dramatic performance of theme-related songs). The term padavali, also transliterated as padaabali or padaboli, literally means 'gathering of songs'. See Joseph T. O'Connell, 'Tracing Vaishnava Strains in Tagore', *The Journal of Hindu Studies*, 4/2 (2011), 144–64. Here 146–8.

linked to a single author? Does it mean faithfulness to an original text (however defined) in a philological sense? Who or what guarantees authenticity? And, perhaps more importantly, who decides that authenticity is one of the foremost attributes of literature? Why is the return to the 'original' described in terms of purification, whether with regard to the logic of arguments and semantics or with regard to what is to be understood as the form intended by the author? And why are translators who explicitly advocate postcolonial and poststructuralist translation techniques still reassuring their readers that their translation is as close to the original as a translation could possibly be?

There is a discrepancy between the rhetoric presented to the readers in the paratext ('this is a text nearly as good as the original') and a critical discourse superimposed onto the act of translation that emerged from my personal contact with the two translators. I asked both translators about their stance on the relationship between original and target texts and for their opinions about the 'authenticity claim' made by Radice and Desai about Surendranath's version. Nivedita Sen had the following to say:

> Those of us who have engaged with [Surendranath's translation] as teachers often wonder how [Rabindranath] could have advocated or approved of the deletion of important passages that leave the novel high and dry. The entire theory of Nikhilesh, focusing on his realization that there is a whole world of suffering people whose problems are not solved by the slogans and mindless violence of nationalism, gets sidetracked, deflected, often erased from that text. There could have been some complex reason connected with [Rabindranath's] concern that his foreign audience should not know too much about people like Ponchu whose suffering he thought we might not be able to alleviate irrespective of whether we gained our independence from colonial rule. This is indeed a grey area, but if that translation was tailored according to his instructions, there must have been some reason.[118]

Sen then refers to the Indian translation theorist Tejaswini Niranjana who claims that the postcolonial desire to retranslate is linked to the desire to rewrite history: 'Niranjana would read into every translation like mine the appropriation of the text in a way that is subsumed within the post-colonial

118 Nivedita Sen, personal correspondence with Marion Dalvai. 4 January 2010.

theory of resistance. But she would also say that that is what translation in the post-colonial context is all about'.[119] Srishti Publishers leave the shaping of the paratext in Nivedita Sen's hands. Her voice clearly comes through in the introduction, the glossary and the 'Translator's Note'. While Sen engages with the puzzling deletions in the 1919 text, both on a paratextual level in the translation and in her correspondence with me, and is slightly uneasy about Rabindranath's professed textual interventions, Sreejata Guha is more categorical in her answer regarding the 'authenticity' of that particular text:

> I happen to belong to the school of thought that translation is 'the most intimate act of reading' (sic Spivak). Hence an endorsement from the author of the Bangla original to me is just another reading, no more and no less 'authentic' than the next reading. [...] I do believe that in the post-structuralist world that I inhabit, following in the footsteps of Fish, Iser, Barthes and others before and since who have imparted agency to the reader and the text s/he creates by the act of reading, 'fidelity' to an 'original' becomes a reductive and absolutist concept which may have its uses in certain contexts, but in the larger perspective of the praxis of translation, it fails to validate its position. A SL [source language] text is not a static entity; it is shaped and reshaped in every new reading and similarly, each and every translation in a TL [target language] breathes new life into yet another avatar of the same (and yet not the same) SL [source language] 'original'.[120]

Both translations, and the Penguin India translation especially, advocate the translation's closeness and faithfulness to the original. The two voices at the paratextual level in the Penguin India translation, however, do not include the translator's (who, as we have just seen, does not believe in the categories of 'authenticity', 'completeness' or 'faithfulness'). The introduction and notes are by Swagato Ganguly and the reader is also presented with a brief 'Publisher's Note': it is here where the claim of proximity to the original is made. There seems to be a divergence between academic discourse on translation, which critically engages with issues of translatability, closeness and faithfulness, on the one hand, and the commercial

119 Sen, personal correspondence with Marion Dalvai. 4 January 2010. See Tejaswini Niranjana, *Siting Translation: History, Post-Structuralism, and the Colonial Context* (Berkeley: University of California Press, 1992).

120 Sreejata Guha, personal correspondence with Marion Dalvai. 17 April 2012.

presentation of translations to the reading public, on the other. In my view, this is not simply a marketing strategy. As I have already demonstrated in several cases, the assumption seems to be that the general readers should not be troubled with the reality of how translated texts are shaped; they are not deemed capable of appreciating an item that is not and cannot be 'authentic' or 'faithful' to a proclaimed original.

Tagore's case is by no means as drastic as Carver's case discussed in Chapter 2: although the 2004 and 2005 translations are more complete and therefore slightly longer, they are still recognizably related to the 1919 version. Yet, as the paratextual comments to the different editions have shown, the quest for authenticity in literature is far from over. Whether one considers the author dead or come back to life again, whether one believes in the relative stability of literary texts or strongly asserts their instability, the issue of authenticity must be a central one in the debate on textual interventions.[121]

Restoring Tagore in the English-speaking West

Tagore was an important – if not the *most* important – figure to have emerged from the Bengal Renaissance. His works have seen a second renaissance in the English-speaking West in the last thirty years, culminating in several sesquicentenary celebrations of 2010–2012. What agents and factors are responsible for this ongoing restoration of his literary importance?

It seems to me that the restoration of Tagore as a visible member of world literature in its English-language implementation started towards the end of the 1970s. In 1978, Edward Said published the influential

121 For a detailed engagement with the proclaimed death of the author and his/her return, see Sean Burke, *Authorship: From Plato to Postmodern. A Reader* as well as Burke's *The Death and Return of the Author: Criticism and Subjectivity in Barthes, Foucault and Derrida* (Edinburgh: Edinburgh University Press, 1998).

Orientalism, from which emerged a multiculturalist interrogation of the traditional Eurocentric canon. In an attempt to redefine the East and itself, the West turned its interest towards forgotten names like Tagore's again. In the early 1980s, a new generation of Indian authors writing in English helped shape a new literary image of the subcontinent and in the process also kindled interest in earlier Indian writers. Two prominent examples are Salman Rushdie and Anita Desai. Rushdie was awarded the Booker Prize for *Midnight's Children* in 1981. Desai was shortlisted twice during the 1980s, in 1980 for *Clear Light of Day* and in 1984 for *In Custody*.[122]

Tagore found a strong academic advocate during the 1970s and 1980s in the late Mary Lago who continued to publish articles and books about the Bengali writer into the twenty-first century. In the late 1980s, Lago demanded 'more translations of previously translated works, more translations more faithful to the Bengali originals and free of the awkwardness and crippling deletions that discourage the modern reader'.[123] This call for new translations has not gone unanswered. Amongst recent Tagore translators into English we find Pratima Bowes, William Radice, Ketaki Kushari Dyson and the late Sujit Mukherjee. Thirty translators contributed to *The Essential Tagore*, an 800-page anthology of Tagore's work, published by Harvard University Press in 2011, the sesquicentenary year of Tagore's birth. Clearly, the decision of Indian universities to teach Indian writers in English translation has played a crucial role in kindling interest in Tagore from academics and translators alike. Western readers have undoubtedly profited from the rapid expansion of English-language publishing in India since 1990.[124]

This restoration process is still ongoing – Tagore's work is so multifaceted and multilayered that we can expect more translations of his work and a diversified and challenging critical response in the coming decades, both from Eastern and Western scholars. The interest in Tagore, however,

122 Desai was shortlisted a third time in 1999 for *Fasting Feasting*.

123 Lago, 'Restoring Tagore', 21–2.

124 On the changing publishing trends in India, see Suman Gupta, *Globalization and Literature* (Cambridge and Malden, MA: Polity, 2009), 162–4.

has not been confined to academics. Other institutions have also played a role in putting Tagore back onto the map. The Tagore Centre UK with its head office in London and a branch in Glasgow has financed and actively encouraged a variety of publications since its foundation in 1985. Marino Rigon, an Italian monk working in Bangladesh since the mid-1950s, has translated many of Tagore's works into Italian and established the 'Centro Studi Tagore' in Venice in the early 1990s. The Indian Cultural Centre in Berlin, founded in 1994, is called the Tagore Centre and while it is not specifically dedicated to the Bengali writer, he is clearly seen as a unique symbol of India. While these Tagore Centres all differ in scope and outreach, they want to see themselves as reminders of the importance of Rabindranath.

The latest addition to the growing interest in Tagore has been the foundation of the first Tagore Centre attached to a university, *ScoTs* (The Scottish Centre of Tagore Studies) at Edinburgh Napier University with the establishment of a chair in Tagore Studies in 2012, held by Professor Indranath Chaudhuri, Academic Director of the Indira Gandhi Institute. The Indian Council for Cultural Relations funds the Chair as well as two PhD fellowships. There are two distinct factors that seem to be behind this particular upsurge of institutional interest in Tagore. First, chairs and fellowships in Tagore Studies form part of the strategic agenda of European and US universities seeking to establish and strengthen links with institutions in Asia.[125] Second, Tagore's iconic status and position as an Indian

125 In April 2011, a delegation from Trinity College Dublin participated in a trade mission to India organized by Enterprise Ireland. 'Potential links for key areas of collaboration were explored in the areas of the digital humanities, history, law and business, and political science. Institutions visited in Delhi were the University of Delhi, to follow up on the MoU signed there last November, and Jawaharlal Nehru University. A memorandum of understanding was signed with the Indian Institute of Management, Bangalore'. See 'Vice-Provost/CAO signs memorandum of understanding with Indian Institute of Management, Bangalore', 19 April 2011 <http://www.tcd.ie/vpcao/latest-news.php> accessed 25 January 2015. In the last few years, several such MOUs were signed, for example, between the University of Northhampton and the University of Madras and between the University of Dhaka and Indiana University. See 'University of Northampton Signs MoU with University of Madras' <http://www.jamshedsiddiqui.com/2012/04/university-of-northampton-uk-signs-mou.

writer with a complex history of international reception are being used by Indian institutions and government agencies to enhance the profile of Indian culture globally through their funding of research. The coincidence of interest emerges quite clearly from the statements given by Joan Stringer of Edinburgh Napier University and Suresh Goel of the Indian Council for Cultural Relations:

> Professor Dame Joan Stringer, Principal & Vice-Chancellor of Edinburgh Napier University, said: 'The spirit of Rabindranath Tagore continues to inspire the entire world and it is with great honour that we sign this MoU with the Indian Council for Cultural Relations. It represents a significant step towards the opening of Scotland's first centre for Tagore Studies at Edinburgh Napier, which we hope will attract research interest from both near and far and, in the spirit of the man himself, will be outward looking, inclusive and visionary'.
>
> Suresh Goel, Director General of the Indian Council for Cultural Relations (ICCR), said: 'The ICCR considers this collaboration with the University to be of great importance since it will promote an academic exchange between India and Edinburgh Napier. It has been the philosophy of the ICCR that this kind of co-operation contributes to the civilisation of dialogue and understanding on a much more durable basis'.[126]

Concluding remarks: All is well that ends well? Tagore through English

Over the last three decades, it would seem, Rabindranath Tagore has been reintroduced into the canon of world literature with some vehemence. More English translations by the Bengali writer are in print now than

html> and 'IBA and Indiana University Sign MOU' <http://iba-du.edu/index.php/media/index/78> both accessed 25 January 2015.

126 'Opportunities Around the World', *The Deccan Herald*. <http://www.deccanherald.com/content/211694/opportunities-around-world.html> accessed 11 January 2015.

ever before. Although in a traditional bookshop in the West readers are still presented with the first translations rather than the new translations from India, internet bookshops stock the new translations and ship them from India in a relatively short time. In late February 2015, amazon.co.uk even had two new copies of Guha's translation in stock that were eligible for next day delivery and also offered six copies of Sen's translation via third-party sellers.

More Western scholars engage with the writer Tagore and with his œuvre and, subsequently, several of his works are now a mainstay of world literature syllabuses in European and US universities.[127] Still, there are some critical voices that doubt the importance of Tagore and the impact of his literary writing. This becomes apparent in the press coverage of the Tagore celebrations in 2011 in two leading UK newspapers, the *Guardian* and the *Times Literary Supplement*.

In an article written for the *Guardian* in May 2011, Ian Jack suggests that 'perhaps the time has come for us to forget Tagore was ever a poet, and think of his more intelligible achievements'.[128] Jack then summarizes what aspects we should concentrate on: Tagore as an essayist, an educationist, an opponent of terrorism, a secularist, an ecologist, a critical nationalist and a writer who understood women. We should, in short, forget about a large percentage of Tagore's literary output. The same week, J. C. wrote in the *Times Literary Supplement*:

> Who reads Rabindranath Tagore now? Not many, it is safe to say. Yet, a century ago, Tagore, whose 150th anniversary falls this year, was all the rage. [...] If your Bengali is good enough, you might tell us that to read Tagore in the original is to be transported; in English, the tune that was once so new is now apt to sound quaint.[129]

127 For example, at Amherst College, Rice University, Rutgers and University of Texas in the United States and at Warwick University and the University of Zagreb in Europe.

128 Ian Jack, 'Rabindranath Tagore Was a Global Phenomenon, So Why Is He Neglected?', *The Guardian*, 7 May 2011. <http://www.guardian.co.uk/commentisfree/2011/may/07/rabindranath-tagore-why-was-he-neglected> accessed 25 January 2015.

129 J. C, 'In Another Time', *The Times Literary Supplement*, 13 May 2011. <http://www.the-tls.co.uk/tls/reviews/other_categories/article724824.ece> accessed 25 January 2015.

In September 2011, however, Seamus Perry was more affirmative in his *TLS* review of four Tagore texts: William Radice's new translation of *Gitanjali*, *The Essential Tagore* and Radha Chakravarty's translations of *Boyhood Days* and of *Farewell Song*:

> A welcome flurry of publications, arriving in time for the 150th anniversary of his birth, seeks to remedy the neglect into which Tagore has fallen among those of us who cannot read him in the original. For even allowing for the losses of translation [...] he remains a wonderful writer, humane and unsparing, above all a superb analyst of human longing and its capacity both to transform and to distort the lives it touches.[130]

In the last days of Tagore's 150th birthday anniversary, the editorial of the *Guardian* asks the question why 'the scant press coverage accorded to him this past year, has, ironically, focused on why he is so neglected'.[131] The editorial then chastises the *Times Literary Supplement* author J. C. of parochialism for his 'Who reads Rabindranath Tagore now' comment but fails to mention the scathing view of the literary translations of Tagore's works expressed by the *Guardian*'s own Ian Jack. After praising the work of translators such as Radice and Kushari Dyson, the editorial concludes with the following words: 'His 150th anniversary is as good a time as any for readers to rediscover just how various and interesting a man Tagore was'. The new translations of Tagore's work definitely will play a crucial part in this rediscovery.

The issue whether and how much we need to retranslate, however, has not been resolved, as I have indicated in my discussion of the translations of *The Home and the World*. Even if we agree that Tagore needs to be retranslated, we should ask how many times over the same work should be translated: do we really 'need' three new translations of *Chokher Bhali* in the space of a few years? While readers worldwide able to read English clearly profit from the increase in English-language translations and publications coming out of India, Ketaki Kushari Dyson expresses uneasiness

130 Perry, 16 September 2011.

131 'Rabindranath Tagore: The Poet at 150', *The Guardian*, 29 April 2012. <http://www.guardian.co.uk/commentisfree/2012/apr/29/rabindranath-tagore-poet-india> accessed 25 January 2015.

about the way in which English now dominates translation in India. What seems equally troublesome is the prevalence of English as an academic language. Will Tagore scholars (and Indian scholars in general) decide to simply write in English rather than their native Bengali (or other Indian language) in the future? Kushari Dyson writes of an alarming trend:

> If today I write a book on Tagore in Bengali, no matter how path-breaking it may be, it will not be reviewed in an English-language paper, not even in Kolkata, though if I am lucky, I may be interviewed about it. To be reviewed in such a paper the book has to be in English. What can one say about this kind of neo-colonialism?[132]

The danger of this kind of neo-colonialism is indeed a topic that is not willingly broached in Tagore Studies at the moment. While I agree with Peter Hitchcock that the use of English for Academic Purposes can actually dislocate and decolonize English from its rootedness in a specifically Eurocentric location, the imperatives of international academia do not seem to give non-native English speakers much of a choice when it comes to the international visibility or the funding of their research.[133] While the positive changes in Tagore's literary reputation are certainly to be welcomed, and while the increase in English-language translations and critical writing will win the Bengali writer more readers in the future, the danger of an imbalance in favour of English-language engagement with his works cannot be denied. Will the afterlife of Tagore outside Bengal become a primarily English-language affair?

132 Ketaki Kushari Dyson, 'The Phenomenal Legacy of Rabindranath Tagore', *Asian and African Studies*, 14/1 (2010), 37–44. Here 43–4.

133 Peter Hitchcock, 'Decolonizing (the) English', *South Atlantic Quarterly*, 100/3 (2001), 749–71.

CHAPTER 4

'I now lay before you the book, the inkwell, and the pens': Tahar Ben Jelloun's *The Sand Child* in English-Language Criticism

> Every critical affirmation contains, on the one hand, a recognition of the value of the work which occasions it [...] and on the other hand an affirmation of its own legitimacy. All critics declare not only their judgment of the work but also their claim to the right to talk about it and judge it, in short, they take part in a struggle for the monopoly of legitimate discourse about the work of art, and consequently in the production of the value of the work of art.[1]

While I have given a general overview of agents and factors that shaped the reception of Tagore's *The Home and the World* in Chapter 3, this chapter focuses on a single aspect of the reception process: academic criticism. Tahar Ben Jelloun's 1985 novel *L'enfant de sable*, translated into English by Alan Sheridan in 1987 as *The Sand Child*, will serve as my case study.[2] This chapter gives an overview of items of literary criticism about the novel written in English between 1987 and 2014. Leaving aside newspaper reviews and other forms of more 'popular' readers' reactions, the aim is to foreground a specific category of gatekeepers, literary critics who publish academic – generally peer-reviewed – articles and books. The analysis is twofold: in concentrates on specific readings of Ben Jelloun's novel as well as on the

1 Pierre Bourdieu, *The Field of Cultural Production. Essays on Art and Literature*, trans. Claude DuVerlie et al. (Cambridge: Polity, 1993), 35.

2 Tahar Ben Jelloun, *L'enfant de sable* (Paris: Seuil, 1985). *The Sand Child*, trans. Alan Sheridan (Baltimore, MD and London: Johns Hopkins University Press, 2000). When reproducing French quotes as they appear in some of the critical works, I use the abbreviation *ES* for *L'enfant de sable*.

cross-fertilization between individual critical readings and critical discourse across cultures.

Academic writing is perhaps the mode of writing most obviously based on generative reading. Using the tools of the text, literary critics construct an interpretation of the work in question, according to specific rules that are (more or less) well-established in their particular academic field (for example, postcolonial studies or narratology). Peer-reviewed academic articles, book chapters and monographs thus are the result of a 'working consensus', which is not an agreement in any absolute sense but a tentative agreement within a specific school of thought.[3] The concept is particularly useful in the realm of literary criticism: scholars may agree to disagree on certain interpretations presented to them in academic papers but they will generally accept that, when it comes to focus and methodology, other scholarly interpretations follow the standards set out in their particular area of literary criticism.

Another factor apart from the working consensus that plays a crucial role in the cross-cultural exchange of ideas of literary criticism is the habitus of individual and institutional gatekeepers. Habitus is a set of dispositions that generates practices and perceptions of which we are not always consciously aware. It is the result of a long process of inculcation that eventually becomes second nature (see Chapter 1). Rather than seeing each interpretation of works of literature as the expression of a subjective viewpoint, my approach is perspectivist: it focuses on individual contributions within several 'branches' of literary criticism and also takes into account the combative nature of the academic field, which, *pace* Bourdieu, is the site of an ongoing struggle over classification:

> The university field is, like any other field, the locus of a struggle to determine the conditions and the criteria of legitimate membership and legitimate hierarchy, that is, to determine which properties are pertinent, effective and liable to function as capital so as to generate the specific profits guaranteed by the field. The different sets of individuals (more or less constituted into groups) who are defined by these

3 I borrow the term from Goffman. See Erving Goffman, *The Presentation of Self in Everyday Life* (London: Penguin, 1990).

> different criteria have a vested interest in them. In proffering these criteria, in trying to have them acknowledged, in staking their own claim to constitute them as legitimate properties, as specific capital, they are working to modify the laws of formation of the prices characteristic of the university market, and thereby to increase their potential for profit.[4]

Like the wider academic field, the field of literary criticism is the territory of Bourdieu's *homo academicus*, 'supreme classifier among classifiers'.[5] Literary criticism always embodies the specific interests of groups of intellectuals who share a particular vision of and approach to literature.

For over three decades, Tahar Ben Jelloun has been a constant presence on the international book market. Winner of the Prix Goncourt in 1987 and the International IMPAC Dublin Literary Award in 2004, Ben Jelloun has published well over forty works that have been translated into several dozens of languages. Although Ben Jelloun's first language is Arabic he has published his entire œuvre in French. He also works as a translator from Arabic into French.[6] Many of Ben Jelloun's novels are set in Morocco and he has been praised for bringing the Maghreb closer to French and Western audiences. However, Ben Jelloun has also been attacked – mostly, but not exclusively, by North African scholars and fellow writers – for not writing in his mother tongue and for oversimplifying Maghrebian customs and culture in order to please his audience. For example, in a brief review essay, Hedi Abdel-Jaouad writes: 'No one has more consciously and artfully capitalized on cultural syncretism and cosmopolitan idealism than Ben Jelloun', yet admitting that 'he is not the only one to have jumped on the cross-cultural bandwagon'.[7] Indeed, several voices in the West tend to

4 Pierre Bourdieu, *Homo Academicus*, trans. Peter Collier (Cambridge: Polity Press, 1988), 11.

5 Ibid., 1.

6 On Ben Jelloun as a translator of Mohamed Choukri, see Mustapha Ettobi, 'Cultural Representations in Literary Translation: Translators as Mediators/Creators', *Journal of Arabic Literature*, 37/2 (2006), 206–29.

7 Hedi Abdel-Jaouad, 'Sacrilegious Discourse', *Middle East Report*, 163 (1990), 34–6. Here 34.

idealize Ben Jelloun as an apostle of a new cosmopolitanism, as this extract from a *Companion to the World Novel* shows:

> [Tahar Ben Jelloun] writes fiction to comment on Moroccan society and try and change its archaic structures. Inspired by the French ideals of secularism, equality and social justice, Jelloun militates for a free, egalitarian, and secular society in which religion does not interfere in politics and where men and women have equal rights. His novels focus on Morocco, which he criticizes for its 'feudal' institutions based on tyranny, sexual and religious hypocrisy, and women's oppression.
>
> A fervent social critic, Jelloun is an *intellectuel engagé* (engaged intellectual) involved in world politics and in issues relating to Morocco, North Africa and the Middle East [...].
>
> An honored novelist and a respected intellectual, Jelloun is a humanist and a man of dialogue, urging understanding and fraternity between people.[8]

Bernard R. Périsse portrays Ben Jelloun in a similar light in his 2003 comparative thematic study of Nabokov's *American Works* and Ben Jelloun's novels. After stating that Nabokov was against the treatment of social themes in literature, Périssé quotes from Ben Jelloun's interview with Thomas Spear in which he described his writerly duty: 'to be a witness to [...] reality, an engaged witness, personal and sentimental and all that, but a witness nevertheless'.[9] Thus, Périssé describes Ben Jelloun as 'an independent thinker and a sincere enthusiast for liberty and justice' who has no hesitation 'in criticizing and condemning what he considers as a major impediment to human dignity and to human rights'. For Périssé, 'it

8 Amar Acheraiou, 'Tahar Ben Jelloun', in Michael D. Sollars, ed., *Companion to the World Novel. 1900 to the Present.* (New York: Infobase Publishing, 2008), 403–5. Here 404.

9 Bernard R. Périssé, *Solitude and the Quest for Happiness in Vladimir Nabokov's American Works and Tahar Ben Jelloun's Novels* (Berne and New York: Peter Lang, 2003), 167n5. Périssé sporadically refers to Ahmed's mother in *The Sand Child* in Chapter 4 'Women and Solitude', 120–40.

is obvious that as a novelist, he denies himself any temptation to comply rigidly with the Art for Art's sake principle and give all his attention and energy to form only'.[10]

Ben Jelloun's *The Sand Child* lends itself to a thorough investigation of the mechanics of academic criticism as it is a highly self-reflexive piece of fiction that is sufficiently complex to give rise to completely opposing interpretations. It is therefore worthwhile not only to analyse which lines of argument available to the scholarly community working mainly in English are accepted as meaningful, but also to investigate whether the arguments put forward in English acknowledge or adopt arguments present in Ben Jelloun criticism in French. If so, which arguments travel across cultural and linguistic borders into English easily and which arguments do not? I am aware of the fact that one cannot simply equate a shared language with a shared culture. In the specific case of literary criticism focused on a specific author or novel, however, one can argue that most literary critics who are interested in 'Francophone' or 'Maghrebian' literature and writing about it in English share enough of a common background to engage in a meaningful exchange about the significance of a particular book/author and the existing criticism on these. I also assume that, within a particular school of thought, critics labour towards establishing a working consensus on issues that are important to them. That is to say, they form part of the same reading community.

Before we can engage with the critical works that deal specifically with *The Sand Child*, however, an overview of Ben Jelloun's life and œuvre as well as of the novel's complex narrative structure are necessary.

10 Ibid., 116–18.

Tahar Ben Jelloun, a Moroccan writing in French

Ben Jelloun was born into a poor family in Fez, Morocco in 1944, when the country was still a protectorate of both Spain and France. He attended a Koranic primary school in Fez until his family moved to Tangiers, a city 'naturally projected towards Europe, yet deeply rooted in Africa'.[11] Here, Ben Jelloun attended French secondary school before moving on to the University of Rabat to study philosophy. In 1966, because of his involvement in a student protest against King Hassan II, Ben Jelloun was sent to two different internment camps for eighteen months, an experience he drew on in *This Blinding Absence of Light*, for which he won the IMPAC prize in 2004. After his release, Ben Jelloun worked as a philosophy teacher while also contributing to *Anfas/Souffles*, a cultural magazine in Tangiers founded by Abdellatif Laâbi in 1966. When the Moroccan government decided that philosophy was to be exclusively taught through Arabic, Ben Jelloun left for Paris to read for a doctorate in social psychiatry. He started writing poetry and novels, as well as articles for *Le Monde*. His first essay *La plus haute des solitudes* [The greatest solitude] (1977) investigates the Moroccan immigrant community in France and their misery. It draws on his doctoral dissertation, which researched sexual impotence among North African migrants at the Dejerine Centre for Psychosomatic Medicine. Ben Jelloun's first bestseller, the novel *Harrouda* (1973), had already won him critical acclaim from Samuel Beckett and Roland Barthes.

Ben Jelloun sees himself as a public figure and his writing tends to be interpreted as politically committed. Two titles stand out in particular in this regard: *French Hospitality* (1984) and *Racism explained to my daughter* (1998).[12] The first work has been widely criticized, although it was

11 Abdellatif Attafi, 'Tahar Ben Jelloun (1944–)', in Alba Della Fazia Amoia and Bettina Liebowitz Knapp, eds, *Multicultural Writers since 1945: An A-to-Z Guide* (Westport, CT: Greenwood Press, 2004), 75–8. Here 75.

12 On the public figure of the writer, see Ben Jelloun's semi-autobiographical *L'écrivain publique* [The Public Writer] (Paris: Seuil, 1983).

republished in 1997 (English translation 1999) with a new introduction in which Ben Jelloun responds to some of the original criticism and reiterates key points about the difference between the concept and practice of hospitality in France and Morocco. *Racism explained to my daughter*, on the other hand, became an instant bestseller and has been translated into over thirty languages.[13]

In the Maghrebian context, Ben Jelloun's decision to write in French rather than Arabic is by no means an exception. He is part of a growing number of North African writers who choose to write in French and like a growing number of writers from the former colonies he does not want to be described as a Francophone, but a Moroccan writing in French. Ben Jelloun is one of forty-four writers who signed a manifesto that aspired to replace the term Francophone literature with the term *littérature-monde en français* [world-literature in French] which appeared in *Le Monde* in 2007. Nobody speaks 'francophone', the manifesto argues, and it is high time to free language from 'its exclusive pact with the nation' and all other powers 'but the powers of poetry and the imaginary'.[14] One of the aims is to break down the hierarchy of French and francophone literature. The co-signers opt for the term 'world-literature in French' because

> Literatures in French around the world today are demonstrably multiple, diverse, forming a vast ensemble, the ramifications of which link together several continents. But 'world-literature' also because all around us these literatures depict the world that is emerging in front of us, and by doing so recover, after several decades, from what was 'forbidden in fiction', what has always been the province of artists, novelists,

13 Tahar Ben Jelloun, *French Hospitality: Racism and North African Immigrants* (New York and Chichester: Columbia University Press, 1999); *Racism Explained to My Daughter* (New York: New Press, 1999).

14 Michel Le Bris, et al., 'Towards a "World-Literature" in French', in Alec G. Hargreaves, Charles Forsdick and David Murphy, eds, *Transnational French Studies. Postcolonialism and* Littérature-monde (Liverpool: Liverpool University Press, 2010), 296–300. Here 300. The translation of the manifesto by Daniel Simon first appeared in *World Literature Today*, 83/2 (March-April 2009), 54–6. It is also reprinted in David Damrosch, ed., *World Literature in Theory* (Oxford and Malden, MA: Wiley Blackwell, 2014), 271–5.

> creators: the task of giving a voice and a visage to the global unknown – and to the unknown in us.[15]

Ben Jelloun has described writing in French as liberating, and the association of Arabic with the Koran as a barrier to experimentation.[16] His novels, however, constantly bring him back to a Moroccan setting, which is also the case with *The Sand Child*. The novel's sequel, *La Nuit Sacrée* (1987), translated by Sheridan as *The Sacred Night* in 1989, won the coveted *Prix Goncourt*. According to William Cloonan, Ben Jelloun fit the pattern

> for a *goncourable* author. He was in the preferred age category, about forty-one years old, had written articles for *Le Monde*, and had previously published six books with Seuil. He was already a literary figure of some prominence whose taste in fiction corresponded, at least in some areas, with traditional Goncourt thinking. [...] The confluence of a noteworthy novel, a climate of opinion, and an established author allowed the jurors to make an award that permitted them to champion progress without making any significant changes in the essential Goncourt philosophy.[17]

In the last twenty years, Ben Jelloun has published dozens of works and has won a myriad of literary and non-literary prizes, including the IMPAC prize in 2004 and the Erich-Maria-Remarque peace prize in 2011.

In Ben Jelloun's fictions, readers are confronted with references to sociology, psychology, politics and the everyday life of outsiders (prostitutes, androgynes, madmen) as well as a strong reliance on mythology and the supernatural. In terms of narrative techniques, Ben Jelloun excels at constantly blurring literary genres and at playfully engaging with and distorting traditionally accepted narrative devices. This mix of realism and myth and

15 Ibid., 299.

16 'I often say that the fact of writing in French is a way for us to be somewhat bold and also to be relevant, because when one writes in Arabic, one is slightly intimidated by the language of the Koran'. Thomas Spear and Caren Litherland, 'Politics and Literature: An Interview with Tahar Ben Jelloun', *Yale French Studies*, 82/2 (1993), 30–43. Here 34.

17 William Cloonan, 'The Politics of Prizes: The Goncourt in the 1980s' in Joseph Brami, Madeleine Cottenet-Hage and Pierre Verdaguer, eds, *Regards sur la France des Années 1980* (Saratoga, CA: ANMA Libri, 1994), 215–22. Here 220.

the unwillingness to adopt a single specific narrative strategy may confuse many readers, but Ben Jelloun has a growing readership worldwide: many of his novels have become part of the curriculum at secondary school level and at university level. His novels can, for example, be found on the school syllabuses in the final year in secondary schools in France and Germany, as well as on several world literature courses (including at Northwestern and Columbia universities in the United States). The complexity of Ben Jelloun's polyphonic writing clearly also makes a perfect playground for literary criticism.

The Sand Child

The protagonist of the novel is a child who is born into a family already 'cursed' with seven girls. Thus, the eighth child, although biologically a girl, is presented to the world as a boy by the name of Ahmed. Seven different narrators tell often conflicting versions Ahmed's growing awareness that he is different and his painful journey towards a new identity, Zahra. In the sequel, *The Sacred Night*, Zahra rises to speak herself.

The basic narrative structure of *The Sand Child* shows a constant tension between two ways of storytelling: the spoken and the written word. Not only do we have a variety of storytellers who give us different versions of the protagonist's life; there is an underlying question: what makes a good, authentic story? While some narrators derive the right to speak from their possession of the protagonist's diary (for them, authenticity is conferred by the written word), others derive the right to speak from personal experience (this applies especially to the only female storyteller, Fatuma). Some narrators, however, argue that authenticity – conventionally understood as correspondence to what really happened – has nothing to do with a good story.

There are seven narrators telling the story of the sand child. Three of them claim to have access to the protagonist's diary.

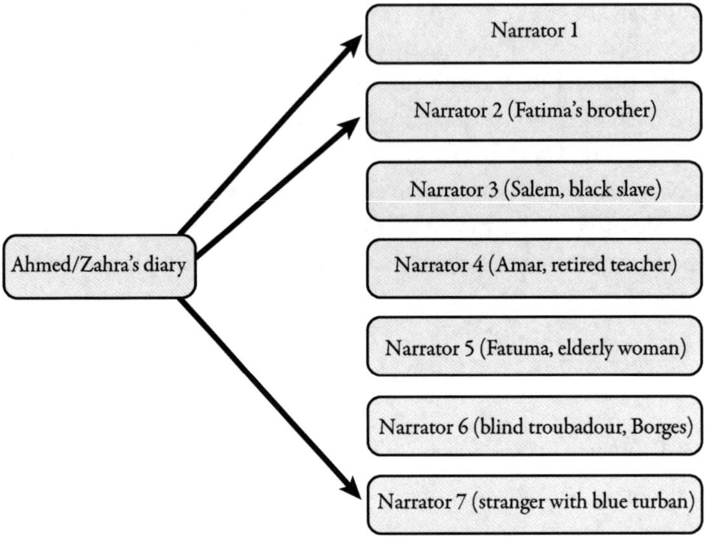

Figure 3: Narrators in *The Sand Child*.

There is no consensus amongst Ben Jelloun scholars on the exact number of narrators or the names of the first and the second narrator. Marrouchi, for example, wrongly states that there are six storytellers: the teller devoured by his own sentences, the man with female breasts, the woman with the poorly shaved beard, Salem, Amar and Fatuma.[18] There is a chapter in the novel entitled 'The Woman with the Badly Shaven Beard' but there is no indication that the narrator of this story is indeed a woman. The confusion as to the names of narrator 1 and narrator 2 is even greater. There is a reference to a certain Si Abdel Malek in the text (Salem is told that he does not have 'the gifts of Si Abdel Malek, may God have his soul…' when he wants to tell his version of the story) but critics are unclear about whether Si Abdel Malek is the name of narrator 1 or narrator 2.[19] Laila Ibnlfassi calls

18 See Mustapha Marrouchi, 'Breaking up/down/out of the Boundaries: Tahar Ben Jelloun', *Research in African Literatures*, 21/4 (1990), 71–83. Here 81n5.

19 Ben Jelloun, *Sand Child*, 105.

the first narrator Si Abdel Malek; Memmes claims that Si Abdel Malek is the name of Fatima's brother and suggests that the first narrator is called Bouchaïb.[20] Memmes further believes that narrator 1 actually corresponds to narrator 7; in which case he faked his own death.[21] Shona Elizabeth Simpson states that the last storyteller is in fact a fictionalized Ben Jelloun and that 'as he speaks, we realize that he was also the first, the man who "dared to recount the story and destiny of the eighth birth"'.[22] Similarly, Ibnlfassi argues that, by 'putting himself more into his work', Ben Jelloun 'leaves no doubt as to the identity of the speaker when he writes: "Ma vie fut principalement consacrée aux livres. J'en ai écrit, publié, détruit, lu, aimé… toute ma vie avec des livres". [*ES*, p. 187]').[23]

The above diagram hints at the complexity of the narrative but it cannot make apparent the various narrative layers. Not only do readers have to negotiate different unreliable storytellers and contradicting versions of Ahmed/Zahra's life; each narrator inserts comments on the nature of storytelling into their tales so readers have to deal with metanarrative comments as well as a chaotic plot and changing narrative voices. I have myself tried to summarize the nineteen chapters of the novel according to structure, plot development and metatextual commentary (see Appendix I). There are so many layers in this narrative which sometimes overlap but

20 Laila Ibnlfassi, 'The Ambiguity of Self-Structure. Tahar Ben Jelloun's *L'enfant de sable* and *La nuit sacrée*', in Kamal Salhi, ed., *Francophone Voices* (Exeter: Elm Bank Publications, 1999), 157–69. Abdallah Memmes, 'Démarche interculturelle dans *L'enfant de sable* de Tahar Ben Jelloun', in Abdellah Madrhri Zeggaf and Ahmed Alaoui, eds, *L'interculturel au Maroc. Arts, langues, littératures et traditions populaires* (Casablanca: Afrique Orient, 1994), 61–74. Here 72. Bouchaïb is the name of a character who appears again at the start of *The Sacred Night*.

21 Memmes, 'Démarche interculturelle', 72n17.

22 Shona Elizabeth Simpson, 'One Face Less: Masks, Time, and the Telling of Stories in Tahar Ben Jelloun's *The Sand Child*', in Anna-Teresa Tymieniecka, ed., *Allegory Revisited: Ideals of Mankind* (Dordrecht, Boston, London: Kluwer Academic Publishers, 1994), 325–32. Here 329.

23 Ibnlfassi, 169. Alan Sheridan renders the quote as follows: 'My life had been devoted mainly to books. I had written them, published them, destroyed them, read them, loved them – I had spent all my life in books'. Tahar Ben Jelloun, *The Sand Child*, 147.

more often contradict one another, and which cast doubt on every single enunciation uttered by any of the seven narrators. It also seems virtually impossible to detect a clear authorial voice or intent behind the myriad of voices surging from the text. How, then, do literary critics, set in their habitual approaches to literature, deal with the complexity of *The Sand Child*?

Ben Jelloun uses narrative devices that could easily pertain to the Western tradition of novel writing, especially the *nouveau roman*, as well as to Arab letters and to Moroccan oral tradition (the storyteller and the *halqa*, the circle of listeners surrounding the storyteller on the public square). As we have seen, the combination of these narrative traditions results in polyphony, intertextuality, and an outright refusal of narrative closure. The indeterminacy of the text allows for a variety of interpretations from all angles of literary criticism (*inter alia*, gender studies, postcolonial studies and psychoanalytical criticism). The different interpretations ask and very often struggle to answer some of the following questions. Can one read Ben Jelloun's novel as a document regarding the real Morocco? Is he criticizing colonialism and patriarchy or is he more interested in narrative structures? Is Ben Jelloun primarily a postmodern or postcolonial writer? What weighs more heavily, the narrative (plot) or the metanarrative (metafictional elements)? What sources does Ben Jelloun use (Western and/or Arab)? Are the novel's unreliable narrators signs of the 'foreignness' of Maghrebian culture or rather a tribute to writers such as Queneau, Borges and Calvino? Is Ben Jelloun indebted to Berber orality or is this a postmodern novel that wants to break with both Western and Maghrebian tradition?

In the thirty years following the publication of *L'enfant de sable*, several MA and PhD theses, but very few monographs have been dedicated to this complex novel, or indeed to Ben Jelloun. This is especially true of criticism available in English.[24] There are, however, over forty articles and book chapters written in English on the novel. Most of these concentrate

24 Predictably, the situation is different where French-language criticism is concerned. See Appendix II for a preliminary list of academic articles, book chapters and books

exclusively on *The Sand Child*, but some pair the book up with other novels by Ben Jelloun, mainly its sequel *The Sacred Night* or with novels written by French, African or Asian writers.

In my survey, the aim is not to give detailed summaries of all the items of criticism dealing with *The Sand Child*, but to take a closer look at the mechanisms of cross-fertilization of certain strands of interpretation within English-language criticism and between English- and French-language criticism, and to account for the presence or lack of such cross-fertilization. In this context, the first few articles to introduce a specific thought within a quite narrowly defined field of interest will be given particular attention. This 'zooming in' on specific articles and the *modus operandi* of their authors will show how working consensus is achieved in the specific practice of academic peer-reviewed publishing. As all academic criticism is an act of persuasion, I also include (sometimes quite substantial) quotations from the articles to give readers a feel of the argumentative style and language adopted by the different critics.

Document, commentary or aesthetic object?

The interpretations of *The Sand Child* depend on 1) the critic's repertoire and on the critical angle adopted (such as gender studies, sociology of literature, postcolonial studies or semiotics) and 2) more general assumptions about literature that form part of the critic's habitus and strategies of rhetorical hermeneutics, as outlined in Chapters 1 and 2. The large majority of criticism of *The Sand Child* in English reads the novel through the lens of either postcolonial or gender studies, or both. A smaller, second strand of Ben Jelloun criticism shifts the focus from the level of the plot and its

written in French on or relevant to *The Sand Child* (the list does not include MA or PhD theses).

possible criticism of reality to the convoluted narrative structure of the novel, trying to make sense of the text's intricate polyphony.

Broadly speaking, we can distinguish three approaches to *The Sand Child*: there is a small group of critics who interpret the novel as a socio-political critique of Moroccan society, especially its treatment of women, and therefore share the view that literature has a documentary function. The novel is not just an individual's commentary on social reality but can be used as a document which, alongside historical and sociological documents, tells us something about the 'real' Morocco. At the opposite end of the spectrum we find a small group of critics who see the novel as an aesthetic exercise. The working consensus amongst critics who interpret the novel along the lines of the *nouveau roman* and Postmodernist writing techniques is that literature is fundamentally an autonomous field of artistic production that has no significant correspondence to reality. Most critics who have written on the novel seem to position themselves somewhere between these two extreme poles, claiming that the novel is a commentary on Moroccan society (not to be confused with a document, as I have explained in Chapter 1).

Both extreme tendencies are present in Ben Jelloun criticism and at several times they seem to exclude one another. When Tamara El-Hoss argues that *The Sand Child* is mainly concerned with the plight of Moroccan women, she treats the novel as a linear narrative coherently told by an authorial narrator.[25] The documentary modes of literary criticism at times seem to struggle to make a convincing argument if they mention in too much detail the multiple contradicting narrative voices. At the same time, one cannot simply argue the opposite either: the array of metafictional and magical elements do not preclude that the work might actually criticize aspects of Moroccan life.[26] One thing is certain: the text of *The Sand Child*

25 Tamara El-Hoss, 'Veiling/Unveiling in Tahar Ben Jelloun's *The Sand Child*: Disguise and Deception of the Female Protagonist', in Leslie Boldt-Irons, Corrado Federici, and Ernesto Virgulti, eds, *Disguise, Deception, Trompe-L'œil: Interdisciplinary Perspectives* (Berne and New York: Peter Lang 2009), 149–60.

26 This is particularly true of the Maghrebian novel, according to Rachida Saigh Bousta: 'Certes, une œuvre purement esthétique reste dans sa conception même incompatible

offers such a wide variety of hooks onto which to latch an interpretation that the resulting apparatus of literary criticism resembles the original text in its complexities and contradictions.

In very general terms, critics approaching the novel from a postcolonial critical angle are interested in the representation of the effects that French colonialism has had on Morocco. According to postcolonial theory (represented by the writings of, *inter alia*, Frantz Fanon, Edward Said and Homi Bhabha), formerly colonized societies that have undergone foreign political rule have experienced a forced modernization of certain areas of public life, while the bond with the indigenous culture and tradition has been severed.[27] In the case of *The Sand Child*, the parallels between Franco-Moroccan relations and gender relations in the novel constitute one major focus of analysis from the postcolonial angle. Several critics position Ben Jelloun in a transnational space of (world) literature, either alongside other subaltern writers writing in French or alongside other writers 'from the margins' who, in a famous phrase coined in the field of postcolonial studies, write *back* to the centre.

The novel has proved especially fertile ground for interpretations within the gender studies paradigm. It lends itself to an analysis of biological and acquired gender, female and male identity and sexuality, as well as androgyny. Major sources are Hélène Cixous and Judith Butler, but also North African intellectuals, such as the late Assia Djebar and the sociologist Fatima Mernissi.

---

avec la sphère socio-culturelle de l'intellectuel maghrébin'. [Admittedly, a purely aesthetic work seems conceptually irreconcilable with the socio-cultural sphere in a Maghrebian intellectual's life.] Rachida Saigh Bousta, *Lecture des récits de Tahar Ben Jelloun: écriture, mémoire et imaginaire* (Casablanca: Afrique Orient, 1992), 10. Evan Maina Mwangi raises a similar claim about African literature in general: 'A purely formalistic approach to literature that ignores the sociological and political contingencies ordering the production of art would be untenable in the study of African literature'. Evan Mwangi, *Africa Writes Back to Self: Metafiction, Gender, Sexuality* (New York: State University of New York Press, 2009), 14.

27 For a detailed overview of postcolonial theory, see Bill Ashcroft, Gareth Griffiths, and Helen Tiffin, *The Empire Writes Back: Theory and Practice in Post-Colonial Literatures* (London: Routledge, 2002).

Within these two broad categories, one can distinguish a tendency to focus on one or several of the following issues:

1. *Gender roles*: criticism that sees Ben Jelloun as portraying the status of women in Muslim societies and as attacking misogyny within Moroccan society.
2. *Structuring values in Moroccan society*: criticism that links gender issues, especially the discrepancy between biological and social gender, to larger political issues such as the colonization and decolonization of Morocco. A typical argument runs as follows: just as the West has historically defined the non-West as object, women continue to be posited as objects/non-subjects in postcolonial Morocco.
3. *Corporeality (of protagonist and text)*: criticism that argues for a strong connection between the body of the text and the body of the protagonist. Sexuality plays a major role in this context: there is a hidden power in Ahmed's discovery of sexuality, just as there is a hidden power in the fluidity of the narrative.
4. *Language and identity*: criticism that argues for a strong connection between language and identity. Basing itself mainly on poststructuralist theories of language, this approach concentrates on the social function of language and on its function in constructing the categories of gender, race, class and ethnicity. In the case of a protagonist who is both a man (socially) and a woman (biologically) and who is presented as speaking (of) him/herself, one can analyse the interdependence of language, discourse and identity.

Other critics state that the plot of *The Sand Child* is of secondary importance and that one should focus on the narrative techniques employed by Ben Jelloun. On this view, this is a work of metafiction which constantly draws attention to its own artificial nature and exposes different techniques of tale-telling.[28] There is a playfulness in metafiction that seems to be at

28 On general theory and practice of metafiction, see Patricia Waugh, *Metafiction: The Theory and Practice of Self-Conscious Fiction* (London: Methuen, 1984). On metafiction in African literature, see Mwangi, *Africa Writes Back to Self*.

odds with the seriousness of the questions of gender and power analysed by critics mainly interested in the novel's plot, as well as an impressive degree of self-reflexivity that, again, seems to contradict the socio-political criticism detected by some critics. Critical engagement with the apparently postmodern narrative techniques used in *The Sand Child* focuses on one or more of the following aspects:

1. *Metafiction*: criticism that sees the text as metacommentary on the structuring of narratives. Critics focus on the different diegetic levels of the narrative as well as on the metafictional commentary provided by the seven narrators. The use of metafictional elements is seen either as in line with mainstream French and European postmodern forms of writing or as specifically Maghrebian.
2. *Intertextuality*: criticism concentrating on the novel's links to other texts, mainly to Borges and *The 1001 Nights*. The text's evident intertextuality is sometimes linked to the 'intersexuality' of the protagonist: just as the protagonist is in-between sexes, the text consciously takes up an in-between position, on the threshold to European literature, in a transnational space that escapes narrow definition.
3. *Techniques of magical realism*: criticism interested in a transnational network of 'marginal' writers, such as Rushdie and Borges, who subvert the categories of writing established by the Western centre by merging realism with fantastical narrative elements.

Before we move on to the arguments made by English-language critics, I must draw attention to the *venues* of this criticism: most peer-reviewed articles in English dealing with Ben Jelloun's novel have been written by academics associated with North American universities and have been published in North American journals. Most book chapters on the novel have also been published by North American publishers. The journal with the highest number of *Sand Child* articles is the *French Review*, published by the American Association of Teachers of French (three articles in English, four in French), followed by *Research in African Literatures*, published by Indiana University Press (three articles in English). Other North American journals have published only one contribution on the novel to date, for example: *World Literature Today* (University of Oklahoma), *boundary 2* (Duke University Press), *Yale French Studies* (Yale University Press), *Dalhousie French Studies* (Dalhousie University Press), *Comparative Literature* (University of Oregon) and *differences: A Journal of Feminist Cultural Studies* (Duke University Press). It was in 2000 that a peer-reviewed journal based in Europe, *Neophilologus*, published an article on *The Sand Child*, fourteen years after the first such article in North America. It is perhaps not surprising that most contributions in English should be published in North America which contains most of the world's English-language publishing houses specialized in the humanities; what is striking, though, is the consensus on the literary approach to be adopted towards the novel.

Since the early 1990s, the critical engagement with literature considered 'marginal' has featured high on the agenda in Western academic circles. While this has helped rethink the definition of literature, it might also have helped to commodify 'subaltern' culture and ultimately resulted in the Western education system assimilating so-called marginal culture for its own interest.[29] Graham Huggan warned against this commodification over a decade ago:

> It seems worth questioning the neo-imperialist implications of a postcolonial literary/critical industry centred on, and largely catering to, the West. English is, almost exclusively, the language of this critical industry, reinforcing the view that postcolonialism is a discourse of *translation*, rerouting cultural products regarded as emanating from the periphery toward audiences who see themselves as coming from the centre.[30]

29 Gayatri Chakravorty Spivak has voiced this concern several times, for example in 'Theory in the Margin: Coetzee's *Foe* Reading Defoe's *Crusoe/Roxana*', in Jonathan Arac and Barbara Johnson, eds, *Consequences of Theory* (Baltimore: Johns Hopkins University Press, 1991), 154–80.

30 Graham Huggan, *The Postcolonial Exotic. Marketing the Margins* (London and New York: Routledge, 2001), 4.

Introducing Ben Jelloun: Mortimer, Thacher, Abdalaoui and Marrouchi

Ben Jelloun's *The Sand Child* was first mentioned in a brief review article in *World Literature Today* in 1986. The author of the review, Mildred Mortimer, is one of the first American scholars to have engaged with Maghrebian literature from the late 1970s onwards. In 1986, none of Ben Jelloun's other writings had yet been translated into English, and the translation of *L'enfant de sable* was still in the making. According to Mortimer, Ben Jelloun's novel is 'both an episodic Oriental tale told by a traditional storyteller and a disquieting journal of a solitary soul in distress'.[31] Mortimer interprets the ambiguity of Ahmed/Zahra's sexual identity as a representation of the consequences of a loss of identity, 'whether linguistic, cultural or political. In this highly poetic, imaginative novel, the writer reminds us that to assume the mask of "the other" is to face pain, isolation, and finally self-destruction'.[32]

When Alan Sheridan's translation for the New York publisher Harcourt Brace Jovanovich appeared in 1987, Ben Jelloun was still known to relatively few English-speaking academics. He was in fact erroneously described as an Algerian writer in an overview of French literary events in 1987 which could not fail to mention who had won the Prix Goncourt.[33]

Alan Sheridan's translation was reviewed the following year by Jean-Louise Thacher alongside eight other examples of so-called 'Arabic fiction'.[34] Thacher can accord each novel relatively little space, yet she manages succinctly to describe what she finds most intriguing in *The Sand Child*:

31 Mildred Mortimer, '*L'enfant de sable* by Tahar Ben Jelloun', in *World Literature Today*, 60/3 (1986), 509.

32 Ibid.

33 See Jack Kolbert and Nancy L. Cairns, 'L'année littéraire 1987', *French Review*, 61 (1988), 845–58. The 'Algerian' Ben Jelloun is mentioned (twice) on 857.

34 Jean-Louise Thacher, 'Recent Translations of Arabic Fiction: Review Article', *Middle East Journal*, 42/3 (1988), 481–5.

> Tahar Ben Jelloun's *The Sand Child* [...] is based firmly on culture/tradition, but the plot is influenced by and developed with the aid of literary legacy, legend, and the vivid imagination of the author. [...] This novel is perhaps the most complex of those under review here, because of the many levels on which the story is told and because of its conspicuous oral and traditional heritage. [...] The novel is sensitive and perceptive when one of the listeners describes Ahmed Mohammed's struggle with the feminine side of 'his' nature. The work is also violent, fantastic, convoluted in style, rich in images, and filled with metaphors and the metaphysical. It is to be hoped that its sequel, *The Sacred Night*, will soon be available in English and that is will contain the answers to some of the questions aroused by this strange masterpiece.[35]

Due to their brevity, these two introductory review essays only manage to draw attention to and provide quite generalized comments about the writer and the novel. Full-length critical essays started to appear at the beginning of the 1990s: two of the first contributions were by Maghrebian critics who most probably had been familiar with Ben Jelloun's work for over a decade.

Very little material is available in English about Ben Jelloun's position amongst French-language writers from Morocco or the larger Maghreb. The notable exception seems to be M'hamed Alaoui Abdalaoui's 1992 overview 'The Moroccan Novel in French' which positions Ben Jelloun in a specific historical context, that of Moroccan writers of an earlier generation, such as Ahmed Sefrioui, Driss Chraïbi, Kateb Yacine and Abdellatif Laâbi.[36] It also provides readers with an overview of Ben Jelloun's early œuvre. Of *The Sand Child* and *The Sacred Night*, Abdalaoui says:

> These two novels make their way among myths, legends and reality, between the masculine and the feminine, between being and its double; it is an itinerary on the outer edges of ourselves, where what we assume to be certain is only an illusion, or

35 Ibid., 482–3.

36 M'hamed Alaoui Abdalaoui, 'The Moroccan Novel in French', *Research in African Literatures*, 23/4 (1992), 9–33. Houssaine Afoullous also sees Ben Jelloun as part of a tradition of Maghrebian writers rather than influenced by European literary standards. See Houssaine Afoullous, 'Three Generations of Francophone North African Writers in Exile: Driss Chraïbi, Tahar Ben Jelloun and Medhi Charef', in Anthony Coulson, ed., *Exiles and Migrants: Crossing Thresholds in European Culture and Society* (Brighton: Sussex Academic Press, 1997), 144–53.

> just one image in a mirror. Both novels can be read as offering a view of Muslim society, a defense of the woman who is not only 'walled in' but forbidden to exist (which did not fail to captivate the imagination of Western readers and critics – with whose tastes, moreover, the author is not unfamiliar).[37]

In half a paragraph, Abdalaoui manages to suggest the complexity of the plot as well as to imply criticism of the author's familiarity with Western literary tastes and his presumed exploitation of them. However, Abdalaoui locates Ben Jelloun's narrative techniques within a specifically Moroccan tradition:

> When Khaïr-Eddine announced his intention, in the first issue of *Souffles* (1966), 'd'écrire un roman complexe où poésie et délire seraient un' (7) [to write a complex novel in which poetry and delirium would be one], he unwittingly pointed toward what would become a standard procedure not only in his work but also in the work of other novelists from his generation – novelists such as Ben Jelloun and Laâbi as well as Algerians such as Rachid Boudjedra. Because the itinerary of delirium is in total contradiction with an organized universe, it authorizes a number of transgressions – authorial, social, religious, and sexual.[38]

The critic's recommendation is clear: Ben Jelloun's style should be seen not as an emulation of Western postmodernist techniques but in line with Maghrebian tradition and, more specifically, with a poetics of delirium developed by Moroccan writers.

The first academic article in English dedicated exclusively to Ben Jelloun's novel is a detailed investigation of the author's narrative techniques: Patricia Geesey's translation of an article by Mustapha Marrouchi, published two years before Abdalaoui's contribution, in 1990.[39] Drawing heavily on examples from the twin novels, the article provides many English-speaking readers who have little or no knowledge of certain aspects of Moroccan life with an explanation of, for example, the importance of orality and

37 Abdalaoui, 26.

38 Ibid., 15.

39 Patricia Geesey is a scholar and translator who has also translated other critical essays on Moroccan literature, such as Zohra Mezgueldi, 'Mother-Word and French-Language Moroccan Writing', *Research in African Literatures*, 27/3 (1996), 1–14.

the *halqa* [round table of listeners]. The novels are not interesting for their plots, Marrouchi claims, as the theme of both *The Sand Child* and *The Sacred Night* can be summarized in a single sentence: 'My aunt is a man'. Rather, both novels are reflections about the blurring boundaries of narration, exercises in metafiction. Ever since *Moha le fou, Moha le sage* [Madman Moha, Wiseman Moha] (1980), Ben Jelloun has drawn attention to the self-representational nature of narrative, borrowing from a variety of sources: 'If Ben Jelloun draws inspiration from the collective imaginary of a Maghrebian culture in which one finds a hodge-podge of elements borrowed from the Koran, the worship of Saints, Muslim mystics [...] and popular traditions [...], certain obsessive images plunge us into his personal mythology and his own hallucinations'.[40] Marrouchi defends Ben Jelloun's style, describing his language as 'clear and simple'; and although Ben Jelloun very often writes fragmented sentences, 'he obviously refuses to elaborate his writings for the sake of writing. In short, it is as if Ben Jelloun has been unaffected by the fashions of French literature. Gratuitous literary games are the antithesis of his work as writer'.[41] In Marrouchi's view, then, critics should focus on the self-representational narrative act and metafiction. Marrouchi does not concern himself with the politics of the body, gender matters or decolonization, topics that are paramount to many critics writing subsequently about *The Sand Child*.

Both Abdalaoui and Marrouchi stress the centrality of narrative techniques in Ben Jelloun's writing. Marrouchi returns to Ben Jelloun in his 2002 article 'My Aunt is a Man: Ce "je"-là est multiple'. The Francophone Maghrebian author faces problems of definition, Marrouchi states at the beginning of his essay: 'He or she is described and redescribed, sloganized and falsified, until, for the howling combatants, he or she almost ceases to exist. He or she becomes a sort of a myth, an empty vessel into which the world can pour its prejudices, its poison, and its hate'.[42] In 2002, Marrouchi

40 Marrouchi, 'Breaking up/down/out', 74–5.

41 Ibid., 77.

42 Mustapha Marrouchi, 'My Aunt is a Man: Ce "je"-là est multiple', *Comparative Literature*, 54/4 (2002), 325–56. Here 326.

reiterates what he had said in his 1990 article, yet also integrating some of the critical readings of Ben Jelloun from the 1990s:

> Ben Jelloun is not immediately easy to read: he does not really provide plots to follow or characters with whom to identify. His terrain is that of the dispossessed; his characters remain exiled from family, gender, tribe, or nation. His reputation outside the Francophone world is largely based on two intertwined narratives of the fantastic, which have earned him inevitable comparisons with Marquéz, Borges, and Rushdie. The distinctive feature of his work is, however, a consuming obsession with language. Dense with allusion, metaphor, and echoes of his native Arabic, his texts are deeply inscribed with his migrant sensibility. His work takes, therefore, a little training, and some time spent on counterpoint (or variational) writing helps us to read this foreign, strange and 'difficult' writer, who is also one of the few authentic voices to have risen to meet the challenge of 'leaving home'.[43]

Marrouchi then performs such a contrapuntal reading of Ben Jelloun but without referring to *The Sand Child* specifically.

Other articles written on the novel in English in the early 1990s, however, focus on the plot more than on narrative techniques in an attempt to analyse the representation of gender.

Questions of gender in *The Sand Child*: Cavenaze and Corredor

The first article in English to examine gender matters in *The Sand Child* is Odile Cazenave's 1991 'Gender, Age, and Narrative Transformations in *L'enfant de sable* by Tahar Ben Jelloun', published in the *French Review*.[44] The article actually does broach the matter of gender and misogyny, but in its use of Althusser's Ideological State Apparatuses (ISAs) it is more interested in the

43 Ibid., 327.

44 Odile Cazenave, 'Gender, Age, and Narrative Transformations in *L'enfant de sable* by Tahar Ben Jelloun', *French Review*, 64/1 (1991), 437–50.

construction of identity on an abstract level. Cazenave starts out by claiming that 'in North-African Literature, factors of age and gender appear to be key elements in determining the role and status in society for a given character', thus positioning herself along the theoretical lines of gender studies.[45]

As the article progresses, however, Cazenave indiscriminately uses phrases such as 'the character's true identity' and 'not only does the character deny her gender but also her ethnic background and national heritage'.[46] She seems to imply that gender and ethnic/national affiliation are stable entities rather than constructed and fluid (as generally accepted within the field of gender studies). Cazenave's argument appears to me to be weakened by her unreflected use of gender studies vocabulary: 'Once aware of the artificiality of her status as he-subject, she conquers her true subjectivity as an individual in deciding that, precisely, she will be that he-subject that has been forced upon her'.[47] There is no attempt to define 'subjectivity' in this case, let alone 'true' subjectivity. Other statements seem equally troublesome: Ahmed and Fatima are 'both sick, one due to natural biological causes, the other due to his/her own choice [...] In its very essence, Ahmed's infirmity is more severe than the cousin's'.[48]

Cazenave's engagement with the multiplicity of narrative voices is also informed by her main concern, the construction of identity:

> Just as the image of woman is broken down into a myriad of facets in cubist art, so Ben Jelloun reflects Ahmed's image through the assemblage of the multiple strategies of the narrative [...] Through this device, the author rounds out his character while demonstrating at the same time that he cannot be seized in his totality.[49]

As a critic concerned with the 'true identity' of the novel's protagonist, Cazenave's other concern is with the authenticity of the narrative, where authenticity is linked to the ownership of the story. She sees a parallel between the impossibility of establishing an authentic narrative voice and

45 Ibid., 437.
46 Ibid., 440–1.
47 Ibid., 442.
48 Ibid., 440.
49 Ibid., 445.

Ahmed/Zarah's impossible quest for his/her 'true' identity. Towards the end of her contribution, Cazenave also establishes a similar link to the 'problem' of Maghrebian literature in French: 'Until very recently, Maghrebin [sic] authors writing in French were traumatized since, on the one hand, they denied their *true identity* and, on the other, this effort gained them only marginal acceptance and attention in French literature'.[50] In Cazenave's analysis, the narrative complexities seem to be subordinated to the plot or rather, they are meant to accentuate the 'message' of the novel: this is a novel about a disturbed individual struggling to find his/her identity, living in a society or culture struggling to find its identity after decolonization.

As a first contribution to Ben Jelloun criticism from the critical angle of gender studies, this article makes some valid points that will be taken up and developed by other critics. Yet, the recurring use of expressions such as 'true identity' sets it at odds with the tenets of gender studies, namely that identity is a construct and not an innate state of being. While using certain catchwords of gender studies in order to position herself within that particular field, Cazenave does not refer directly to gender studies theory: in fact, all she uses are two chapters from a collection of essays entitled *Feminist Criticism and Social Change. Sex, Class and Race in Literature and Culture*, and the bibliography includes no more than eight titles.

The following year, the *French Review* published an article by Eva L. Corredor on father figures in Maghrebian fiction.[51] Besides Ben Jelloun's twin novels, Corredor also analyses Rachid Boudjedra's *Pour ne plus rêver* [In order to stop dreaming] (1965) and Mourad Bourboune's *Le Muezzin* [The Muezzin] (1968) in light of the representation of the autocratic position of the father and its effects on the protagonists. She sees *The Sand Child* as a critique of Muslim society which values a male heir to such an extent that it forces the father to play God: 'Instead of Allah, the father will be the "god" who determines not only his own place in society, and thus his worldly destiny, but also the sex of his eighth child, who, again, is

50 Ibid., 450. Emphasis added.

51 Eva L. Corredor, '(Dis)Embodiments of the Father in Maghrebian Fiction', *French Review*, 66/2 (1992), 295–304.

a girl'.[52] Ahmed/Zahra's body is 'an embodiment of schizophrenia, a body sacrificed to the ego of the father and the folly of society'.[53] Corredor conceals the fact that there are several narrators telling the protagonist's story in order to be able to ground her findings about father-child relations in both psychoanalytical and sociological terms.

> The fictional process of self-discovery here leads to a multitude of possible solutions that are all more or less 'surreal', as are Ahmed's being and authenticity within his society. [...] Once the protagonist becomes fully aware of his/her existential predicament, he seems to run away from home – or, at least we think so; it may all just be in his imagination, a surrealistic journey within his prison, without his ever leaving the glass cage. In the course of these fantastic journeys, Ahmed leads the life of a transvestite, a circus attraction as a man with a woman's breasts. His imagined possible destinies are multiple and we could add our own.[54]

The 'fantastic journeys' in question are not the protagonist's hallucinations but versions delivered by different storytellers. At the time of writing this article Corredor must have had access to Marrouchi's 1990 article on narrative techniques and metafictional elements in Ben Jelloun in English, as well as to several contributions in French written about the novel between 1986 and 1991, some of which also engage with the complexity of the narrative aspects. None of these are mentioned; in fact, only three books are cited in the bibliography besides the four novels discussed in the article: a book and an article by Michel Foucault and a book by Charles Bonn on Algerian literature. Is it conceivable that Corredor simply misread the presence of the different narrators as 'personifications' of the protagonist's hallucinations? It strikes me that narrative complexities have been suppressed because they did not serve the argument.

While Cazenave and Corredor see Ben Jelloun's novel as expressing a particularly African or Maghrebian consciousness that aims to write back to France and Europe, other critics align his writing with Western literary models.

52 Ibid., 300.

53 Ibid., 301.

54 Ibid.

Confessional voices: Meyer

The starting point for Meyer's 1992 analysis of two 'Arab' novels, *Season of Migration to the North* by Tayeb Ṣalih and *The Sand Child*, is the argument that postcolonial literature tends to 'mimic the minority strain of subjectivity and ambivalence that characterizes much of late colonial literature'.[55] Both novels, Meyer argues, are confessional as they 'combine the aims of expressing both subjectivity and ambivalence' and are shaped as personal histories in which 'the search for personal and social identity is the overriding theme'.[56] Thus, the subjectivity of the confessional voice reflects the search for identity, both national and cultural. The ambivalence stands for the crisis in the social, political and cultural spheres of life. While Salih's novel is a 'crisis' narrative (the protagonist moves from abstract idealism towards romantic disillusionment), *The Sand Child* is a 'developmental' confessional narrative (the protagonist moves from an initial state of disillusionment towards a new-found sense of values). Comparing the subordinated position of women in decolonized countries to the subordinated position of the country during colonization, Meyer describes Ahmed/Zahra's story as a national parable: the 'ambiguity of gender imposed on the main character in childhood can be taken to represent the colonial experience in which Arab society has been forced to adopt the persona of a foreign culture'.[57] While one should not describe these works as feminist in orientation, Meyer continues, both novels leave openings for a feminine voice. The issue of women's status in society, Meyer concludes, is a 'touchstone of social critique, one which produces an ambivalence and a sense of complicity similar to that

55 Stefan G. Meyer, 'The Confessional Voice in Modern Arab Fiction: *Season of Migration to the North* by Tayeb Salih and *The Sand Child* by Tahar Ben Jelloun', *Estudos Anglo-Americanos*, 16 (1992), 137–47. Here 140.

56 Ibid., 140.

57 Ibid., 144.

which we can detect in late Western colonial literature with respect to the issue of colonialism'.[58]

Linking female and narrative bodies: Erickson, Simpson and Zanzana

In 1993, John D. Erickson published the first of several critical engagements with *The Sand Child* in which he deals with questions of gender identity and the narrative complexities of the novel.[59] The difference when compared to the first contributions discussing gender issues is striking. Erickson's article

58 Ibid., 146. In his article, Meyer gives an overview of the then current disputes in postcolonial studies and therefore his 'Works Cited' contain the following names: Said; Ashcroft, Griffith and Tiffin; Babha; Jameson; and Ahmad. There are only two items on *The Sand Child:* Cazenave's scholarly article and a review in the *Times Literary Supplement.*

59 John D. Erickson, 'Veiled Woman and Veiled Narrative in Tahar Ben Jelloun's *The Sand Child*', *boundary 2*, 20/1 (1993), 47–64. Erickson had already mentioned aspects of intertextuality in a previous article: 'Writing Double: Politics and the African Narrative of French Expression', *Studies in Twentieth-Century Literature*, 15.1 (1991), 101–22. A French translation of the 1993 article appeared the same year: 'Femme voilée, recit voilé dans *L'enfant de sable* de Ben Jelloun', in Antoine Régis, ed., *Carrefour de cultures: Mélanges offerts à Jacqueline Leiner* (Tübingen: Narr, 1993), 287–96. Erickson reworks his ideas on *The Sand Child* in chapter 3 of his monograph *Islam and the Postcolonial Narrative* (Cambridge: Cambridge University Press, 1998). He also uses the novel as example in 'Metoikoi and Magical Realism in the Maghrebian Narratives of Tahar Ben Jelloun and Abdelkebir Khatibi' in Lois Parkinson Zamora and Wendy B. Faris, eds, *Magical Realism: Theory, History, Community* (Durham, NC and London: Duke University Press, 1995), 427–50. Erickson has established himself as an expert in the field, as his contribution to the *Companion to Magical Realism* shows: 'Magical Realism and Nomadic Writing in the Maghreb', in Stephen M. Hart and Wen-Chin Ouyang, eds, *A Companion to Magical Realism* (Woodbridge and Rochester, NY: Tamesis, 2005), 247–55. Here, Ben Jelloun's novel also serves as a major example.

published in *boundary 2* is more theoretically grounded: he refers to several dozen books and articles, by North African scholars and writers such as Fatima Mernissi, Assia Djebar and Abdelwahab Bouhdiba as well as significant figures on the Western literary scene such as Maurice Blanchot, Jacques Derrida and Jacques Lacan. Also, the article engages in detail – a first for English-language Ben Jelloun criticism – with both aspects of the novel, the plot *and* the narrative structure. The veil is used in the title as a linking metaphor between the two: this is a novel about a veiled woman and about a veiled narrative.

> The voices of the storytellers and the omniscient narrator appear to tell things in a telling way, to order and organize things as they are or are conventionally expected to be in regard to the telling; that is, the revelation of truths, of the identity of the subject, of the adherence of things and events within the novel to the system of things and events as they 'ought to be' outside the novel – Islam custom and law, in the first instance; the Western law of the narrative and the discourse of power, in the second.[60]

Describing the male semiotics ruling Maghrebian society, Erickson mentions Fatima Mernissi's *Beyond the Veil* which posits the male, European gaze as the dominant gaze: 'Just as the Western discourse of the father circumscribes the North African male, and just as the male colonial gaze fixes the female, so Islamic discourse fixes and circumscribes the Arab woman.'[61] The gaze of the Arab woman is bound by religious belief. In order to avoid 'zina ul-ayni' [fornication of the eye], there is the moral imperative for veiling. Zahra resists the male gaze and therefore cannot be fixed by it. However, while it is true that this is a story about the

> unmaking and the remaking of the female subject [...] [it] also evolves around the unmaking/remaking of the traditional narrative of legitimation, as well as the relentless deconstruction of a coherent (male) subject/narrative. In an extended sense, Zahra becomes for Ben Jelloun a privileged metaphor for the postcolonial author striving to reconstruct an idiom expressive of his own perceptions and cultural specificity out of the shards and artefacts of the discourse, inherited from his French colonial antagonists, which he has undertaken to deconstruct.[62]

60 Erickson, 'Veiled', 51.

61 Ibid., 53.

62 Ibid., 52.

Erickson suggests that the novel is a double attempt at liberation: the North African woman is trying to liberate herself from the chains of patriarchy while the postcolonial Maghrebian writer attempts to free him/herself from the constraints of Eurocentric narrative. Thus, while 'Ben Jelloun's narrative ostensibly takes as its project the undermining of structuring values in Islamic society', it simultaneously undermines traditional Western narrative conventions.[63] Yet Erickson also warns us not to read the novel as a 'simple' act of writing back to Europe:

> How different is difference if it responds to the difference already posited in a certain Western discourse on counternarration, running from Mallarmé to such contemporary writers as Lyotard, Derrida, and Foucault – all of whom, among other critics, have used the convention of discourse against itself.[64]

In his analysis of *The Sand Child*, Erickson accords space to several strands of literary criticism: gender studies (Mernissi, Irigaray and Nancy Miller), postcolonial studies (Said and Fanon) and postmodernism (Derrida, Barthes, Lacan). He introduces his readers to a variety of ideas from Western and non-Western thinkers concerned with sexuality, identity, narration and counternarration. Rather than attempting to present the narrative as more linear and coherent than it is (as did Cavenaze and Corredor), Erickson describes Ben Jelloun's novels as a 'narrative of impossibility, which speaks the secret languages of the Arab woman and the postcolonialist writer, for which there are no adequations, no equivalents'.[65]

The following year, 1994, saw the publication of a short book chapter on the novel by Shona Elizabeth Simpson, a strongly individual interpretation that – in sharp contradiction to Erickson's theory-laden contribution – contains not a single note or reference to other works. Simpson describes *The Sand Child* as an 'allegory about the act of storytelling itself [that] draws into question the dominant principles of the culture which

63 Ibid., 58.
64 Ibid., 61.
65 Ibid., 64.

produced it – and eventually its own authority as a work'.[66] Because the protagonist must hide his/her corporeality from the world, he/she takes refuge in journal writing: 'Written words themselves are given a corporeality which the spoken word does not have'.[67] Yet, even the written words disappear or are misappropriated. Therefore, the fact that all narrators lack authority and than no version of the protagonist's story can be called authentic is of vital importance for Simpson's analysis.

> By a confusing and circuitous route, *The Sand Child* has arrived at a fluidity of existence where individual identity and time are also circular, contrasting with the traditional Aristotelian ideas of linear time. This Western idea of linear narrative – and thus of the act of writing itself – comes under criticism by the end of *The Sand Child*.[68]

This fluidity is no longer granted in *The Sacred Night* where Ahmed/Zahra speaks for herself, in a traditional, linear narrative, claiming that all narrators of *The Sand Child* got his/her story wrong. As a result, Simpson argues, 'while the first book presents gender as socially constructed, the sequel destroys all the multiplicity such a view creates, making a woman sex-less'. Simpson concludes her argument by criticizing Ben Jelloun for 'giving in to his critics and pinning down the fluidity, the multiplicity of sexuality and voices he left so intriguingly open in *The Sand Child*'.[69]

In 1998, Erickson returned to his previous work on *The Sand Child* in chapter 3 of a monograph entitled *Islam and Postcolonial Narrative*. The chapter is split into two sections, one entitled 'Veiled woman and veiled narrative' (a reworking of his 1993 article) and a second untitled part which, using Todorov, deals with the interpenetration of characters, narrators and authors as well as with the folds of the narrative (based on his 1991 article). Action is not an illustration of Ben Jelloun's narrators or characters, Erickson argues; they should rather be seen as 'subserving the action, such that we encounter what Tzvetan Todorov has called an a-psychological

66 Simpson, 326.
67 Ibid., 327.
68 Ibid., 330.
69 Ibid., 332.

narrative [which] throws into relief the *event* itself. [...] Character comes to represent thereby a story that is in the making or is potential – the story of the character's own life'.[70]

An a-psychological narrative results in 'embedding and embedded narrative' in which characters migrate from one story to another, in which stories are embedded in other stories 'to such a degree that levels meld; barriers separating characters and creators/tellers are breached and become traversable, fused, confused; and narrators/characters pass freely from one level to another'.[71]

In his conclusion, Erickson describes the novel as an 'inside/outside, postcolonial text' that also resembles the

> deconstructionist text described by Derrida, constructed around a network of differential traces referring endlessly to something other than itself, scene of a spillover having no respect for margins, frames, or partitions, actively engaged in breaking down those infrastructures of resistance supporting ideological and literary systems that attempt to assign limits in accord with a male Eurocentric discourse of power. [...] Ben Jelloun's tale points up the historical illusion of, the philosophical and epistemological insistence on, a fixed center, source or origin.[72]

In Erickson's view, *The Sand Child* is an amalgam that might represent a new way of writing which is simultaneously postcolonial and postmodern, and in which the body of the protagonist and the body of the text manage to forge an identity for themselves that escapes a traditional, binary definition (European versus Other).

In his 1999 article, Habib Zanzana wants to 'probe the enigmatic relationship between the construction of the self (male, female or perhaps both), the contested body of the text and the concept of identity'.[73] In a society that silences women, the protagonist chooses to write a journal

70 Erickson, *Islam and the Postcolonial Narrative*, 86.

71 Ibid., 87–8.

72 Ibid., 91.

73 Habib Zanzana, 'Gender, Body and the Erasure of the Feminine in Tahar Ben Jelloun's *L'enfant de sable*', *RLA: Romance Languages Annual*, 10/1 (1998), 194–8. <http://tell.fll.purdue.edu/RLA-Archive/1998/french-html/Zanzana,%20Habib.htm> accessed

which 'speaks of her alienation from the feminine and her inability to identify with the world of her mother and sisters'.[74] Keeping a journal, according to Zanzana, is an 'act of textual and sexual creation, a rebirth of gender and a deliberate unveiling of body and desire. It is also an act of survival that recalls Scheherazade'.[75]

The fragmented nature of the narrative reflects the fragmented construction of the feminine and, as a result, 'the narrative account of Zahra's life is a suspect document in the eyes of many story-tellers and audience members who presume that it is either false or grossly inaccurate (just like her gender and identity)'.[76] However,

> [t]he truth about Zahra's identity, like the truth of the text, is deferred and disseminated but not lost. It is constantly recuperated and dispersed in the incessant flow of narrative voices that compete for the right to tell the true story of her life and reveal the secrets of her gender, body and sexuality.[77]

The journal is not to supposed to counteract the multitude of narrators or to establish itself as a dominant discourse, rather its aim is to 'hand the reader an original narrative fragment loosely connected but solidly attached to the construction of self, to a woman's voice, body and text'.[78] Ultimately, Zanzana argues, the highly self-referential text advocates an alternative notion of gender, one that 'incorporates the constant shifting of the self and that embraces the instability of the sign'.[79]

Zanzana mentions several French theorists (Irigaray, Kristeva, Cixous, Barthes, de Beauvoir), as well as Fedwa Malti Douglass (on gender and discourse in the Islamic world). The only existing Ben Jelloun criticism he includes is Erickson's 1993 contribution in French.

---

14 September 2012. No pagination. When quoting from the article, I indicate the paragraphs instead of page numbers.

74 Ibid., para. 8.

75 Ibid., para. 26.

76 Ibid., para. 10.

77 Ibid., para. 21.

78 Ibid., para. 30.

79 Ibid., para. 11.

The prominence of postcolonial thinkers and the absence of articles such as Marrouchi's and Abdalaoui's (not to mention of several articles in French, which similarly posit metafictional elements as central) from these first contributions already point towards an emerging 'trend' in Ben Jelloun criticism in English. Even in articles that engage with both plot and narrative techniques, the narrative techniques are often described as subordinated to the plot.

Ahmed/Zahra operated on: Flaugh

As we have seen above, Erickson uses the metaphor of the veil as the basis of his analysis of *The Sand Child*. In his 2009 article and 2012 monograph, Christian Flaugh uses the metaphor of 'operation' to establish a similar link.[80] 'Reading narrative as "operating narrative"', Flaugh explains, 'involves the study of identity as it is informed by the enforcing or operation of related norm-driven narratives'.[81] Operating narrative, as understood by Flaugh, is both a process and a product that embodies 'the fundamental unreliability of any one master narrative in that its "being read" reveals efforts to perpetuate the narrative'. Ben Jelloun's twin novels, thus, are 'narratives about narrative, be it the narrative of gender, of ability, or of narrative itself' which interrogate the traditional operations (constructed mechanisms) of those same categories: gender, ability and narrative.[82] Flaugh proceeds to analyse Ahmed/Zahra's mother and father in light of the identity categories of man and woman just defined, before

80 See Christian Flaugh, 'Operating Narrative: Words on Gender Disability in Two Novels by Tahar Ben Jelloun', *Forum for Modern Language Studies*, 45/4 (2009), 411–26 and *Operation Freak. Narrative, Identity, and the Spectrum of Bodily Abilities* (Montreal and Kingston: McGill Queen's University Press, 2012).

81 Flaugh, 'Operating', 412.

82 Ibid., 413.

discussing Ahmed's feigned circumcision in *The Sand Child* and Zahra's actual circumcision (a genital mutilation performed by her sisters as an act of revenge) in *The Sacred Night*. Flaugh claims that both operations are discursive and rhetorical as well as physical. Within the Maghrebian master narrative of clear distinctions between man and woman, disabled bodies, such as Ahmed's and Fatima's, are automatically read in pejorative terms. Yet, Flaugh sees Fatima's character as a counter-example in which 'disability becomes a living subjectivity that demonstrates physical and mental productivity and that requires us to review the ways in which cultures and those who populate them see, hear and think bodily ability and its relationship to identity'.[83]

Chapter 3 of Flaugh's 2012 monograph, entitled 'Regenerating Family Fortune: Incising Religious Orders of Gender and Procreation in Tahar Ben Jelloun's *L'enfant de sable* and *La nuit sacrée*', expands on his earlier article. Here, Flaugh does engage with French-language criticism on the novels that does not seem to have been picked up by English-language critics before, such as Carine Bourget and Marc Gontard. Flaugh also refers to several French texts on issues of gender in Islam, such as Fatima Mernissi, Nadia Tazi and Malek Chebel, a welcome and necessary supplementation to his earlier argument.

However, Flaugh overuses the term 'operation' and its cognates at times which has the effect of flattening out his argument, or even producting an unintended effect of self-parody, as in the following excerpt: 'The same texts also help us to think anew the operability and thus malleability that surfaces in *L'enfant de sable* and *La nuit sacrée*, particularly on the part of operating agents who call upon and thereby operate multiple sociocultural narratives to frame and justify their operations to the body.'[84]

83 Ibid., 422.

84 Flaugh, *Operation Freak*, 136.

Intertextuality and the presence of Borges: Aizenberg and Fayad

Not surprisingly, intertextuality is one of the features that critics have focused on in the polyphonous narrative of *The Sand Child*, although they have done so in quite different ways. The fact that one of the narrators of *The Sand Child*, the blind troubadour, is a fictionalization of Borges, an author who insisted that all writing was rewriting, and that all literature was a single continuous text, suggests that intertextuality is a major concern for Ben Jelloun in this novel.

Derived from the Latin *intertexto*, meaning to intermingle while weaving, intertextuality is a term introduced by Julia Kristeva in the late 1960s. Kristeva argued that is was time to break with traditional notions such as the 'influences' on an author and a text's 'sources'. Rather, all signifying systems are constituted by the manner in which they transform earlier signifying systems. A literary work, therefore, is not simply the product of a single author but also defined by 1) its relationship to other texts and 2) its relationship to the structures of language itself: 'Any text is constructed of a mosaic of quotations; any text is the absorption and transformation of another'.[85]

In her 1992 article on Borges as a postcolonial precursor, Edna Aizenberg mentions Ben Jelloun's *The Sand Child* alongside fictions by Rushdie and Shammas, as Borges features in novels by these authors as a character as well as a source of inspiration for 'postmodernist' writing.[86] What makes Ben Jelloun a disciple of Borges, according to Aizenberg, is a distinct 'poetics of pastiche':

> As in the master, the shock of discourses insinuates a postcolonial heterotopia, but one that takes Borges's undermining strategies even further, because it is more

85 Julia Kristeva, *Revolutions in Poetic Language*, trans. Margaret Waller (New York: Columbia University Press, 1997), 37.

86 Edna Aizenberg, 'Borges, Postcolonial Precursor', *World Literature Today*, 66/1 (1992), 21–6.

> heterotopic, embracing more multifarious and more far-flung cultural ingredients. The 'empire' that 'writes back' to the 'center' has been enlarged, as has the notion of what is the 'center', which may now be not only the culture of Europe or North America, but dominant cultures within the 'margin' itself. Concomitantly, there are enlarged possibilities for irreverence with fortunate consequences.[87]

This poetics of pastiche, Aizenberg seems to suggest, is particularly adept at voicing concerns from the 'margins' in a way that is congenial both to a postcolonial and a postmodernist stance towards literature. Not surprisingly, Aizenberg references postmodernist thinkers (Fokkema, Hutcheon, McHale) as well as postcolonial thinkers (Ashcroft, Griffiths and Tiffin; Ngũgĩ wa Thiong'o) in her bibliography, implicitly placing Ben Jelloun in a transnational space of world literature, alongside Rushdie and Shammas. This is the space that Graham Huggan has labelled the 'postcolonial exotic', which consciously and successfully markets its own marginality on the international book market.

In 1993, the *French Review* published a contribution by Marie Fayad on the fictional Borges in *The Sand Child*.[88] In the first paragraph of her article, Fayad does not gloss over the narrative complexities of the novel but rather explains why she focuses on one single narrator: all narrators belong to the Moroccan milieu, except for the blind troubadour who narrates chapters 17 and 18. The troubadour is recognizable as Borges when he uses the words 'j'ai passé ma vie à falsifier ou altérer les histoires des autres' [I spent my life falsifying or altering other people's stories, *ES*, 171].[89] This is the first of several instances of textual closeness between the words of the fictional Borges and those of the factual Argentinean writer.[90] Fayad argues

87 Ibid., 25.

88 Marie Fayad, 'Borges in Tahar Ben Jelloun's *L'enfant de sable*: Beyond Intertextuality', *French Review*, 67/2 (1993), 291–9.

89 In *A Universal History of Infamy*, Borges used the same turn of phrase to describe himself as a young man 'who dared not write stories and so amused himself by falsifying and distorting [...] the tales of others'. Jorge Luis Borges, *A Universal History of Infamy*, trans. Norman Thomas Di Giovanni (New York: E. P. Dutton, 1972), 13. Quoted in Fayad, 292.

90 For further examples, see Fayad, 'Borges in Ben Jelloun', 293–7.

that Ben Jelloun's strategy moves beyond intertextuality 'since the character who delivers the "hypertext" (the ulterior text) is the very same author who is the source of the "hypotext" (the model, or original text)'.[91] While Fayad concentrates on chapters 17 and 18, she suggests that the Borgesian influence permeates the entire novel, 'starting with the title, reminiscent of Borges's short story "The Book of Sand"'.[92]

Fayad uses the French edition of the novel and lists six works by Borges in her bibliography. She also includes four pieces of secondary literature on Borges, as well as Cavenaze's article and a 1988 French article about the reception of *The Sacred Night* in the European press.

While Aizenberg interprets Ben Jelloun's use of intertextuality and the fictionalization of Borges as a marker of postcoloniality, Fayad claims that the Moroccan writer uses 'Borgesian devices to pay homage to Borges' and thus suggests that Ben Jelloun has a more personal relationship with and indebtedness to Borges.[93]

The Sand Child as an allegory of the postcolonial condition of Morocco: Lowe and Lezra

In her 1993 article published in *Yale French Studies*, Lisa Lowe asserts that postcolonial Francophone literatures of North Africa and South-East Asia 'are not only symptomatic sites of the struggles and contradictions analysed by Fanon and others, but in certain cases, the literatures also offer narrative allegories of these struggles and contradictions'.[94] Lowe interprets *The Sand Child* alongside Pham Van Ky's *Des femmes assises çà et là* as narratives

91 Fayad, 295.

92 Ibid., 297.

93 Ibid., 298.

94 Lisa Lowe, 'Literary Nomadics in Francophone Allegories of Postcolonialism: Pham Van Ky and Tahar Ben Jelloun', *Yale French Studies*, 82 (1993), 43–61. Here 44.

that visit and revisit the question of 'colonialist' and 'nativist' nationalism. Lowe refers to the different ways one can read the two novels and explains why she has chosen a different path:

> I do not read the ultimate placelessness of either protagonist as signifying the fluctuating indeterminacy of postcolonial or postmodern culture; nor do I read their postcolonial placelessness romantically, as a poignant flight of the forever exiled. Indeed, each of these novels could be read in these ways. Rather, I interpret the nomadic movements of both narratives and their protagonists as suggesting strategies for imagining resistance to the logics of cultural imperialism, logics which manage nativist reaction as the binary complement to cultural domination.[95]

Using the notion of *heterotopia* (Foucault) and the concept of the *nomadic* (Deleuze and Guattari), Lowe's declared intent is to disrupt the 'binary schemas which tend to condition the way in which we read and discuss not only postcolonial literature, but postcolonial situations in general'.[96]

According to Lowe, *The Sand Child* is a novel which 'allegorizes problems of colonial domination, nativist reaction, and nomadic resistance in the protagonist's ambivalent relationship to sexuality and gender roles' in which French colonial subjugation is allegorized in the figure of Ahmed/Zahra who is confronted with an impossible choice between two polar positions: male – female.[97] This binarism corresponds to the nativist-colonialist binarism facing the newly formed nation of Morocco.

Lowe identifies two major *topoi* in Ben Jelloun's narrative. First, she sees Ahmed/Zahra's 'fetishistic' belief in his/her simultaneous male and female sexuality as an allegory of the 'splitting of the subject under colonialism' and of the 'coexistence of contrary currents of personality which correspond to entirely different cultural systems'.[98] Second, Lowe explains the *topos* of nomadic wandering as mirroring the novel's 'dispersed modes of narration'.[99] Three narrators are vital in this regard: the ending of Amar's

95 Ibid., 45.
96 Ibid., 47.
97 Ibid., 54.
98 Ibid., 56.
99 Ibid., 57.

story reflects a 'nativist' logic (Ahmed finds peace and redemption through the study of Islamic religious texts), while Salem's violent account of Zahra's rape and death is meant to represent the worst allegory of colonialism. Fatuma, the only female narrator and a nomadic being herself, constitutes an alternative to the binary model 'nativist' versus 'colonialist': 'through her extensive travels, she has moved away from her past dilemma of ambivalent gender and sexuality; she is also no longer confined to colonial or native territories, and describes her freedom to dwell in any site she wishes'.[100]

Lowe sees *The Sand Child* as a novel that thematizes '*the colonized subject as an important site of cultural and political contestation*' and which subverts the Oedipal discourse as a powerful instrument of colonialism.[101] It refigures and displaces

> privileged psychoanalytical explanations of gender acquisition, including castration anxiety, disavowal, and fetishism, and therefore suggests the importance of our attendance to the various sites of splitting in the colonized subject as one part of theorizing colonial and postcolonial resistances to domination.[102]

Through its use of sources and argument, Lowe's contribution locates itself within postcolonial studies (quoting Fanon and Bhabha) and postmodernism (Deleuze and Guattari, Soja). Lowe also refers to the Oedipus complex (Freud and Lacan) as well as the Anti-Oedipal projects of Deleuze and Guattari and of feminists such as Katja Silverman and Jessica Benjamin.[103] However, Lowe does not refer to a single French contribution on *The Sand Child* or by a Maghrebian writer or critic. The only exception is a brief mention of the Tunisian writer Albert Memmi.

100 Ibid., 58.

101 Ibid., 61. Emphasis in the original.

102 Ibid.

103 Aparna Halpe argues that the issue of gendered subjectivity in *The Sand Child* is best understood through a Freudian paradigm. She sees the novel as a reworking of Freud's theories of Eros and Thanatos (life and death drives). See Aparna Halpe, 'The Problem of Eros in Tahar Ben Jelloun's *The Sand Child*', *Canadian Review of Comparative Literature/Revue Canadienne de Littérature Comparée*, 32/3–4 (Sep–Dec 2005), 400–19.

Overall, Lowe positions Ben Jelloun's œuvre in a transnational space of literature that is both 'postcolonial' and 'Francophone'. This literature is written in French by writers from the former colonies and it engages with issues of domination and subordination in an innovative way that describes but no longer subscribes to the reactive model (Europe versus its Other). Rather, Lowe argues, alternatives to this binarism can be found in the nomadic figures such as Fatuma and in the fragmented narrative techniques.

In a book chapter published in 2008, Esther Lezra reads *The Sand Child* in a similar way: as 'articulating violent subjection of [...] peripheral bodies as a necessary moment in the disruption of the unifying and inevitably stifling structures of the neo-colonial and gender discourses around Moroccan independence (1956)'.[104] Just as Lowe had done, Lezra also uses a second text, *The Pagoda* by Patricia Powell, to strengthen her argument. Both texts use 'the errant and cross-dressing body as a metaphor for the act of outlining an alternative subjectivity' which points 'to a common preoccupation with taking a critical position vis-à-vis the oppressive elements in the ideological makeup of colonialist and national structures that rely on notions of fixed and normative identities'.[105] At the start of her article, Lezra partly distances herself from Lowe's approach to *The Sand Child*:

> Lowe understands the father's nationalist utterance as an imposition of the neo-colonial will onto the female body, while I would like to read the imposition of masculinity onto the female body as a gesture that 'takes back' and rewrites what dominant European discourses have represented as the figure of the colonized-feminized and penetrated body of Morocco.[106]

The multiple and complex narrative strands are seen as serving a specific purpose: 'to reclaim a community voice and assert heterogenous subjectivities

104 Esther Lezra, '[Ab]Errant Bodies/[Ab]Erring Stories/Remembering Bodies/Disordering Stories in *The Pagoda* and *The Sand Child*', in Robert Cancel and Winifred Woodhull, eds, *African Diasporas: Ancestors, Migration and Borders* (Trenton, NJ: Africa World, 2008), 80–106.

105 Ibid., 102–3.

106 Ibid., 102n1.

in the face of external, flattening colonial aggression'.[107] In Lezra's view, Ben Jelloun draws on specific narrative devices in order to 'map a collective space not entirely defined by colonization within which the community that he addresses might be able to refashion itself'.[108] The destruction of the marketplace and the disappearance of the first narrator are seen as a 'neocolonial attempt to eliminate [a] generative knot of cultural activity' which is however 'countered by the emergence of a multiplicity of narrators that come forth to replace the eliminated teller'.[109] Narrative authority is decentred, yet a community forms around a 'sense of collective and individual responsibility to each other as well as to the story and its characters'.[110] The story is (and has to be) retold several times 'in what seems to be a deliberate act – on the part of those who take over the retelling – of rebuilding a destroyed community'.[111] Thus, Lezra concludes her analysis of *The Sand Child*,

> the disorder and errancy with which [Ahmed/Zahra's] story is inflected can be understood in terms of an act of resistance to destructive neocolonial structures. This resistance itself enacts violence on the female body, for it is the body upon which the violent processes of narrating, erasing and re-membering are played out.[112]

To strengthen her argument, Lezra uses texts by Anderson (on imagined communities), Butler (on identity), Woodhull (on feminism and decolonization in the Maghreb), Mignolo (on coloniality and border thinking) and Mernissi (on Islam and democracy). She also references theoretical writings on the Caribbean and the Subcontinent as subaltern, postcolonial spaces. Only two items of Ben Jelloun criticism are present in the 'Works Cited':

107 Ibid., 82.
108 Ibid., 83.
109 Ibid., 86.
110 Ibid., 87.
111 Ibid., 88.
112 Ibid., 89.

a monograph by Jarrod Hayes (2000) who also reads the representation of gender as a national allegory (see below), and Lowe's article.[113]

Lowe and Lezra both see Ben Jelloun's novel as exemplifying the post-colonial condition in general and as an act of writing and resisting the grievances of a specific, Moroccan, 'reality'.

Intertextuality and intersexuality: Harvey

In 1997 Robert Harvey contributed an article on *The Sand Child* to an edited collection of essays on gender studies and French-language writing.[114] Starting off with the familiar criticism that Ben Jelloun '(perhaps yielding to his market) had honed [*The Sacred Night*] into a prize-winning, euphonic, and seamless parody of Arabic narrative traditions', Harvey praises *The Sand Child* as a 'generalized intertext on the verge of cacophony' struggling with the 'instability of intersexuality'.[115] In order to describe the social conditioning that Ahmed/Zahra undergoes, Harvey resorts to the metaphor of 'coinage', which is also used in the novel itself: the protagonist's maleness is stamped upon him/her just as a coin is stamped but then the coinage fades.

113 Jarrod Hayes, *Queer Nations. Marginal Sexualities in the Maghreb* (Chicago and London: The University of Chicago Press, 2000).

114 Robert Harvey, 'Purloined Letters: Intertextuality and Intersexuality in Tahar Ben Jelloun's *The Sand Child*' in Dominique D. Fisher and Lawrence R. Schehr, eds, *Articulations of Difference: Gender Studies and Writing in French* (Stanford: Stanford University Press, 1997), 226–45. Harvey also published a Portuguese version of the article in 2000: 'Cartas e letras roubadas: intertextualidade e intersexualidade em *L'enfant de sable* de Tahar Ben Jelloun', *Estudos Neolatinos*, 2/1 (2000), 73–96.

115 Harvey, 'Purloined Letters', 226. Erickson also expresses the view that *The Sacred Night* is inferior to *The Sand Child* and that Ben Jelloun might have deliberately changed his writing strategy for the sequel in order to 'specifically appeal to the Goncourt jury, the general public, and the popular press' (Erickson 'Veiled', 48n2).

In his discussion of the Borgesian intertext, Harvey refers to two previous articles on intertextuality by Erickson and Gontard.[116] Harvey states that Ben Jelloun comes very close to actually plagiarizing Borges ('unavowed literary borrowing') and that 'Borges is not just *any* author to steal from, since most of his work questions the concept of originality in literature, the significance of the signature, and the very notion of authorship'.[117] Ben Jelloun has adopted a technique of 'intertextual deviation' that imitates 'the nomadic survival tactics that the intersexual sand child adopts'.[118]

Harvey weaves together several strands of literary criticism: psychoanalytical criticism (Freud and Kristeva), postmodernism (Deleuze and Guattari) and postcolonial studies (comparing Ben Jelloun's narrative strategies to those of other Maghrebian writers, such as Abdelkebir Khatibi and Assia Djebar). According to Harvey, the intertextuality in Ben Jelloun

> results less from postmodern paralogism or metafiction than from the author's incorporation of the Berber oral tradition of his native Morocco and from the intertwining of speaking and writing in Islamic culture. Thus the Koran and the *1001 Nights* – two paradigmatic Islamic texts of the voice – have massive presence in *The Sand Child*.[119]

Ultimately, Harvey argues, it does not matter whether we define the intertextuality of this rhizomatic novel as 'the apotheosis of modernism or an exemplum of the postmodern': what is important in the work stretches the 'limits of decipherability'.[120] By making Borges a central character, Ben Jelloun reclaims him for the 'decentering project of minor literature' as

116 Harvey refers to Erickson's 1991 article which briefly touches on *The Sand Child* but fails to mention Erickson's contributions that deal exclusively with the novel. The other source quoted is Marc Gontard, 'Le récit meta-narratif chez Tahar Ben Jelloun' in Mansour M'Henni, ed., *Tahar Ben Jelloun. Stratégies d'écriture* (Paris: L'Harmattan, 1993), 99–118. Gontard argues that Ben Jelloun merges Moroccan tradition and postmodern writing practices. On the Borgesian intertext, see 112–15. Aizenberg and Fayad go unmentioned.

117 Harvey, 'Purloined Letters', 229. Emphasis in the original.

118 Ibid., 230.

119 Ibid., 241.

120 Ibid., 244.

defined by Deleuze and Guattari: 'By shunning [...] the genealogy of culture fostered and nurtured in the salons of European capitals, Ben Jelloun transplants Borges into the rhizome where his Morocco can easily connect with the *criollo* quarters of Latin American medinas'.[121]

Harvey seems to suggest that, while intertextuality and intersexuality mirror one another, the narrative techniques are at least as important as, if not more important than, the plot developments. While agreeing on the general working consensus that seems to have established itself by the late 1990s – '*The Sand Child* is best read as an example of postcolonial literature investigating gender and national identity and which uses disruptive narrative techniques', – Harvey is prone to accentuate the narrative techniques over the novel's proclaimed political stance on issues of gender and national identity. He does not, however, refer to Marrouchi, Abdalaoui or items of criticism written in French that argue along similar lines. Overall, articles that investigate gender identity still prevail, as the next few sections will show.

Masculinity and virility: Ouzgane

Lahoucine Ouzgane's 1997 article and his 2011 reworking thereof aim to redress the lack of critical work on masculinity (rather than femininity) in criticism of Maghrebian literature.[122] Most of the attention in gender studies has been on the construction of Islamic femininity, Ouzgane argues, and the rare existing studies of Islamic masculinities concentrate on homosexuality

121 Ibid., 245.

122 Lahoucine Ouzgane, 'Masculinity and Virility in Tahar Ben Jelloun's Work', *Contagion: Journal of Violence, Mimesis, and Culture*, 4 (1997), 1–13. 'The Rape Continuum: Masculinities in the Works of Nawal El Saadawi and Tahar Ben Jelloun', in *Men in African Film and Fiction* (Woodbridge: Currey, 2011), 68–80.

and homoeroticism. Patriarchal structures of society do not only marginalize women but shape the

> violent hierarchies structuring the relationships between men themselves [...]. Because women are not the centre of men's experience (other men are), misogyny is actually fuelled by something deeper – by the fear of emasculation by other men, the fear of humiliation, the fear of being not so manly.[123]

The male characters in Ben Jelloun's novels all reduce masculinity to virility, Ouzgane argues, a state of affairs that can only be sustained through recurring acts of violence.

Ouzgane gives two examples from *The Sand Child*: the rivalry between Ahmed's father and his brothers and the story of Antar, a woman disguising herself as man and known as a ruthless warrior chieftain. In a society in which virility is a synonym for manhood, not being able to procreate or being able to produce only girls is a sign of weakness. In fact, the North African Arabic words for 'manhood' and 'virility' are almost interchangeable.[124] Through Antar's character, 'Ben Jelloun offers us the spectacle of the most masculine of men, the soldier, elaborately arrayed, in transgression of gender fixities'.[125]

Ouzgane even cites the example of serial rapist Hajji Hamid Tabet (sentenced to death in 1993 for having raped over five hundred women in the space of thirteen years) as evidence that Ben Jelloun's texts are 'indeed inseparable from their context'.[126] For Ouzgane, literature clearly fulfils a documentary function, describing mentalities and gender constructions in a particular society. As a consequence of Ouzgane's emphasis on the interpretation of plot, the aesthetic dimension of the novel is downplayed.

123 Ouzgane, 'Rape Continuum', 69.

124 See Ouzgane, 'Rape Continuum', 78n7.

125 Ouzgane, 'Masculinity and Virility', 11.

126 Ibid., 12.

Genuineness, authority and authenticity: Gauch

In her 1999 article, which also forms the basis of chapter 3 of her 2007 monograph, Suzanne Gauch criticizes some of the accepted notions of postcolonial studies, namely 'the emasculating effects of colonization upon the colonized' and the acknowledgement of 'colonialism's role in furthering the oppression of colonized women' as they fail to question 'occluded assumptions regarding the body, particularly the female body'.[127] While Gauch agrees that *The Sand Child* is a novel that combines 'elements of sexual difference, dominance, independence and national identity, and postcolonial consciousness' she wants to counteract a tendency in previous Ben Jelloun criticism that took for granted the femininity of Ahmed:

> Relying upon a notion of biology as naturally determinative of gender, such readings designate the colonial period as the unnatural suppression of some authentic female essence. To overcome the unnatural effects of colonialism is to recover or remake a 'natural' female subject. Such reasoning implicitly predicates the liberation of Ahmed's female subjectivity on the recreation of an authentic sociocultural identity uncontaminated by the aberrant structures of colonialism.[128]

Gauch takes up position by criticizing other interpreters, Erickson and Lowe in particular, for contending that 'Ahmed/Zahra is a woman cruelly forced to disavow her female body and desires, with her socialization as a male either, in Erickson's view, contesting the colonizer's emasculation of the colonized, or alternately, in Lowe's reading, reflecting French colonial policies of assimilation'.[129] In Gauch's view, the protagonist does not have innate female desires; rather, the text actually condemns notions of sexual

127 Suzanne Gauch, 'Telling the Tale of a Body Devoured by Narrative', *differences: A Journal of Feminist Cultural Studies*, 11/1 (1999), 179–202. Here 179. 'A Story without a Face', in *Liberating Shahrazad. Feminism, Postcolonialism, and Islam* (Minneapolis and London: University of Minnesota Press, 2007), 55–80.

128 Gauch, 'Telling the Tale', 180.

129 Ibid., 183.

identity exclusively linked to biology and unsettles 'categories long taken for granted by analyses of colonialism, offering an important glimpse into the gendering of postcolonial identity'.[130] Using Butler's concept of performativity, Gauch argues that Ahmed actually revels in the narratives that constrain him as they heighten his perception of the constructedness of gender. It is not his body but his crippled wife Fatima who provokes Ahmed to question his identity.

In the second part of her article, Gauch moves from an engagement with the genuineness of the protagonist's gender to the question how the different narrators claim authority, as both symbolize the struggle of decolonized nations to recuperate a 'genuine' identity.[131] Ben Jelloun exposes different ideas about authenticity and authority as the novel progresses: authority derived from the possession of the protagonist's diary, authority derived from one's proclaimed position as an eyewitness, authority derived from a shared fate. The blind troubadour's function is to make a mockery of the 'quest for narrative resolution'.[132] The narrative strategies deployed by Ben Jelloun in this novel, Gauch concludes her 1999 article, serve to destabilize the binaries of masculinity and femininity as well as to put in question simplistic formulations of postcolonial national identities.

In the 2007 book chapter, Gauch includes an analysis of the trends in criticism of *The Sand Child* up to that point in time:

> Scholars have discerned in the story of Ahmed/Zahra allegories of bicultural or nomadic postcolonial identities, a critique of Islam's influence on the psyches of its adherents, a condemnation of colonialism's impact on gendered social relations, a commentary on the gender insubordination at the root of national identity, and a reflection of a culturally specific, postcolonial, gender theory.[133]

130 Ibid., 181.

131 Here, Gauch's claim resembles that of Lowe and Erickson whom she had criticized earlier on in her contribution.

132 Gauch, 'Telling the Tale', 198.

133 Gauch, 'Story Without a Face', 59.

As examples, Gauch quotes Lowe, Erickson, Brand and Hayes (for the latter two, see below) but she does not refer to any of the existing French-language contributions about the novel of which there are several dozens by 2007 (see Appendix II). She does, however, refer to the 'usual suspects' of postcolonial and gender studies (Fanon, Butler) and to Fatima Mernissi as a representative voice from the Maghreb. Although some critics, such as Gauch and Harvey, have sufficient competence to prefer their own translations of the French novel to Sheridan's, they do not find it necessary to incorporate more than token items of criticism on the novel written in French.

As Gauch's monograph uses Shahrazad [Scheherazade] as a copula, she argues that *The Sand Child*, 'building on what Mernissi deemed the insolent lesson of Princess Budur – that the difference between the sexes is but a matter of dress –' proposes that we need to reimagine the construct of sex. Gauch argues that narratives such as *The Sand Child* expose the 'fantasy of rigid and impermeable boundaries between Occident and Orient, the West and the Arab world' which is especially difficult for postcolonial writers when 'regional particularism is assumed to dominate their aesthetics'.[134] Thus, Gauch concludes in 2007, 'through his many doubles, the storytellers, Ben Jelloun entices those readers in search of an ethnographic performance of Moroccan authorship and then, through a radical foregrounding of fictionality, turns such a project to ridicule'.[135]

Gauch suggests that *The Sand Child* is a most interesting narrative for exactly its foregrounding of fictionality. While she is not alone in advocating this stance, questions of gender emerging from the plot seem to be more important to many other critics: the arrival of the new millennium saw more articles on queer sexuality and queer nationality, on the masking and unmasking of gender, as well as on androgyny.

134 Ibid., 67.
135 Ibid., 79–80.

The Sand Child as allegory of gender: Hayes

Although I have already discussed gender approaches I want to treat Jarrod Hayes separately as he is the first to apply queer theory while also stressing the literariness of the novel (which Cazenave, Corredor and El-Hoss fail to do). In a chapter of his monograph on marginal sexualities in the Maghreb, 'Becoming a Woman: Tahar Ben Jelloun's Allegory of Gender', Hayes describes the twin novels as telling 'not only the story of one individual's becoming a woman, but also the story of gender, a narration of the process through which gender is stamped onto the bodies and minds of those belonging to the "second sex".'[136] Hayes proposes to read *The Sacred Night* through the lens of *The Sand Child* (rather than the other way round) in an attempt to reopen questions seemingly closed in the second, linear, narrative: 'Instead of narrating the liberation of a female from the imposed gender of man, instead of narrating the return to the roots of womanhood, *La nuit sacrée* is about the impossible task of such a narrative'.[137]

Hayes also sees his own reading as challenging the interpretations seemingly authorized by Ben Jelloun, who in an interview stated that he wanted to describe a process of emancipation, 'a woman's struggle to become what she should have been had she not been the victim of an aggression against her sexuality and all her being'.[138] Becoming a woman, Hayes argues, involves forgetting the violence at the origin of gender, 'the violent stamping of the body by language'. Thus, 'for the gender system to work, gender as performance must be forgotten, replaced by gender naturalized and joined to its source, biology'. Zahra's decision to live as a woman also means giving up the status of a full citizen and accepting that of a servant.[139]

136 Jarrod Hayes, 'Becoming a Woman: Tahar Ben Jelloun's Allegory of Gender', in *Queer Nations*, 165–81. Here 165.

137 Ibid., 173.

138 See Philippe Gaillard, 'Tahar le fou, Tahar le sage', *Jeune Afrique*, 1404 (1987), 44–6. Translation quoted from Hayes, 172.

139 Hayes, 174–9.

Towards the end of the chapter, Hayes engages with Lowe's reading of the novel as an allegory of the nation.[140] While Lowe's reading seems to imply the notion of the protagonist's journey towards womanhood as liberation (an interpretation that Hayes questions), he is especially interested in what Lowe calls 'literary nomadics' as one way of resisting both colonialism and nationalism and of 'disrupting narratives of a return to national origins'.[141] Both gender and nation are performative: gender is an individual, nation a collective performance; neither are naturally given, they are both internalized. National identity as performance

> both uses the origin of official nationalist discourse and disrupts the centrality of that origin. National identity, still useful in this concept, becomes a sort of drag. [...] Ben Jelloun's model of the performance of gendered identity is thus simultaneously a model of national identity, where the Nation involved is inescapably queer. In this vision of becoming/performing woman, the relation between nation and Woman is one of exclusion: The more Zahra becomes woman, the more she is denied an officially recognized identity.[142]

Comparing Ahmed/Zahra and Silence: Ramond Jurney and Hess

In her 2001 article on the masking and unmasking of gender, Florence Ramond Jurney analyses *The Sand Child* in tandem with a text from the thirteenth century, *Le roman de Silence*, as both narratives deal with the socio-political origins of transvestism and its consequences.[143] There are

140 In the 'Works Cited' of the monograph, we find four of the previous items of criticism on the novel written in English (Cazenave, Lowe, Marrouchi and Mehta) and four written in French (Déjeux, Erickson, Maazaoui and Saigh Bousta).

141 Hayes, 180.

142 Ibid., 180–1.

143 Florence Ramond Jurney, 'Secret Identities: (Un)Masking Gender *in Le roman de Silence* by Heldris de Cournouaille and *L'enfant de sable* by Tahar Ben Jelloun', *Dalhousie French Studies*, 55 (Summer 2001), 3–10.

three ways in which the protagonists (both biologically female but raised as males) are masked: by naming (an act exercised by the fathers with the complicity of the mothers); by the ritual of clothing (wearing clothes reserved to men and hiding female bodily characteristics) and by the usurpation of education (education is subverted by females to learn and do what is usually reserved to men). While the masking is initiated by the masculine, the protagonists are soon 'decrowned' (Bakhtin's term) and can be 'symbolically seen as clowns who usurp the power of the King in that they usurp the power of the masculine'.[144] The process of unmasking is aimed at proclaiming the importance of Nature over Nurture, Ramond Jurney concludes, yet everything returns to the order defined by the masculine. Therefore, 'neither *Le roman de Silence* nor *L'enfant de sable* is a feminist success: Ahmed/Zahra dies in exile without giving the reader many more details, and Silence's wedding is followed by a very abrupt ending'. Yet, Ramond Jurney argues, Nurture wins over Nature in Ben Jelloun's novel: 'the mask that was deceiving in one way (physically) can continue to deceive in another (culturally), leaving the feminine with the possibility of shaking patriarchal society enough so that it can assert the multiple expressions of its identity independent of the authority and the schemes of the masculine'.[145]

In a by now familiar move, Ramond Jurney glosses over the existence of multiple narrators and states that Ahmed/Zahra has died, failing to mention that this is only one of several versions of the protagonist's life and that Zahra actually rises to speak herself in the sequel.

The 'Works Cited' consists of five items: besides the two novels at the centre of the article, Ramond Jurney quotes Bakhtin's study of Rabelais, an article on the *Roman de Silence* by Elizabeth Waters and Cazenave's 1991 article treated above. However, remarkably, no mention is made of a previous critical comparative study of the two novels in question: in 1998, Erica Hess had published an essay entitled 'Passing the Test of Truth: Gender as Performance in Two French Narratives, Medieval and Modern' which

144 Ibid., 8.

145 Ibid., 9.

also discusses the thematic and linguistic hybridity of the two protagonists, Silence and Ahmed.[146]

Hess starts by stressing that both texts portray a 'debate between Nature and Nurture, or Culture (made explicit in the *Roman de Silence*, implied in *L'enfant de sable*)' which echoes the identity struggle of Ahmed and Silence.[147] Following Butler's theory that gender is a discursively constrained performative act, Hess shows in several examples how both Silence and Ahmed *pass* as males in society. However, as far as *The Sand Child* is concerned,

> with increasing frequency, narrative ruptures and conflicts draw the reader's attention to the inconstancies of appearances and to the inadequacies of reason. In an explicit and rigorous fashion, this novel underscores physical and narrative instability at every juncture. The 'truth', always suspect and qualified, can only ever be that which passes for true. And nothing *passes* for long.[148]

The forces of Nature and Nurture seem to want to compel both protagonists into a single gender and constantly 'work to reposition both Silence and Ahmed away from his/her hybrid *third space*'. Nature's/Nurture's resistance to their hybridity, Hess concludes, 'indicates the degree to which the suggestion of multiple "foundational categories of identity" (Butler) – sex, gender, the body – disturbs and threatens the accepted regimes of power and discourse'.[149]

Besides seven items of criticism on the *Roman de Silence* and Butler's *Gender Troubles*, Hess refers to a book on the formation of Islamic laws of inheritance and two histories of women in the Middle East. The 'Works Cited' also include Simpson's 'One Face Less' and Erickson's article in French as well as another article in French by Anne Chevalier (see Appendix II).

146 Erica Hess, 'Passing the Test of Truth: Gender and Performance in Two French Narratives, Medieval and Modern', *Cincinnati Romance Review*, 17 (1998), 42–8.

147 Ibid., 42.

148 Ibid., 46.

149 Ibid., 47.

Both Jurney Ramond and Hess provide a survey of the theme of gender identity in medieval and modern literature written in French. Neither critic reflects on the fact that theirs is an undertaking that presumes a dubious continuity. Can the two texts in question simply be called 'French narratives', as Hess does in her title and how far do the perceived thematic similarities (women forced to pose as men) really constitute a valid departure point for comparison? Comparing *The Sand Child* to another text which deals with a similar theme is common practice, though, as the next section shows.

The Sand Child as androgynous construct: Brand

Hanita Brand describes the aim of her 2000 article as an analysis of the production of meaning in literature that involves androgynous constructs, with a particular focus on three aspects: the paraliterary (the 'why'; connections between author and protagonist), the metaliterary (the 'how'; literary themes in cultural and social debates) and the literary (the 'what'; historically charged narratives).[150] As examples of literary works interested in androgyny, Brand uses *The Sand Child* and a short story by Isaac Bashevis Singer, 'Yentl, the Yeshiva Boy'. According to Brand, these two texts are 'remarkably close in their perspective, theme and literary approach': they are both tales of women who 'masquerade' [Brand's term] as men.[151] Later, Brand is forced to admit that while Yentl chooses to masquerade as a man, Ahmed is never given that choice.

150 Hanita Brand, "Fragmentary, but Not Without Meaning": Androgynous Constructs and Their Enhanced Signification', *Edebiyât: The Journal of Middle Eastern Literatures*, 11/1 (2000), 57–83.

151 'Brand, 58. Interestingly, Brand refers to *The Sacred Night* not as the sequel of *The Sand Child*, but as 'a novel that has the same theme' (81 n2).

On the paraliterary level, Brand argues, one notices a special relationship 'between the (male) authors and their (originally female) protagonists' which is easily explained: 'Both Tahar Ben Jelloun and Isaac Bashevis Singer are culturally transplanted authors. Theirs is not a gendered androgyny but a cultural one'.[152] On the metaliterary level, Brand continues, 'these texts can help us grasp the social and psychological dimensions of androgyny, both in their problems and possibilities. As literary texts, the plots present, on the whole, a mirror image of reality – in this case, a distorted mirror image'.[153]

As far as the literary level is concerned, Brand uses Annis Pratt's distinction between male and female matrices of the *Bildungsroman*: the male grid describes a linear development from childhood to adult life that results in the acceptance of social rules; the female grid entails disruption and indeterminate endings.[154] If one observes *The Sand Child* and 'Yentl' carefully, Brand proceeds, their formal features reveal

> that the meta-literary thematic elements have corresponding literary manifestations. The structural 'marriage of opposites' throughout the stories is built around the polarity androgyny-vs-society, as one is constantly played out against the other in a power struggle, with few ideal moments of easy balance. The stories oscillate between a regular plot situation, with a main character and a social background (i.e., a male plot line), and an unconventional situation, with a retreat of the protagonist on the one hand and society's coming to the fore on the other (i.e., a female plot line).[155]

In both narratives, the first half is male-gridded and things proceed in a regular, smooth manner 'as the youngsters act fast and have the upper hand, deceiving society, getting married, and settling into the regular social patterns of their milieu'. Later, in the female-gridded part, disaster strikes and 'Ahmed withdraws to his room, refusing to see anyone, awaiting death'.[156]

152 Ibid., 60.

153 Ibid., 65.

154 See Annis Pratt, *Archetypal Patterns in Women's Fiction* (Bloomington: Indiana University Press, 1981).

155 Brand, 'Fragmentary', 72–3.

156 Ibid., 73.

Sixteen pages into her article, Brand has not mentioned the multiple narrators yet and makes the plot appear more straightforward than it is. Next, Brand develops her methodology based on semiotic concepts: the reader is given definitions of Umberto Eco's 'reverse entropy' and Riffaterre's concept of the 'hypogram' as well as an explanation for the author's preference for the term 'paragram'. Confusingly, the reader is asked to understand the latter more like Riffaterre's hypogram than Saussure's paragram.[157]

Nineteen pages into her article, Brand is obliged to admit that 'the narration concerning Ahmed's life is 'set inside a "framework plot" which denies its status as reality. This is achieved by causing the inner plot to be understood as some kind of a folk tale being told in a town square by a series of raconteurs'.[158] The frame story, as Brand calls it, sends readers mixed messages, at times affirming 'the existence of an attainable inner story (in a male plot line)', at times denying it (in a female plot line).[159] The focus on Ahmed's life story, which is portrayed as more linear than it is, results in the neglect of the novel's narrative complexity. In her conclusion, Brand shows her understanding of the nature and function of literature: formal elements, plot line and theme join each other 'to engage in the most enriching dialogue of all – that between literature and life'.[160]

Besides items of feminist criticism dealing with androgyny (Phyllis Rackin, Marilyn French, Ben Agger, Shulamit Firestone and Elaine Showalter) and some texts about semiotics, Brand refers to three critical studies on Singer in the 'Works Cited'. However, there is not a single item of Ben Jelloun criticism in either English or French.

157 Ibid., 73–6.
158 Ibid., 76.
159 Ibid., 77.
160 Ibid., 80–1.

Language, sexual identity, gender: Rye, Hamil and Saunders

In her 2000 article, Gill Rye establishes a strong link between language and sexual identity in *The Sand Child*.[161] Relying on Cixous and Freud as well as gendered reader response theory, Rye's main argument is that language plays a crucial role in the construction and de-construction of sexual identity. Ben Jelloun's main aim, she claims, is to encourage his readers to challenge their own assumptions about sexual identity. Following Cixous, Rye sees reading as a gendered activity, 'a dialogue which takes place within a framework of (changing) power relations'.[162] *The Sand Child* explores the 'biological, socio-cultural, psychological and linguistic dimensions of gender'.[163] Rye also addresses the fact that it is a male writer who constitutes the protagonist as a (female) speaking subject: 'the woman is given voice only with the permission and by the action of a man'. Rye suggests that rather than enabling marginal voices to speak for themselves, Ben Jelloun's intercession actually achieves the opposite effect: it feeds into and reinforces patriarchal and Eurocentric perspectives of Moroccan women as exotic sexual objects.[164]

In a 2000 book chapter, Mustafa Hamil asks the question whether socio-political revolts can only be launched from the site of the woman's body and language. The female body is seen as a space where religious, cultural, economic, sexual and political discourses intersect. 'No displacement [...] of the Law/Name-of-the-Father can be better achieved than through the evocation of woman's body'.[165] While Rye sees Ben Jelloun's adoption of a female voice as questionable, Hamil approves of the author's strategy:

161 Gill Rye, 'Uncertain Readings and Meaningful Dialogue: Language and Sexual Identity in Anne Garréta's *Sphinx* and Tahar Ben Jelloun's *L'enfant de sable* and *La nuit sacrée*', *Neophilologus*, 84/4 (2000), 531–40.

162 Ibid., 532.

163 Ibid., 534.

164 See Rye, 'Uncertain Readings', 536 and 539n11.

165 Mustafa Hamil, 'Rewriting Identity and History. The Sliding *Barre(s)* in Tahar Ben Jelloun's *The Sacred Night*', in Mildred P. Mortimer, ed., *Maghrebian Mosaic: A Literature in Transition* (Boulder, CO: L. Rienner, 2000), 61–80. Here 64.

> Through the act of writing-the-woman, Ben Jelloun embarks on a triple journey: an ontological, linguistic, and historical exploration of his own voice and identity. When the woman speaks, her voice, like that of the author, sounds like her voice but not quite, and her desires and fantasies cast on the plane of writing function as a metadiscourse intended to disrupt the discourse of the Other/Father.[166]

Hamil deploys French theorists such as Lacan, de Certeau, Derrida, Barthes and Deleuze and Guattari alongside Bakhtin and Todorov to bolster his argument. He also refers to Rachid Boudjedra's writing as similar to Ben Jelloun's and points out the similarities between *The Sand Child* and Rushdie's *Midnight's Children*: the birth of the protagonists is linked to the birth of their nations; they are both condemned to a fragmented life. Several Maghrebian critics appear in the 'Works Cited': one item written in English (an article on mother-son relationships by Hedi Abdel-Jaoud) and three in French published in North Africa (Boughali, Memmes and Mezgueldi; see Appendix II). While European theorists still feature prominently, Hamil is one of the few critics to include more than the token Maghrebian critic.

In 'Decolonizing the Body: Gender, Nation, and Narration in Tahar Ben Jelloun's *L'enfant de sable*' (2006), Rebecca Saunders explicitly places the novel 'in a theoretical dialogue with postcolonial and gender studies', arguing that Ben Jelloun's aim is to show how gender is a colonization of the body or how both gender and colonization are mechanism aimed at fabricating subjects.[167] Saunders claims that Ben Jelloun establishes a 'kind of fluid triangulation in which the body is the nation, the nation is the narrative, and the narrative is the body'.[168] Ahmed's life is linked to the life of Morocco, and in the newspaper announcement after Ahmed's birth, the two are already put in relation to one another. The protagonist's troubled gender identity mirrors the troubled Moroccan decolonizing process. Saunders also suggests parallels to Salman Rushdie's *Midnight's Children*.

166 Ibid., 62.

167 Rebecca Saunders, 'Decolonizing the Body: Gender, Nation, and Narration in Tahar Ben Jelloun's *L'enfant de sable*', *Research in African Literatures*, 37/4 (2006), 136–60. Here 136.

168 Ibid., 138.

The fundamental question that Ahmed asks himself ('From what forces do I need to liberate myself?') applies to Morocco, as well. In this interpretation, Salem's, Amar's and Fatuma's alternative endings to Ahmed/Zahra's story allegorize possible developments for Morocco. In a further development, the body becomes indistinguishable from the narrative. The main narrator claims that he alone has access to the story, that in a quite cannibalistic act, he has merged with the book.

The similarities between gender and colonization/colonized subjects, according to Saunders, are several: first, both women and colonies are relegated to childlike status (they both need to be taken care of); second, their status as human beings is defined in terms of relation to men/masters; third, attempts to define women and colonies are negative only: uncivilized, abnormal, underdeveloped; fourth, they are often described as deficient beings. So perhaps the question whether Ahmed is trapped in the wrong 'sex' is not the right one to ask, Saunders suggests. Rather, we should ask ourselves whether Ben Jelloun is actually criticizing the whole gender system as such.

Saunders merges gender and postcolonial theory (Butler and Bhabha) to argue that gender and culture are not *a priori* existing categories but normative ideals. These ideals are reiterated in common usage (therefore *performativity* is a key concept) and the question of agency cannot be ignored. Precisely because identity comes into being through repetition, it can be altered. Rather than losing the language of the body (whether female or national), we should see these concepts as forces of discursive demands with the capacity to draw out the materiality of the body.

Disguising gender? El-Hoss

In a similar vein to several other critics interested in identity formation in *The Sand Child*, Tamara El-Hoss's 2009 contribution to an edited volume dedicated to disguise, deception and trompe-l'œil also fails to mention the narrative complexities. Tamara El-Hoss wants to 'investigate the manner in which, through various stages of deception and disguise, and with his father's "blessing", Ben Jelloun's protagonist succeeds in building his masculine identity (Ahmed), only to discard it after his father's death, thus allowing his female persona (Zahra) to emerge'.[169] Using Mernissi, El-Hoss gives a brief overview of the role of women in Arab Muslim society before describing how Ahmed's existence is regulated by a double veil: 'the first is a symbolic veil he wears (in public as well as in private) to mask his biological gender, while the second is the physical veil (the *hijab* in Arabic) he does not wear as long as his father is alive, be it in private or in public, since Ben Jelloun's protagonist is perceived to be a man'.[170] El-Hoss follows up this textual example by citing the Koran, Asmas Barlas, professor at Ithaca College, and Nawal El Saadawi, an Egyptian feminist and activist. Then she analyses the motif of the *hammam* (though failing to acknowledge Jurney Ramond's 2004 contribution about the *hammam* in *The Sand Child* written in French; see Appendix II), and the importance of the character of Fatima for Ahmed's reflection on gender issues (not quoting any of the previous criticism on this topic, either in English or in French). El-Hoss does quote Erickson's monograph as well as Hayes's book. Ultimately, the critic seems to suggest that the novel is a more or less mimetic representation of gender insubordination in a Muslim society:

> By disguising her biological gender in *The Sand Child* and deceiving everyone around her, Zahra has transgressed numerous boundaries within a Muslim society and has caused a *fitna*. As a consequence, she has upset the order established by Allah. Her punishment for such a transgression is to live her life as someone unable to experience sexual pleasure (sexual pleasure is unattainable after a clitorodectomy), an asexual being *in-between* genders (she is, after all, a bearded woman), banned from the universe of women (since she is not a 'real' woman) as well as from the universe of men (since she is socially no longer a man), a fact/reality she accepts without tears.[171]

169 El-Hoss, 149.
170 Ibid., 151.
171 Ibid., 159.

Queer Postcolonial Ethics of Witnessing: McCormack

In 2014, Donna McCormack published a monograph entitled *Queer Postcolonial Narratives and the Ethics of Witnessing* in which *The Sand Child* serves as a case study alongside Shani Mootoo's *Cereus Blooms at Night* and Ann-Marie MacDonald's *Fall on Your Knees*. In the chapter 'Monstrous Witnessing in Tahar Ben Jelloun's *L'enfant de sable*', McCormack merges postcolonial and queer theories with Felman's, Laub's and Caruth's thoughts on trauma and memory. Focusing on the collective sense of responsibility for the narrative, the compulsive desire to keep the story going 'opens up the possibility of bearing witness to the multiple, discordant histories of colonial and familial violence'.[172]

McCormack also sees Ahmed/Zahra as the embodiment of the transition from colonialism to an independent Moroccan state but she suggests that the performative character of both the narrative and of queer bodies does more than simply elucidate the constructedness of nations and bodies: it enacts 'the very vulnerability of being'. In this context, McCormack defines the *queer* as signifying 'morphologically diverse, disabled, non-normative desires and gender expressions, and perverse and freaky practices'. [173]

The ethics of witnessing in *The Sand Child* is quite physical: the storytellers and the audience share an epistemology connected to the senses. They experience language through their bodies. One of the reasons why the narrators take over from one another might be that remembering a traumatic event is painful and destructive, a burden better shared: 'there is a finite call to respond to a history that must be told and heard, but there is also an infinite call to take responsibility for this narrative by keeping the telling going and by being open to different, even infinite, versions'.[174]

172 Donna McCormack, *Queer Postcolonial Narratives and the Ethics of Witnessing* (New York and London: Bloomsbury, 2014), 81.

173 Ibid., 79.

174 Ibid., 118.

McCormack is the first critic to apply an 'ethics of witnessing' paradigm to *The Sand Child*. Besides other critics working in that paradigm, she refers to critical work on disability and non-normative embodiment. Postcolonial thinkers and eight of the contributors mentioned in this chapter (Erickson, Hayes, Gauch, Harvey, Cazenave, Ibnlfassi, Lowe and Saunders) are also mentioned. Along with Hayes's work, therefore, McCormack's contribution shows the most evidence of cross-fertilization and the widest range of engagement with relevant scholarship, even if it is not with criticism written in French, as is the case with Hayes.

Magical realism: Erickson

We have encountered John D. Erickson before as one of the first critics to write on the corporeality of protagonist and narrative. In fact, he is the most prolific critic writing in English on Ben Jelloun, having established himself as a specialist on nomadic writing and magical realism in the Maghreb.

Erickson uses Franz Roh's definition of the term 'magical realism' ('depiction of the supernatural in a realistic setting') as well as the more common usage of the term for narratives by Latin-American writers that merge fantasy and reality.[175] Erickson claims that Ben Jelloun's writings from the 1980s, and *The Sand Child* especially, 'best exemplify magical realism and its Maghrebian form of nomadic thought'.[176] In adopting techniques of magical realism that remind the reader of Julio Cortázar, Raymond Queneau and Gabriel García Márquez, Ben Jelloun 'levels' narrative [Erickson's term]: he deprives the master discourse (Western, linear, realistic mode of narration) of its value and privileged position and makes this form of narration one amongst many possible discourses. Time and space collapse, gender distinctions are blurred over and over, characters

175 Erickson, 'Metoikoi and Magical Realism', 427.
176 Erickson, 'Magical Realism and Nomadic Writing', 250.

and objects are thus destabilized and become tainted with surreality. The narrative levels interpenetrate one another (is Fatuma really Ahmed/Zahra, her avatar or a symbol of all Moroccan women?) to a level that causes nothing but indeterminacy. North African narratives such as Ben Jelloun's and Abdelkebir Khatibi's are remarkably close to 'postcolonial discourses from other non-Western cultures in Africa and other areas of the world'.[177] In the narrative universe of Ben Jelloun the coexistence of fantasy and reality mark 'his special brand of magical realism and, more generally, the alternative postcolonial discourse of the "non-Greeks", the *metoikos*, the *métèques*'.[178]

Erickson devotes a portion of his 1995 article to an analysis of chapters 17 and 18, narrated by the blind troubadour, to elucidate the narrative complexities of the novel. The blind troubadour operates on multiple levels:

> a fictional replication of the historical author Jorge Luis Borges, he functions as one of the second-level (intradiegetic) narrators and is in that role a character in the tale of the first-level (extradiegetic) narrator; he functions also on various metadiegetic levels in his direct interactions with the character of the mysterious woman visitor. [...] The dream related in chapter 18 leaves us to speculate that the BT [sic] also may be dreamt by another, by Zahra, the character of another storyteller, and that he might consequently inhabit a still more remote level – a meta-meta-metadiegetic level![179]

This interpenetration of narrative levels, according to Erickson, is a distancing mechanism adopted by Ben Jelloun and his fellow Maghrebian writers as a 'protective covering that allows them to lead their own existence equidistant from sameness (assimilation) and otherness (alienation), to exist in the face of the power play of Western culture as well as traditional Islamic culture'.[180]

In an effort to rewrite the language of the colonizer, Erickson concludes, both Khatibi and Ben Jelloun efface all metanarratives: they start anew, replacing pseudo-African (neocolonialist) discourses with an African discourse. The magical realism of *The Sand Child* is one form of narrative

177 Erickson, 'Metoikoi and Magical Realism', 428.

178 Ibid., 444.

179 Ibid., 440–1.

180 Ibid., 441.

renewal under the auspices of the larger project of creating a counterliterature that does not follow Western imperatives.

Concluding remarks: Worldliness in literary criticism

The survey of English-language criticism on *The Sand Child* developed in this chapter has shown that critics primarily frame the novel within the discourse of postcoloniality. This seems inevitable, Nasrin Qader argues, because

> the critical and theoretical discourse on African literatures, both within and without the continent, has been dominated by the political, social, or anthropological, rendering texts documents. Even those who admit that the literary is not the same phenomenon as the social, the political, or the cultural have not always managed to escape the pitfalls of appropriating literature for these domains.[181]

In 1992 Abdalaoui argued along similar lines:

> In France (and elsewhere in the West), Moroccan novels are still universally read as sociological documents (the most highly prized being those that deal with the condition of Muslim women). This propensity reinforces ethnocentric views and expectations inherited from the previous century. [...] The criteria that prevail on both sides of the Mediterranean are highly arbitrary: in France, critics argue about whether a text has literary merit; in Morocco, they debate whether to label it 'authentic', whether to admit it into the national cultural canon.[182]

Abdalaoui points towards the major difference between French and Moroccan criticism. My survey of English-language literary criticism shows that, here too, the prevailing tendency is to read Ben Jelloun's novels as related to the social, the political, or the cultural (either seeing literature

181 Nasrin Qader, *Narratives of Catastrophe. Boris Diop, Ben Jelloun, Khatibi* (New York: Fordham University Press, 2009), 1.

182 Abdalaoui, 31.

as document or commentary on those spheres of life). Discussions about the literary merit of Maghrebian literature (common in French-language criticism) are rare. This is because French-language criticism is motivated by different interests: those connected with the consecration of new authors and their admission into the canon of Francophone literature. Also, there seems to be a tendency in the criticism surveyed in this chapter to accept Ben Jelloun's narrative as 'authentically' Moroccan, Maghrebian, African or Francophone (very often an issue with Maghrebian critics). The organizing trope of postcolonial studies presents Ben Jelloun's work as a site of struggle and, even when it acknowledges the narrative complexities, very often sees these as strategies in line with the trope of resistance.

Perhaps it is not so surprising then that Ben Jelloun criticism in English very much functions in parallel to French Ben Jelloun criticism: there is hardly any significant cross-fertilization.[183] French thought does travel across into English-language criticism but it is canonical critics such as Deleuze, Guattari, Derrida, Kristeva or Cixous whose theories are used in conjunction with prominent names of postcolonialism (Fanon, Said, Bhabha) and gender studies (Butler). The only notable exception seems to be Fatima Mernissi's works on the status of women in Islam. As Mernissi is a sociologist by training, her approach chimes with the major currents in postcolonial criticism and gender studies. What does not make the transition is the body of textual interpretations that plays a key part in constituting a French-language reading community.

Ultimately, what emerges quite clearly is that critics arguing for the value of a given literary text simultaneously argue for the value of the particular stance in literary criticism they advocate and for their own

183 The same seems to be true in reverse, perhaps because French-language critics are known to have to date resisted most of postcolonial theory which, as we have seen, is the dominant way in which English-language academics read novels coming from the 'margins'. See Michal Krzykawski, 'Réticences françaises à l'égard des *Postcolonial Studies*: entre le soubresaut républicain et le hoquet francophone', *Romanica Silesiana* 6 (2011), 76–88. It also seems to hold true that is mostly critics from an Anglophone background who promote Transnational French Studies with a specific focus on postcolonial theory.

position as experts in the field. In an environment in which novels such as *The Sand Child* are portrayed as voicing the concerns of the 'Other' (the silenced woman, the writer from a former colony writing against dominating Western discourse), some of the critics also claim to have an ethical duty to write about this 'special' kind of literature:

> As critics, readers and writers, we contribute to the disordering of dominant discourses by recognizing, pointing to and pushing the limits that dominant narratives would impose. We contribute to the remembering of erased and forgotten experiences and voices by pointing to the traces and echoes left by these acts of violence and historical forgetting.[184]

Lezra's claim that literary criticism is a powerful and morally robust exercise conceals two aspects that have emerged quite clearly from the analysis in this chapter: 1) the critical readings are also informed by the wish of the academics to position themselves within the academic field of literary studies; 2) while postcolonial and gender studies were initially established to counteract and subvert dominant ways of reading literature, they have by now themselves become dominant forms of critical discourse. Far from being subversive, postcolonial readings of *The Sand Child* as a site of struggle for gender and national identity are constitutive of a disciplinary system or working consensus when they are performed dozens of times. Even when such studies disagree with one another on a point of interpretation, the extent to which studies published within a reading community agree on the terms of criticism is striking. These terms sharply distinguish one reading community from another. Postcolonial and gender studies have undoubtedly established themselves as dominant approaches in the case of Ben Jelloun's novel; and academics working through this critical lens seem to be largely ignoring contributions that offer a different approach (those that read the novel as a singular instance of storytelling) and which do not fit into their agenda.

An important part of the habitus of practitioners of world literature is *worldliness*, which I understand as openness to the world, its literature

184 Lezra, 102.

and opinions about it. Yet, when it comes to taking account of criticism written in other languages and other countries, much research seems rather parochial. If criticism in French, one of the foremost languages of academic discourse, fails to be registered, then the chances of research written in lesser-known languages being picked up is negligible. The noticeable lack of engagement with other criticism (either written in another language or from a different viewpoint) raises the question whether some critics are not more often interested in promoting their own field of study rather than achieving a multi-faceted understanding of the object of study.

In cases where the scholarship on a particular author has proliferated to an extent where it can scarsely be adequately surveyed, disregarding previous work may be a vital step for a critic establishing his or her own approach. This is the case where W. B. Sebald is concerned, an author whose works have spawned a veritable academic industry. However, the scholarship on Ben Jelloun is not yet so prolific that it cannot be concisely surveyed. Moreover, since Ben Jelloun is a contemporary author who has entered the critical canon it is desirable that knowledge about his work be consolidated. Such consolidation, for instance in a monograph, is an essential step in a process that would carry Ben Jelloun's work into posterity. The Louvre museum is said to remove an artist's work from the contemporary art section upon his or her death and store it for a period of ten years before deciding whether to admit the artist to the pantheon of immortals. In order for Ben Jelloun to enter the pantheon of literary immortals it will be necessary for some consolidation of knowledge about his development and overall cultural significance, an aspect that is so far absent from Ben Jelloun scholarship in English. Such a consensus exists about the pre-eminence of Dario Fo in world theatre, despite doubts about his status as a literary author.

CHAPTER 5

Who is Afraid of Dario Fo? Translation and Adaptation Strategies in English-Language Versions of *Accidental Death of an Anarchist*

> Translations act as a form of intercultural communication, making what is alien to a culture come into contact with what is peculiar to it. [...] Since it is generally the receiving system that initiates the cultural contact, a translator's decisions will be largely determined by the translation and cultural norms prevalent in the target polysystem.[1]

> Translation in general and theatre translation in particular has changed paradigms: it can no longer be assimilated to a mechanism of production of semantic equivalence copied mechanically from the source text. It is rather to be conceived of as an appropriation of one text by another. Translation theory thus follows the general trend of theatre semiotics, reorienting its objectives in the light of a theory of reception.[2]

In the last chapter, I dealt with a specific aspect of cross-cultural reception, academic criticism. The aim of this final chapter is to analyse yet another specific aspect of the reception process: the paratextual and metatextual commentary provided by several agents involved in the production of the English translations and adaptations of one of Dario Fo's best known plays,

1 Marta Mateo, 'Translation Strategies and the Reception of Drama Performances: A Mutual Influence', in Mary Snell-Hornby, Zuzana Jettmarová, and Klaus Kaindl, eds, *Translation as Intercultural Communication* (Amsterdam: John Benjamins, 1997), 99–110. Here 99.

2 Patrice Pavis, 'Problems of Translation for the Stage: Interculturalism and Post-Modern Theatre', in Hanna Scolnicov and Peter Holland, eds, *The Play out of Context: Transferring Plays from Culture to Culture* (Cambridge: Cambridge University Press, 1989), 22–45. Here 41.

Morte accidentale di un anarchico [Accidental Death of an Anarchist]. Concentrating on the visible traces these agents leave within the covers of a book allows me to flesh out the translation and adaptation strategies pertaining to this particular case study, and to link these to the wider politics at work in the transposition of theatre texts and theatrical traditions.

Morte accidentale di un anarchico has been translated into many languages and staged in over fifty countries. The plot is based on a true story: in 1969, a railway worker, Giuseppe Pinelli, was accused of being involved in the bombing of the Piazza Fontana in Milan. During the police questioning, Pinelli fell to his death from a window on the fourth floor, raising the question as to whether he jumped or was pushed. In the play, the central figure called 'Il Matto' – variously translated as 'the Maniac' or 'the Madman' – resorts to playing different roles (a high court judge, a police officer, a bishop) in order to show that the true culprits were the policemen interrogating the anarchist. Thus, Pinelli's case served Fo in his endeavour to attack the manner in which the Italian state reacted to what was perceived to be a real Communist threat: the so-called 'strategy of tension'. In no other West European country did the Communist Party count so many members as it did in Italy after 1945. Following international political events such as Kennedy's election in 1960, the Europe-wide political tensions of 1968 and domestic developments such as the growing power of the unions, closely linked to the left-wing parties, the possibility that the Italian Communist Party might actually achieve power and force the Christian Democratic Party into opposition was thought to be very real. The Italian domestic and foreign secret services therefore decided to resort to a strategy of terrorism in order to prevent this from happening. In the three years from 1969 to 1972, Italy was shaken by several indiscriminate bomb attacks, which were blamed on left-wing terrorist groups, but which were actually carried out by right-wing terrorist groups and secret service agents. Counting on the fact that terror increases the population's desire for security at the expense of their desire for change, the Italian state decided to destabilize the country in order to stabilize it.[3]

3 For a brief overview of the 'strategy of tension' employed during the 1960s and 1970s in Italy, see Martin J. Bull and James Newell, *Italian Politics: Adjustment*

Fo used his political theatre to present the Italian population with counter-information about the events that shaped those years. He pursued this endeavour in several other plays which, however, have not been as successful in English translation as *Morte accidentale di un anarchico*. Six different English translations or adaptations of this particular play were published in the twenty-five years between 1978 and 2003 – as many as of Pirandello's *Six Characters in Search of an Author* over the course of ninety years. There have also been various unpublished translations. In this chapter, I engage with several questions: 1) Where does the need to attempt yet another English-language translation of *Morte accidentale di un anarchico* come from? 2) How present are the agents involved in the translation and adaptation process on a paratextual level? 3) What clues does this case study provide with regard to the cross-cultural transfer of theatrical texts and traditions?

Fo is known to encourage theatre directors and actors alike to adapt and change his texts as they see fit. He insists that the audience is in fact a co-producer and actors are authors in their own right. The authenticity of the dramatic experience, he suggests, is more important than authenticity intended as faithfulness to the source text. In what way, then, has Fo's permission to freely adapt his texts influenced the English-language versions of his play? As Jennifer Lorch points out, Fo is 'quite relaxed about his relationship with his text but not so relaxed as to have no attachment to his work'.[4] What I am interested in here is how Fo's permission to freely adapt his texts has influenced the English-language translations and adaptations of *Accidental Death of an Anarchist*.

As we have seen in Chapter 1, there is no consensus on what exactly distinguishes a translation from an adaptation, which is usually defined quite broadly: 'Adaptation may be understood as a set of translative interventions which result in a text that is not generally accepted as a translation

under Duress (Cambridge and Malden, MA: Polity, 2005), 101–4. On strategies of counter-information such as the ones adopted by Dario Fo, see Aldo Giannuli, *Bombe a inchiostro* (Milan: BUR Rizzoli, 2008).

4 Jennifer Lorch, '*Morte Accidentale* in English', in Joseph Farrell and Antonio Scuderi, eds, *Dario Fo. Stage, Text, and Tradition* (Carbondale and Edwardsville: Southern Illinois University Press, 2000), 143–60. Here 144.

but is nevertheless recognized as representing a source text'.[5] In this chapter, I make do with the appellations the published texts are given: three are called translations, three are called adaptations. I use the umbrella term 'version' to subsume both translations and adaptations.

How, if at all, do the agents involved in the production of the various English-language versions engage with the freedom accorded to them? Deciding to publish a theatrical text automatically means giving the text a fixity that was never intended, as Stuart Hood points out: 'What one must recognize is that by editing and printing the version of the text as it stands today one is fixing, as an entomologist fixes a butterfly or moth, a theatrical event which ought not to be subject to closure of this kind'.[6]

The many faces of Dario Fo

Dario Fo was born in 1926 in Sangiano on the shores of Lago Maggiore in Northern Italy. Having been called up to military service in 1944, he deserted and joined the Resistance. After the Second World War had ended, Fo studied architecture in Milan but was soon strongly attracted to the theatre world. His talent first emerged in radio sketches entitled *Poer Nano* [Poor Dwarf] in the early 1950s. In 1953, Fo's review *Il dito nell'occhio* [A finger in the eye] was put on at the Piccolo Theatre in Milan. In 1954, Fo married Franca Rame who came from a family with a long acting tradition. Rame became Fo's most faithful collaborator, acting alongside him, editing his plays and other writings, and at all times critically engaging with, explaining and defending their theatrical practices.

5 Georges L. Bastin, 'Adaptation', in Mona Baker and Gabriela Saldanha, eds, *Routledge Encyclopedia of Translation Studies* (London: Routledge, 2009), 5–8. Here 5.

6 Stuart Hood, 'Open Texts: Some Problems in the Editing and Translating of Dario Fo's Plays', in Christopher Cairns, ed., *The Commedia Dell'Arte from the Renaissance to Dario Fo* (Lewinston, NY: Mellen, 1989), 336–52. Here 348–9.

From the mid-1950s until the end of the 1960s, Fo and Rame put on their plays in established commercial theatres across Italy and were also invited to host the popular TV show *Canzonissima*, which combined music with sketches. However, the strict censorship of many of their sketches led Fo and Rame to abandon scripted television shows. They also became increasingly disillusioned with commercial theatre and decided, in 1968, to create a new theatre company on a cooperative basis, called *Nuova Scena* [New Scene]. The aim was to reach a different audience, that of the working class. Fo and Rame therefore started performing in factories, public squares, tents, workers' clubs and the *case del popolo* [Communist Party centres].

In 1970, Fo and Rame finally broke with the Communist Party (they were never active members) and established another theatre initiative, *La Comune* [The Commune]. The premiere of *Morte accidentale di un anarchico* was staged in a warehouse in Via Capannone in Milan in December 1970. Between 1970 and 1981, Fo put on many political plays besides *Morte accidentale*, such as *Pum Pum! Chi è? La polizia!* [Knock Knock! Who's There? Police!, 1972], *Non si paga, non si paga!* [We can't pay! We won't pay, 1974], *Il Fanfani rapito* [Fanfani abducted, 1975] and *Clacson, trombette e pernacchie* [Trumpets and Raspberries, 1981]. Fo calls this type of theatre 'un teatro da bruciare' [throw-away theatre]. Yet it is his political theatre, with perhaps the exception of *Mistero Buffo* [The Comic Mysteries] (1968), which has travelled across languages and cultures most successfully, despite being steeped in a particular situation pertinent to Italian political and social history.

The 1980s and early 1990s saw several successful plays staged in Italy, amongst which notably *Coppia aperta – quasi spalancata* [The Open Couple, 1984] and *Johan Padan a la descoverta de le Americhe* [Johan Padan and the Discovery of the Americas, 1992], as well as some theoretical works on theatre practices. Fo also stage designed and directed operas, including Rossini's works *The Barber of Seville* (1987) and *The Italian Woman in Algiers* (1994). In 1995, Fo suffered a stroke from which he recovered nearly completely; he returned to the stage and to writing soon afterwards.

Fo seems to have been taken by surprise by the award of the Nobel Prize for Literature in 1997. The award also stunned many Italian intellectuals who did not see Fo as a primarily literary figure. Several critics, including

Umberto Eco and Giulio Ferroni, discussed the meaning of the awarding of the prize to somebody who was generally perceived to be a great actor but not necessarily a great author in a variety of newspapers, from *Liberazione* via *La Stampa* to *La Repubblica*. The most negative reaction came from the Vatican's paper, *L'Osservatore Romano*, which wrote that 'Fo is the sixth Nobel from Italy after Carducci, Deledda, Pirandello, Quasimodo, [and] Montale. After these sages, a clown'.[7]

Fo's functions do indeed multiply: not only does he direct and star in the plays he writes, he also composes songs and works as a visual artist. Is he an actor who also writes or an author who also acts? Fo plays on this uncertainty in *Fabulazzo*: 'Authors refuse to accept me as an author and actors refuse to accept me as an actor. Authors say I am an actor trying to be an author, while actors say I am an author trying to be an actor. Nobody wants me in their camp. Only the set designers tolerate me'.[8] Translators and adaptors of Fo's texts are confronted with a figure that often seems to be larger than life. Yet, as the Nobel Prize Committee stated:

> One cannot hold it against Fo that he is a first-rate actor. The decisive thing is that he has written plays which arouse the enthusiasm of actors and which captivate his audiences. The texts are chiselled in an interplay with the spectators and have often been given their final shape over a long time. Rapidly changing situations give impetus to the plays and shape the characters. The rhythm of the actors' lines, the witty wording and the aptitude for improvisation combine with strong intensity and artistic energy in the profoundly meaningful, steady flow of his flashes of wit. The printed texts can also give you this feeling if you give free range to your imagination. Fo's work brings to the fore the multifarious abundance of the literary field.[9]

Fo has continued to write plays since the Nobel Prize, bringing his total theatrical œuvre to over seventy plays. Two plays have

7 Quoted in Ron Jenkins, *Dario Fo and Franca Rame. Artful Laughter* (New York: Aperture, 2001), 194.

8 Dario Fo, *Fabulazzo*, ed. Lorenzo Ruggiero and Walter Valeri (Milan: Kaos, 1992), 21. English translation by Antonio Scuderi. See Walter Valeri, 'An Actor's Theatre', in Farrell and Scuderi, eds, *Dario Fo. Stage, Text and Tradition*, 19–29. Here 19.

9 'Presentation by Sture Allén', reprinted in *Nobel Lectures: Literature. 1996–2000* (Stockholm: Nobel Foundation, 2002), 17–21. Here 18.

been particularly successful with the audience and critics alike: *L'anomalo bicefalo* [The Two-Headed Anomaly, 2003], a scornful satire of then prime minister Silvio Berlusconi and *Lu santo jullàre Françesco* [The Holy Jester Francis, 1999] in which Fo presents his interpretation of Saint Francis as a representative of the *giullare* tradition.

The most central figure in Fo's theatre is a re-elaboration of the medieval Italian fool figure called *giullare*. The term is often misleadingly translated into English as *jester*, yet a jester is first and foremost connected to the court and aristocracy. The Italian *giullare*, however, is a travelling solo performer who entertains the people on public squares, in the street and on market places. Not only the bearer of news, he also publicly criticizes the social injustice he sees around him and, in his role of a fool and outsider, usually gets away with speaking the truth.[10] Fo uses the device of the fool speaking the truth both in *Mistero buffo*, his first and most famous *giullarata* [fool play], and in *Morte accidentale di un anarchico*. The Maniac/Madman is a modern *giullare* who bears a medical certificate which attests to his insanity. He is the only character with a fool's licence and therefore the only one who can get at the truth without being seriously harmed.

In its presentation speech, the Nobel Prize Committee highlights exactly these two pieces of writing (*Mistero Buffo* and *Accidental Death*) centred around the figure of the *giullare*. Sture Allén said the following about *Accidental Death*:

> The play is about the cross-examining following on the supposed accident. By and by the questioning is taken over, through a brilliantly carried out shift, by a Hamlet-like figure – il Matto – who has the kind of madness that exposes official falsehoods. All in all there are many topical allusions in Fo's plays, but the texts transcend everyday situations and are given a far wider range of application.[11]

Despite referring to a specific event in Italian history and despite being an example of Fo's 'throwaway theatre', *Accidental Death of an Anarchist* struck

10 For a detailed account of Fo's lifelong engagement with the carnival tradition and the figure of the fool, see Antonio Scuderi, *Dario Fo: Framing, Festival, and the Folkloric Imagination* (Lanham, MD: Lexington Books, 2011).

11 'Presentation by Sturé Allen', 18.

a chord with many theatre-makers in Europe and elsewhere. Translators and theatre-makers all over the world were attracted to the play for various reasons: the political character of the play, the brilliant protagonist that is the 'Matto' figure or Fo's distinct brand of humour that merges popular forms of farce with the political and social concerns of modern life. Amongst the first European countries to stage *Accidental Death* were Denmark, Norway, Sweden, Germany and Austria, countries that had a strong tradition of staging a certain kind of political theatre (associated with authors such as Brecht and Mayakovsky).[12] In the English-speaking world, the term 'political theatre' has quite different connotations, which, as we shall see, in turn influenced the reading(s) of Fo's work. The transposing of the play into the British or American context poses particular problems which will be at the centre of my investigation.

Issues of translation

Perhaps one of the most difficult facts about Dario Fo to transmit to a non-Italian audience is that he is revolutionary and radical where politics are concerned, yet 'an intransigent conservative in poetics', that is to say, deeply steeped in the tradition of Italian popular theatre.[13] Also, as we have seen, Fo is not simply a playwright and an actor: 'Continuing the Italian

12 The Fiol Teater in Copenhagen was the first to stage a translated version of the play in their 1972/73 season, followed by Trondelag Teater (Trondheim, Norway) in 1975/76. Towards the end of the 1970s, more countries followed: Sweden (Narren Teatern in Stockholm, 1978/79), Germany (several theatres) and Austria (with nearly 490 shows over two seasons from 1978 to 1980 at the Ensemble Theater in Vienna). The first staging in France happened in 1979. For a preliminary list of foreign stagings of *Accidental Death* and other plays, see 'Gli spettacoli di Dario Fo e Franca Rame nel mondo' <http://www.archivio.francarame.it/estero.aspx> accessed 26 January 2015.

13 Joseph Farrell and Antonio Scuderi, 'Introduction: The Poetics of Dario Fo', in Farrell and Scuderi, eds, *Dario Fo. Stage, Text, and Tradition*, 1–19. Here 19.

tradition of an actor-dominated theatre, in which actors applied themselves to all aspects of their trade, he directs, designs sets and costumes, and choreographs his own productions'.[14] Fo's theatre is didactic without being cathartic: it is intended to make the audience reflect on serious political and societal issues while being entertaining at the same time. It is didactic not in the sense of pedantry but sees its function as that of counter-information stimulating thought processes in the audience. Fo does not want to create a liberating emotional release in his audience; he wants his audience to leave the theatre with anger still inside them which can be carried forward into their socio-political struggle.[15]

This double bind poses a problem for translators and adaptors who find themselves struggling with the task of merging Fo's particular brand of humour that refers back to a typically Italian tradition of popular theatre with the political fervour of the plot. As so many of Fo's other plays, *Morte accidentale di un anarchico* refers to a specific historical event that requires a considerable amount of background knowledge. Should translators and adaptors attempt to communicate this context to a non-Italian audience or reading public and if yes, how to do so without overburdening them?

What further complicates the issue is the way in which the written versions of Fo's texts are achieved. There is no such thing as a single source text, a scripted play that a translator could refer back to. While this is certainly the case with many plays, Fo's case is particularly complex. He starts off with a rough copy of a play which he constantly changes during rehearsals. In the case of *Morte Accidentale*, Fo was still changing lines and scenes while on tour from 1970 to 1972 to keep up with developments in

14 Scuderi, *Framing*, 1.

15 'Noi non vogliamo liberare nella indignazione – lo diciamo alla fine – la gente che viene. Noi vogliamo che la rabbia stia dentro, resti dentro e non si liberi, che diventi operante, che faccia diventare razionante il momento in cui ci troviamo, e portarlo nella lotta'. [We always say at the end that we do not want to liberate our audience into indignation. We want the anger to stay inside, stay inside unable to free itself, so that it will become effective, so that it may develop into a partaking in the moment in which we find ourselves, and carry on over into the fight.] Dario Fo, *Compagni Senza Censura*, vol. 2 (Milan: Collettivo Teatrale La Comune, 1973), 189.

the trial of policemen involved in the Pinelli affair happening at that very moment. After each performance, Fo discusses the play with his audience in what he calls 'third acts'. Along with the introductory monologue that he provides before the play (lasting about fifteen to twenty minutes), these third acts are important features of a Fo performance that never make it into the written versions of his texts in their entirety. Fo is known to have rewritten parts of his playtexts after such exchanges with his audience. In theatrical circles, a playtext refers to the finished blueprint of the final presentation. I consciously use this term to point towards the draft-like nature of Fo's 'originals'.

Fo is not interested in the theatrical text as a *primarily* written document: 'Fo's scripts are not elaborate literary or verbal constructs but texts at the service of performance'.[16] The existing published Italian versions of *Morte Accidentale* have been collated from a variety of sources; and the Italian text acknowledges Fo's late wife, Franca Rame, as the editor of the play. Not surprisingly, in a familiar move which aims to assign a 'unique voice' to literary works, not one of the English translations mentions Rame's involvement, and this despite the immense influence she has had on all of Fo's work.

> Her influence in the shaping and modifying of their theatre had always been considerable and [...] received more generous notice on the covers of the printed version. It could be said that if the plays began as his, they ended as hers. [...] She intervenes substantially from the beginning of rehearsals. It is also she who administers the companies and prepares the changing versions of the script into something that could be distributed to the company and later delivered for publication.[17]

Also, any translator has to refer to one of the three editions of the text available in Italian: the 1970 version published by Bertani Editore, the 1973 edition published by Mazzotta Editore and the 1974 version published by Einaudi (reissued in 1976, 1988, 2000, 2004 and 2007).

16 Farrell and Scuderi, 'Poetics of Dario Fo', 13.

17 Ibid., 7.

The three Italian editions present the reader with two different versions of Fo's drama. The first resorts to a framing device, setting the story in 1921 in New York, where another anarchist, Andrea Salsedo, fell out of a window during police questioning. This framing device is dropped in the second version. The main difference between the two texts is the ending. The first ends with an explosion and prolonged screaming which the audience witnesses in complete darkness. Shortly afterwards, the actor playing the 'Matto' reappears on stage as the true judge come to conduct the enquiry (this is the ending used in the latest 2004 and 2007 Einaudi editions). The second text ends with a socialist critique of society, namely with the words, uttered by the 'Matto': 'Siamo nello sterco fino al collo, è vero, ed è proprio per questo che camminiamo a testa alta' [It's true – we're in the shit up to our necks, and that's precisely the reason why we walk with our heads held high].[18]

Yet another matter to consider is the practice of translating plays for the theatre. In the Western tradition, there are two dominant ways of translating for the theatre: there is a stage-oriented tradition which concerns itself with a specific staging at a particular time in history aimed at a specific audience and there is a reader-oriented tradition, mainly concerned with philological exactness and literary values.[19] The first tradition produces performance or theatre texts while the second tradition produces so-called drama texts. A drama text is supposed to be mainly read – the German term *Buchdrama* [book drama] and the French *théâtre dans un fauteuil* [armchair theatre] are telling in this regard – while a theatre text is supposed to be mainly performed. Most of the published English versions of Fo's play are theatre texts based on the final blueprints of the English-language

18 Translation from Ed Emery in Fo, *Plays: 1*, ed. Stuart Hood, trans. Ed Emery, et al., Methuen Drama (London: Methuen, 2006), 206.

19 See Manuela Perteghella, 'A Descriptive-Anthropological Model of Theatre Translation', in Sabine Coelsch-Foisner and Holger Klein, eds, *Drama Translation and Theatre Practice* (Berne: Peter Lang, 2004), 1–23. On the two traditions, see 6. On non-Western translation traditions, see Eva Hung and Judy Wakabayashi, eds, *Asian Translation Traditions* (Manchester: St. Jerome Publishing, 2005).

production (playtexts); only one is a drama text (not written with a specific staging in mind).

Joseph Farrell points out that Fo himself draws a distinction between 'theatre' and 'dramatic literature':

> He consigned Pier Paolo Pasolini to the domain of 'dramatic literature' on the grounds that he had no feeling for the rhythms of theatre, no sense of dramatic tension, no understanding of the primacy of the actor, no grasp of the demands of immediate communication with an audience in real time. If all theatrical texts occupy an indeterminate, intermediate space between literature and performance, not all lie on the same meridian between those two poles. Fo's preference is for those plays that incline towards performance and away from literature, as his own do. Put differently, Fo's scripts have much in common with the canovaccio of commedia dell'arte: they are, of course, more than outline plots intended as a prompt for improvisation, but they are less than the finished, polished scripts produced by such other Nobel Prize-winning dramatists as Bernard Shaw or Eugene O'Neill.[20]

How is a translation of a theatre text produced in the English-speaking world? A theatre company commissions what they call a 'literal' translation from a translator (who is not necessarily mentioned in the programme or, indeed, decently remunerated for his or her efforts). Then the company hires an adaptor: this may be the director or the principal actor, or the adaptation may be a collaborative work. An adaptor then changes the text in order to make it more audience-oriented; he or she makes the text work for the particular show that is being set up. In the case of Fo, some adaptors do not speak Italian and are therefore unable to check the translated text they are given against the source text or to refer back to the source text at all. The practice of commissioning translations done by a famous, usually monolingual playwright is accepted in the UK but it is frowned upon in other countries, such as France. Lately, the situation in the UK seems to be changing as well: the international project 'Channels', initiated by the National Theatre Studio in London, sponsors the collaboration of

20 Joseph Farrell, 'Variations on a Theme: Respecting Dario Fo', *Modern Drama*, 41/1 (1998), 19–29. Here 22.

author, translator and adaptor.[21] The English version of *Habitats*, staged by the Gate Theatre in London in 2002, for example, was written during a residency sponsored by 'Channels' that allowed the French playwright Philippe Minyana, the translator Christopher Campbell and the translator-playwright Steve Waters to collaborate on the project. Here, as in more traditional practices of adaptation that do not involve an input from the author of the source text, the assumption seems to be that a literary translator working on the literal translation does not know enough about theatre practices to make the text work *as a theatre text* in the first place.

In the case of *Morte accidentale di un anarchico* in English translation, we have a proliferation of agents involved, starting with the author, Dario Fo, who constantly changes his texts and his wife, Franca Rame, who collates all the different existing versions into another, publishable, version that is printed as the 'original' Italian drama text. This text is then translated 'literally' into English by an (often unnamed) translator; this literal translation is subsequently adapted by one or more people into a theatre text. If the play is successful enough, the theatre text is then fixed again in a published version. The UK theatre publisher Methuen has published four of the six available printed versions of Fo's play in English. Their interest in the playwright and their policy of translation have fundamentally shaped the reception of Fo's works in the British literary and theatrical polysystems.[22]

Before I move on to the editing voices in the various translations' paratextual corpus, that is to say the voices we hear in the prefaces, introductions, footnotes, and commentary of a metatextual nature strewn here

21 See Phyllis Zatin, *Theatrical Translation and Film Adaptation: A Practitioner's View* (Clevedon: Multilingual Matters, 2005), 60–1. On the Channels project, also see Perteghella, 'Descriptive-Anthropological Model of Theatre Translation', 17.

22 'An example of a culture where the contemporary theatrical system exercises some influence over the publication of drama is provided by contemporary England, where the most important publisher of drama, Methuen, prefers 'stage' to 'page' translations, that is, translations where the focus is on the expectations of the receiving stage rather than on the careful repetition of the details of the source text'. Sirkku Aaltonen, *Time-Sharing on Stage: Drama Translation in Theatre and Society* (Clevedon and Buffalo, NY: Multilingual Matters, 2000), 39.

and there in the playtexts proper, let us have a closer look at the translation history of *Morte accidentale di un anarchico* into English.

Translating and adapting *Morte accidentale di un anarchico* into English

There are six published translations of the text available in English, four of which published in the Methuen Modern Drama series and two published in the United States. In chronological order, these are:

- Gavin Richards's 1979 adaptation based on Gillian Hanna's literal translation, first published by Pluto Press and then by Methuen;
- Susan Cowan's translation for the periodical *Theater* in 1979;
- Richard Nelson's 1983 adaptation of Cowan's translation, published by Samuel French Inc.;
- Alan Cumming and Tim Supple's 1991 adaptation for the National Theatre, published by Methuen;
- Ed Emery's translation (not written with an immediate staging in mind), published in a 1992 Methuen collection of plays by Dario Fo; and
- Simon Nye's 2003 translation for the National Theatre, published by Methuen in two versions: the playtext with no commentary and a student edition with over sixty pages of commentary.

In the following sections, I will focus on the paratextual corpus and on comments of a metatextual nature in five of the six versions, leaving aside Suzanne Cowan's translation for *Theater*, as it never was widely available to readers outside academic and theatre circles. Cowan's translation is mainly based on the 1973 Mazzotta edition, but she also consulted the other two published versions. The translation is preceded by a short introductory essay on Fo's life and significance in Italian theatre, the background of the play and a short discussion of the main features of the play. This essay also incorporates five still photographs of Fo during a performance as examples of his particular facial expressions and body language.[23] Viewing the pictures in Cowan's essay recalls Stuart Hood's image of the entomologist fixing the moth. I am also not including in my analysis any versions that did not result in a published text, such as Robyn Archer's adaptation of the 1991 UK text for an Australian audience or the translation used by Luca Giberti for his 2005 staging at the Oxford Playhouse.[24]

The published versions of any Fo translations and adaptations need to satisfy a variety of 'clients' who read the text with different sets of expectations. The play has made it onto a variety of syllabuses in quite diverse college courses: whether in Italian studies, theatre studies, world literature, comparative literature, or cultural studies. In the autumn of 2010, for example, NYU in Florence offered a course entitled 'Italy since 1815' which features Fo's *Accidental Death of an Anarchist* (no particular translation/adaptation specified) alongside Paul Ginsborg's history of Italy and his book on Silvio Berlusconi, Tomasi di Lampedusa's *The Leopard*, a biography of Mussolini and Vittorio de Sica's 1948 film *The Bicycle Thief*.[25] Reading Fo's text in this context is clearly different from reading it with a view of a possible staging, alongside other examples of political theatre or for a paper on theatrical practices. In what versions, if at all, does the paratextual corpus take into consideration the diversity of the readership?

23 Suzanne Cowan, 'Dario Fo, Politics and Satire: An Introduction to *Accidental Death of an Anarchist*', in *Theater*, 10/2 (Spring 1979), 6–11. Dario Fo, *Accidental Death of an Anarchist*, trans. Suzanne Cowan, in *Theater*, 10/2 (Spring 1979), 12–46.

24 Textual strategies adapted by Archer are described in Tim Fitzpatrick and Ksenia Sawczak, 'Accidental Death of a Translator: The Difficult Case of Dario Fo', *About Performance: Translation and Performance. Working Papers*, 1 (1995), 15–34. On Giberti's staging see Rosie Hetherington , 'Review: *Accidental Death of an Anarchist* at the Oxford Playhouse' <http://www.bbc.co.uk/oxford/stage/2005/02/accidental_death_of_an_anarchist_review.shtml> accessed 22 February 2015.

25 See 'Italy since 1815' course programme <http://www.nyu.edu/content/dam/nyu/globalPrgms/documents/florence/academics/syllabi/V57.9168_V42.9163_V59.9868_Travis.pdf> accessed 22 February 2015.

There seems to be a general consensus amongst British theatre makers that there are particular obstacles to be overcome in a theatre production based on translation, especially translations coming from 'the South'. Stefania Taviano argues that these perceived obstacles (high emotionality, stronger folk tradition, more diversified local customs and dialects) are not so much innate to Italian theatre, but rather exaggerated by a general British attitude towards the Mediterranean, in particular Italy: the British are drawn towards the 'cradle of civilization' but at the same time tend to establish their cultural superiority over the chaotic Mediterraneans.[26] There are two ways of dealing with these obstacles, and both are visible in the translation choices adopted towards *Morte accidentale*: either one adheres to a stereotypical image of Italian culture, thus reducing characters to caricatures or one transfers the plot to a British milieu, the assumption being that domestication is what the audience wants (or the only translation strategy the audience can cope with). However, this domestication results in heavily adapted translations. Perhaps as a reaction to this practice of heavy adaptations, in a reversal, 'critical discourse surrounding British productions of Italian theatre continues to be characterized by a normative approach built around concepts such as faithfulness, authenticity and truthfulness to the original'.[27] This critical discourse often happens on the paratextual and metatextual levels surrounding a printed playtext, which therefore merit closer analysis.

26 Stefania Taviano, 'British Acculturation of Italian Theatre', in Andrew Chesterman, Natividad Gallardo San Salvador, and Yves Gambier, eds, *Translation in Context: Selected Papers from the EST Congress, Granada 1998* (John Benjamins, 2000), 339–50. Here 340.

27 Ibid.

Gavin Richards

Gavin Richards's adaptation of Gillian Hanna's translation was commissioned by Belt & Braces Roadshow Company in 1978. In January 1979, the premiere at Dartington College saw Fred Molina in the role of the Maniac. After initial success, the production moved to London, first to the Half Moon Theatre, then to Wyndhams Theatre where Richards took over the main role as well as continuing his position as director. Pluto Press first published the English playtext in 1980; a corrected edition appeared as part of the Methuen Modern Drama series in 1987. The 1987 text was republished in 2001. On the upper right corner on the cover of this latest edition, we find a timeline from the 1930s to 2000. The 1970s are marked by a bold outside border, thus helping the unknowing reader to place the text in time.

The paratext in the Methuen edition is considerable: we have an eight page introduction by Stuart Hood, a five page contribution by Dario Fo exclusively written for the 1980 English text, and a five page postscript by Dario Fo (this is Ed Emery's translation of the postscript of the Italian 1974 text). Except for three footnotes by Emery in the postscript, there are no footnotes to explain specific cultural references. On a paratextual level, the reader is confronted with just two voices, Hood's and Fo's. We do not hear directly from the 'literal' translator Hanna or the adaptor Richards. Thus there is no explanation provided for several of Richards's (some would say debatable) decisions: from where arose the need to add and cut scenes? Why the abundance of stage directions, not to be found in the Italian play? Why name the character of the *commissario sportivo* [casually dressed inspector] Pissani? Do these choices really contribute to the 'performability' of the play? This seems to be one of those cases described by Susan Bassnett when she points out that 'performability' is a concept that is often used 'to excuse the practice of handing over a supposedly literal translation to a monolingual playwright, and [...] to justify substantial variations in the target language text, including cuts and additions'.[28] While Richards's voice is not visible in the paratext, it becomes audible in several metatextual comments strewn within the playtext which I will analyse shortly.

The postscript is a translation of the preface to the Italian 1974 version of the play. It concentrates on the context that led to the Italian production of *Accidental Death of an Anarchist* and describes the changes to the text during Fo and Rame's two-year tour of Italy. As this text was written with an Italian audience in mind, Emery adds three footnotes to explain to English-language readers who Inspector Calabresi is (the real life *commissario sportivo*), who Feltrinelli is (an Italian publisher who was killed in mysterious circumstances), and the location of La Comune's theatre at the time. In the postscript, Fo states that adaptations are always necessary. While on tour with the play, 'the spiral of the [Italian government's – M. D.] strategy of tension has increased, and has created other victims: the play has been brought up to date, and its message has been made more explicit'.[29] Adaptors therefore, Fo advocates, are free to change the playtext *as long as* their aim is to make the message clearer and the didactic function of theatre more effective. This is a crucial condition notionally binding on any translator or adaptor of the playtext.

In the introduction (written in 1986), Stuart Hood provides a short biography of Fo and an overview of his and Rame's theatrical practices. He accords *Accidental Death* half a page, thus focusing mainly on positioning this play within Fo's larger œuvre. Hood's personal view of Fo's importance as a political playwright emerges in the final paragraph:

> Dario Fo and Franca Rame have a world-wide reputation. The Scandinavian countries were among the first to welcome them as performers and to produce their work. The whole of Western Europe has by now acknowledged their importance and virtuosity. Ironically the Berliner Ensemble, the theatre founded by Brecht to whom Fo owes so much, found Fo's rock version of *The Beggar's Opera* too difficult to take in

28 Susan Bassnett, 'Translating for the Theatre: The Case against Performability', *TTR (Traduction, Terminologie, Redaction)*, 4/1 (1991), 99–111. Here 102.

29 Dario Fo, 'Postscript', in *Accidental Death of an Anarchist*, adapt. Gavin Richards (London: Methuen, 2001), 76–80. Here 79.

> spite of Brecht's advice to treat famous authors with disrespect if you have the least consideration for the ideas they express.[30]

Hood's self-effacement in the introduction leaves room for a more critical voice, Dario Fo's own, in the 'Author's Note'. The note serves several purposes. First, Fo defines his play as a 'farce of power'. Second, the note justifies the need for three different Italian editions published within a short time frame. Finally, in the note Fo points out the difference between the Italian and English audiences:

> The English public, seeing this play in its present adaptation, obviously cannot feel the real, tragic, tangible atmosphere which the Italian public brought with them when they came to the performance. It can share this only by the act of imagination or – better still – by substituting for the violence practised by the powers in Italy (the police, the judiciary, the economy of the banks and the multinationals) equally tragic and brutal facts from the recent history in England.[31]

Dario Fo is an advocate of freedom for translators and adaptors in their work, and has himself freely adapted Brecht's work. Yet he is critical of Richards's adaptation for quite specific reasons:

> I have the impression – more than an impression – that some passages which have been skipped in Gavin Richards's version may have produced some erosion at a satirical level, that is to say in the relationship of the tragic to the grotesque, which was the foundation of the original work, in favour of solutions which are exclusively comic.[32]

Satire is part of Fo's didactic theatre; simple slapstick comedy is not. Actually, Fo had to be restrained when he saw Richards's production in London for the first time. Although he hardly speaks English, he could see that the didactic qualities of his theatre had been neglected in favour of slapstick comedy and stereotypical representation of Italians. Farrell notes that '[s]everal people tried to explain to him the differences between British and Italian traditions of comic writing and performance, attempting to placate

30 Stuart Hood, 'Introduction', in Fo, *Accidental Death* [Richards] vii–xiv. Here xiv.
31 Fo, 'Author's Note', *Accidental Death* [Richards], xvi–xvii.
32 Ibid., xvi–xvii.

him – for he needed placating – by talking of the vibrancy of a music hall tradition which had provided the inspiration of the British production.' But Farrell is not simply trying to excuse Fo's behaviour as he then asks a very valid question: 'Was Fo, of all authors, entitled to his annoyance?'[33] While Fo is advocating the adaptor's freedom in theory, in this particular instance he was quite clear in stating that Richards's adaptation had lost in translation.

Fo is not alone in this judgment; several theatre and literary scholars with knowledge of Italian agree that by opting for entertainment the Richards version has left the defining didactic and satirical elements in Fo's theatre out of the equation. As early as in 1986, Tony Mitchell argues that 'Richards's adaptation and the style of his direction of the piece [...] severely distorted the meaning and intention of the original, cutting it extensively and adding speeches and stage business which often went completely against the grain of Fo's play'. Similarly, Stefania Taviano argues that 'Fo's revolutionary theatre is reduced to theatre with a political content [...]. Taken out of its Italian context, the political content of Fo's theatre can be maintained, while its function and efficacy tend to be altered. Thus the theatrical quality of Fo's plays is given priority over its political role'. In her 2007 comparative article on the comic voice in the original Italian and Richards's version, Brigid Maher also argues that the changes made by the adaptor result in a change of the protagonist's character. As a result, the play's brand of humour and its message are altered.[34]

Tellingly, Fo ends his 'Author's Note' with a popular Sicilian song from the nineteenth century in which a madman laughing at a king escapes punishment because the people know 'it is great bad luck to kill a madman protected as they are by the pity of St Francis "the great madman of God"'. Fo introduces the song with the following words: 'We [in Italy – M. D.] are

33 See Farrell, 'Variations', 24.

34 Tony Mitchell, *Dario Fo. People's Court Jester* (London: Methuen Theatrefiles, 1986), 98–9. Stefania Taviano, 'Translating Political Theatre: The Case of Dario Fo and Franca Rame', in Sabine Coelsch-Foisner and Holger Klein, eds, *Drama Translation and Theatre Practice* (Berne: Peter Lang, 2004), 325–40. Here 328–9. Brigid Maher, 'The Comic Voice in Translation: Dario Fo's *Accidental Death of an Anarchist*, *Journal of Intercultural Studies*, 24/8 (2007), 367–79.

not yet a sufficiently modern nation to have forgotten the ancient feeling for satire. That is why we can still laugh, with a degree of cynicism, at the macabre dance which power and the civilization that goes with it performs daily, without waiting for carnival'.[35] Fo suggests that, historically, the popular understanding of social hierarchies and the handling of satire in Italy are radically different to those in other European countries. The link between the Maniac and the marginalized figure of the *giullare*, 'a *fool*, with that special brand of madness that allows him to speak the truth and criticize others, even his betters' is deliberate.[36] To summarize, the 'Author's Note' defines the play in terms of genre (political farce) that belongs to both the specific tradition of Italian satire and to a more universal tradition of carnival figures who possess jester's licence. Fo charges the Richards version with being less effective both didactically and satirically than its Italian original. Yet, he is willing to accept that this might not be exclusively the adaptor's fault but due to fundamental differences in theatre practices and political cultures.

The paratextual apparatus aims to provide readers with as much contextual information as possible about the author, authorial intention and the history of the play itself. It is quite strange, then, to see that the playtext proper in the Richards version not only provides very little context but also sometimes sharply contradicts the aims expressed in the paratext. In my view, there are two metatextual moments in particular that reveal a certain degree of uneasiness on the part of the adaptor regarding the freedom accorded by Fo.

Right at the start of the play, in an added scene, inspector Bertozzo introduces himself to the audience as 'Francesco Giovanni Batista Giancarlo Bertozzo of the Security Police' and informs them that he has been struggling to do his daily work because of the public outrage following a 'sordid little incident a few weeks ago when an anarchist, under interrogation in a similar room a few floors above, fell through the window'.[37] Then, before he starts questioning the Maniac – which is how the Italian play starts – he

35 Fo, 'Author's Note' [Richards], xviii.

36 Scuderi, *Framing*, 6.

37 Fo, *Accidental Death* [Richards], 1.

directs these words at the audience: 'I ought to warn you that the author of this sick little play, Dario Fo, has the traditional, irrational hatred of the police common to all narrow-minded left-wingers and so I shall, no doubt, be the unwilling butt of endless anti-authoritarian jibes'.[38]

Belt & Braces was known in the UK as a left-wing theatre. Ideally, the audience would interpret the first dig at Fo as tongue-in-cheek or as irony in line with Fo's permission to freely adapt his texts. Yet, the words 'sick little play' and 'traditional, irrational hatred' may also be understood as markers of distance: are the adaptor and actors perhaps distancing themselves from some of the political messages contained in the play? Ultimately, Richards seems to be undermining the didactic function of Fo's theatre for a single laugh from his audience.

In my view, this first scene twists another of Fo's intentions, that of portraying the Italian police as he perceived it to be: violent, unpredictable, and corrupt. The first few scenes of the play in Italian are ambiguous: it is not yet clear who will triumph over whom, who will be the butt of the joke in the end. Richards does not leave any doubt about who is going to be ridiculed all along. This is unfortunate because, as Tony Mitchell points out:

> It is important to stress that the police characters [...] are no mere caricatures or stereotypes – a factor which makes many foreign productions of the play inaccurate. Although Fo makes them the butts of comedy and farce, this is inherent in the inconsistencies of their statements and behaviours, which is in fact that of devious, dangerous types who show the abuses of power the police exerted in brazenly cracking down on the Italian left, frequently without a shred of evidence, often resorting to wildly trumped-up accusations.[39]

By presenting the audience with the 'right' interpretation of the role assigned to the policemen in the play, Richards flattens out some of the deliberate ambiguity.

Towards the end of the play, there is a further metatextual moment: the Maniac uses as examples Anthony Blunt and Guy Burgess, clearly English references, at which point the 'Superintendent' addresses the

38 Ibid., 2.

39 Mitchell, 62.

actor who is playing the Maniac by name saying: 'This isn't Dario Fo'. The Maniac replies that he knows but that he does not care. There follows a heated exchange:

PISSANI:	This is an unheard of distortion of the author's meaning!
MANIAC:	He'll get his royalties. Who's moaning?
PISSANI:	Get back to the script!
SUPERINTENDENT:	This is an insult to Dario Fo!
FELETTI:	Good. I've got a bone to pick with him. Why is there only one woman's part in his blasted play? I feel marooned!
MANIAC:	The author's sexist?
FELETTI:	He's pre-historic!
BERTOZZO:	Then why are we bothering?
MANIAC:	He's a pre-historic genius! On with the dance![40]

Though reminiscent of techniques such as Brecht's *Verfremdungseffekt* [estrangement effect] and consistent with Fo's anti-illusionistic tendencies, the contrived departure from the script seems to me to actually undermine the didactic function of Fo's theatre. If the gag had stopped at 'This isn't Dario Fo' it might have served its purpose better: reminding the audience that this is an Italian play in translation and that therefore it is not an exact equivalent, that this is not 100 per cent Dario Fo. Even more interestingly perhaps, this metatextual moment expresses Richards's struggle to find a balance between the freedom granted to him by the author who will 'get his royalties' anyhow and the restrictions imposed by cultural conventions regarding the nature of translation. These conventions tend to demand a return to an authorized or original script.

What is the most important aspect of Fo's theatre that Richards wanted to transpose in his adaptation? As Richards's voice is not present on a paratextual level, let me quote briefly from an interview:

> The most important point about the play is that it is what popular theatre is about, not only in Italy but also in this country. What we haven't really succeeded in doing is adapting a popular form successfully for a larger audience without writing something which either condescends to sexism or racism, or which falls back on easy jokes, the

40 Fo, *Accidental Death* [Richards], 68.

> extremely vicious anti-people edges of humour. Fo is an important lesson for us (in left-wing political theatre) because, effortlessly, he destroys the invisible fourth wall and creates live theatre again.[41]

In an effort to transplant Fo's live and popular theatre to British soil, Richards ends up falling back on what he criticizes in popular British theatre: racism (stereotyping Italians must qualify as such), easy jokes and the recurrence to vulgar language (Fo rarely uses cuss words; most English translations and adaptations use them abundantly). Belt & Braces provided information about the Italian context and the political message of the original in the programme where they also referred to similar cases of injustice in the British system. However, with this information relegated to the epitext (the programme in the event of a staging) and the paratext (in the published version), the English playtext proper no longer fulfils the function that *Morte accidentale di un anarchico* had fulfilled in Italy: its satire is less effective, the message is less radical and, overall, the play is less didactic. It is a different kind of funny, as well. No matter how persuasively the paratextual commentary tries to argue for equivalence, translations and adaptations are not about equivalence. Every translation clearly has to move away from the original and create a new text capable of embodying the spirit of the source text in a guise acceptable to the receiving culture. This idea of translation as embodiment is caught exactly by Tagore's use of the metaphor of reincarnation for his work in English.

The Richards adaptation was highly successful – it defined how Fo would be seen in the UK for a very long time. If one only reads the playtext without any of the commentaries in the paratext or any other knowledge of Fo's theatre, the text in itself works. Yet, as we have seen, there are discrepancies between the message of the play proper and the message given to us in the paratext. When publishing an adaptation, perhaps greater care should be taken to bring the text and paratext more in line with one another. The published text would be more coherent if Richards

41 *Time Out*, 16–22 March 1979, 17. Quoted in Mitchell, 99.

had explained his adaptation strategies in a paratextual contribution or if certain discrepancies between the Italian texts and the translation had been explained in footnotes.

Richard Nelson

The first and only version of *Accidental Death* to have appeared in a North American publishing house (Samuel French) in 1987 contains a limited paratextual corpus, none of which can be assigned to a single identifiable individual. The first page provides biographical and bibliographical information about both Fo and Nelson. Another two pages are dedicated to copyright acknowledgements and 'Important Billing & Credit Requirements' which are very detailed, specifying the size of type and prominence of credit to be accorded in the event of a restaging to the playwright, adaptor and theatre that first staged the version in the United States. A further two pages reproduce the programme and cast list of the Broadway show. The final two pages of paratext preceding the playtext proper consist of a note on the text and a brief prologue which mentions the Pinelli and Salsedo cases. Uneasiness about the involvement of a variety of agents and the ensuing proliferation of voices is palpable in the note, which deserves to be quoted at length:

> The version printed in this volume was first created by Richard Nelson in 1983 for a production at Arena Stage. His adaptation was based on Suzanne Cowan's literal translation, published in *Theater* Magazine in 1979. For the Arena Stage production and the subsequent Broadway production, both directed by Douglas Wager, Nelson revised the dialogue for the American stage, and added some references to current politics. Dario Fo approved his adaptation. Subsequently, Fo asked for further changes in the text, which were made by Ron Jenkins and Joel Schechter, in collaboration with Fo and Franca Rame. His changes included some new political references, and dialogue closer in meaning to that of the original Italian text. These changes were made with the consent of Richard Nelson, who remains credited as the American adaptor

> of the play. Future productions of the text may require further alteration of political references, unless our President is elected for a life term, and outlives the century.[42]

Conscious of Fo's negative reaction to Richards's version, the American team of adaptors tried very hard to respect authorial intent, asking for Fo's advice and enrolling major theatre experts such as Schechter. The issue of authoritativeness is of utmost importance: while everyone involved in the shaping of the text is mentioned (even the literal translator – a practice that is quite uncommon in the United Kingdom), special attention is drawn to the fact that all changes were made in agreement with the author and adaptor.

The play was successful in San Francisco and in Washington D. C., but on Broadway it closed after twenty performances and fifteen previews. Fo's involvement in the 'politicization' of the play may have resulted in a version closer to the Italian, but it failed to inspire audiences. Taviano has suggested that this may be due to a very specifically American understanding of 'political' and 'political theatre'. Political theatre in the United States is perceived to be broadly equivalent to propagandistic and didactic theatre, starting with the Federal Theatre Project (FTP) under Roosevelt's New Deal. Founded in 1935, the FTP served a double aim: to provide work for unemployed actors and to draw in people who would not usually go to the theatre. In a new dramatic form, the 'Living Newspaper', this kind of political theatre focused on social issues (such as housing, health care and labour unions). Several other political theatre groups emerged over the decades (such as Group Theatre, Moscow Art Theatre, Living Theater, the Performance Group) which were also perceived to be 'both agit-prop and [...] dealing with social and identity issues'. In the United States, therefore,

> political has come to mean anything which is not highly commercial, which does not correspond to Broadway's standards and is not staged in mainstream theatres.

42 Dario Fo, *Accidental Death of an Anarchist*, adapt. Richard Nelson (New York: Samuel French, 1987), 6.

> The definition of political theatre functions as a handy label, a category to identify theatre texts that are disturbing, challenging and therefore difficult to stage.[43]

Based on these criteria, the categorization of Fo's play as 'political' perhaps made its failure on Broadway in the 1980s inevitable. Other stagings, in smaller, non-mainstream theatres, have been relatively profitable. In the summer of 2011, a version of the play closely based on Emery's 2003 translation was successfully staged in New Jersey.[44]

Alan Cumming and Tim Supple

In 1990, Alan Cumming and Tim Supple wrote another adaptation of Fo's play for the National Theatre which toured the UK before moving to London in January 1991. The adaptation, published in 1991, was advertised both in the jacket text and on the first page as a 'fresh new version, faithful to the clear-sighted insanity of the original'. In terms of language and political intent, this version is closer to the Italian published texts than the Richards or Nelson versions. Yet, this adaptation was received less well than its predecessor. By then, the Richards version had made its way onto syllabuses at UK universities, thereby attaining the status of an 'original' in its own right, both for audiences and (many) critics. Cumming and Supple stress that their version is different in many ways from Richards's: in a similar move to Nelson, they invited Fo during the rehearsals and got 'a few gags' from him.[45] No literal translator is mentioned in this version, and despite the reference to the original, the adaptors do not reveal what

43 See Stefania Taviano, *Staging Dario Fo and Franca Rame. Anglo-American Approaches to Political Theatre* (Aldershot and Burlington: Ashgate, 2005), 66–9. Here 69.

44 See Anita Gates, 'Searching for Truth, Under Cover of Lies', *The New York Times*, 12 August 2011 <http://www.nytimes.com/2011/08/14/nyregion/accidental-death-of-an-anarchist-at-drew-university-review.html> accessed 22 February 2015.

45 Andrew Burnett, 'Rebirth of an Anarchist', *List*, 26 October 1990.

Italian editions they worked with (or if they worked with Italian texts at all). Cumming and Supple clearly also worked with Richards's and Nelson's versions: they too decide to name the *commissario sportivo* of the Italian version: however, the inspector loses a letter in his name and is no longer called *Pissani* but *Pisani,* most probably in an effort to make his name less of a laughing matter for an English-speaking audience.

By 1991, Stuart Hood, the author of the introduction to the 1987 Methuen text, had become series editor of the Methuen Modern Drama series. As such, he was in a position to decide what sort of paratext would be published alongside the new adaptation. Unlike the Richards adaptation, the 1991 text contains neither an author's note nor a translation of any of the available Italian prefaces, introductions or postscripts by Fo. Instead, the paratext consists of two introductions, one by Hood himself, one by Christopher Cairns, another literary scholar, a short 'Note on the Present Text' by the adaptors, as well as two texts that follow the playtext: the lyrics to the song used at the end of Act 1 and a list of changes made while on tour. While we had heard twice from Fo in the 1987 version and not at all from the adaptor, here the adaptors get to say their share while Fo is only ever quoted.

Hood's introduction is exactly the same as the one in the Richards version of 1986 with no further additions to comment on developments in Fo's life or œuvre between 1986 and 1991. In his contribution, Cairns expands on the historical facts of the Pinelli case and also explains Fo's credo that 'everything must be done through irony' and that it is the ironic role reversal, which he calls a 'rising crescendo from the realistic through the implausible to the grotesque' that makes *Accidental Death* special.[46] Cairns quotes Fo's criticism of directors who choose the easy way of entertainment while leaving aside the political message expressed in his *Dialogo provocatorio sul comico, il tragico, la follia e la ragione* [Provocative dialogue on the comic, the tragic, folly and reason]:

46 Christopher Cairns, 'Introduction', in Dario Fo, *Accidental Death of an Anarchist,* adapt. Alan Cumming and Tim Supple (London: Methuen, 1991), xv–xxi. Here xvii.

> This game of grotesques, of paradox, of madness, is a device quite capable of standing on its own without the political message. So much so that some directors (heaven forgive them) concerned to create pure entertainment, have taken out of the play all the real conflict, they have built up the comedy to the point of making it into an exchange between clowns, arriving, in the end, at a kind of surreal *pochade*, where everyone splits their sides laughing, and goes out of the theatre quite empty of political anger or indignation'.[47]

The British audience might now better understand Fo's point, Cairns continues, with the handling of the judicial cases of the Guildford Four and the Birmingham Six, for example. Cumming and Supple themselves add a note, a short page and a half, which starts off with the following statement:

> From the outset we knew that a revival of *Accidental Death of an Anarchist* must grow directly from Fo's original text. Even in literal translation, we were aware of an uncomplicated satire [...] that we had not recognised in other English adaptations. We understood how, as Fo put it, tragedy had been turned into farce: the farce of power.[48]

Having learned from Richards's and Nelson's shortcomings, Cumming and Supple claim that their characters are never caricatures but reveal themselves through action and situation. While they clearly wanted the audience to laugh, they never lost sight 'of the target, [to] release the anger and indignation contained in the play'. They seem to have taken on board Fo's message in the 'Author's Note' to the Richards version: this is a play 'born out of classic satirical principles and the deepest roots of comedy, shaped by a master of performance into a modern political farce'.[49]

The content of the play was sadly familiar, because Britain had its own farces of power, and therefore the aim had to be to 'show Italy through a British filter and so [...] to see both clearly'. Foregrounding Fo's belief that theatre is continuous substitution, Cumming and Supple continue: 'We trust that any future production will be as free with our version as we were

47 Ibid., xix.

48 Alan Cumming and Tim Supple, 'A Note on the Present Text', in Dario Fo, *Accidental Death of an Anarchist*, adapt. Alan Cumming and Tim Supple (London: Methuen, 1991), xxiii–xxiv. Here xxiii.

49 Ibid., xxiii.

with Fo's original in these areas [topical and linguistic references to Britain in 1990 – M. D.]'.[50]

With future shows based on their adaptation in mind, Cumming and Supple add at the end of their script a list of changes made to the script as well as the song adopted at the end of Act 1 during the touring production. The text is very much seen as a fluid product that needs to be adaptable according to a director's and an actor's needs and expectations. At the same time, Cumming and Supple also advocate a stronger reliance on the original text as well as a deeper understanding and the thorough implementation of Fo's intentions. However, in the paratext, the voice of Fo is heard only in quotation and not in a more substantial form, such as an author's foreword.

Because Cumming and Supple engage with authorial intentions and their adaptation strategies in the paratext, there are no striking examples of metatextual engagement with these issues of the kind found in the playtext of Richards's version. The play starts as it does in Italian, with Bertozzo questioning the Madman (no longer called a Maniac, as in the previous versions). Act 1 is preceded by a short prologue that gives the audience facts about the incident behind the play in a neutral register:

> Milan, Italy. Police Headquarters: Some months ago, a man, a self-confessed anarchist, fell from a window on the fourth floor. He was found dead on the pavement below. The police said it was suicide; an enquiry, however, said it was accidental. But we begin on the second floor, in the office of Inspector Bertozzo.[51]

In the 1991 version, one can also note the tendency to let the lead actor take centre stage, a typical characteristic of Fo's theatre which relies extensively on monologues. Richards, on the other hand, perceived this as an imbalance that he redressed by adding lines for other actors, making the whole play more dialogical.

50 Ibid., xxiv.

51 Fo, *Accidental Death* [Cumming and Supple], 1.

Ed Emery

Ed Emery's 1992 translation of *Morte accidentale di un anarchico* shares the first volume of Dario Fo's plays published by Methuen Drama with four other plays: *Mistero Buffo* and *One Was Nude and One Wore Tails* (also translated by Emery), *Trumpets and Raspberries* (translated by R. C. McAvoy and A.-M. Giugni) and *The Virtuous Burglar* (translated by Joe Farrell). The volume was reissued in 1994 and 1997.

The latest edition contains a chronology with the most important events in Fo's life up to the Nobel Prize in 1997. In his introduction, series editor Stuart Hood explains the most important figures of Italian popular theatre that are central to Fo's poetics: Pulcinella and Arlecchino from the Commedia dell' Arte, the *giullari* and *Zanni* [a Venetian clown]. Then he moves on to describe in what manner each of the texts chosen for the collection was important in a political and/or theatrical sense. The power of *Accidental Death of an Anarchist*, Hood argues, derives 'from the tension which Fo deliberately sets up between the comedy arising from confusions of identity, always one of the principal elements of farce, and the tragic circumstances surrounding the death of an innocent man'.[52]

Emery's text is the closest to the published versions of the Italian text. This closeness to the originals might be due to the fact that it was not translated with an immediate staging in sight. In the 'Translator's Note', Emery explains very briefly his translation strategies: he has maintained all the original references (to Italian political scandals rather than finding equivalents in the UK) and he has also avoided swearwords 'which may or may not be characteristic of the constabulary world-wide, but which are not characteristic of Dario Fo'.[53] Emery is aware of the fact that his text might be adapted and updated: 'There is by now a tradition with the staging of Fo's plays: theatre companies take the original texts and adapt the political and cultural references to suit their own circumstances. You

52 Stuart Hood, 'Introduction', in Dario Fo, *Plays: 1*, ix–xv. Here xi.

53 Ed Emery, 'Translator's Note', in Dario Fo, *Plays: 1*, 124.

are invited to use your own imagination and creativity accordingly'.[54] As a literary translator, Emery sticks as closely to the original as possible: the *commissario sportivo*, for example, is rendered as *Inspector in the sports jacket* and all references to Italian place names, legal procedures and other culture-specific elements are kept as in the original. Yet Emery also acknowledges (perhaps rather grudgingly) the necessity of adapting the drama text into a theatre text.

The paratext in this version of Fo's play consists of a translator's note, a translation of Dario Fo's prologue from the 1973 edition, the postscript by Fo written for the 1974 edition and a page of notes to the translation. As Emery decides to translate every single cultural reference in the play, he needs, of course, to explain who some of the public figures mentioned are and also expand on some locations. However, there are no more than nine endnotes which seems to suggest that an English-speaking audience is able to cope with a literal translation very well. The need to adapt the text, therefore, seems to stem from theatrical practice rather than from a quality innate to the text that renders it incomprehensible to a foreign audience. The publishers at Methuen Drama clearly are aware of this fact: otherwise they would not have commissioned and published yet another, the third, translation of the play in less than fifteen years – and a translation that is faithful in a philological sense.

Emery's 'Translator's Note' is only half a page long, briefly mentioning the strategies adopted for the translation: all original references are kept, expletives are avoided and, as usual, closeness to the original is asserted. The translator's self-effacement is evident in the footnotes as well, which are kept short and to the point. The paratextual apparatus is quite short; besides Hood's introduction, which only briefly mentions the historical situation in Italy in the 1960s and 1970s, the readers are not given much socio-historical context. The text, it seems, is deemed to be powerful enough to speak for itself.

54 Ibid.

Simon Nye

Although Simon Nye's 2003 text is the only version unequivocally set in Britain and therefore a profoundly domesticated text, it is not called an adaptation but a translation. It was first performed at the Donmar Warehouse in London in February 2003 with Rhys Ifans in the role of the Maniac. The plain playtext consists of ninety pages, following a one-page introduction written by an anonymous person. There is no postscript, either. In a departure from the editing practices of the Methuen Drama series up to that point, there is no paratextual apparatus to speak of: on a single page, we find a short paragraph about the play that describes how Fo's 'skill at writing farce and his gifts as a clown brilliantly serve his politics' and which also states that 'this new translation by playwright and screenwriter Simon Nye is faithful to the Italian version'.[55] Interestingly, at the beginning of a new millennium, translation is still presented in terms of faithfulness and equivalence. A very brief biography of Fo mentioning plays that were successfully performed in England is also provided. As pointed out above, neither the paragraph dedicated to the play nor the biography are signed.

The near complete absence of paratextual commentary in the 2003 edition is redressed in the 2005 student edition. However, neither a translator's note nor an author's note of the kind contained in the earlier editions is included in this version. Yet the paratextual corpus is the most considerable in an English-language version to date: about sixty pages of commentary on author, plot, background, difficulty of translation and a further thirteen pages of notes on the text by Joe Farrell as well as questions for further study. The proliferation of paratext is not surprising: it is clearly motivated by its intended audience, students of drama and world literature classes. While the translation does mirror the Italian original in a way similar to Emery's translation, Simon Nye is also the only Fo translator/adaptor to set

55 Dario Fo, *Accidental Death of an Anarchist*, trans. Simon Nye (London: Methuen, 2003), unpaginated page.

the play unequivocally in Britain. As a consequence, Nye drops the name Pisani and renames the journalist Felkin. However, Nye's Englishing is not consistent, as Bertozzo gets to keep his name. The *commissario sportivo* is simply called *Inspector*. Also, the *bersaglieri* [alpine troops] in Fo and Emery become the Gurkhas. In these as in many other cases of divergence, Farrell's footnotes prove helpful as they explain Nye's translational choices in relation to the Italian play.

As was the case with the Richards version, the paratextual commentary often works in a different direction, providing a complementary perspective to the playtext proper. In the Nye version, the paratextual commentary reminds the reader that this is an originally and deeply Italian text. However, rather than just presenting text and paratext alongside one another, the notes and detailed commentary provided by Farrell engage with the inherent discrepancies between these two types of text and carefully construct a double perspective. This is a first in the translation history of the play. This double perspective, however, is available only to the reader of the student edition. For a theatregoer attending a performance of Nye's version of the play or a reader of the version published in 2003 that has virtually no commentary at all, the links to an Italian context are weak and diluted (in the first case perhaps necessarily so, as a performance cannot include explanations of the kind provided in the paratext).

In his introduction, Farrell, a professor of Italian at Strathclyde University, uses interviews and theoretical texts by Fo to argue his case. He terms Fo's style of drama 'didactic farce'.[56] Farce makes catharsis impossible: it leaves the spectator or reader with anger alongside a specific, defiant type of laughter. Farrell includes a long section on the situation in Italy in 1969 (over fifteen pages), thus providing the reader with a deeper understanding of the genesis of the Italian text(s). Since the translation is set in contemporary Britain none of the events described in the historical section form part of the action of the play. Farrell also engages with the particular difficulties in staging works by the Italian playwright:

56 Joe Farrell, 'Commentary', in Dario Fo, *Accidental Death of an Anarchist*, transl. Simon Nye (London: Methuen, 2005), xxiii–lxiii. Here xxiii.

> There are two specific difficulties in the case of Fo: finding a means of communicating to a non-Italian audience the information on political events Fo was able to take for granted with his own audiences, and finding a way of combining his own brand of humour with the political fire. The end product must be stimulating and entertaining for an audience whose cultural expectations are different.[57]

Farrell also engages with the reasons why Fo seems to need an adaptor more than other foreign playwrights:

> An adaptation involves a wider switch, where the adaptor, who in Britain is likely to be different from the translator, makes alterations designed to update, to change setting, to alter the topic of any discussion of satire, to modify character or in some other way to domesticate and make more familiar what is foreign and strange.[58]

Yet another innovation of the Nye version is Farrell's overview of the different versions available in the UK (Richards, Cumming and Supple, Emery). According to Farrell, the Richards adaptation 'involved a switch of theatrical culture, from an Italian *commedia dell'arte* style to a messier style based on British music hall. It was not Fo and was more vacuous than the original, but it had a fire, a drive and a comic force of its own'. Cumming and Supple chose 'an imprecise setting, half-Italy and half-England' but then used the play to point out political injustices in Britain.[59] In his brief discussion of Emery's translation, Farrell implies that Nye's translation is similarly faithful in a philological sense to the Italian versions of the play. The major difference between the two is that Emery sets the play in Italy while Nye sets the play unambiguously in Britain, employing Anglo-American references: the *bersaglieri* become Ghurkas, the university of Padua becomes the university of Des Moines, references to Venice and other Italian locations disappear completely or are replaced by English locations (Huddersfield instead of Vibo-Valentia Calabrese). Also, the references to the Inspector's possible involvement with the Nazis are updated: he is now suspected to have been running a mercenary outfit in Bosnia.

57 Ibid., lix.
58 Ibid., lx.
59 Ibid., lxii.

The final paragraph of Farrell's extensive commentary to the Nye version is dedicated to the poor reception of *Accidental Death* in the United States, attributed to 'the poor quality of the adaptations and the productions. In all cases, companies have sought to emphasise the comedy at the expense of the politics'. Farrell fails to mention that Nelson and his fellow adaptors called in Fo for help and thus produced what they thought to be a 'faithful' rendering of the Italian original and that there might be other factors involved, as pointed out in Taviano's work. In comparison to the American versions, Farrell states, Nye's version is a 'witty and lively translation'.[60]

All of the versions analysed in this chapter clearly assert their status as a translation or adaptation. Yet, readers still manage to ignore the translated status of works of literature, as the following example shows.

When translated texts are not perceived as such: Misreading Fo

Why is it important to stress, in the paratext or elsewhere, the mediated status of translations and to distinguish the different voices that shape a text in translation? Let us have a closer look at a specific case, an essay by a theatre critic on *Accidental Death*, which fails to reflect on the mediated status of translations.

In a 1990 article published in *Modern Drama*, Jolynn Wing struggles with exactly the 'This isn't Dario Fo' metatextual moment in the Richards adaptation that I have analysed above, linking it to issues of authority and authorization.

> In the process of enactment [...] it becomes clear that more than one notion of author/authority/authorized has been set in motion. On the one hand, the authority of

60 Ibid., lxiii.

> Dario Fo, the author of the play, is challenged by the very characters he has created (for example, at one point the lone female actor exclaims, 'Why is there only one woman's part in this blasted play?' [p. 41]). Concomitantly, Fo's ostensible [...] fiction in turn challenges the officially authorized version of Pinelli's fall. Meanwhile, the authority of theatrical representation itself is subverted by a series of disruptive strategies which persistently undermine the integrity of the performance text.[61]

As we have seen, the disruptive strategy of invoking Dario Fo's inadequacy as an author deplored by Wing does not come from Fo himself, but from his English adaptor. The failure to distinguish between the Italian and English versions of the play also lead Wing to claim that a 'performance *glissage* is apparent from the moment Fo appears onstage, in the guise of "The Maniac", and an actor playing the police inspector, Bertozzo, announces: "I ought to warn you that the author of this sick little play, Dario Fo, has the traditional, irrational hatred of the police common to all narrow minded left-wingers"'.[62] Two things become immediately clear: Wing does not have access to the Italian play; and she assumes that translations are *exact* replica of source texts. While not having access to a text in the original does not automatically disqualify the reading of a translated text, failing to acknowledge the translated nature of a text with which one is critically engaging, however, is problematic. If Fo were playing the Maniac, it would be in an Italian version of the play, which would certainly not contain the intervention by Bertozzo that Wing sees as an example of performance *glissage*. Wing's inadequate sense of the agents involved in the production of the text leads to an interpretive faux pas.

If academics fail to acknowledge the possibility that what is usually perceived as a single distinctive voice in a literary text may actually be the result of the voices of several agents merging in more or less successful ways, it is perhaps not surprising that general readers very often tend to do the same.

61 Jolynn Wing, 'The Performance of Power and the Power of Performance: Rewriting the Police State in Dario Fo's *Morte accidentale di un anarchico*', *Modern Drama*, 33/1 (1990), 139–49.

62 Ibid., 141.

Concluding remarks: Listening out for voices in translation

According to Scuderi and Farrell, critics who have written extensively on Fo, one of the problems with the English Fo is that there is no 'official' Fo translator who could give his writings a certain consistency in the target language.[63] It might help to give Fo one voice in English rather than many; yet, as the practice of adapting plays is accepted and widespread, and as Fo himself believes in the need to update political theatre, fixing his voice in a uniform published edition of his major works would still only be a philological rather than a theatrical success.

One simple explanation for the many translations and adaptations of a single play such as *Accidental Death* (with one publisher producing five different versions in several editions in less than three decades!) is that – to put it bluntly – each new production represents an opportunity to reissue this bestselling play. Further, because it is a theatre text and a text by a playwright who advocates artistic freedom, it can reinvent itself on a regular basis in a variety of ways. This reinvention must, however, be justified in a culture which still judges translations in terms of authenticity and faithfulness. There is, as we have seen, a conflict between the adaptor's freedom granted by Fo and the demand for fidelity to the original, a conflict that is quite visible on the paratextual level. My close reading of the paratexts has also shown another issue in this regard: while Fo advocates the adaptor's freedom in theory, in practice his credo sometimes falters, as

63 Farrell and Scuderi, 'Editors' Preface', in Farrell and Scuderi, eds, *Dario Fo. Stage, Text, and Tradition*, unpaginated page. In a 1999 interview, however, Ed Emery claimed: 'I have a stormy relationship with my bosses – Dario and Franca, I mean. Periodically they sack me and cast me into outer darkness, but then we argue and shout, and now I have been appointed their more or less official translator into English'. See Jim Mulligan, 'Interview with Ed Emery: Translating Dario Fo's *Devil in Drag*' <http://www.jimmulligan.co.uk/interview/ed-emery-dario-fo-the-devil-in-drag> accessed 22 February 2015. However, in the last decade, several other translators have translated Fo's work into English.

his critical position towards some translations and his active involvement in the shaping of others shows.

While the author's position towards the translations is inconsistent, this may also be true of the publisher. There exists no single editing strategy when it comes to translated plays, not even in the Methuen Drama series. Translated plays are accompanied by a varying amount of paratext, yet there does not seem to be a standard procedure for deciding whose voices should be heard in the paratext: those of the author, the translator, the adaptor, literary critics? Within a single publishing house and within a single series there probably should be a clearly defined strategy when it comes to the presentation of texts. Ideally, the aim would be to provide the reader with as rounded a picture as possible by allowing all major agents involved in the production of the text to have their say. An introduction by a specialist in the field that focuses on the genesis of the text and its impact in the original culture is always helpful. So are notes from the adaptors and translators, as they engage with translation and adaptation strategies and thus make readers more aware of voices besides that of the author. If, as is accepted practice in the UK and the USA, the playtext appears in conjunction with or after a specific staging, the paratext could also include extracts or a facsimile of the programme (this form of epitext can be used to contextualize a play). Ultimately, the author should also be heard, whether in a translation of an original preface or introduction, or – as is the case with the Richards version – in a text specifically written for the translation or adaptation in which an author is given space to comment on the new version of the text.

The repeated attempts at an English-language *Accidental Death* make one think of Erika Fischer-Lichte's remark that acts of translation and adaptation are egotistical because they do not primarily serve the purpose of getting to know another culture but rather reinforce one's own culture:

> The starting point of intercultural performance is […] not primarily interest in the foreign, the foreign theatre form or foreign culture from which it derives, but rather a wholly specific situation within the own culture or a wholly specific problem originating in the own theatre. The net of relationships which an intercultural performance weaves between the own theatre, own culture, and the foreign theatre

> traditions and cultures from which it adopts elements, is thus clearly dominated by the 'familiar'.[64]

In the case of *Accidental Death*, the overall translation and adaptation trend has been one of domestication. Jennifer Lorch has claimed that 'it is not possible to produce a version of this play that aims both to be faithful to the author's intentions of the period and to make of it a viable play for the English/American stage, whether fringe or mainstream, because the difference in political culture is simply too great'.[65]

Farrell is less negative in his assessment. He argues that 'there is the same need with Fo as with other, more obviously "serious" playwrights, to identify the inner vision and to respect that vision as well as the quirks, oddities, idiosyncrasies and comic predilections of the surface'.[66] However, he also argues that out of Fo's entire œuvre the versions of *Accidental Death of an Anarchist* have to date been the most successful. The heavily domesticated text may refer to

> the plight of airport protesters in Japan or spy-scandals in Britain, but this has prevented it suffering the fate of *Uncle Tom's Cabin* or *Gulliver's Travels*, both works that began life as political satires. The international success of that play is a testimony to the theatrical mastery of Fo, to his skill in imagining original theatrical situations and to his expertise in devising structures marrying the extra-theatrical passion to appropriate theatrical techniques, but also to the value of a process which, combining translation and adaptation, conveys all these qualities to other cultures. The result might be, for purists, a variation on a theme, but the music is Fo's.[67]

Some may argue that the case of Fo's political theatre as exemplified by *Accidental Death* is quite unique; and the play does pose a particular set of problems, as we have seen. However, I contend that the proliferation of voices that is quite visible in the English versions of Fo's play (author,

64 Erika Fischer-Lichte, 'Staging the Foreign as Cultural Transformation', in Erika Fischer-Lichte, Josephine Riley, and Michael Gissenwehrer, eds, *The Dramatic Touch of Difference: Theatre, Own and Foreign* (Tübingen: Narr, 1990), 277–87. Here 283.

65 Lorch, '*Morte Accidentale*', 157.

66 Farrell, 'Variations', 28.

67 Ibid., 29.

translator, adaptor, academic, editor) is actually the rule rather than the exception in most translations. It may be time for readers, academic and general, to make a conscious effort to acknowledge and differentiate the various voices in (translated) literature, and the distinct strategies these voices advocate.

BY WAY OF CONCLUSION

Why Investigate Acts of Cross-Cultural Reading?

The aim of this study has been to describe real, tangible acts of cross-cultural reading and increase awareness of the negotiations performed by translators, publishers, editors, literary critics and academics, on the one hand (they way in which specific works of world literature are currently read) and to point to the potential of reading these texts differently, based on contextual knowledge, an acknowledgement of the silenced voices in translation and an attitude of wordliness towards works of world literature, on the other. Readers have a tendency to assign the books they read a single, distinctive, 'authentic' voice, effacing the voices of agents other than the author who have helped shape a given version of a text. This book reverses that process in an effort to evoke the polyphony excluded by the focus on a single authorial voice.

In the introduction, I noted that in a highly competitive world in which 'international visibility' is often equated with 'translation into English', a literary work's transnational standing as a work of world literature is fundamentally shaped by how it is presented in its English implementation. It is therefore necessary to investigate the network of agents involved in these processes of cultural transfer, both on a theoretical level as well as in a sample of quite diverse works of world literature in translation. By focusing on politico-cultural agents and factors that shape works of world literature in English translation, I have shown how literary texts undergo a series of transformations even before they reach the reading public in the receiving culture; and I have explored how publishers, reviewers, translators and academics act as gatekeepers, including or excluding works from cultural discourse. The agents' hermeneutical and rhetorical skills influence the way in which they mediate and translate specific texts and larger cultural systems. My study also shows that, consciously or not, most readers are still committed to an ideal of the author's originary genius that emerged in European Romanticism and that authenticity is a matter of importance both for general readers and for the agents responsible for the presentation and representation of works of literature in translation.

In the three case studies, I engaged with different agents responsible for the way in which each of the translated texts is presented to and received by the English-speaking readership, as their specific strategies and methods of decision-making and their discursive practices fundamentally influence the standing of a text in the receiving culture. In each case, my focus has been slightly different in order to show the versatility of the model developed here. As we have seen, the model can be applied either to give a bird's-eye view of the reception of a literary work over a relatively prolonged period of time (Rabindranath Tagore's *The Home and the World*), to 'zoom in' on one particularly revealing aspect of reception, such as the academic criticism on a specific work (Tahar Ben Jelloun's *The Sand Child*), or to examine the paratextual apparatus for traces of agents other than the author within the covers of a published text (Dario Fo's *Accidental Death of an Anarchist*).

The Western interest in world literature over the last two centuries is crucially connected to the long-term growth in the number of foreign books in translation from the late eighteenth and the early nineteenth centuries onwards. The term 'world literature' eludes clear definition, yet – defying all efforts to abolish or replace it – it remains firmly established in critical and pedagogical practice. I analysed the discursive politics visible in several academic monographs that approach 'world literature' in one of five ways: as a mode of circulation, reading, researching and teaching (Damrosch, Rosendahl Thomsen); as a teaching practice in need of a metatheoretical and historicizing approach (Pizer); as an autonomous space following its own rules (Casanova); as a paradigm best applied to a new kind of hybrid literature (Sturm-Trigonakis); or as a flawed practice that stubbornly refuses to focus on what is untranslated and untranslatable (Apter). My perspective on world literature complements – and sometimes contradicts – these critical stances foregrounding a myriad of agents, events and factors that make for the contingencies of canonization (or the lack thereof). By adopting a multi-centred model of literature, polysystem theory, I have opted for a description of literary space that is much better equipped to deal with the reality of a transnational network of literary influence and with the real workings of the international book market and academic engagement with literature than Casanova's model.

Readers in a given receiving culture share a sphere of experience that, in turn, will influence how they read and interpret a work of literature in translation. There are several co-existing reading communities, more or less clearly defined groups of people who share a common way of approaching literature, linked by similar strategies and methods of decision-making. Such reading communities share interpretive strategies (they read texts in similar ways, using similar tools) and rhetorical strategies (they use arguments that are persuasive in that particular context). Specific members of the reading community invested with discursive and rhetorical authority (writers, translators, editors, publishers, academics and literary critics) will fundamentally shape the manner in which the entire reading group approaches a literary text: they influence the general consensus by deploying specific discursive practices and recur to rhetorical strategies that seem the most plausible to the majority of members of a specific reading community.

The acts of cross-cultural reading which publishers, translators, adaptors, editors, literary critics and academics perform are never disinterested: they are informed by an understanding of literature specific to a given time and place, and inculcated by specific experiences of socialization and education (*habitus*), and they relate to other works of literature that form the *repertoire* of individual readers and reading communities alike. Agents are also deeply connected to *institutions* (publishing houses, universities, theatrical traditions, but also 'schools of thought' within academia); and their acts of reading and rewriting reflect those connections. E. M. Forster and Gyorgy Lukács were members of distinct reading communities invested with particular discursive and rhetorical power, and their scathing reviews of *The Home and the World* most probably dissuaded many readers from approaching the text or, alternatively, influenced the manner in which readers who trusted their judgment would approach the text.

Where the discursive and rhetorical power of such agents becomes most evident in this book is in my investigation of the reception of Ben Jelloun's *The Sand Child* through the lens of English-language criticism. Not only did I discover an overall trend to subsume the novel (and other works by Ben Jelloun) under the heading of postcolonialism, with a special interest in gender issues, but such positioning of the text is clearly linked to the desire and need of academics to position themselves in a way that fits emerging or current trends in scholarship. Similarly, the growing number of retranslations into English of Fo's *Accidental Death of an Anarchist* is also best explained by pointing to the particular link that exists between the theatre scene in the United Kingdom and the theatre publisher Methuen. Ultimately, cross-cultural acts of reading are a worthwhile object of investigation because they make visible the temporal and spatial location of all agents involved in shaping works of literature as well as accepted ideas about (world) literature in specific reading communities.

What emerges quite powerfully from an overview of the international book market is that textual interventions from agents other than the author are rarely spoken about in a candid fashion. The reactions to the revelations about Raymond Carver's strained relationship with his first editor, Gordon Lish, caused by Lish's editorial practices serve as a striking example of the general unease felt when it comes to discussing how literary texts attain the shape in which they are presented to the readership. Editors and other agents involved in the publishing process will more often than not suggest changes to the text before it is published (although such changes rarely alter the text in the fundamental way in which Carver's first collection was reshaped): this is common practice and yet it is difficult to accommodate this practice to our understanding of literature as the 'original', creative output of a single mind that should not be tampered with.

Lawrence H. Schwartz's investigation of the literary reputation of a now well-known figure of world literature, William Faulkner, engages with the workings of the literary market from a slightly different angle. In this case, it is not so much a question of textual interventions before publication but of how historical and political circumstances can shape the fortune of a writer or a book within a relatively short time span. Schwartz shows that commercial innovations, a shift in critical reception and in literary aesthetics as well as changes in the political agenda after 1945 significantly contributed to a radical change in the way in which the American public (and subsequently, other readerships) viewed Faulkner: from a difficult-to-read, nihilistic writer to distinctly American moralist voice that expressed a new, post-war aesthetic.

The ongoing restoration of Tagore as an important representative of world literature in English is another example of how the coincidence of historical and literary developments with personal and institutional interests can result in the redefinition of the standing of an author and his literary output. It was a combination of academic interest in Tagore, India and the Orient on the part of Mary Lago, William Radice, Edward Said and others and a growing public appetite for the works of authors from the Indian subcontinent that helped rekindle the Western interest in Tagore which, in turn, has resulted in a flurry of new translations of Tagore's works by translators such as Pratima Bowes, William Radice, Ketaki Kushari Dyson and Sujit Mukherjee. Finally, one notices a growing institutional interest in Tagore in the Western world: from the Tagore Centre UK with its head office in London and a branch in Glasgow that has financed and actively encouraged a variety of publications since its foundation in 1985 via the 'Centro Studi Tagore' in Venice established by Mario Rigon (who incidentally has translated dozens of Tagore titles into Italian) to the first Tagore Centre attached to a Western university, *ScoTs* (The Scottish Centre of Tagore Studies) at Edinburgh Napier University. Most Tagore scholars welcome the positive changes in Tagore's literary reputation and admit that the increase in English-language translations and critical writing will most likely win the Bengali writer more readers in the future. However, when one takes a closer look at the discourse surrounding translation, another aspect of the readership's unease with agents other than the author emerges.

We have repeatedly seen translators being criticized for the failure of a particular book or author in a receiving culture. Around 1920, English-speaking readers, academics and general readers alike, were quick to blame Surendranath Tagore for what they perceived to be a 'faulty' translation of *The Home and the World*. Surendranath continues to be faulted whenever it is argued that there exists a need for a new translation of the novel, notably in the paratext of the two latest English translations of the novel (Sen's for Srishti Publishers and Guha's for Penguin India). Similarly, each new translation of Dario Fo's *Accidental Death of an Anarchist* has claimed in some form or other to be faithful to the original text, or at least to be more faithful than its predecessors. Faulting the translator takes place not only when the relation between original and translation is being discussed; it also spills over into the critical apparatus surrounding translated texts. Some literary critics who have access to both the language of the original and the translation express their frustration at the shortcomings of the translation, as we have most strikingly seen in the case of *The Sand Child*. Translation is still very often presented as being about equivalence between two texts or languages and about faithfulness to an 'original' which is often positioned superior to the translated version of the text by virtue of its priority. The overall sense seems to be that the practices of editing and translating are actually interfering with what is an authentic, genuine article and therefore automatically result in a loss of quality, a loss of intensity, or a loss of literary specificity.

Thus, there is still a widespread tendency to see the text as a single author's property and not as the product of an interaction that involves several inputs from different sources (author, editor and/or translator and reader). Bourdieu has called this tendency an 'ideology of charisma', which is interested in the 'apparent producer' of a work of art and not in the agents in the field of cultural production who shape the work of art and legitimize and authorize both the work and the author. Michel Foucault points out that the notion of 'author' coincides with a privileged moment of *individualization* in human history: the Romantic idea of poetry as the creative, spontaneous and genuine expression of the individual. Tampering with the authentic work of a genius automatically and inevitably reduces the work's value. Even today, many Western readers are heirs of Romanticism in the sense that they believe that the text reveals (a smaller or larger part of) its author, where 'author' is more often than not understood as the Romantic archetype of the natural genius producing an original, authentic work.

The Greek *authentikos* translates as 'one acting on one's own authority' and therefore already contains the germ of that individual and individualistic aspect of authorship that shapes the Romantic definition of an author. In the domain of literary translation, consequently, any source text is automatically perceived to be superior to its translation. Also, a translator is not expected to act on his or her own authority, since it is the original that is authoritative. Originals are perceived to be organic entities (the 'real' thing) while translations are represented routinely as manufactured articles or constructions (the ersatz). The uneasiness about the perceived inauthentic (or less authentic) nature of any translated text usually reinforces the need to reassure the reader of the translation's philological equivalence and faithfulness to the language and literariness of the original. This is the case with the two latest translations of *The Home and The World* which argue that the text at hand is closer to the Bengali original than Surendranath's translation. Similarly Ed Emery's translation of *Accidental Death of an Anarchist* is framed by paratextual argument that asserts the claims of a literal translation by criticizing the domesticating strategies pursued in earlier adaptations of Fo's play. While Emery seems to advocate authenticity as closeness to the original, other theatre translators and theatre makers would argue that changing the text into something that the receiving audience can relate to better means creating an 'authentic' experience for the audience.

However, the concern with recouping authenticity does not stop at the discussion of the linguistic equivalence between original and translation; it actually carries over into a second domain of literary criticism, as well. There is a recurring preoccupation with authorial intention: a translation needs to be not only faithful to the 'words on the page' of the original; it should also convey the meaning the author intended for the text in the source culture. As we have seen, Joe Farrell argues that Simon Nye's translation of Fo's play is faithful to the original in this sense. Nye may well set the play in contemporary England, but by doing so he respects Fo's intentions far more than previous versions of the play that followed different translation and adaptation strategies. Similarly, Penguin India and Srishti Publishers both argue that their translations are more complete, including passages left out in the 1919 translation, and that the authorial intention expressed in the textual choices made for the original Bengali text is for the first time preserved in these retranslations. William Radice, on the other hand, argues that we should respect the authorial intentions behind Tagore's decision to change the text for a different audience in the 1919 translation. By not retranslating the text, the argument goes, one preserves the authenticity of a new, hybrid text that was never intended to be a word-for-word translation of the Bengali original.

A third kind of engagement with authenticity in the presentation of works in translation has emerged over the course of my study: instances when literary works are presented and dealt with as socio-anthropological documents that provide authentic and reliable information about a given culture. In what looks like a partial reversal of the Western obsession with the Romantic genius, the spontaneous creative outpouring of an individual author makes room for the perception of the author as the representative of a social reality in a given (usually non-Western) culture. This has emerged most clearly in my discussion of *The Sand Child*, which is often taken to represent the reality of Moroccan life (however defined): the assumption is that Ben Jelloun seems to be using literature to critique the political and social reality of Moroccan life. Ben Jelloun's case is not isolated; it actually points towards a more general trend in postcolonial and gender studies approaches to literature. However, whether this approach is actually doing any favours to so-called emerging literatures is up for discussion: as a result of this 'documentary' approach there seems to be a tendency to emphasize content over form as if these were separable, to the detriment of a fuller discussion of the literary work. The organizing trope of postcolonial studies presents Ben Jelloun's work as a site of struggle and, even when it acknowledges the complexities of narrative, very often sees these as strategies in line with the trope of resistance. The different focus of English-language Ben Jelloun criticism (a mostly postcolonial stance with an emphasis on gender issues) and French-language Ben Jelloun criticism (mostly directed at language issues and literariness) lies at the heart of the general lack of cross-fertilization between these two bodies of criticism. The search for 'authentic' material that would explain a different culture results in an essentialization of that culture and in literary texts being treated as if they were historical, sociological and ethnographic documents. However, as Wolfgang Riedel points out, there is a danger in equating literary texts with the culture they are thought to represent, as this stance tends to neglect the aesthetic component of literature and therefore fails to acknowledge that literature is in fact a discourse quite distinct from history, sociology or ethnography. Riedel's view of the literary text not as a document but rather a commentary on the culture and reality it stems from, written from an aesthetic and reflective distance, is useful in the context of world literature in translation as it allows one to relativize the idea that the main value of such literature consists in its ability to provide privileged knowledge of that culture.

The insistence on authorial intention and authenticity that permeates all three case studies points towards a wider issue. It seems to me that the *author* or the *text* (both intended as absolute authority, a *locus* of authenticity) emerge as demand-driven functions that are foregrounded so that we, as readers, do not have to remind ourselves of the complex processes that shape the books that we read. We have in reality a complex process that involves a variety of crafters, politico-cultural agents with specific degrees of rhetorical power: translators, publishers, editors, reviewers, critics and academics. They all shape texts before they reach the reading public and have the power to include or exclude works from cultural discourse once they are published. I deliberately use the term crafters because all of the agents involved in shaping the final product, a book of world literature in translation, are adepts of a specific craft tradition and are invested with a varying degree of authority by virtue of their position within that tradition. It may be time for readers, academic and general, to make a conscious effort to acknowledge and differentiate the various voices in (translated) literature, and the distinct strategies these voices advocate. We should, therefore, systematically think of world literature in translation as a 'cultural category produced through institutions and processes.'[1]

In the three case studies, world literature has been revealed as a field of forces, an interactive arena where cross-cultural discourse is possible, yet largely within channels shaped by agents whose politico-cultural, especially rhetorical, powers should not be underestimated. Mapping a literary text's transnational trajectory in light of the changing positions adopted by politico-cultural agents towards that particular text reveals the processual nature of all cultural transfers. The three case studies elucidated here serve as examples of general trends in literary reception and my findings are by no means exhaustive. I think, however, that I have succeeded in showing

1 James F. English, *The Economy of Prestige: Prizes, Awards, and the Circulation of Cultural Value* (Cambridge, MA: Harvard University Press, 2005), 311.

that by focusing on prominent empirical findings (para- and metatextual elements, epitexts such as interviews, newspaper reviews and academic criticism) we can shed light on the preferred ways in which literature in translation is seen at particular junctures in the history of a receiving culture. Only by considering the agents involved in creating the text and the factors that influence the reception of a text are we able to account for both the *effect* and the *affect* of literature in translation: the text's effect on the reader and the affective relationship of text and reader.

The model developed here distinguishes itself by its wide applicability: it can serve investigations of a virtually unlimited number of texts in translation. I have applied this model to world literature in English for very specific reasons. World literature in English is a transnational polysystem that is more resistant to translation than other national and transnational polysystems. A closer look reveals that the polysystem of world literature in translation is made up of a publishing subsystem, a teaching subsystem and a subsystem of criticism, and that there exists a tension within the polysystem: academics are at least nominally committed to translation while members of the publishing subsystem are less willing to invest in translation. The model of the polysystem is, however, adaptable enough for the analysis of other literary markets that are less resistant to translation. It might be interesting to analyse different polysystems, for example the polysystem of world literature in German, to investigate whether the presence of a more vibrant translation culture and better access to world literature *in practice* is actually linked to a decreased interest in world literature *in theory*.

The model could also be developed further by applying it to other kinds of literature, such as literature written by women, so-called popular literature and children's literature – from more than one polysystem – in order to investigate the changes in the presentation and representation of literature once we move away from 'high' literature written by men and marked as relevant to a specific tradition.

While I have focused here on those members of a reading community who are invested with rhetorical power and whose acts are more visible and therefore tracable for a reception historian, the process of consecration in contemporary literary circles is changing. It is true that many middle-sized publishers have been bought up by international conglomerates. However, it is also true that the last decade has seen dozens of small English-language publishers exclusively focusing on translated works. While these may not be immediately visible to readers and certainly struggle to get their books stocked in a chain book shop, they have developed a variety of strategies to attract clients: they offer subscription plans whereby readers get sent a fixed number of translated works per year; they organize literary events such as salons; they use social media to advertise their products and even set up stands outside supermarkets to draw in customers and to draw attention to translated literature.[2] More of these projects get funding from national and international bodies and foundations and will hopefully be able to create a niche market for themselves in the future.

This study aimed at increasing awareness among professional and general readers of the unfulfilled potential of world literature in English. This potential remains to be fulfilled in the subsystem of publishing by increased openness to translation, and in the system of criticism by heightening cross-fertilization with critical work in other polysystems. Fostering an ethic of worldliness among readers will enable that potential to be realized. In this sense, my study is both realistic and idealistic.

2 'Die deutsche "Pereine"-Verlegerin Meike Ziervogel [...] greift [...] zu ungewöhnlichen Strategien: Sie transferiert die Foren der Vergangenheit in die Zukunft, lädt zu literarischem Kaffeeklatsch und Salons ein, in deren Mittelpunkt jeweils ein Autor steht. Sie setzt auf Subskriptionen, Social Media, starkes Branding und aussergewöhnlich gestaltete Buchumschläge. Selbst für den Verkauf am Marktstand vor dem lokalen Supermarkt ist sie sich nicht zu schade [Meike Ziervogel, the founder and director of Pereine publishing house, uses unusual strategies: she has returned to literary forums of the past, inviting readers to coffee parties and literary salons focused on a specific author. She concentrates on subscriptions, social media, strong branding and exceptionally designed book covers. And she does not think it beneath herself to sell her books outside local supermarkets either]. See Marion Löhndorf 'Die Stieftocher emanzipiert sich. Neue deutschsprachige Literatur such ihren Platz in Grossbritannien', *Neue Zürcher Zeitung*, 19 November 2012 <http://www.nzz.ch/aktuell/feuilleton/literatur/neue-deutschsprachige-literatur-sucht-ihren-platz-in-grossbritannien-1.17817151> accessed 28 February 2015.

The standing of English as the foremost international academic language is, at least for the time being, an undisputed fact. This predominance may pose a threat of cultural levelling to a hegemonic standard but it may also be an opportunity for those agents involved in shaping 'world literature in English' to work towards a higher degree of what I call worldliness: openness to the world, its literature and opinions about it. As it stands, literary criticism of world literature in English is not particularly worldly. It should, and can, be more worldly but in order to achieve this, more engagement with literature and criticism written in languages other than English is required. It also seems to me that translation needs to be depicted more energetically as a craft that adds value to a receiving culture. Who can picture what the Anglo-American landscape of academic criticism would look like if Derrida, Bakhtin or Agamben had remained untranslated from French, Russian and Italian? Clearly, these translations have added to, stimulated and changed the receiving culture. They have, in fact, become thoroughly integrated in the Anglo-American intellectual landscape. Yet, there are many more such works that deserve to be translated into English (and other languages). Similarly, how many brilliant works of literature lie undiscovered because they remain untranslated in a publishing reality that allows less and less room for translations? World literature in general, and world literature in its English implementation in particular, can only gain from an increase in translation, both of fictional and non-fictional works.

APPENDIX I

Summary of *The Sand Child*

All page numbers refer to the English translation.

Content of narrative	*Information about protagonist*	*Self-reflexive metanarrative elements/ strategies deployed by narrators*
Chapter 1: Homme/The Man		
Storyteller explains that he received Ahmed's journal when the latter was an elderly man.	Ahmed, now old, lives an isolated life in the family home and writes about his secret(s) in the journal to say that he had 'ceased to be' (5).	Presenting storyteller as source of information and necessary presence for true understanding: A.'s journal is described as having 'seven gates pierced in a wall' (6) and storyteller promises key to open them.
Chapter 2: La porte du jeudi/The Thursday Gate		
A.'s father decision: his eighth child will be a boy. Bribes midwife. The baby, a girl, is presented to the world as Hajji's son.	The midwife announces A.'s birth thus: 'It's a man, a man, a man' (16).	Creating complicity with the audience: 'I do not tell stories simply to pass the time. [...] I need to get them out of my body in order to make room for new stories. I need you. I make you part of my undertaking' (8).
Chapter 3: La porte du vendredi/The Friday Gate		
Father's ruses at circumcision. A. raised as a boy. Traumatic Hammam experience (being moved from women's to men's bath).	A.'s childhood was mainly happy – some minor instances where behaviour is branded male/female and the latter has negative connotations.	Underlining the authenticity of the storyteller's account: First instance of use of A.'s journal – extensive reading from it.

Content of narrative	*Information about protagonist*	*Self-reflexive metanarrative elements/ strategies deployed by narrators*
Chapter 4: La porte du samedi/The Saturday Gate		
Storyteller admits that there are blank pages in the journal so he does not know about certain aspects of A.'s adolescence. Soon he proceeds to reading from the journal again.	A. is traumatized at finding stained sheets in his bed, 'imprints of a fact about my body [...]' (30). Relief at not having breasts.	Blurring between storyteller and narrator. *Readers* (not the listeners) addressed directly. Several interpretations are anticipated (disguised as opinions voiced amongst the storyteller's audience). 'Adolescence is a very obscure period [...] that we must imagine, a blank space left for the reader to fill in as he will' (27). Then the storyteller reclaims authority by reading from A.'s journal again.
Chapter 5: Bab El Had		
Storyteller now describes a 20-year-old A. trying to fit into the role assigned to him: he becomes a petty tyrant to his mother and sisters. Always isolated, A. writes about his misery in his journal and in letters to a (real or imaginary?) friend.	A. chooses to keep up appearances (growing a moustache, wearing European clothes, getting married): 'Father, you've made me a man. I must remain one' (35).	Pleading with the audience to stick with the narrative though it may be strange, creating complicity in not understanding: 'I read on your faces embarrassment and anxiety. This confession both enlightens us and distances us. It makes the character even more strange'. (41) Then, the narrator prepares the audience for the 'decisive ordeal' in A.'s fate and the story.

Content of narrative	*Information about protagonist*	*Self-reflexive metanarrative elements/ strategies deployed by narrators*
Chapter 6: La porte oubliée/The Forgotten Gate		
Storyteller starts telling about A. taking over the household after father's death. He is interrupted by a man claiming to be A.'s brother-in-law who accuses him of not telling everything and of not possessing A.'s journal. He then takes over the narration, informing the audience that he stole the diaries when A. passed away.	A. behaved strangely when laying down the conditions for his life with Fatima, quoting philosophers and talking to himself: 'For a long time now I have laughed at myself and at the other who is now talking to you, whom you think you see and hear. [...] You will have news of me on the exact day of my death. It will be a splendid, sunny day, the day when the bird inside me will sing ...' (49).	One storyteller exposing another as fraud but journal (written word) still seen as proof of authenticity: 'Our storyteller is pretending to read from a book that Ahmed is supposed to have left behind him. That is untrue! Of course the book exists, but it is not that old notebook [...] Bravo! What courage, what deception! I am the one who has Ahmed's diary [...] I stole it the day after his death. Here it is. It is covered with a newspaper of the time. You can read the date – does it not coincide with that of his death? [...] Listen to me, I belong to this story' (50).
Chapter 7: La porte emmurée/The Walled-up Gate		
Fatima's brother reads from A.'s journal: recollections of A.'s short married life.	A. is first relieved that Fatima wants to live like brother and sister. But her presence soon starts to disturb him. In fact, shortly before dying, she reveals that she has known his secret all along: 'I am your wife and you are mine... You will be a widower and I... Let's say that I was a mistake' (58–9).	First-person narrative, written word is supposed to confer authenticity to the narrative.

Content of narrative	*Information about protagonist*	*Self-reflexive metanarrative elements/ strategies deployed by narrators*
Chapter 8: Rebelle à toute demeure/The Houseless Woman		
As a reaction to the claim that widowhood was painful for A., a member of the audience tells the story of a warrior-chieftain, Antar, who was actually a woman. Then the plot returns to A. and the journal.	A. becomes more isolated, writing in his room. Letters from secret correspondent resume: they annoy and challenge him.	Narrator allows audience to participate but then retakes control of the story. Relies heavily on the journal, but also comments on the written word: 'Friends, I close the book here, open up my heart, and appeal to my reason. During that period of retirement, no one saw him' (66).
Chapter 9: 'Bâtir un visage come on élève une maison'/'Construct a face as one constructs a house'		
The story moves briefly to the other members of the family: the mother is going insane; the sisters want to harm A. in any way possible. Then it is back to the journal entries.	A. experiences an orgasm for the first time. 'I have lost my body's language; indeed, I never possessed it. I ought to learn it, starting out by speaking as a woman. [...] This will require a journey'. (72). A. starts speaking about him/herself in the third person female. 'Something trembles within me. It must be my soul' (79).	Move from third person narration to first person narration (journal entries).

Content of narrative	*Information about protagonist*	*Self-reflexive metanarrative elements/ strategies deployed by narrators*
Chapter 10: Le conteur dévoré par ses phrases/The Storyteller Devoured by His Words		
This chapter is entirely meta-narrative, discussing the fragmentary nature of all narratives: 'The manuscript I wanted to read to you falls to pieces whenever I try to open it and free its words. [...] Fragmentary, it possesses me, obsesses me, and brings me back to you, you who have the patience to wait' (81).	No progress in A.'s story, no new information about the character.	Directly addresses the dwindling audience: 'Not many of you have followed me through this man's story, but the number is not important' (80). The audience/reading public is necessary, however: 'Our character is about to get up. We catch a glimpse of him, but he does not see us. He thinks he's alone. He does not feel spied upon. All the better. Let us listen to his steps, follow his breathing, draw the veil from his tired soul' (82).
Chapter 11: L'homme aux seins de femme/The Man with a Woman's Breasts		
The storyteller reads from A.'s journal again.	A. decides to 'go out. It is time to be born again. I am not actually going to change, but will simply return to myself'. (83) On the journey, A. explores her body in a conscious way for the first time. A. meets Um Abbas and joins her circus. A. is named 'Zahra, Amirat Lhob' (princess of love).	For the first time, the entire chapter is in the first person (Ahmed writes down his decision to go on a journey and how he became Zahra).

Content of narrative	*Information about protagonist*	*Self-reflexive metanarrative elements/ strategies deployed by narrators*
Chapter 12: La femme à la barbe mal rasée/The Woman with the Badly Shaven Beard		
A., or Lalla Zarah, does not seem to mind the circus life and slowly learns how to be a woman.	'Sometimes a man, sometimes a woman, our character was moving toward the reconquest of his being' (96). The 'Anonymous One' starts writing letters again.	Narrator points out the fragility of narrative: 'The story that I am telling you is an old piece of wrapping paper. It will need only a match, a torch, to confine everything to nothingness' (96).
Chapter 13: Une nuit sans issue/A Night Without Escape		
Zahra has recurring nightmares about her parents. Tries to find positive female role model but fails.	Zahra is struggling to redefine her entire life. 'I cannot understand the meaning of all this commotion' (102).	The next chapter starts thus: 'It is now eight months and twenty-four days since the storyteller disappeared' (103). The storyteller has died, clutching the journal. Therefore 'we shall never know the end of this story. Yet a story is written to be told to the end' (104).
Chapter 14: Salem		
Salem describes the shock and panic when A.'s family discover upon his death that he was a woman. Then he describes his violent death.	Rumoured to have become a saint after death who grants only male children, Z. died a violent death: knowing that she would be raped again by the circus owner, she placed razor blades between her buttocks, killing him and herself.	Audience satisfaction comes before authenticity: Salem delivers an end to the story but his audience (Amar and Fatuma) are not satisfied: 'You're not going to get out of it like that. [...] I know the end of this story. I found the manuscript the storyteller was reading to us. I shall bring it along tomorrow. I salvaged it from the nurses at the morgue' (111).

Content of narrative	*Information about protagonist*	*Self-reflexive metanarrative elements/ strategies deployed by narrators*
Chapter 15: Amar		
Amar agrees with his predecessors that A. left his family home. 'He was tempted to go along with the circus adventure, but I believe he did something else' (114). Amar gives us an alternative account of A.'s death, a peaceful, gentle death.	A. escapes from the circus and goes looking for Fatima's grave. He wanders around, confused and ghostlike – mirrors no longer returning his image. Or has he actually never left his room and all the adventures reported in the journal are hallucinations? A. dies surrounded by religious books.	Salem and Fatuma look convinced but then Salem tries to justify his own ending. This results in a discussion about differing interpretations between the two men. When Fatuma is asked for her opinion, she complains about the fact that nobody listens to women. In fact, she is the only female storyteller.
Chapter 16: Fatouma/Fatuma		
Fatuma strongly identifies with Ahmed/Zarah so that it is quite impossible to tell whether it is her own story and thoughts she is voicing or A/Z.'s. Perhaps she is the protagonist come to tell his/her story?	If Fatuma is A., this is how she feels: 'I admit that I took great pleasure in listening to the storyteller and then to you: it gave me the privilege of reliving certain stages in my life, twenty years later' (133).	Completely different ending and interpretation of A.'s story. First person narrative that could be Fatuma's or Ahmed/Zahra's. Yet another possible ending: A/Z. is alive and had assisted to the versions of her life story all along. But another storyteller is about to take over and will change A/Z.'s story again.

Content of narrative	*Information about protagonist*	*Self-reflexive metanarrative elements/ strategies deployed by narrators*
Chapter 17: Le troubadour aveugle/The Blind Troubadour		
The Troubadour tells of his encounter with a mysterious woman who shows him an old coin. She proceeds to tell him that he alone is capable of understanding her story. She starts telling him about herself – the Troubadour, however, digresses on how she reminded him of a woman he met 30 years previously. She disappears before she has told her story and now the Troubadour is looking for her (and her story) – she has left signs for him to decipher.	A./Z. is dressed like a woman and has left Morocco for Argentina where she manages to meet the troubadour, after having falsified letters to him from an old friend in order to be able to meet him (she does not know the friend passed away).	Narrating = falsifying: 'All you need to know is that I have spent my life falsifying or altering other people's stories' (134). Aim of book(s): 'A book – at least that's how I see it—is a labyrinth created on purpose to confuse men, with the intention of ruining them and bringing them back to the narrow limits of their ambitions' (140). Creation of suspense: the audience is growing, other people in the café are interested. 'Suddenly a man got up and said, "You are welcome here. Tell us about this woman who gave you the coin. What did she tell you?"' (145). Deciphering: just as the troubadour sets out to decipher A./Z.'s signs, so the audience must decipher signs.

Content of narrative	*Information about protagonist*	*Self-reflexive metanarrative elements/ strategies deployed by narrators*
Chapter 18: La nuit andalouse/ The Andalusian Night		
Story of how troubadour ended up in Morocco. Dreams and reality about the Alhambra in Granada mix in the narrative. The audience seems doubtful (silence).	A./Z. appears in the Alhambra episode but it is not clear whether this really happened or whether it is a hallucination. Recites the Arabic alphabet and tries to strangle the troubadour.	Fact and fiction, memory and dreams are entwined and cannot be separated.
Chapter 19: La porte des sables/The Gate of the Sands		
Storyteller with blue turban (perhaps first storyteller returning?) admits that his story is in fact the story of Bey Ahmed from Alexandria who lived his life as a man but biologically was a woman and that he thought about 'what I could do with this material, and how it could be adapted to our country' (164). The moonlight has erased Bey Ahmed's diary so it is gone forever.	No new information.	Edifice of narration: 'A story is like a house, an old house, with different levels, rooms, corridors, doors, and windows. Locks, cellars, useless spaces. The walls are its memory. Scratch the stone a little, hold your ear to it, and you will hear things! Time gathers together what the day brings and what night disperses. It keeps and holds. Stone is the witness. Each stone is a page of writing, read and crossed out. A story. A house. A book. A desert. A journey' (163).

APPENDIX II

Untapped Resources: A Provisional Bibliography on Tahar Ben Jelloun's *The Sand Child* in French

Accad, Evelyne, *Des femmes, des hommes et la guerre: fiction et réalité au Proche-Orient* (Paris: Indigo & Coté-femmes Éditions, 1993).

Amar, Ruth, *Tahar Ben Jelloun. Les stratégies narratives* (Lewiston, NY: Edwin Mellen Press, 2005).

Ammar, Sonia, 'De quelques exilés sociaux dans l'univers romanesque de Tahar Ben Jelloun', *Les Lettres Romanes*, 61/1–2 (2007), 75–87.

Antle, Martine, 'Voix et voiles dans *L'enfant de sable* de Tahar Ben Jelloun', in Joseph Brami, Madeleine Cottenet-Hage and Pierre Verdaguer, eds, *Regards sur la France des Années 1980* (Saratoga, CA: ANMA Libri, 1994), 75–82.

Babana-Hampton, Safoi, 'L'image et le texte entre déconstrution et construction dans *L'enfant de sable* et *Le fond de la jarre*', *French Review*, 84/3 (2011), 541–53.

Bargenda, Angela, 'Le theme du double chez Tahar Ben Jelloun', *Revue Francophone de la Louisiane*, 8/2 (1993), 19–27.

Bengt, Novén, *Les mots et le corps. Etude des procès d'écriture dans l'œuvre de Tahar Ben Jelloun* (Uppsala: Acta Universitatis Upsaliensis, 1996).

Bouanane, Kahina, 'Le corps en cris et écrits dans *L'enfant de sable* de Tahar Ben Jelloun', *Synérgies*, 4 (2009), 303–10.

Boughali, Mohamed, *Espaces d'écriture au Maroc* (Casablanca: Afrique Orient, 1987).

Bounfour, Abdellah, 'Langue, identité et écriture dans la littérature francophone du Maghreb', *Cahiers d'études africaines*, 140 (1995), 911–23.

Bourkhis, Ridha, 'Tahar Ben Jelloun: Graphèmes français, culture arabe', *IBLA: Revue de l'Institut des Belles Lettres Arabes*, 57/1 (1994), 23–38.

——, 'Tahar Ben Jelloun: un auteur et son œuvre', *IBLA: Revue de l'Institut des Belles Lettres Arabes*, 67/2 (2004), 195–200.

Bousta, Rachida Saigh, *Lecture des récits de Tahar Ben Jelloun. Ecriture, mémoire et imaginaire* (Casablanca: Afrique Orient, 1999).

Boza Araya, Virginia, '*L'enfant de sable* de Tahar Ben Jelloun: Apprendre le français et découvrir le Maghreb', *Français dans le monde*, 341 (2005), 35–7.

Chanfrault, Bernard, 'Figure du corps et problématique de l'oralité dans *L'enfant de sable* de Tahar Ben Jelloun', *Revue de la Faculté de Lettres et des Sciences Humaines de Marrakech*, 3: *Littérature marocaine de langue française: récits et discours* (1989), 41–61.

Chevalier, Anne, "Le voile des fables" dans *L'enfant de sable* de Tahar Ben Jelloun', in Ernstpeter Ruhe, ed., *Europas islamische Nachbarn. Studien zur Literatur* (Würzburg: Königshausen & Neumann, 1993), 61–70.

Chossat, Michèle, Ernaux, *Redonnet, Bâ et Ben Jelloun. Le personnage féminin à l'aube du XXIème siècle* (Berne & New York: Peter Lang, 2002).

Clavaron, Yves, 'La vie d'Ahmed/Zahra ou la mise en crise de la masculinité chez Tahar Ben Jelloun', in Gary Ferguson, ed., *L'homme en tous genres. Masculinités, textes et contextes* (Paris: L'Harmattan, 2009), 149–61.

Clement, Jean-François, 'Tahar Ben Jelloun, un passeur de cultures', *Horizons maghrébins: Le droit à la mémoire*, 56 (2007), 98–106.

Dahouda, Kanate, 'Tahar Ben Jelloun. L'architecture de l'apparence', *Tangence*, 71 (2003), 13–26.

Déjeux, Jean, 'Les romans de Tahar Ben Jelloun ou 'Le territoire de la blessure', in Antoine Régis, ed., *Carrefour de cultures: Melanges offerts a Jacqueline Leiner* (Tübingen: Narr, 1993), 273–86.

Denans, Julien, '*L'enfant de sable*: De la culture à une écriture de la différence', *Topique*, 118/1 (2012), 93–106.

Devaux-Fargues, Claire, '*L'enfant de sable* de Tahar Ben Jelloun', *Recherches sur l'Imaginaire* 18 (1988), 277–84.

Djaouti, Fatima, 'Oralitude esthétisée *dans L'enfant de sable* et *La nuit sacrée*', in Andrée Mansau, ed., *Mises en cadre dans la littérature et dans les arts* (Toulouse: PU du Mirail, 1999), 135–47.

El Qasri, Jamal, 'Tahar Ben Jelloun. Les mots du corps', *Francofonía*, 19 (2010), 48–69.

Elbaz, Robert, *Tahar Ben Jelloun ou l'inassouvissement du désir narratif* (Paris: L'Harmattan, 1996).

—— and Ruth Amar, 'De l'oralité dans le récit benjellounien', *Maghreb Littérature*, 1/1 (1997), 35–53.

Erfani, Amin, 'Le Texte errant: la Textualité incarnée dans *L'Enfant de sable*', *Nouvelles Etudes Francophones*, 21/1 (2006), 79–94.

Farouk, May, *Tahar Ben Jelloun. Etudes des enjeux réflexifs dans l'œuvre* (Paris: L'Harmattan, 2009).

Gallouet-Schutter, Catherine, 'Nouveaux dilemmes du roman: Tahar Ben Jelloun', in Ginette Adamson and Jean-Marc Gouanvic, eds, *Francophonie plurielle* (Montreal: Hurtubise, 1995), 105–13.

Gaudin, Françoise, *La fascination des images. Les romans de Tahar Ben Jelloun* (Paris: L'Harmattan, 1998).

Girardini, Elisa, '*L'enfant de sable* de Tahar Ben Jelloun', in Maria Teresa Puleio, ed., *Letterature e civiltà dei paesi africani di lingua francese* (Catania: CUECM, 1990), 183–91.

Gontard, Marc, *Le moi étrange: Littérature marocaine de langue française* (Paris: L'Harmattan, 1993).

——, 'Effets de métissage dans la littérature marocaine de langue française', *Francographies: Bulletin de la Société des Professeurs Français et Francophones d'Amérique*, 2 (1993), 65–72.

——, 'Le récit meta-narratif chez Tahar Ben Jelloun', in Mansour M'Henni, ed., *Tahar Ben Jelloun. Stratégies d'écriture* (Paris: L'Harmattan, 1993), 99–118.

Hadjadj, Dany, 'Chercher la voie, trouver la voix. De *L'enfant de sable* à *La nuit sacrée* de Tahar Ben Jelloun', in Simone Bernard-Griffiths and Stéphane Michaud, eds, *Révolutions, Résurrections et Avènements. Mélanges offerts à Paul Viallaneix* (Paris: Sedes, 1991), 277–89.

Hafez-Ergaut, Agnès, 'Le déracinement: Introduction à l'étude de l'œuvre de Tahar Ben Jelloun', *Revue Frontenac*, 12 (1995), 67–89.

——, 'L'espace clos dans trois ouvrages de Tahar Ben Jelloun: *La réclusion solitaire*, *L'écrivain public* et *L'enfant de sable*: Littérature et résistance', *Présence francophone*, 50 (1997), 113–33.

——, 'Jeux de masques: *L'enfant de sable* et *La nuit sacrée* de Tahar Ben Jelloun', *Mots pluriels et grands thèmes de notre temps*, 10 (1999). <http://www.arts.uwa.edu.au/MotsPluriels/MP1099ahe.html> accessed 30 January 2015.

Heiler, Susanne, 'Jorge Luis Borges chez Tahar Ben Jelloun et Leonardo Sciascia', *Cahiers de l'association internationale des etudes françaises*, 7/1 (2005), 377–91.

Hollosi, Szonja, 'Réinterprétation de l'androgyne, du stéréotype aux métamorphoses dans l'imaginaire maghrébin francophone', in Micéala Symington and Béatrice Bonhomme, eds, *Libres horizons. Pour une approche comparatiste. Lettres francophones. Imaginaires* (Paris: L'Harmattan, 2008), 165–71.

Jurney Ramond, Florence, 'Le Hammam dans *L'enfant de sable* de Tahar Ben Jelloun et *Halfaouine: L'enfant des terrasses* de Ferid Boughedir', *French Review*, 77/6 (2004), 1128–39.

Laouissi, Farida, 'Tératologie borgesienne dans *L'enfant de sable* de Tahar Ben Jelloun', in Charles Bonn and Arnold Rothe, eds, *Littérature maghrébine et littérature mondiale* (Würzburg: Königshausen & Neumann, 1995), 175–81.

Maazaoui, Abbes, '*L'enfant de sable* et *La nuit sacrée* ou le corps tragique', *French Review*, 69/1 (1995), 68–77.

Masmoudi, Ikram, 'La catégorie du genre en français: fonctionnement et transgressions dans *L'enfant de sable* et *La nuit sacrée* de Tahar Ben Jelloun, *Langues: Cahiers d'études et de recherches francophones*, 2/1 (1999), 14–21.

——, 'Aventure et itinéraire d'un nom proper arabe dans *L'enfant de sable* de Tahar Ben Jelloun', *Arabica*, 49/2 (2002), 235–44.

Maury, Pierre, 'Tahar Ben Jelloun: Deux cultures, une littérature', *Magazine Littéraire*, 329 (1995), 107–11.

Mayer, Linda, 'Reflexions sur le discours intercultural actuel de la littérature marocaine de langue française chez Tahar Ben Jelloun et Abdelkebir Khatibi', in Lidia Anoll and Marta Segarra, eds, *Voix de la Francophonie (Belgique, Canada, Maghreb)* (Barcelona: Universidad de Barcelona, 1999), 373–87.

Memmes, Abdellah, *Littérature Maghrébine de langue française. Signifiance et interculturalité* (Rabat: Editions Okad, 1992).

——, 'Démarche interculturelle dans *L'enfant de sable* de Tahar Ben Jelloun', in Abdellah Madrhri Zeggaf and Ahmed Alaoui, eds, *L'interculturel au Maroc. Arts, langues, littératures et traditions populaires* (Casablanca: Afrique Orient, 1994), 61–74.

Mezgueldi, Zohra, *Corps au féminin* (Casablanca: Le Fennec, 1991).

M'Henni, Mansour, ed., *Tahar Ben Jelloun. Stratégies d'écriture* (Paris: L'Harmattan, 1993).

Michel-Mansour, Thérèse, 'La Portée esthétique du voile dans la littérature maghrébine', in Claude Bouygues, ed., *Texte africain et voies/voix critiques* (Paris: Harmattan, 1992), 157–70.

Natij, Salah, 'Dialogue interculturel et complaisance esthétique dans l'œuvre de Tahar Ben Jelloun', in Charles Bonn, ed., *Poétiques croisées du Maghreb. Vol 14: Itinéraires et contacts de cultures* (Paris: L'Harmattan, 1991), 35–41.

Pagan Lopez, Antonia, 'Subversion et transgression de l'écriture. Tahar Ben Jelloun: *L'enfant de sable*', in Lidia Anoll and Marta Segarra, eds, *Voix de la Francophonie (Belgique, Canada, Maghreb)* (Barcelona, Spain: Universidad de Barcelona, 1999), 407–12.

Perraudin, Pascale, 'Subversion de l'autorité dans *L'enfant de sable* de Ben Jelloun: la narration comme alternative', *Francographies: Bulletin de la Société des Professeurs Français et Francophones d'Amérique*, 2 (1995), 137–46.

Quintiliano, Deise, 'Le 'Double-Singulier': L'inscription du tragique dans *L'enfant de sable* de Tahar Ben Jelloun', *Nouvelles Etudes Francophones*, 25/1 (2010), 148–60.

Rahali, Ali, 'Représentation de la femme dans le roman marocain: le cas de Tahar Ben Jelloun', *Communication Interculturelle et Littérature*, 4/12 (2010), 23–30.

Reynaud, Patricia, 'Sexualité et identité dans Tahar Ben Jelloun', in Edris Makward, Mark Lilleleth and Ahmed Saber, eds, *North-South Linkages and Connections in Continental and Diaspora African Literatures* (Trenton, NJ: Africa World, 2005), 404–22.

Rosa da Silva, Edson, '*L'enfant de sable*. La reécriture du destin', *Bulletin of Francophone Africa*, 8 (1995), 37–45.

Rosenberg, Iona, 'Hypostases de l'anti-réalisme dans *L'enfant de sable* et *La nuit sacrée* de Tahar Ben Jelloun', *International Journal of Francophone Studies*, 9/2 (2006), 167–84.

Sadiq, Abdelhaï, 'D'une rive à l'autre: l'errance du traducteur de *L'enfant de sable*, de Tahar Ben Jelloun à Med Chergui', *Revue de la Faculté de Lettres et des Sciences Humaines de Marrakech*, 14: *L'interculturel: problématique et espace de création* (1996), 183–98.

Sardin, Pascale, '"Trouble dans le genre" – de la traduction anglo-américaine de *L'enfant de sable* de Tahar Ben Jelloun', *Transatlantica*, 1 (2009). < http://transatlantica.revues.org/4355> accessed 30 January 2015.

Spiller, Roland, 'L'intertextualité circulaire ou le désir dans la bibliothèque: Ben Jelloun lit Borges, lecteur de Cervantes', in Charles Bonn and Arnold Rothe, eds, *Littérature maghrébine et littérature mondiale* (Würzburg: Königshausen & Neumann, 1995), 165–74.

Stepniak, Maria, 'Quelques aspects du tragique dans le roman maghrébin de langue française des annees quatre-vingts', *Kwartalnik Neofilologiczny*, 38/2 (1991), 127–51.

Stone McNeece, Lucy, 'Discours à la dérive: Figures metanarratives chez Khatibi et Ben Jelloun', in Amadou Koné, Christiane Ndiaye and Josias Semujanga, eds, *De paroles en figures. Essais sur les literatures africaines et antillaises* (Paris: Harmattan, 1996), 113–24.

Tamm, Susanne, 'Fonction du portrait de Borges dans *L'enfant de sable* ou: la realisation de la liberté dans l'écriture', in Charles Bonn and Arnold Rothe, eds, *Littérature maghrébine et littérature mondiale* (Würzburg: Königshausen & Neumann, 1995), 155–64.

Urbani, Bernard, 'Si par une nuit sacrée un enfant de sable', *Recherches sur l'Imaginaire*, 22 (1991), 474–90.

Zdrada-Cok, Magdalena, 'L'hybridité dans *L'écrivain public* et *L'enfant de sable* de Tahar Ben Jelloun, *Romanica Silesiana*, 6 (2011), 160–80.

Bibliography

Aaltonen, Sirkku, *Time-Sharing on Stage: Drama Translation in Theatre and Society* (Clevedon and Buffalo, NY: Multilingual Matters, 2000).

Abdalaoui, M'hamed Alaoui, 'The Moroccan Novel in French', *Research in African Literatures*, 23/4 (1992), 9–33.

Abdel-Jaouad, Hedi, 'Sacrilegious Discourse', *Middle East Report*, 163 (1990), 34–6.

Abrams, M. H., *The Mirror and the Lamp: Romantic Theory and the Critical Tradition* (Oxford and New York: Oxford University Press, 1971).

Acheraiou, Amar, 'Tahar Ben Jelloun', in Michael D. Sollars, ed., *Companion to the World Novel. 1900 to the Present* (New York: Infobase Publishing, 2008), 403–5.

Afoullous, Houssaine, 'Three Generations of Francophone North African Writers in Exile: Driss Chraïbi, Tahar Ben Jelloun and Medhi Charef', in Anthony Coulson, ed., *Exiles and Migrants: Crossing Thresholds in European Culture and Society* (Brighton: Sussex Academic Press, 1997), 144–53.

Aizenberg, Edna, 'Borges, Postcolonial Precursor', *World Literature Today* 66/1 (1992), 21–6.

Alberge, Dalya, 'British Readers Lost in Translations as Foreign Literature Sales Boom' *The Guardian*, 24 August 2014. <http://www.theguardian.com/books/2014/aug/24/british-readers-translations-foreign-literature-sales-boom-stieg-larsson-jo-nesbo> accessed 21 January 2015.

Allén, Sture, and Kjell Espmark, *The Nobel Prize in Literature. An Introduction* (Stockholm: Swedish Academy, 2001).

Altick, Richard D., *The English Common Reader: A Social History of the Mass Reading Public, 1800–1900* (Columbus, OH: Ohio State University Press, 1998).

Anderson, Amanda, *The Way We Argue Now: A Study in the Cultures of Theory* (Princeton, NJ and Woodstock: Princeton University Press, 2006).

Andringa, Els, "For God's and Virginia's Sake Why a Translation?" – Virginia Woolf's Transfer to the Low Countries', *Comparative Critical Studies*, 3/3 (2006), 201–26.

'Appendix 3: Tagore's Writings Published from Britain between 1912 and 1941', in Kundu, Bhattacharya and Sircar, eds, *Imagining Tagore: Rabindranath and the British Press (1912–1941)* (Kolkata: Shishu Sahitya Samsad, 2000), 628–9.

'Appendix B', in James Joyce, *Ulysses*, ed. Jeri Johnson (Oxford: Oxford University Press, 1993), 740–5.

Apter, Emily, *Against World Literature: The Politics of Untranslatability* (London & New York: Verso Books, 2013).

Ashcroft, Bill, Gareth Griffiths, and Helen Tiffin, *The Empire Writes Back: Theory and Practice in Post-Colonial Literatures* (London: Routledge, 2002).

Assmann, Aleida, 'The Curse and Blessing of Babel; or, Looking Back on Universalisms', in Budick and Iser, eds, *The Translatability of Cultures: Figurations of the Space Between* (Palo Alto, CA: Stanford University Press, 1996), 85–104.

Attafi, Abdellatif, 'Tahar Ben Jelloun (1944 –)', in Alba Della Fazia Amoia and Bettina Liebowitz Knapp, eds, *Multicultural Writers since 1945: An A-to-Z Guide* (Westport, CT: Greenwood Press, 2004), 75–8.

Bangha, Imre, 'From 82-Year-Old Musicologist to Anti-Imperialist Hero: Metamorphoses of the Hungarian Tagore in East Central Europe', *Asian and African Studies*, 14/1 (2010), 57–70.

——,'Tagore's Reception and His Translations in Hungary', in Sanjukta Dasgupta and Chinmoy Guha, eds, *Tagore. At Home in the World* (New Delhi, Thousand Oaks, CA and London: SAGE, 2013), 25–37.

Barck, Simone, and Siegfried Lokatis, eds, *Fenster zur Welt: Eine Geschichte des DDR-Verlages Volk und Welt* (Berlin: Christoph Links Verlag, 2003).

Bassnett, Susan, 'Translating for the Theatre: The Case against Performability', *TTR (Traduction, Terminologie, Rédaction)*, 4/1 (1991), 99–111.

Bastin, Georges L., 'Adaptation', in Mona Baker and Gabriela Saldanha, eds, *Routledge Encyclopedia of Translation Studies* (London: Routledge, 2009), 5–8.

Ben Jelloun, Tahar, *L'écrivain publique* (Paris: Seuil, 1983).

——, *L'enfant de sable* (Paris: Seuil, 1985).

——, *French Hospitality: Racism and North African Immigrants* (New York and Chichester: Columbia University Press, 1999).

——, *Racism Explained to My Daughter* (New York: New Press, 1999).

——, *The Sand Child*, trans. Alan Sheridan (Baltimore, MD and London: Johns Hopkins University Press, 2000).

Bernheimer, Charles, ed., *Comparative Literature in the Age of Multiculturalism* (Baltimore: Johns Hopkins University Press, 1995).

Bhabha, Homi K., *The Location of Culture* (London: Routledge, 1994).

Bhattacharya, Sabyasachi, 'Introduction', in Rabindranath Tagore, *One Hundred Poems of Kabir* (London: Orient Blackswan, 2004), 1–29.

Bhatti, Anil, 'Culture, Diversity and Similarity: A Reflection on Heterogeneity and Homogeneity', *Social Scientist*, 37/7–8 (2009), 33–49.

Birus, Hendrik, 'The Goethean Concept of World Literature and Comparative Literature', in Steven Tötösy de Zepetnek, ed., *Comparative Literature and Comparative Cultural Studies* (Lafayette: Purdue University Press, 2003), 11–22.

Blaskovics, Jozsef, and Dusan Zbavitel, *Baren Basu: Zsoldosok* (Pozsony: Magyar Kiado, 1953).

Bloom, Harold, *The Western Canon: The Books and School of the Ages* (New York and London: Harcourt Brace, 1994).

Borges, Jorge Luis, *A Universal History of Infamy*, trans. Norman Thomas Di Giovanni (New York: E. P. Dutton, 1972).

Boruszko, Graciela, and Steven Tötösy de Zepetnek, eds, 'New Work about World Literatures', Special Issue, *CLCWeb: Comparative Literature and Culture*, 15/6 (December 2013).

Bourdieu, Pierre, *Outline of a Theory of Practice* (Cambridge: Cambridge University Press, 1977).

——, *Distinction: A Social Critique of the Judgement of Taste*, trans. Richard Nice (London: Routledge, 1984).

——, *Homo Academicus*, trans. Peter Collier (Cambridge: Polity, 1988).

——, *The Logic of Practice*, trans. Richard Nice (Cambridge: Polity, 1990).

——, *The Field of Cultural Production: Essays on Art and Literature*, trans. Claude DuVerlie et al. (Cambridge: Polity, 1993).

——, *The Rules of Art*, trans. Susan Emanuel (Cambridge: Polity Press, 1996).

Bousta, Rachida Saigh, *Lecture des récits de Tahar Ben Jelloun: Ecriture, mémoire et imaginaire* (Casablanca: Afrique Orient, 1992).

Brand, Hanita, '"Fragmentary, but Not Without Meaning": Androgynous Constructs and Their Enhanced Signification', *Edebiyât: The Journal of Middle Eastern Literatures*, 11/1 (2000), 57–83.

Bruns, Gerald L., *Hermeneutics Ancient and Modern* (New Haven, CT: Yale University Press, 1992).

Budick, Stanley, and Wolfgang Iser, eds, *The Translatability of Cultures: Figurations of the Space Between* (Palo Alto, CA: Stanford University Press, 1996).

Bull, Martin J., and James Newell, *Italian Politics: Adjustment under Duress.* (Cambridge and Malden, MA: Polity, 2005).

Burke, Kenneth, *A Rhetoric of Motives* (Berkeley and London: University of California Press, 1969).

Burke, Sean, *Authorship: From Plato to Postmodern. A Reader* (Edinburgh: Edinburgh University Press, 1995).

——, *The Death and Return of the Author: Criticism and Subjectivity in Barthes, Foucault and Derrida* (Edinburgh: Edinburgh University Press, 1998).

Burnett, Andrew, 'Rebirth of an Anarchist', *List*, 26 October 1990.

Buzelin, Hélène, 'Agents of Translation', in Yves Gambier and Luc van Doorslaer, eds *Handbook of Translation Studies* (Amsterdam and Philadelphia: John Benjamins Publishing Company, 2011), 6–12.

Cairns, Christopher, 'Introduction', in Dario Fo, *Accidental Death of an Anarchist* (London: Methuen, 1991), xv–xxi.

'La casa y el mundo' <http://www.plataformaeditorial.com/ficha/269/1/3725/la-casa-y-el-mundo.html> accessed 26 January 2015.

Casanova, Pascale, *The World Republic of Letters* (Cambridge, MA and London: Harvard University Press, 2004).

——, 'Literature as a World', *New Left Review*, 31 (2005), 71–90.

Cazenave, Odile, 'Gender, Age, and Narrative Transformations in *L'enfant de sable* by Tahar Ben Jelloun', *French Review*, 64/1 (1991), 437–50.

Chabal, Patrick, and Jean Pascal Daloz, *Culture Troubles: Politics and the Interpretation of Meaning* (London: C. Hurst and Co., 2006).

Chatterjee, Kalyan Kumar, '*The Home and the World.* Tagore's Ghandi Novel', in Kundu, *The Home and the World. Critical Perspectives* (Kolkata: Shishu Sahitya Samsad, 2000), 109–16.

Chattopadhyay, Jayanti, '*Ghare Baire* and Its Readings', in Datta, *Rabindranath Tagore's The Home and the World. A Critical Companion* (London: Anthem Press, 2005), 187–204.

Chaudhuri, Amit, 'Introduction', in *The Picador Book of Modern Indian Literature* (London: Picador, 2001), xvii–xxxiv.

Cloonan, William, 'The Politics of Prizes: The Goncourt in the 1980s', in Joseph Brami, Madeleine Cottenet-Hage and Pierre Verdaguer, eds, *Regards sur la France des Années 1980* (Saratoga, CA: ANMA Libri, 1994), 215–22.

Codde, Philippe, 'Polysystem Theory Revisited: A New Comparative Introduction', *Poetics Today*, 24/1 (2003), 91–126.

Coelsch-Foisner, Sabine, and Holger Klein, eds, *Drama Translation and Theatre Practice* (Berne: Peter Lang, 2004).

Cohen, Philip, 'Textual Instability, Literary Studies, and Recent Developments in Textual Scholarship', in *Texts and Textuality: Textual Instability, Theory, and Interpretation* (New York and London: Garland, 1997), xi–xxxiv.

Cohen, Ralph, ed., 'Literary History in the Global Age', Special Issue, *New Literary History*, 39/3 (Summer 2008).

Collins, Michael, 'Rabindranath Tagore and Nationalism: An Interpretation', *Heidelberg Papers in South Asian and Comparative Politics*, Working Paper No. 42 (2008), 1–37.

——, *Empire, Nationalism and the Postcolonial World: Rabindranath Tagore's Writings on History, Politics and Society*, Edinburgh South Asian Studies Series (London: Routledge, 2011).

——, 'Rabindranath Tagore and the Politics of Friendship', *South Asia: Journal of South Asian Studies*, 35/1 (2012), 118–42.

Corredor, Eva L., '(Dis)Embodiments of the Father in Maghrebian Fiction', *French Review*, 66/2 (1992), 295–304.

Cowan, Suzanne, 'Dario Fo, Politics and Satire: An Introduction to *Accidental Death of an Anarchist*', *Theater*, 10/2 (Spring 1979), 6–11.

Culler, Jonathan, 'Literary Competence', in Jane P. Tompkins, ed., *Reader Response Criticism. From Formalism to Post-Structuralism* (Baltimore and London: The Johns Hopkins University Press, 1992), 101–17.

——, *Structuralist Poetics: Structuralism, Linguistics and the Study of Literature* (London: Routledge Classics, 2002).

Cumming, Alan, and Tim Supple, 'A Note on the Present Text', in Dario Fo, *Accidental Death of an Anarchist* (London: Methuen, 1991), xxiii–xxiv.

D'haen, Theo, David Damrosch and Djelal Kadir, eds, *The Routledge Companion to World Literature* (Abingdon and New York: Routledge, 2011).

D'haen, Theo, César Domínguez and Mads Rosendahl Thomsen, eds, *World Literature. A Reader* (Abingdon and New York: Routledge, 2012).

Damrosch, David, *What Is World Literature?* (Princeton, NJ and Woodstock: Princeton University Press, 2003).

——, 'World Literature in a Postcanonical, Hypercanonical Age', in Haun Saussy, ed., *Comparative Literature in an Age of Globalization* (Baltimore: Johns Hopkins University Press, 2006), 43–53.

——, ed., *World Literature in Theory* (Oxford and Malden, MA: Wiley Blackwell, 2014).

Darnton, Robert, 'What Is the History of Books?', *Daedalus*, 111/3 (1982), 65–83.

——, *The Kiss of Lamourette: Reflections in Cultural History* (New York: Norton, 1990).

Das, Sisir Kumar, ed., *The English Writings of Rabindranath Tagore* (New Delhi: Sahitya Akademi, 1996).

Das Gupta, Uma, ed., *A Difficult Friendship. Letters of Edward Thompson and Rabindranath Tagore 1913–1940* (New Delhi: Oxford University Press, 2003).

——, *Rabindranath Tagore: A Biography* (New Delhi: Oxford University Press, 2004).

Dasgupta, Subrata, *The Bengal Renaissance: Identity and Creativity from Rammohun Roy to Rabindranath Tagore* (Delhi: Permanent Black, 2007).

Datta, Amaresh, *The Encyclopaedia of Indian Literature. Volume One: A to Devo* (New Delhi: Sahitya Akademi, 2006).

Datta, Pradip Kumar, ed., *Rabindranath Tagore's* The Home and the World. *A Critical Companion* (London: Anthem Press, 2005).

——, 'Introduction', in *Rabindranath Tagore's The Home and the World. A Critical Companion* (London: Anthem Press, 2005), 1–27.

Desai, Anita, 'Introduction', in Tagore, *The Home and The World* (London: Penguin, 2005), xxi–xxviii.

Devine, Caroline, and B. Venkat Mani, eds, 'What Counts as World Literature?', Special Issue, *Modern Language Quarterly: A Journal of Literary History*, 74/2 (2013).

Dimock Jr, Edward C., 'Rabindranath Tagore: The Greatest of the Bauls of Bengal', *The Journal of Asian Studies*, 19/1 (1959), 33–51.

Donahaye, Jasmine, 'Three Percent? Publishing data and statistics on translated literature in the United Kingdom and Ireland' (2013), <http://www.lit-across-frontiers.org/wp-content/uploads/2013/03/Publishing-Data-and-Statistics-on-Translated-Literature-in-the-United-Kingdom-and-Ireland-A-LAF-research-report-March-2013-final.pdf> accessed 8 February 2015.

Donald, David Herbert, 'Afterword: The Posthumous Novels of Thomas Wolfe', in *Look Homeward: A Life of Thomas Wolfe* (Cambridge, MA and London: Harvard University Press, 2002), 464–85.

Dutta, Krishna, and Andrew Robinson, eds, *Selected Letters of Rabindranath Tagore* (Cambridge and New York: Cambridge University Press, 1997).

——, *Rabindranath Tagore: The Myriad-Minded Man* (London: Tauris Parke Paperbacks, 2009).

Dyson, Ketaki Kushari, 'The Phenomenal Legacy of Rabindranath Tagore', *Asian and African Studies*, 14/1 (2010), 37–44.

——, 'Rumbling Empires and Men Speaking to Storms' (April 2012), <http://www.parabaas.com/rabindranath/articles/brKetaki_Collins.html> accessed 19 February 2015.

Eco, Umberto, *The Role of the Reader: Explorations in the Semiotics of Texts* (Bloomington: Indiana University Press, 1984).

El-Hoss, Tamara, 'Veiling/Unveiling in Tahar Ben Jelloun's *The Sand Child*: Disguise and Deception of the Female Protagonist', in Leslie Boldt-Irons, Corrado Federici and Ernesto Virgulti, eds, *Disguise, Deception, Trompe-L'œil: Interdisciplinary Perspectives* (Berne and New York: Peter Lang 2009), 149–60.

Eliot, Thomas Stearns, 'Tradition and the Individual Talent', in Lawrence S. Rainey, ed., *Modernism: An Anthology* (Malden, MA and Oxford: Blackwell, 2005), 152–5.

Emerson, O. B., *Faulkner's Early Literary Reputation in America* (Ann Arbor, MI: UMI Research Press), 1984.

Emery, Ed, 'Translator's Note', in Dario Fo, *Plays: 1* (London: Methuen), 124.

Engdahl, Horace, 'A Nobel Sensibility', *World Policy Journal*, 27/3 (2010), 41–5.

Engel, Elliot, *How Oscar Became Wilde and Other Literary Lives You Never Learned About in School* (London: Robson Books Limited, 2005).

English, James F., *The Economy of Prestige: Prizes, Awards, and the Circulation of Cultural Value* (Cambridge, MA: Harvard University Press, 2005).

Erickson, John D., 'Writing Double: Politics and the African Narrative of French Expression', *Studies in Twentieth-Century Literature*, 15/1 (1991), 101–22.

——, 'Femme voilée, récit voilé dans *L'enfant de sable* de Tahar Ben Jelloun', in Antoine Régis, ed., *Carrefour de cultures: Mélanges offerts à Jacqueline Leiner* (Tübingen: Narr, 1993), 287–96.

——, 'Veiled Woman and Veiled Narrative in Tahar Ben Jelloun's *The Sand Child*', *boundary 2*, 20/1 (1993), 47–64.

——, 'Metoikoi and Magical Realism in the Maghrebian Narratives of Tahar Ben Jelloun and Abdelkebir Khatibi', in Lois Parkinson Zamora and Wendy B. Faris, eds, *Magical Realism: Theory, History, Community* (Durham and London: Duke University Press, 1995), 427–50.

——, *Islam and the Postcolonial Narrative* (Cambridge: Cambridge University Press), 1998.

——, 'Magical Realism and Nomadic Writing in the Maghreb', in Stephen M. Hart and Wen-Chin Ouyang, eds, *A Companion to Magical Realism* (Woodbridge and Rochester, NY: Tamesis, 2005), 247–55.

Ettobi, Mustapha, 'Cultural Representations in Literary Translation: Translators as Mediators/Creators', *Journal of Arabic Literature*, 37/2 (2006), 206–29.

Even-Zohar, Itamar, 'Polysystem Theory', *Poetics Today*, 11/1 (1990), 9–26.

——, 'Factors and Dependencies in Culture: A Revised Outline for Polysystem Culture Research', *Canadian Review of Comparative Literature*, 24 (1997), 15–34.

Farrell, Joseph, 'Variations on a Theme: Respecting Dario Fo', *Modern Drama*, 41/1 (1998), 19–29.

——, 'Commentary', in Dario Fo, *Accidental Death of an Anarchist* (London: Methuen, 2009), xxiii–lxiii.

Farrell, Joseph, and Antonio Scuderi, eds, *Dario Fo. Stage, Text, and Tradition* (Carbondale and Edwardsville: Southern Illinois University Press, 2000).

——, 'Introduction: The Poetics of Dario Fo', in *Dario Fo. Stage, Text, and Tradition* (Carbondale and Edwardsville: Southern Illinois University Press, 2000), 1–19.

Faulkner, William, *Essays, Speeches and Public Letters*, ed. James B. Meriwether (New York: Random House, 1965).

Fayad, Marie, 'Borges in Tahar Ben Jelloun's *L'enfant de sable*: Beyond Intertextuality', *French Review*, 67/2 (1993), 291–9.

Finkelstein, David, 'History of the Book, Authorship, Book Design, and Publishing', in Charles Bazerman, ed., *Handbook of Research on Writing. History, Society, School, Individual, Text* (New York and Abdingdon: Taylor and Francis 2008), 65–80.

Finkelstein, David, and Alistair McCleery, *An Introduction to Book History* (London and New York: Routledge, 2005).

Finkelstein, David, and Alistair McCleery, eds, *The Book History Reader* (London and New York: Routledge, 2006).

Fischer-Lichte, Erika, 'Staging the Foreign as Cultural Transformation' in Erika Fischer-Lichte, Josephine Riley and Michael Gissenwehrer, eds, *The Dramatic Touch of Difference: Theatre, Own and Foreign* (Tübingen: Narr, 1990), 277–87.

Fish, Stanley Eugene, *Is There a Text in This Class?* (Cambridge, MA and London: Harvard University Press, 1998).

——, 'Interpreting the *Variorum*', in David Finkelstein and Alistair McCleery, *The Book History Reader* (London and New York: Routledge, 2005), 450–8.

Fitzpatrick, Tim, and Ksenia Sawczak, 'Accidental Death of a Translator: The Difficult Case of Dario Fo', *About Performance: Translation and Performance. Working Papers*, 1 (1995), 15–34.

Flaugh, Christian, 'Operating Narrative: Words on Gender Disability in Two Novels by Tahar Ben Jelloun', *Forum for Modern Language Studies*, 45/4 (2009), 411–26.

——, *Operation Freak. Narrative, Identity, and the Spectrum of Bodily Abilities* (Montreal & Kingston: McGill Queen's University Press, 2012).

Fo, Dario, *Compagni Senza Censura*, Volume 2 (Milan: Collettivo Teatrale La Comune, 1973).

——, *Fabulazzo*, ed. Lorenzo Ruggiero and Walter Valeri (Milan: Kaos, 1992).

——, *Accidental Death of an Anarchist*, trans. Suzanne Cowan, *Theater*, 10/2 (Spring 1979), 12–46.

——, *Accidental Death of an Anarchist*, adapt. Richard Nelson (New York and Toronto: Samuel French, Inc., 1987).

——, *Accidental Death of an Anarchist*, adapt. Alan Cumming and Tim Supple, Methuen Modern Plays (London: Methuen, 1991).

——, *Accidental Death of an Anarchist*, adapt. Gavin Richards, Methuen Modern Plays (London: Methuen, 2001).

——, *Accidental Death of an Anarchist*, trans. Simon Nye, Methuen Drama (London: Methuen, 2003).

——, *Plays: 1*, trans. Ed Emery, Joe Farrell, R. C. McAvoy and A.-M. Giugni, ed. Stuart Hood, Methuen Drama (London: Methuen, 2006).

——, *Accidental Death of an Anarchist*, trans. Simon Nye, Methuen Drama Student Editions (London: Methuen, 2009).

——, 'Postscript', in *Accidental Death of an Anarchist*, adapt. Gavin Richards (London: Methuen, 2001), 76–80.

Forster, Edward Morgan, *Abinger Harvest* (Harmondsworth: Penguin, 1983).

Foucault, Michel, 'What is an Author?', in Josué V. Harari, ed., *Textual Strategies: Perspectives in Post-Structuralist Criticism* (Ithaca: Cornell University Press, 1979), 141–60.

Friedman, Susan Stanford, 'Towards a Transnational Turn in Narrative Theory: Literary Narratives, Traveling Tropes, and the Case of Virginia Woolf and the Tagores', *Narrative*, 19/1 (2011), 1–32.
Gadamer, Hans-Georg, *Wahrheit und Methode. Grundzüge einer philosophischen Hermeneutik* (Tübingen: Mohr, 1965).
——, *Truth and Method*, trans. rev. Joel Weinsheimer and Donald Marshall (New York: Crossroad, 1989).
Gaillard, Philippe, 'Tahar le fou, Tahar le sage', *Jeune Afrique*, 1404 (1987): 44–6.
Gambier, Yves, and Luc Van Doorslaer, eds, *Handbook of Translation Studies* (Amsterdam and Philadelphia: John Benjamins Publishing Company, 2011).
Gates, Anita, 'Searching for Truth, Under Cover of Lies', *The New York Times*, 12 August 2011.
<http://www.nytimes.com/2011/08/14/nyregion/accidental-death-of-an-anarchist-at-drew-university-review.html> accessed 22 February 2015.
Gauch, Suzanne, 'Telling the Tale of a Body Devoured by Narrative', *differences: A Journal of Feminist Cultural Studies*, 11/1 (1999): 179–202.
——, 'A Story without a Face' in *Liberating Shahrazad. Feminism, Postcolonialism, and Islam* (Minneapolis and London: University of Minnesota Press, 2007), 55–80.
Genette, Gérard, 'Introduction to the Paratext', *New Literary History*, 22/2 (1991), 261–72.
——, *Paratexts: Thresholds of Interpretation* (Cambridge: Cambridge University Press, 1997).
Gentry, Marshall Bruce and William L. Stull, eds, *Conversations with Raymond Carver* (Jackson: University Press of Mississippi, 1990).
Ghosh, Tapobrata, 'The Form of *The Home and the World*', in Datta, *Rabindranath Tagore's* The Home and the World. *A Critical Companion* (London: Anthem Press, 2005), 68–81.
Giannuli, Aldo, *Bombe a inchiostro* (Milan: Rizzoli, 2008).
Gill, Stephen Charles, *The Cambridge Companion to Wordsworth* (Cambridge and New York: Cambridge University Press, 2003).
Gillespie, Gerald Ernest Paul, *By Way of Comparison: Reflections on the Theory and Practice of Comparative Literature* (Paris: Champion, 2004).
Gillespie, Stuart, 'Translation and Canon-Formation', in Stuart Gillespie and David Hopkins, eds, *The Oxford History of Translation in English* (Oxford and New York: Oxford University Press, 2005), 7–20.
Ginzburg, Carlo, *The Cheese and the Worms: The Cosmos of a Sixteenth-Century Miller* (Baltimore: Johns Hopkins University Press, 1992).
Goethe, Johann Wolfgang, *Conversations with Eckermann (1823–32)*, trans. John Oxenford (New York: North Point Press, 1984).

——, *Sämtliche Werke. Briefe, Tagebücher und Gespräche* ['Frankfurter Ausgabe'], 40 volumes, ed. Friedmar Apel, Hendrik Birus et al. (Frankfurt/Main: Suhrkamp, 1986–1999), volume 25.

Goffman, Erving, *The Presentation of Self in Everyday Life* (London: Penguin), 1990.

Gontard, Marc, 'Le récit meta-narratif chez Tahar Ben Jelloun', in Mansour M'Henni, ed., *Tahar Ben Jelloun. Stratégies d'écriture* (Paris: L'Harmattan, 1993), 99–118.

Grannis, Chandler B., *What Happens in Book Publishing* (New York and London: Columbia University Press, 1967).

Groenland, Tim, 'My Words, Your Words', *Dublin Review of Books* 19 (2011), <http://www.drb.ie/essays/my-words-your-words> accessed 22 February 2015.

Grossman, Edith, *Why Translation Matters* (New Haven and London: Yale University Press), 2010.

——, 'A New Great Wall. Why the Crisis in Translation Matters', *Foreign Policy* (May/June 2010). <http://www.foreignpolicy.com/articles/2010/04/26/a_new_great_wall> accessed 5 October 2014.

Guillory, John, 'Canon', in Frank Lentricchia and Thomas McLaughlin, eds, *Critical Terms for Literary Study* (New York: Octagon Books, 1995), 233–49.

Gupta, Suman, *Globalization and Literature* (Cambridge and Malden, MA: Polity, 2009).

Gürçaglar, Sehnaz Tahir, 'Paratexts', in Gambier and Van Doorslaer, *Handbook of Translation Studies* (Amsterdam and Philadelphia 2011), 113–16.

Haas, Willy, 'Lesehilfen für notorisch faule Leser', *Die Welt*, 27 December 1971.

Hajer, Maarten, and David Laws, 'Policy in Practice', in Michael Moran, Martin Rein and Robert E. Goodin, eds, *The Oxford Handbook of Public Policy* (Oxford University Press, 2006), 409–25.

Halpe, Aparna, 'The Problem of Eros in Tahar Ben Jelloun's *The Sand Child*', *Canadian Review of Comparative Literature/Revue Canadienne de Littérature Comparée*, 32/3–4 (Sep-Dec 2005), 400–19.

Hamil, Mustafa, 'Rewriting Identity and History. The Sliding *Barre(s)* in Tahar Ben Jelloun's *The Sacred Night*', in Mildred P. Mortimer, ed., *Maghrebian Mosaic: A Literature in Transition* (Boulder, CO: L. Rienner, 2000), 61–80.

Harder, Hans, 'Rabindranath Tagore, Übersetzen und (Miss-)Verstehen zwischen den Kulturen', *Translation as Cultural Praxis. Yearbook 2007 of the Goethe Society of India* (2007), 74–91.

Harvey, Robert, 'Purloined Letters: Intertextuality and Intersexuality in Tahar Ben Jelloun's *The Sand Child*', in Dominique D. Fisher and Lawrence R. Schehr, eds, *Articulations of Difference: Gender Studies and Writing in French* (Stanford: Stanford University Press, 1997), 226–45.

——, 'Cartas e letras roubadas: intertextualidade e intersexualidade em *L'enfant de sable* de Tahar Ben Jelloun', *Estudos Neolatinos*, 2/1 (2000), 73–96.

Hayes, Jarrod, 'Becoming a Woman: Tahar Ben Jelloun's Allegory of Gender, in *Queer Nations. Marginal Sexualities in the Maghreb* (Chicago and London: The University of Chicago Press, 2000), 165–81.

Hereford, C. H., 'Rabindranath Tagore and His Work', *The Manchester Guardian*, 28 March 1918.

Herrnstein Smith, Barbara, *Contingencies of Value: Alternative Perspectives for Critical Theory* (Cambridge, MA and London: Harvard University Press, 1988).

Hess, Erica, 'Passing the Test of Truth: Gender and Performance in Two French Narratives, Medieval and Modern', *Cincinnati Romance Review*, 17 (1998), 42–8.

Hetherington, Rosie, 'Review: *Accidental Death of an Anarchist* at the Oxford Playhouse' <http://www.bbc.co.uk/oxford/stage/2005/02/accidental_death_of_an_anarchist_review.shtml> accessed 22 February 2015.

Hitchcock, Peter, 'Decolonizing (the) English', *South Atlantic Quarterly*, 100/3 (2001), 749–71.

Hoesel-Uhlig, Stefan, 'Changing Fields: The Directions of Goethe's Weltliteratur', in Christopher Prendergast, ed., *Debating World Literature* (London and New York: Verso, 2004), 26–53.

Holub, Robert C., 'Reception Theory: The School of Constance', in Raman Selden, ed., *The Cambridge History of Literary Criticism. Volume 8: From Formalism to Post-Structuralism* (Cambridge: Cambridge University Press, 1995), 319–46.

Hood, Stuart, 'Open Texts: Some Problems in the Editing and Translating of Dario Fo's Plays', in Christopher Cairns, ed., *The Commedia dell'arte from the Renaissance to Dario Fo* (Lewinston, NY: Mellen, 1989), 336–49.

——, 'Introduction', in Fo, *Accidental Death of an Anarchist* (London: Methuen, 2001), vii–xiv.

——, 'Introduction', in Fo, *Plays: 1* (London: Methuen, 2006), ix–xv.

Huggan, Graham, *The Postcolonial Exotic. Marketing the Margins* (London and New York: Routledge, 2001).

Hung, Eva and Judy Wakabayashi, eds, *Asian Translation Traditions* (Manchester: St. Jerome Publishing, 2005).

Hurwitz, Harold M., 'Yeats and Tagore', *Comparative Literature*, 16/1 (1964), 55–64.

'IBA and Indiana University Sign MOU' <http://iba-du.edu/index.php/media/index/78> accessed 25 January 2015.

Ibnlfassi, Laila, 'The Ambiguity of Self-Structure. Tahar Ben Jelloun's *L'enfant de sable* and *La nuit sacrée*', in Kamal Salhi, ed., *Francophone Voices* (Exeter: Elm Bank Publications, 1999), 157–69.

Iser, Wolfgang, *The Act of Reading: A Theory of Aesthetic Response* (Baltimore: Johns Hopkins University Press, 1980).

——, *Prospecting: From Reader Response to Literary Anthropology* (Baltimore: Johns Hopkins University Press, 1989).

——, 'The Emergence of a Cross-Cultural Discourse: Thomas Carlyle's Sartor Resartus', in Stanley Budick and Wolfgang Iser, eds, *The Translatability of Cultures: Figurations of the Space Between* (Palo Alto, CA: Stanford University Press, 1996), 245–64.

——, *The Range of Interpretation* (New York and Chichester: Columbia University Press, 2000).

——, *How to Do Theory* (Oxford: Blackwell Publishing, 2006).

'Italy since 1815' Course Programme <http://www.nyu.edu/content/dam/nyu/globalPrgms/documents/florence/academics/syllabi/V57.9168_V42.9163_V59.9868_Travis.pdf> accessed 22 February 2015.

J. C., 'In Another Time', *The Times Literary Supplement*, 13 May 2011 <http://www.the-tls.co.uk/tls/reviews/other_categories/article724824.ece> accessed 25 January 2015.

Jack, Ian, 'Rabindranath Tagore Was a Global Phenomenon, So Why Is He Neglected?', *The Guardian*, 7 May 2011 <http://www.guardian.co.uk/commentisfree/2011/may/07/rabindranath-tagore-why-was-he-neglected> accessed 25 January 2015.

Jasinski, James, *Sourcebook on Rhetoric: Key Concepts in Contemporary Rhetorical Studies* (Thousand Oaks and London: Sage Publications, 2001).

Jauss, Hans Robert, 'Der Leser als Instanz einer neuen Geschichte der Literatur', *Poetica*, 7/3–4 (1975), 325–44.

——, *Toward an Aesthetic of Reception* (Minneapolis: University of Minnesota Press, 1994).

Jelnikar, Ana, 'Sreçko Kosovel and Rabindranath Tagore: Points of Departure and Identification', *Asian and African Studies*, 14/1 (2010), 79–95.

——, 'W. B. Yeats's (Mis)Reading of Tagore: Interpreting an Alien Culture', *University of Toronto Quarterly*, 77/4 (2008), 1005–24.

Jenkins, Ron, *Dario Fo and Franca Rame. Artful Laughter* (New York: Aperture, 2001).

Johnson, R., 'Juan Ramon Jiménez, Rabindranath Tagore, And "La Poesia Desnuda"', *Modern Language Review*, 60/4 (1965), 534–46.

Juvan, Marko, ed., 'World Literatures from the Nineteenth to the Twenty-First Century', Special Issue, *CLCWeb: Comparative Literature and Culture*, 15/5 (December 2013).

Kaegi, Werner, *Jacob Burckhardt: Eine Biographie*, 7 vols (Basel: Schwabe, 1947–82), III: 750–56.

Kämpchen, Martin, *Rabindranath Tagore and Germany: A Documentation* (Kolkata: Goethe-Institut, 1991).

——, *Rabindranath Tagore* (Hamburg: Rowohlt, 1992).

——, *Rabindranath Tagore in Germany: Four Responses to a Cultural Icon* (New Delhi: Indian Institute of Advanced Study, 1999).

——, *Rabindranath Tagore und Deutschland*, Marbacher Magazin (Marbach am Neckar: Deutsche Schillergesellschaft, 2011).

——, 'Rabindranath Tagores Rezeption in Deutschland, Österreich und der Schweiz', in Gabriele Fois-Kaschel, ed., *Rabindranath Tagore. Ein anderer Blick auf die Moderne – Un autre regard sur la modernité* (Tübingen: Narr Francke Attempto, 2013), 17–37.

——, 'Rabindranath Tagore and Germany: An Overview', in Sanjukta Dasgupta and Chinmoy Guha, eds, *Tagore. At Home in the World* (New Delhi, Thousand Oaks, CA and London: SAGE, 2013), 15–24.

Kant, Immanuel, *Critique of Judgment*, trans. Nicholas Walker (Oxford: Oxford University Press, 2007).

Kolbert, Jack, and Nancy L. Cairns, 'L'année littéraire 1987', *French Review*, 61 (1988), 845–58.

Kovač, Miha, Rüdiger Wischenbart, et al., 'Diversity Report 2010. Literary Translation in Current European Book Markets. An Analysis of Authors, Languages, and Flows', <http://wischenbart.com/page-30> accessed 5 October 2014.

Kovala, Urpo, 'Translations, Paratextual Mediation, and Ideological Closure', *Target*, 8/1 (1996), 119–47.

Kripalani, Krishna, *Rabindranath Tagore: A Biography* (Kolkata: Visva Bharati, 1980).

Kristeva, Julia, *Revolutions in Poetic Language*, trans. Margaret Waller (New York: Columbia University Press, 1997).

Krzykawski, Michal, 'Réticences françaises à l'égard des *Postcolonial Studies*: entre le soubresaut républicain et le hoquet francophone', *Romanica Silesiana*, 6 (2011), 76–88.

Kundu, Kalyan, Sakti Bhattacharya, and Kalyan Sircar, eds, *Imagining Tagore: Rabindranath and the British Press, 1912–1941* (Kolkata: Shishu Sahitya Samsad, 2000).

Kundu, Rama, ed., *Rabindranath Tagore's* The Home and the World: *Critical Perspectives* (New Delhi: Asia Book Club, 2001).

——, 'Introduction', in *Rabindranath Tagore's* The Home and the World: *Critical Perspectives* (New Delhi: Asia Book Club, 2001), 11–23.

Lago, Mary M., 'Tagore in Translation: A Case Study in Literary Exchange', *Books Abroad*, 46/3 (1972), 416–21.

——, 'Restoring Rabindranath Tagore', in Mary M. Lago and Ronald Warwick, eds *Rabindranath Tagore: Perspectives in Time* (Basingstoke: Macmillan, 1989), 4–25.

——, *'India's Prisoner': A Biography of Edward John Thompson, 1886–1946* (Columbia: University of Missouri Press, 2001).

Le Bris, Michel, 'Towards a "World-Literature" in French', in Alec G. Hargreaves, Charles Forsdick and David Murphy, eds, *Transnational French Studies. Postcolonialism and* Littérature-monde (Liverpool: Liverpool University Press, 2010), 296–300.

Leavis, Q. D., *Fiction and the Reading Public* (London: Pimlico, 2000).

Lefevere, André, 'Why Waste Our Time on Rewrites? The Trouble with Interpretation and the Role of Rewriting in an Alternative Paradigm', in Theo Hermans, ed., *The Manipulation of Literature* (London and Sydney: Croom Helm, 1985), 215–43.

——, *Translation, Rewriting, and the Manipulation of Literary Fame* (London: Routledge, 1992).

Lentricchia, Frank, and Thomas McLaughlin, eds, *Critical Terms for Literary Study* (New York: Octagon Books, 1995).

Lezra, Esther, '[Ab]Errant Bodies / [Ab]Erring Stories / Remembering Bodies / Disordering Stories in *The Pagoda* and *The Sand Child*', in Robert Cancel and Winifred Woodhull, eds, *African Diasporas: Ancestors, Migration and Borders* (Trenton, NJ: Africa World, 2008), 80–106.

Löhndorf, Marion, 'Die Stieftocher emanzipiert sich. Neue deutschsprachige Literatur such ihren Platz in Grossbritannien', *Neue Zürcher Zeitung*, 19 November 2012 <http://www.nzz.ch/aktuell/feuilleton/literatur/neue-deutschsprachige-literatur-sucht-ihren-platz-in-grossbritannien-1.17817151> accessed 28 February 2015.

Lokatis, Siegfried, 'Ein literarisches Quartett – Vier Hauptgutachter der Zensurbehörde', in Simone Barck and Siegfried Lokatis, eds *Fenster zur Welt: Eine Geschichte des DDR-Verlages Volk und Welt* (Berlin: Christoph Links Verlag), 333–7.

——, 'Nimm den Elefanten – Konturen einer Verlagsgeschichte', in Simone Barck and Siegfried Lokatis, eds *Fenster zur Welt: Eine Geschichte des DDR-Verlages Volk und Welt* (Berlin: Christoph Links Verlag), 15–30.

Longxi, Zhang, *Unexpected Affinities. Reading Across Cultures* (Toronto: University of Toronto Press, 2007).

Lorch, Jennifer, '*Morte Accidentale* in English', in Joseph Farrell and Antonio Scuderi, eds, *Dario Fo. Stage, Text, and Tradition* (Carbondale and Edwardsville: Southern Illinois University Press), 143–60.

Lowe, Lisa, 'Literary Nomadics in Francophone Allegories of Postcolonialism: Pham Van Ky and Tahar Ben Jelloun', *Yale French Studies*, 82 (1993), 43–61.

Lukács, Gyorgy, *Reviews and Articles from 'Die rote Fahne'* (London: Merlin Press, 1983).

Macaulay, Thomas Babington, 'Minute on Indian Education (1835)', in Mia Carter and Barbara Harlow, eds, *Archives of Empire: From the East India Company to the Suez Canal* (Durham and New York: Duke University Press, 2003), 227–38.

McCormack, Donna, *Queer Postcolonial Narratives and the Ethics of Witnessing* (New York and London: Bloomsbury, 2014).

Machor, James L., and Philip Goldstein, eds, *Reception Study: From Literary Theory to Cultural Studies* (New York: Routledge, 2001).

Maher, Brigid, 'The Comic Voice in Translation: Dario Fo's *Accidental Death of an Anarchist*', *Journal of Intercultural Studies*, 24/8 (2007), 367–79.

Mailloux, Steven, *Rhetorical Power* (Ithaca and London: Cornell University Press, 1989).

——, 'Interpretation and Rhetorical Hermeneutics', in James L. Machor and Philip Goldstein, *Reception Study: From Literary Theory to Cultural Studies* (New York: Routledge, 2001), 39–60.

Manguel, Alberto, *A History of Reading* (New York: Viking, 1996).

Manzalaoui, Mahmoud, 'Orientalism. Book Review', *Modern Language Review*, 75/4 (1980), 837–9.

Marrouchi, Mustapha, 'Breaking up/down/out of the Boundaries: Tahar Ben Jelloun', *Research in African Literatures*, 21/4 (1990), 71–83.

——, 'My Aunt is a Man: Ce "je"-là est multiple', *Comparative Literature*, 54/4 (2002), 325–56.

Mateo, Marta, 'Translation Strategies and the Reception of Drama Performances: A Mutual Influence', in Mary Snell-Hornby, Zuzana Jettmarová and Klaus Kaindl, eds, *Translation as Intercultural Communication* (Amsterdam and Philadelphia: John Benjamins Publishing Company, 1997), 99–110.

Max, D. T., 'The Carver Chronicles', *The New York Times Magazine*, 9 August 1998.

Memmes, Abdallah, 'Démarche interculturelle dans *L'enfant de sable* de Tahar Ben Jelloun', in Abdemajid Zeggaf and Abdellah Alaoui, eds, *L'interculturel au Maroc. Arts, langues, littératures et traditions populaires* (Casablanca: Afrique Orient, 1994), 61–74.

Meyer, Stefan G., 'The Confessional Voice in Modern Arab Fiction: *Season of Migration to the North* by Tayeb Salih and *The Sand Child* by Tahar Ben Jelloun', *Estudos Anglo-Americanos*, 16 (1992), 137–47.

Mezgueldi, Zohra, 'Mother-Word and French-Language Moroccan Writing', *Research in African Literatures*, 27/3 (1996), 1–14.

'The Mind of India. The Home and the World. By Rabindranath Tagore', *The Church Times*, 1 August 1919.

Minnis, Alastair J., *Medieval Theory of Authorship: Scholastic Literary Attitudes in the Later Middle Ages* (Philadelphia: University of Pennsylvania Press, 2010).

Mitchell, Tony, *Dario Fo: People's Court Jester*, A Methuen Theatrefile (London: Methuen, 1986).

Moačanin, Klara Gönc, 'Reception of Tagore's Work in Croatia', *Asian and African Studies*, 14/1 (2010), 71–8.

Moretti, Franco, 'Conjectures on World Literature', *New Left Review*, 1 (2000), 54–68.

Mortimer, Mildred, '*L'enfant de sable* by Tahar Ben Jelloun', *World Literature Today*, 60/3 (1986), 509.

Moser, Gerald M., 'The Campaign of Seara Nova and Its Impact on Portuguese Literature, 1921–61', *Luso-Brazilian Review*, 2/1 (1965), 15–42.

Mukherjee, Meenakshi, 'Tagore in the New Millennium', *The Hindu*, 6 June 2004 <http://www.hindu.com/lr/2004/06/06/stories/2004060600160300.htm> accessed 22 February 2015.

Mulligan, Jim, 'Interview with Ed Emery: Translating Dario Fo's *Devil in Drag*' <http://www.jimmulligan.co.uk/interview/ed-emery-dario-fo-the-devil-in-drag> accessed 22 February 2015.

Mwangi, Evan Maina, *Africa Writes Back to Self: Metafiction, Gender, Sexuality* (New York: State University of New York Press, 2009).

Negus, Keith, and Michael Pickering, 'Creativity and Cultural Production', *International Journal of Cultural Policy*, 6/2 (2000), 259–82.

——, *Creativity, Communication and Cultural Value* (Thousand Oaks, London and New Delhi: Sage Publishers Ltd, 2004).

Nemes, Graciela P., 'Of Tagore and Jiménez', *Books Abroad*, 35/4 (1961), 319–23.

Niranjana, Tejaswini, *Siting Translation: History, Post-Structuralism, and the Colonial Context* (Berkeley: University of California Press, 1992).

'The Nobel Prize in 1913. Rabindranath Tagore. Award Ceremony Speech', <http://www.nobelprize.org/nobel_prizes/literature/laureates/1913/press.html> accessed 17 February 2015.

O'Connell, Joseph T., 'Tracing Vaishnava Strains in Tagore', *The Journal of Hindu Studies*, 4/2 (2011), 144–64.

'Opportunities Around the World', *The Deccan Herald*, 14 December 2011, <http://www.deccanherald.com/content/211694/opportunities-around-world.html> accessed 11 January 2015.

Ouzgane, Lahoucine, 'Masculinity and Virility in Tahar Ben Jelloun's Work', *Contagion: Journal of Violence, Mimesis, and Culture*, 4 (1997), 1–13.

——, 'The Rape Continuum: Masculinities in the Works of Nawal El Saadawi and Tahar Ben Jelloun', in *Men in African Film and Fiction* (Woodbridge: Currey, 2001), 68–80.

Pavis, Patrice, 'Problems of Translation for the Stage: Interculturalism and Post-Modern Theatre', in Hanna Scolnicov and Peter Holland, eds, *The Play out of Context:*

Transferring Plays from Culture to Culture (Cambridge: Cambridge University Press, 1989), 22–45.

Pease, Donald E., 'Author', in Frank Lentricchia and Thomas McLaughlin, eds *Critical Terms for Literary Study* (New York: Octagon Books, 1995), 105–17.

Périssé, Bernard R., *Solitude and the Quest for Happiness in Vladimir Nabokov's American Works and Tahar Ben Jelloun's Novels* (Berne and New York: Peter Lang, 2003).

Perry, Seamus, 'Rabindranath Tagore Revived', *The Times Literary Supplement*, 16 September 2011. <http://www.the-tls.co.uk/tls/public/article776938.ece> accessed 19 February 2015.

Perteghella, Manuela, 'A Descriptive-Anthropological Model of Theatre Translation, in Sabine Coelsch-Foisner and Holger Klein, eds, *Drama Translation and Theatre Practice* (Berne and New York: Peter Lang, 2004), 3–23.

Pickford, Susan, 'The Booker Prize and the Prix Goncourt: A Case Study of Award-Winning Novels in Translation', *Book History*, 14/1 (2011), 221–40.

Pizer, John David, *The Idea of World Literature: History and Pedagogical Practice* (Baton Rouge: Louisiana State University Press, 2006).

Pound, Ezra, 'Rabindranath Tagore', *Fortnightly Review*, 1 March 1913, 571–9.

Pratt, Annis, *Archetypal Patterns in Women's Fiction* (Bloomington: Indiana University Press, 1981).

Prendergast, Christopher, ed., *Debating World Literature* (London and New York: Verso, 2004).

'Presentation by Sture Allén', reprinted in *Nobel Lectures: Literature. 1996–2000* (Stockholm: Nobel Foundation, 2002), 17–21.

Prince, Gerald, 'Introduction to the Study of the Narratee', in Jane P. Tompkins, ed. *Reader-Response Criticism. From Formalism to Poststructuralism* (Baltimore: Johns Hopkins University Press, 1980), 7–25.

——, 'Narratology and Narratological Analysis', *Journal of Narrative and Life History*, 7 (1997), 39–44.

Price, Leah, 'Reading: The State of the Discipline', *Book History*, 7 (2004), 303–20.

Qader, Nasrin, *Narratives of Catastrophe. Boris Diop, Ben Jelloun, Khatibi.* (New York: Fordham University Press, 2009).

'Rabindranath Tagore: The Poet at 150', *The Guardian*, 29 April 2012, <http://www.guardian.co.uk/commentisfree/2012/apr/29/rabindranath-tagore-poet-india> accessed 25 January 2015.

Rabinowitz, Peter J., *Before Reading: Narrative Conventions and the Politics of Interpretation* (Columbus, OH: Ohio State University Press, 1997).

——, 'Reading Beginnings and Endings', in Brian Richardson, ed., *Narrative Dynamics. Essays on Time, Plot, Closure, and Frames* (Columbus: Ohio State University Press, 2002), 300–13.

Radice, William, 'Preface', in Rabindranath Tagore, *The Home and the World* (London: Penguin, 2005), vii–xv.

——, 'Tagore the World Over: English as the Vehicle' (2006). <http://www.williamradice.com/Recent%20Events/Tagore_the_world_over.html> accessed 11 September 2012.

——, 'Sum Ergo Cogito: Tagore as a Thinker and Tagore as a Poet, and the Relationship between the Two', *Asian and African Studies*, 14/1 (2010), 17–36.

Radway, Janice A., *A Feeling for Books: The Book-of-the-Month Club, Literary Taste, and Middle-Class Desire* (Chapel Hill, NC and London: University of North Carolina Press, 1997).

Ramond Jurney, Florence, 'Secret Identities: (Un)Masking Gender *in Le roman de Silence* by Heldris de Cournouaille and *L'enfant de sable* by Tahar Ben Jelloun', *Dalhousie French Studies*, 55 (Summer 2001), 3–10.

Rancière, Jacques, *The Politics of Literature* (Cambridge and Malden, MA: Polity Press, 2011).

Raw, Laurence, 'Introduction', in *Translation, Adaptation and Transformation* (London and New York: Continuum, 2012), 1–20.

Ray, Mohit K., 'Tagore on *Ghare Baire*: Aesthetics in Command', in Kundu, *The Home and the World. Critical Perspectives* (Kolkata: Shishu Sahitya Samsad, 2000), 91–104.

——, *Studies on Rabindranath Tagore*. Volume 1 (New Delhi: Atlantic Publishers 2004).

Richards, Thomas, *The Imperial Archive: Knowledge and the Fantasy of Empire* (London and New York, 1993).

Richter, Steffen, *Der Literaturbetrieb. Eine Einführung. Texte – Märkte – Medien* (Darmstadt: Wissenschaftliche Buchgesellschaft, 2011).

Riedel, Wolfgang, 'Literarische Anthropologie: Eine Unterscheidung', in Wolfgang Braungart, Klaus Ridder and Friedmar Apel, eds, *Wahrnehmen und Handeln: Perspektiven einer Literaturanthropologie* (Bielefeld: Aisthesis, 2004), 337–66.

Riffaterre, Michael, *La production du texte* (Paris: Seuil, 1979).

Rorty, Richard, 'Taking Philosophy Seriously', in Sean Burke, ed., *Authorship. From Plato to the Postmodern* (Edinburgh: Edinburgh University Press, 1995), 292–9.

——, *Truth and Progress* (Cambridge: Cambridge University Press, 1998).

Rose, Jonathan, 'Rereading the English Common Reader: A Preface to a History of Audiences', *Journal of the History of Ideas*, 53/1 (1992), 47–70.

Rosendahl Thomsen, Mads, *Mapping World Literature. International Canonization and Transnational Literatures* (London and New York: Continuum, 2010).

——, 'World Famous, Locally: Insights From the Study of International Canonization', 6 March 2014, in *The 2014–2015 Report on the State of the Discipline of Comparative Literature*. <http://stateofthediscipline.acla.org/entry/world-famous-locally-insights-study-international-canonization#sthash.83d8lv6F.dpuf> accessed 1 February 2015.

Rothenstein, William, *Since Fifty: Men and Memories, 1922–1938* (London: Macmillan, 1940).

Rye, Gill, 'Uncertain Readings and Meaningful Dialogue: Language and Sexual Identity in Anne Garréta's *Sphinx* and Tahar Ben Jelloun's *L'enfant de sable* and *La nuit sacrée*', *Neophilologus*, 84/4 (2000), 531–40.

Sanyal, Sovon, 'A Casa e O Mundo: Telo De Mascarenhas's Translation of *Ghare Baire*', *Parabaas* Special Rabindranath Tagore Section (May 2012), <http://www.parabaas.com/rabindranath/articles/pSovon3.html> accessed 25 January 2015.

Sarkar, Sumit, *The Swadeshi Movement in Bengal, 1903–1908* (New Delhi: People's Publishing House, 1973).

Sartre, Jean-Paul, *Jean-Paul Sartre: Basic Writings*, ed. Stephen Priest (London: Routledge, 2001).

Saunders, Rebecca, 'Decolonizing the Body: Gender, Nation, and Narration in Tahar Ben Jelloun's *L'enfant de sable*', *Research in African Literatures*, 37/4 (2006), 136–60.

Saussy, Haun, ed., *Comparative Literature in an Age of Globalization* (Baltimore: Johns Hopkins University Press, 2006).

Schneider, Ute, *Der unsichtbare Zweite: Die Berufsgeschichte des Lektors im literarischen Verlag* (Göttingen: Wallstein Verlag, 2005).

Schwartz, Lawrence H., *Creating Faulkner's Reputation: The Politics of Modern Literary Criticism* (Knoxville: The University of Tennessee Press, 1988).

Scuderi, Antonio, *Dario Fo: Framing, Festival, and the Folkloric Imagination* (Lanham, MD: Lexington Books, 2011).

Sen, Nabaneeta, 'The "Foreign Reincarnation" Of Rabindranath Tagore', *The Journal of Asian Studies* (1966), 275–86.

Sen, Nivedita, 'Translator's Note', in Rabindranath Tagore, *The Home and the World. Ghare Baire* (New Delhi: Srishti Publishers and Distributors, 2004), 312–16.

Sen, S. N., *History of Freedom Movement in India (1857–1947)* (New Delhi: New Age International, 2003).

Sengupta, Saswati, Shampa Roy, and Sharmila Purkayastha, eds, *Towards Freedom. Critical Essays on Rabindranath Tagore's* Ghare Baire/The Home and the World (Hyderabad: Orient Longman, 2007).

Shaffer, Elinor, 'Introduction', *Comparative Critical Studies*, 3/3 (2006), 191–8.

Simpson, Shona Elizabeth, 'One Face Less: Masks, Time, and the Telling of Stories in Tahar Ben Jelloun's *The Sand Child*', in Anna-Teresa Tymieniecka, ed., *Allegory Revisited: Ideals of Mankind* (Dordrecht, Boston, London: Kluwer Academic Publishers, 1994), 325–32.

Smith, Craig, *Adam Smith's Political Philosophy: The Invisible Hand and Spontaneous Order* (London: Taylor and Francis, 2006).

Spear, Thomas and Caren Litherland, 'Politics and Literature: An Interview with Tahar Ben Jelloun', *Yale French Studies*, 82/2 (1993), 30–43.

'Gli spettacoli di Dario Fo e Franca Rame nel mondo' <http://www.archivio.francarame.it/estero.aspx> accessed 26 January 2015.

Spivak, Chakravorty Gayatri, 'Theory in the Margin: Coetzee's *Foe* Reading Defoe's *Crusoe/Roxana*', in Jonathan Arac and Barbara Johnson, eds, *Consequences of Theory* (Baltimore: Johns Hopkins University Press, 1991), 154–80.

——, *Death of a Discipline* (New York: Columbia University Press, 2003).

——, 'The Politics of Interpretations', in *In Other Worlds: Essays in Cultural Politics* (New York and London: Routledge, 2006).

Spivak, Gayatri Chakravorty, and David Damrosch, 'Comparative Literature/World Literature: A Discussion,' in David Damrosch, ed., *World Literature in Theory* (Malden, MA and Oxford: Wiley Blackwell, 2014).

Sturm-Trigonakis, Elke, *Comparative Cultural Studies and the New* Weltliteratur (West Lafayette, Indiana: Purdue University Press, 2013).

Tagore, Rabindranath, *Das Heim und die Welt*, trans. Helene Meyer-Franck (Munich: Wolff, 1920).

——, *La Maison et le Monde*, trans. F. Roger-Cornaz (Paris: Petite Bibliothèque Payot, 2002).

——, *The Home and the World. Ghare Baire*, trans. Nivedita Sen (New Delhi: Srishti Publishers and Distributors, 2004).

——, *Home and the World*, trans. Sreejata Guha (New Delhi: Penguin India, 2005).

——, *The Home and the World*, trans. Surendranath Tagore (London: Penguin, 2005).

——, 'World Literature (1907)', in David Damrosch, ed., *World Literature in Theory* (Malden, MA and Oxford: Wiley Blackwell, 2014), 47–57.

Tatlock, Lynne, 'Introduction: The Book Trade and the "Reading Nation" in the Long Nineteenth Century', in *Publishing Culture and The 'Reading Nation': German Book History in the Long Nineteenth Century* (Rochester, NY: Camden House, 2010), 1–21.

Taviano, Stefania, 'Translating Political Theatre: The Case of Dario Fo and Franca Rame', in Sabine Coelsch-Foisner and Holger Klein, *Drama Translation and Theatre Practice* (Berne and New York: Peter Lang, 2004), 325–40.

——, 'British Acculturation of Italian Theatre', in Andrew Chesterman, Natividad Gallardo San Salvador and Yves Gambier, eds, *Translation in Context: Selected Papers from the EST Congress, Granada 1998* (Amsterdam and Philadelphia: John Benjamins Publishing Company, 2000), 339–52.

——, *Staging Dario Fo and Franca Rame. Anglo-American Approaches to Political Theatre* (Aldershot and Burlington: Ashgate), 2005.

Thacher, Jean-Louise, 'Recent Translations of Arabic Fiction: Review Article', *Middle East Journal*, 42/3 (1988), 481–5.

Thompson Jr, Edward, *Rabindranath Tagore – Poet and Dramatist* (Delhi: Oxford University Press, 1991).

Thompson, John B., *Merchants of Culture: The Publishing Business in the Twenty-First Century* (Cambridge: Polity, 2010).

'Three Percent: A Resource for International Literature at the University of Rochester': <http://www.rochester.edu/College/translation/threepercent/index.php?s=database> accessed 8 October 2014.

Tiwari, Bhavya, 'Rabindranath Tagore's Comparative World Literature' in Theo D'haen, David Damrosch and Djelal Kadir, eds, *The Routledge Companion to World Literature* (Abingdon and New York: Routledge, 2011), 41–8.

Tolstoy, Leo, *What Is Art?* (Letchworth: Bradda Books Ltd., 1963).

Tötösy de Zepetnek, Steven, 'The New Humanities: The Intercultural, the Comparative, and the Interdisciplinary,' *Global Society*, 1.2 (2007), 45–68.

Trivedi, Harish, 'Introduction', in Edward Thompson Jr, *Rabindranath Tagore – Poet and Dramatist* (Delhi: Oxford University Press, 1991), 1–39.

'University of Northampton Signs MoU with University of Madras' <http://www.jamshedsiddiqui.com/2012/04/university-of-northampton-uk-signs-mou.html> accessed 25 January 2015.

Valeri, Walter, 'An Actor's Theatre', in Joseph Farrell and Antonio Scuderi, *Dario Fo. Stage, Text and Tradition* (Carbondale and Edwardsville: Southern Illinois University Press, 2000), 19–29.

Venuti, Lawrence, 'Introduction', in *Rethinking Translation: Discourse, Subjectivity, Ideology* (London: Taylor and Francis, 1992), 1–8.

——, *The Translator's Invisibility: A History of Translation* (London and New York: Routledge, 1995).

'Vice-Provost/CAO signs memorandum of understanding with Indian Institute of Management, Bangalore', 19 April 2011 <http://www.tcd.ie/vpcao/latest-news.php> accessed 25 January 2015.

Wade, Allan, ed., *The Letters of W. B. Yeats* (London: Rupert Hart-Davis, 1954).

Wang, Ning, ed., 'Comparative Literature: Toward the (Re)construction of World Literature', Special Issue, *Neohelicon*, 38.2 (December 2011).

Waugh, Patricia, *Metafiction: The Theory and Practice of Self-Conscious Fiction* (London: Methuen, 1984).

White, Elizabeth H., 'Purdah', *Frontiers: A Journal of Women Studies*, 2/1 (1977), 31–42.

Wing, Jolynn, 'The Performance of Power and the Power of Performance: Rewriting the Police State in Dario Fo's *Morte accidentale di un anarchico*', *Modern Drama*, 33/1 (1990), 139–49.

Wolfe, Thomas, *The Good Child's River*, ed. Suzanne Stutman (Chapel Hill and London: The University of North Carolina Press, 1994).

Wolpert, Stanley A., *A New History of India* (New York and Oxford: Oxford University Press, 2009).

Young, Edward, 'From "Conjectures on Original Composition"', in Sean Burke, ed., *Authorship: From Plato to the Postmodern* (Edinburgh: Edinburgh University Press, 1995), 37–42.

Young, Howard, 'The Invention of an Andalusian Tagore', *Comparative Literature*, 47/1 (1995), 42–52.

——, 'In Loving Translation: Zenobia and Juan Ramón', *Revista Hispanica Moderna*, 49/2 (1996), 486–93.

'zamindar': <http://www.britannica.com/EBchecked/topic/655661/zamindar> accessed 30 January 2015.

Zanzana, Habib, 'Gender, Body and the Erasure of the Feminine in Tahar Ben Jelloun's *L'enfant de sable*', *RLA: Romance Languages Annual* 10/1 (1998): 194–8. <http://tell.fll.purdue.edu/RLA-Archive/1998/french html/Zanzana,%20Habib.htm> accessed 14 September 2012.

Zatin, Phyllis, *Theatrical Translation and Film Adaptation: A Practitioner's View* (Clevedon: Multilingual Matters, 2005).

Unpublished sources

Correspondence with Nivedita Sen. 4 January 2010.

Correspondence with Sreejata Guha. 17 April 2012.

Index

NEW COMPARATIVE CRITICISM

New Comparative Criticism is dedicated to innovative research in literary and cultural studies. It invites contributions with a comparative, cross-cultural, and interdisciplinary focus, including comparative studies of themes, genres, and periods, and research in the following fields: literary and cultural theory; material and visual cultures; reception studies; cultural history; comparative gender studies and performance studies; diasporas and migration studies; transmediality. The series is especially interested in research that articulates and examines new developments in comparative literature, in the English-speaking world and beyond. It seeks to advance methodological reflection on comparative literature, and aims to encourage critical dialogue between scholars of comparative literature at an international level.

New Comparative Criticism publishes the proceedings of *Synapsis: European School for Comparative Studies*.

Proposals are welcome for either single-author monographs or edited collections. Please provide a detailed outline, a sample chapter, and a CV. For further information, please contact the series editor: Florian Mussgnug (f.mussgnug@ucl.ac.uk).

Published volumes

Margherita Laera
Reaching Athens: Community, Democracy and Other Mythologies in Adaptations of Greek Tragedy
2013. ISBN 978-3-0343-0807-6

Florian Mussgnug and Matthew Reza (eds)
The Good Place: Comparative Perspectives on Utopia
2014. ISBN 978-3-0343-1819-8

Marion Dalvai
Politics of Cross-Cultural Reading: Tagore, Ben Jelloun and Fo in English
2015. ISBN 978-3-0343-1881-5